THATCHER'S PEOPLE

JOHN RANELAGH was at the Conservative Research Department, the Party's think-tank, during the Opposition years 1975-9, when Thatcherism was formulated. He was one of the team that established Channel Four Television, and went on to help set up TV2 in Denmark. He is the author of the prize-winning study, *The Agency: The Rise and Decline of the CIA*, which also provided the basis for a major BBC television series.

D1428204

JOHN RANELAGH

Thatcher's People

An insider's account of the politics,
the power and the personalities

Fontana
An Imprint of HarperCollins*Publishers*

To Timothy Dickinson

Fontana
An Imprint of HarperCollins *Publishers*
77–85 Fulham Palace Road,
Hammersmith, London W6 8JB

Published by Fontana 1992
9 8 7 6 5 4 3 2 1

First published in Great Britain by
HarperCollins *Publishers 1991*

ISBN 0 00 637514 6

Set in Linotron Galliard by
Rowland Phototypesetting Ltd
Bury St Edmonds, Suffolk

Printed in Great Britain by
HarperCollins Manufacturing Glasgow

CONTENTS

PREFACE

This book is concerned with Margaret Thatcher and the people who helped her to devise and to implement Thatcherism. It is not about the people who voted for her, or her Cabinets or most of her Ministers and civil servants. It is not about the businessmen who gave financial support to the Conservative Party while she was leader, or about the managers who fought the trade unions and ushered in the privatization of nationalized firms and industries. Nor is it about public figures such as the novelist Jeffrey Archer or Rupert Murdoch or newspaper editors who were widely identified as supporters of Margaret Thatcher. It is about the very small number of individuals who were responsible for the theory and the practice of Thatcherism, which is a particularly British expression of liberal economic and philosophical thinking. It therefore deals also with the classical liberal thinkers whose ideas found practical political form in Thatcherism.

Margaret Thatcher came into power in the Conservative Party in reaction to the performance of Edward Heath's 1970–74 Government. Accordingly, Heath, his 1970 election platform and his 'U-turn' in government are discussed as part of the background necessary for an understanding of some of the motive forces of Thatcher and her people.

The battle for trade union reform, and the battle against inflation leading to the 1981 Budget, were absolutely critical to the success of Thatcher as Prime Minister, and to the success of Thatcherism as a set of policies. Thatcher's people – advisers in Number Ten, particularly in the Policy Unit, and those outside Government – were central to both battles, not least because they convinced Thatcher herself that she could win. Without their systematic planning and analysis, and the personal support they gave to her, it is doubtful whether she would have succeeded against the views of a majority of her first Cabinet and, variously, the studied distance of the civil service, the opposition of the overwhelming mass of professional economists, and the antagonism of the trade unions. The reform of the unions – Thatcher's greatest achievement – had been an election manifesto promise, and it enjoyed the support of a majority of people in Parliament and in the country as a whole. It reflected Thatcher's will, and the struggle Thatcher and her people had with their political colleagues in the 1975–9 Opposition years over the question of trade union reform. In Government they had a second struggle with their colleagues, the Treasury, the Bank of England and the collective wisdom of professional economists over the 1981 Budget. This book deals at some length with these two behind-the-scene battles.

The conflict between the Chancellor of the Exchequer, Nigel Lawson, and the Prime Minister, with Sir Alan Walters, Thatcher's personal economic adviser, acting as the catalyst, which culminated in Lawson's resignation at the end of October 1989, was an affair of great importance to the themes – Thatcher, her people, and how they interact – of this book and thus is also treated at some length. 'Everything has a pre-play,' Enoch Powell observed to me,[1] and the Lawson affair presaged Thatcher's own fall. The affair probed the nature of Thatcher's relationships with advisers and Ministers, and revealed the nature of her style of government. It also demonstrated the role the media can play.

In the mid-1970s, I was a member of the Conservative Research Department (CRD), and so witnessed the formulation of Thatcherism at first-hand. The head of the Department was Christopher Patten, who later became Thatcher's Environment Minister and Major's Chairman of the Conservative Party. He liked to tell the story of when, having worked in John Lindsay's successful 1965 New York City mayoral campaign, he wrote two letters, one to Transport House (then the Labour Party headquarters) and one to Conservative Central Office, asking for a job; Central Office replied first, and that is how he ended up as a Conservative Party official. The message to the Research Department was, 'It's all a game: be flexible and detached.' Thatcher and her people were quite

---

[1] Interview, Rt Hon. J. Enoch Powell, MBE, 1 November 1989.

different. Politics was not a game for them, and they disliked appeals to consensus.

On the occasion of Thatcher's only visit to the Research Department, in the summer of 1975, a friend and colleague, Michael Jones, and I prepared a paper for her meeting with us. We proposed that the Party should adopt a 'Family Policy' – addressing benefits and taxation as they affected the family unit, rather than as they affected an individual – at the 1975 Party Conference. We took the idea from the German Christian Democrats, and in fits and starts such a policy entered the Conservative framework under Thatcher. Another colleague had also prepared a paper arguing that the 'middle way' was the pragmatic path for the Conservative Party to take, avoiding the extremes of Left and Right. Before he had finished speaking to his paper, the new Party leader reached into her briefcase and took out a book. It was Friedrich von Hayek's *The Constitution of Liberty*. Interrupting our pragmatist, she held the book up for all of us to see. 'This,' she said sternly, 'is what we believe,' and banged Hayek down on the table. 'She slammed it down,' remembered Stephen Probyn, who was then responsible for energy matters at the Department. 'Then she delivered a monologue about the British economy, part of which was a sermonette about the miners. But she was factually inaccurate about the miners – I think she said that Heath had not taken steps to reduce the mining workforce when, in fact, he had, largely because oil was so cheap and the National Coal Board couldn't compete. She argued with me about this, and Patten started saying, "That's enough, Stephen," but by then it was too late. I'm sure the whole thing crystallized in her mind that the Research Department was pink, and I think it was the beginning of the end of the Research Department.'[1]

Within CRD and Central Office, Margaret Thatcher's election as Party leader in 1975 was viewed with foreboding. 'My God! The bitch has won!' exclaimed a Vice Chairman of the Party when the news came through. There was a great shrugging of shoulders and an assumption that Thatcher would lose the next election because her policies were 'silly' and out of tune with political realities,

[1] Interview, Stephen Probyn, 30 December 1990.

notably that getting along with the trade unions was a sine qua non of political life. Within the Party bureaucracy it was felt essential to hold on to the respect of the media by indicating privately to journalists that the new leader was an aberration on the part of the MPs who elected her, that she would soon be out and Willie Whitelaw would replace her. In pursuit of these objectives, the Research Department acted as unofficial custodian of the Heath/ Whitelaw flame, arguing against Thatcherite ideas such as free collective bargaining in industrial relations or education vouchers or the replacement of the rating system with a poll tax – all of which were studied and proposed behind the scenes in the 1975–9 period, although they did not become public until many years later. Because of this resistance, CRD, traditionally the Party's Think-Tank, gave way in important respects to the independent, Thatcherite, Centre for Policy Studies, and was not involved with the centrally important work of John Hoskyns (who became the first head of her Policy Unit) and Norman Strauss (who worked with Hoskyns and joined him in the Policy Unit).

Margaret Thatcher made it clear from the outset that she preferred her own people to the Party establishment. She also signalled that she was a new and very different leader. 'One of her great strengths was that she did not mind being a minority of one,' observed one of Thatcher's people. 'Most men hate it. Men need to be reassured that they are doing the right thing. She would ask questions that no man would ask because they would reveal ignorance. She didn't mind looking stupid, ever. The Party establishment hated her for this because it meant she wouldn't go along with things and was always forcing them to justify and explain themselves, which they have never been very good at doing. They always hoped to get rid of her. They thought she was the wrong person and were not prepared to admit that she had done anything good at all. Because she brought in a different group of people, they wouldn't concede that she had done some extraordinary things. And they finally got her.'[1] In fact, her style probably had more to do with Thatcher as a woman being typecast as an outsider and prepared, as a good politician, to exploit that role: to concede

[1] Interview, 2 January 1991.

ignorance but to enforce authority while establishing that she could get to the heart of things.

I was writing this book during the period when Margaret Thatcher resigned as Prime Minister and leader of the Conservative Party. I was struck by the number of Thatcher's people who, before the November 1990 change of leadership, had expressed to me their worry that her time at the top was ending. When I spoke to them about her resignation and the immediate events leading to it, their general opinion was that she had become inflexible. They were upset, but not surprised, by her end. Thatcher's people outside Number Ten also thought that the advice she took from her private secretary, Charles Powell, and her press secretary, Bernard Ingham, contributed significantly to her departure. They were seen as unelected officials cushioned from the brutal realities of political life after years in Downing Street, insufficiently tuned to the feelings of MPs and the man in the street. But what was, perhaps, most surprising was the consistency of view, both before and after November 1990, among Thatcher's people about Thatcher and their part in her story.

I encountered great generosity and friendliness as I spoke to people about their experiences of the Thatcher years. In some cases I agreed to keep identities private, so at times my sources are anonymous. However, I can say that I did speak to most people mentioned in this book.

Carmen Callil suggested this book to me. Timothy Dickinson gave unstintingly of his extraordinary memory and insights, and I owe him a great and characteristic debt of gratitude. Michael Jones gave me his recollections and read and commented on my text. Sir John Hoskyns gave me his time and the benefit of his analysis and criticism (a great deal of which was an attempt to convince me that others deserved whatever credit I gave him). Lord Harris of High Cross reminded me of the intellectual figures of classical economics so important to the development of Thatcherism, and picked me up on countless points of fact and syntax. Sir Alfred Sherman, always stimulating, made available to me his hard-eyed assessments. Norman Strauss found time for energizing conversation and debate. Sir Alan Walters, a mine of refreshment and insight, broke open his hectic schedule to explain crucial points. Lord Wolfson gave shrewd judgements and invaluable recollection in some very enjoyable conversations. Andrew Dickson let me have his acute portraits of a number of people. Jonathan Hill discussed the book with me on many occasions, informed my story, and read and commented with great precision on it. Patrick Uden made several valuable points to me about the consciousness (or lack of it) in Britain in the 1970s of Japan and of the importance of technological development. Once again, John Taft afforded unstinting and unconditional hospitality and support. Stuart Proffitt, my editor, toiled to much purpose to represent the narrative interests of readers less immersed in the themes than the author.

Deirdre McMahon, Michael Shaw, my sister Bawn, and my wife Elizabeth have been involved in nearly everything I have written, and without them none of this would have been possible. But, especially given my debts, I must stress that the opinions and any inaccuracies in the following pages are mine alone.

JOHN RANELAGH
Grantchester, 1991

INTRODUCTION

Everything has a pre-play

Thatcher's people revolved around Margaret Thatcher, rather than the Conservative Party. There were never many of them: fewer than thirty men were responsible for the ideas and the plans that formed Thatcherism. Few were ever in the Cabinet: a vital factor in her resignation in November 1990 was that two-thirds of the Cabinet advised her to go, with four ministers saying that they would have to consider their positions if she decided to try to stay on. It was reported that one – Kenneth Clarke, her Education Secretary – said that 'he had told his wife . . . that either the Prime Minister went or he did'; that another – Chris Patten, her Environment Secretary – said he would not work for her if she fought on, and that Richard Ryder, her Financial Secretary, who had been on her personal staff in the 1970s, and whose political career she 'made', refused to be her campaign manager.[1] Thatcher's people were rarely on the ramparts of Government.

Thatcher's earliest people were the helpers and the thinkers of the 1968–79 period who provided her and Sir Keith Joseph with a base of ideas reaching back into the great tradition of classical liberalism. There were also Thatcher's personal contacts and her husband, Denis, who gave her moral support. From 1979, businessmen and managers with an interest in free enterprise, and some civil servants, entered her circle. Sir Ian MacGregor who, as chairman of the National Coal Board in 1983–6, was in the forefront of the effort by Thatcher and her people to defeat union power, was perhaps the leading representative of this second wave of supporters. MacGregor took the full force of the attempt by the National Union of Mineworkers under Arthur Scargill to bring

[1] Reported by Chris Buckland, 'Inside Politics', *Daily Express*, 20 December 1990.

down the Thatcher Government in 1983–4. Finally, there were those such as Sir John Egan (Jaguar motor cars), Sir Graham Day (Rover cars) and – again – Sir Ian MacGregor (steel) who were involved in the privatization of nationalized industries (and those involved in the mediating institutions between privatized monopolies and consumers) that started during the 1980s.

The earliest of Thatcher's people were far and away the most important, and the fewest in number. Six months after the 1979 election victory, David Wolfson, one of this group and her chief of staff, held a working dinner with an agenda for her and her close colleagues: including Wolfson and Thatcher, only five people were present.[1] The second wave of supporters helped articulate Thatcherism and steeled Thatcher's arguments. The third wave were those who actually implemented Thatcherism. Civil servants and businessmen and managers flesh out any administration and fine-tune policy. This wave had an inevitability to it: if industries are being denationalized, someone has to manage them in the run-up period to privatization and then afterwards. By the end of her second administration in 1987 all her earliest people (with the effective exception of the economist Sir Alan Walters) had left or been dispensed with.

Thatcherism was counter-elitist, but not populist. Margaret Thatcher never tried to be populist. Enoch Powell demonstrated the populist potential of anti-establishment action in the late 1960s: dock workers marched in support of his campaign against immigration, and he influenced the way millions of people voted in three general elections. But he made himself an outcast from the political establishment, and that was something Thatcher never contemplated doing. Unlike her people, she was in many ways a conventional British Conservative politician, always loyal to the Party. She was a loyal Minister under Macmillan, Douglas-Home, and Heath. She shook off the anti-immigration nationalists that Powell had appealed to. She disdained many establishmentarians, but had sufficient Toryism and Conservatism in her to stay within the accepted political boundaries, often to the anger and frustration of

[1] Present were Keith Joseph, John Hoskyns, Norman Strauss. Of her other closest people at the time, Alan Walters was in the United States and Alfred Sherman was not involved in the immediate business in hand inside Number Ten.

her people: they, not she, tended to be anti-establishment. She had an unusual interest in ideas and theories, but on most matters she was a pragmatic and far more traditional politician than many of her people understood. Her promotion of John Major, a man whose life – like hers – has been consumed by politics, who owed her everything, and her endorsement of him as her successor, was quintessentially political.

Sir Ian Gilmour, a leading anti-Thatcherite Tory, sees politics as being about process, and considers that it is distinctly middle-class to have intense notions about competition and economic doctrines. When a theory starts taking control, he has a Tory revulsion. He sees the essence of the Conservative Party as dealing with real situations as they come up, not with formulating abstract designs. Norman Strauss, an early Thatcher person, in contrast, said to Margaret Thatcher in 1977, 'We must create the new history for tomorrow's traditions.'[1]

Thatcher's people believed intensely in ideas, and in the centrality of ideas in Government. They entertained genuinely new opinions, and not simply a different sector of the established spectrum. They sought to apply ideas to a far greater extent than Margaret Thatcher did: she was not identical with her people. Her identity was with the life of politics. She thought certain things were obvious and was reluctant to call them ideas. If asked, she would say that hers were the conclusions of a practical person.

Within Thatcher's people, there were two constituencies: the men of push and go like David Young (a Cabinet Minister from 1984 to 1989) and John Hoskyns; and condition-of-Britain people, full of ideas, like Alfred Sherman (co-founder of the Centre for Policy Studies in 1974 and its director of studies, 1976–84) and Keith Joseph, the man Thatcher credited with making her election as Party leader possible in 1975. They were two layers of a cake. They were united by Thatcher in opposition to British decline. They were not united by doctrine.

The men of push and go were Lloyd Georgian figures, promoted and appointed to do jobs of work. David Lloyd George's 'Garden Suburb' advisers were a parallel case: men such as Sir Joseph

---

[1] Interview, Norman Strauss, 11 December 1990.

Maclay, a great Glasgow shipbuilder. 'I invited from outside a number of men of exceptional capacity who had never held any office in any Government, and most of whom were not even in Parliament, to occupy positions of great responsibility,' remembered Lloyd George. 'I also decided to place men of this type in charge of some of the new departments.'[1] Maclay became Minister of Shipping and a Member of Parliament, but rarely entered the House of Commons: he couldn't have cared less about politicians. There was a war on, and he was fighting it. His was very much the attitude of many of Thatcher's people: tough and self-made, sailing as close to the wind as necessary.

Both layers of Thatcher's people quite consciously set out to act in the real world and not spend much time on airs and graces and polish. And that applied to Thatcher, too. They were people absolutely unembarrassed at not belonging to the Opera set or the Athenaeum, and at not having the appropriately turned quotation on the tips of their tongues in the House of Commons. They were not people who aspired to the established social accoutrements of success and status.

Here, there was another connection with Lloyd George. No one knew whom he was going to bring forward, or could tell whether many of those that he did bring into Government were Liberal or Conservative. Like Maclay, they had not been in the House of Commons or in the House of Lords. Similarly, between 1960 and 1979, there was an increasing overlap between politicians of the two main parties. Except for matters of social background, it was hard to differentiate in terms of policy between Labour and Conservative Ministers and senior officials. Then Margaret Thatcher moved into Number Ten Downing Street and began to bring forward men like David Young and Cecil Parkinson (chairman of the Conservative Party, 1981–3) who were not members of the Athenaeum. With the tension of war and the achievement of victory, Lloyd George had commanding stature, sufficient to curtail grousing about his appointments. Margaret Thatcher lacked this

---

[1] David Lloyd George, *War Memoirs of David Lloyd George* (Boston, Little Brown, 1934), Vol. III, p. 34. The 'Garden Suburb' was the name given to Lloyd George's Cabinet Secretariat (which he created): the members were housed in temporary buildings in the garden of Number Ten.

attribute in 1979. What was more, the Establishment had a genuine bone to pick with her and her people. They correctly understood that Thatcher's people signified her decision to look to outsiders far more interested in effecting radical changes than in maintaining cosy relationships. The 'chattering classes' of the media also had a bone to pick with her and her people, seeing them – correctly – as compromising the idea of 'one nation' by being willing to fight entrenched power blocs and social attitudes. But she was ahead of both groupings.

Winston Churchill had a large responsibility for the post-war 'one nation'/welfare state/cosy establishment/Keynesian consensus that Margaret Thatcher challenged. Churchill's appeasement of labour in the 1950s had been responded to with great moderation. The British labour leaders of the 1950s were like the American labour leaders: they wanted higher wages and better conditions. Churchill put Walter Monckton in as Minister of Labour (1951–5) to buy them off, and the price was easily negotiated. Churchill did not want the works to be jammed at home while he fulfilled his greater dream – an old man's dream – to restore Britain to the place of third power in the world and to achieve the conciliation of Russia. He regarded the State with suspicion, and was sentimentally pro-American. He thought that there were friendships between nations. Enoch Powell made a very funny speech in 1966 attacking Churchill and Macmillan for the amount of damage done to Britain by two Conservative Prime Ministers with American mothers who thus believed in the benevolence of the United States. At home, Churchill established a bipartisan view – the core of the post-war consensus – that social harmony was more important than curbing growing union power.

The post-war Left was concerned with the redistribution rather than the creation of wealth, and they redistributed probably more for the good than the bad. The next generation of the Left, partly owing to Keynesianism and partly owing to ill-concealed communism (usually these did not cohabit in one breast), believed that Britain was losing in the wealth stakes because of the undoubted conservatism and hidebound state of British business, and that having the Left in power would mean greater efficiency through co-operation with powerful trade unions. The 1970–74

Conservative Government of Edward Heath unsuccessfully challenged union power. By 1978 a combination of the activities of hard Left mavericks and a simple failure to deliver the more worthwhile promises – that everyone would be richer and healthier – and the obvious fact that Labour's leadership had no stomach for the revolutionary course, had destroyed Labour's credibility. When matters reached the stage in the Winter of Discontent in 1978–9 that it was impossible to bury the dead, the bankruptcy was apparent and the Left was clearly teetering on the border of political nihilism.

The crisis of the old order was not in 1945 when Churchill was thrown out of office: it was when Heath tried hard to work within the post-war consensus and so found himself unable to govern. That is the genesis of the Thatcher years: a tough, capable Prime Minister – Heath – just not being able to keep order, and a second division Cabinet Minister – Thatcher – emerging as the key player. Minds had been changed by Heath's experience (e.g., in the leadership contest in 1975 or the 1979 general election). In politics, thousands of people may change their minds, but they need someone for their ideas to crystallize around. Thatcher was that person, and she also provided the will to effect change.

Thatcher's people showed with nerve and skill that it was possible to move away from the post-war Keynesian consensus. They thus liberated British economic thinking from some overweight orthodoxies. On the other hand, Thatcherism proved itself prepared to live with a level of inflation (ten per cent in 1990) which would have been shocking even to politicians on the Left a generation earlier. Pragmatism (beliefs, not ideas; mood, not policies) was always dominant in the Thatcher years. She was an employer of ideas, not a servant of them, and she was a politician leading an elected Government, having to be practical at all times if she was to stay on top.

Politicians want freedom from the ordinary trammels of holding office. They want to build power. They know that they are more in office than in power, so they will sacrifice almost anything for power (for example, Nixon going to China and eating twenty years of his words in order to get a freer hand in foreign policy). Margaret Thatcher, above all else, was determined to have power.

*

The following could be counted among Thatcher's People either for part of the time or for all of the time that Margaret Thatcher was leader of the Conservative Party. Some people were Thatcher's People before either they – or she – knew it. It would be wrong, however, to regard the following as an exhaustive list.

TIM BELL A wizard of advertising and public relations, at Saatchi & Saatchi he was responsible for Thatcher's 1979 ('Labour Isn't Working') and 1983 election campaigns. In 1987, having started his own firm, he was called in by David Young to revive Thatcher's flagging campaign, and he did so successfully. Highly respected and admired in the advertising world, he always gave informed and blunt advice, and was a passionate Thatcher supporter. She, in turn, relied on him at key times for political advice and judgement. He is reputed to be the model for 'John Maslama' in Salman Rushdie's *Satanic Verses*.

JOHN BIFFEN A Thatcherite before Thatcher, greatly respected for his intellect and articulateness. He played a key role in securing the acceptance of monetarist policies by the Shadow Cabinet in 1978–9. He was made Leader of the House of Commons in 1982 by Thatcher as part of her attempt to 'Thatcherize' the Cabinet. As a Minister, he differed increasingly from Thatcher about the presentation of policy, and in some cases its implementation, preferring a conciliatory approach to change and reform. He was described by Bernard Ingham as 'semi-detached' from the Government, and was sacked in 1987, but he always regarded himself as a Thatcherite.

MILTON FRIEDMAN The charming and soft-spoken ambassador for monetarism, and chairman of the Mont Pelerin Society, 1970–72. In 1948 at the age of 36 he became Professor of Economics at the University of Chicago, playing a central part in the creation of the 'Chicago School' of monetarist economics. His *Capitalism and Freedom* (1962) has had a major influence on both monetarist and Keynesian economic thinking. Not a libertarian, his (and Hayek's) teachings were at the core of Thatcherism.

IAN GOW Thatcher's first Parliamentary Private Secretary. A generous and witty dog-loving man (his home was called 'The Dog House'). A great admirer of Enoch Powell, he had argued for monetarist policies in the Heath years, and made no secret of his disillusion after the 1971–2 U-turn. He supported Geoffrey Howe's candidacy for the Party leadership in 1975, and did not expect that his association with Thatcher in 1979 would last long. Instead, a great personal bond formed between them, and Gow became renowned for his dedication to her interests in Parliament and the Parliamentary Party. He played an important part in helping Thatcher and Howe withstand Treasury and Bank of England pressure during the run-up to the 1981 Budget. A staunch unionist, he resigned as a junior Minister at the Treasury in protest at the Anglo–Irish Agreement in 1985. Trained as a solicitor, his friendly manner hid a sharp mind. He was murdered by the IRA in 1990: a car bomb killed him at his home in Surrey.

BRIAN GRIFFITHS The last head of Margaret Thatcher's Policy Unit in Number Ten. Professor of Banking and International Finance at the City University, 1977–85. A monetarist economist with a strong religious interest, credited as a major influence on the reorganization of the National Health Service on 'market'principles, and on the 1990 Broadcasting Act that brought in more competitive arrangements. He is a native Welsh speaker, and was a Labour voter in the 1960s.

RALPH HARRIS The energetic, witty, stimulating guiding spirit of the classic liberal Institute of Economic Affairs since 1957, first as general director (1957–86), and then as chairman. He was a lecturer in political economy at St Andrews University, 1949–56, and entered politics as a Conservative in Scotland. In the IEA, however, he firmly eschewed Party politics in a determined effort to convince politicians and opinion formers of all persuasions of the doctrines of classic liberalism and the free market, and of the dangers of over-government. He influenced Keith Joseph's thinking in the late 1960s and mid-1970s, and for over thirty years nurtured a rare centre of intellectual and academic strength in opposition to the post-war Keynesian consensus.

FRIEDRICH VON HAYEK The brilliant author of *The Road to Serfdom* (1944) and *The Constitution of Liberty* (1960), two of the seminal works of modern classic liberalism that influenced Margaret Thatcher and many of her people, and the founder of the Mont

Pelerin Society (1947). He came to England from his native Austria as Tooke Professor of Economic Science and Statistics at the University of London in 1931, and became a naturalized British subject in 1938. He held this chair until 1950 when he went to the University of Chicago as Professor of Social and Moral Science. In esteem, Thatcher made him a Companion of Honour in 1984.

GEOFFREY HOWE Never close to Thatcher personally, he was however at the heart of her leadership both in Opposition and in Government. He was a monetarist before Thatcher. His training as a barrister and his prodigious memory enabled him to be a most effective parliamentarian, and a Chancellor of the Exchequer (1979–83) capable of mastering specialist and technical matters, and debating them with civil servants and experts. Together with Thatcher and Keith Joseph, he founded the Centre for Policy Studies. His working relationship with Thatcher never recovered from her dismissal of him as Foreign Secretary in 1989. His speech to the House of Commons explaining his resignation as Leader of the House and Deputy Prime Minister in November 1990 was regarded as the moment when opinion in the Parliamentary Party moved decisively away from Thatcher.

JOHN HOSKYNS The first head of Thatcher's Policy Unit, 1979–82. A formidable organizer and manager, he co-ordinated policy and its implementation in Thatcher's first Government. He was a Labour voter in the 1960s. He founded the John Hoskyns & Co., computer company, later part of the Hoskyns Group of which he was chairman and managing director. In the late 1970s he had a central role in devising the *Stepping Stones* plans that in Government resulted in the reduction of union power. As director-general of the Institute of Directors in the mid-1980s, he was an acute critic of the civil service.

BERNARD INGHAM Rough, tough, blunt Yorkshireman and outspoken press secretary. He was a journalist and Labour activist in the 1950s and 1960s, entering the civil service as press officer for Harold Wilson's Prices and Incomes Board in 1965. He became Thatcher's press secretary through normal civil service procedures, but rapidly demonstrated his loyalty and commitment both to her and her policies. Always anxious to stress that he operated within the accepted rules of conduct, he was nevertheless accused of undue partisanship and of being too powerful and influential. He left Number Ten and the civil service in November 1990 when Thatcher resigned.

KEITH JOSEPH At the heart of it all: the man whom Thatcher credits with making her successful bid for the Party leadership in 1975 possible. He was a tormented politician, finding public speaking and political debate extremely upsetting and draining. Nevertheless, he forced himself to overcome his inhibitions and public ridicule – not least from several of his Party colleagues – to proselytize for monetarist and classical liberal policies after February 1974. He worked closely with Alfred Sherman, and was the principal 'gatekeeper' of Thatcherism in the 1970s. He is a deeply upright and generous man.

NIGEL LAWSON The combative, effective and longest-serving Treasury Minister of the century (Financial Secretary, 1979–81; Chancellor of the Exchequer, 1983–9) who fell out with Thatcher and Alan Walters over British membership of the European Monetary System. He resigned over this question in 1989, presaging Thatcher's own fall a year later. Until 1987, however, Lawson had been a Thatcher intimate, having been at the heart of Thatcherite economic policy since 1975. In 1966–70 he was a gaullist editor of the *Spectator*. He was one of the few men who successfully transferred from being involved in policy during the Heath years (he wrote the February 1974 Conservative Election Manifesto), to being a Thatcher insider.

ANGUS MAUDE One of Thatcher's most active and influential supporters in the 1975–9 period when he was chairman of the Conservative Research Department. He drafted many of the key Party publications of the period, including *The Right Approach* (1977) and *The Right Approach to the Economy* (1978). In the 1930s he was a financial journalist on *The Times* and the *Daily Mail*. He fought in North Africa during the war, and was a prisoner of war from January 1942 until May 1945. He was elected to Parliament first in 1950, and became an Independent Conservative in 1957–8. He returned to Parliament in 1963 and retired in 1983.

AIREY NEAVE War hero and organizer of Thatcher's election as leader of the Conservative Party in 1975. He was on the right of the Party, and early on as a junior Minister quarrelled with Edward Heath. After Heath became Party leader in 1965, Neave was kept on the backbenches until 1974 when he was made Opposition spokesman on Northern Ireland. He was murdered by the IRA in 1979; a bomb stuck beneath his car exploded and killed him as he drove out of the House of Commons car park. Thatcher was devastated by his death. She trusted his political advice and valued him as a devoted supporter.

CHARLES POWELL One of the two civil servants (the other was Bernard Ingham) completely identified with Thatcher and her policies. A Foreign Office high-flyer, he was reported to have turned down an ambassadorship in order to stay on with Thatcher in Number Ten beyond the regular period of secondment to the Private Office. He was credited with nurturing Thatcher's antipathy to the accumulation of power by the European Commission, and with being anti-German. He was expected to leave Downing Street in November 1990 and either return to the Foreign Office or stay with Thatcher in some capacity, but to the surprise of many he stayed on with John Major until March 1991.

ENOCH POWELL *The* political trailblazer. Many of his views and arguments were deployed by Thatcher and her people. Thatcher shared his concern that Britain's national interests were threatened by membership of the European Community. Privately, she also shared his views about the dangers of large-scale immigration. With Peter Thorneycroft (Chancellor) and Nigel Birch (Economic Secretary), Powell (Financial Secretary) resigned from Macmillan's Government in January 1958 in protest at inflationary policies and the failure to adopt what later was termed a monetarist approach to economic problems. Macmillan called the resignations – unprecedented in British political history – 'a little local difficulty'. Unlike Thatcher, however, Powell was anti-American and less averse to State-led health and social security measures. He was also more sympathetic to the trade unions.

NICHOLAS RIDLEY To many, the unacceptable face of Thatcherism. As Thatcher's Environment Secretary, he demonstrated a greater interest in development than in conservation, in business and jobs than in ecological security. Despite his political unpopularity, Thatcher kept him in her Cabinets: she could depend upon him to support her and her views in debate with colleagues. A Thatcherite before Thatcher, he was the only Minister to resign in protest at Heath's 1971–2 U-turn. Intellectually acute, he was politically naive, and was forced to resign in 1990 following an outspoken interview in the *Spectator* in which he drew parallels between German objectives within the European Community and Adolf Hitler's attempt to dominate Europe fifty years earlier.

ALFRED SHERMAN A central figure in the development of Thatcherism. His ideas, knowledge and energy dynamized a wide range of policies. A journalist, and the first director of studies at the Centre for Policy Studies, which was his idea. The Centre provided Thatcher and Joseph with a bedrock of intellectual and research support, and Sherman was instrumental in drafting many of the most significant speeches by Joseph in the 1970s. Born in the East End of London, as a young man he was a communist and fought on the Republican side in the Spanish Civil War. He was vital in converting Keith Joseph to free market and classical liberal principles, and in pushing him to speak out in 1974.

NORMAN STRAUSS A key planner in the development of Thatcher's policies in the late 1970s and early 1980s. A manager with Lever Brothers, he was brought into Thatcher's inner policy-making group by Keith Joseph. He worked closely with John Hoskyns first to produce *Stepping Stones*, the effective blueprint for the 1979–83 Thatcher Government, and then in the Prime Minister's Policy Unit to co-ordinate the implementation of policies. He left Number Ten in 1982, disenchanted by his experience.

NORMAN TEBBIT The classic Thatcherite MP. A pilot in the Royal Air Force and then with British Overseas Airways, he describes himself as 'upwardly mobile'. A member of the Conservative Party since 1946 when he was 15, he entered Parliament in 1970. He was an early – and ardent – supporter of Margaret Thatcher's bid for the Party leadership against Heath, and worked closely with Airey Neave in the late 1970s helping to brief Thatcher for Parliamentary Questions. Hard-hitting in debate, he entered the

Cabinet in 1981 as Employment Minister and was responsible for much of Thatcher's trade union legislation. He was seriously injured, and his wife was crippled, in the Brighton hotel bombed by the IRA during the 1984 Party Conference. Tebbit grew apart from Thatcher in 1987 when he was Party chairman, feeling that he had been undercut by David Young in the conduct of that year's general election campaign.

DENIS THATCHER Margaret Thatcher's husband and longest-serving Person. Easily – and frequently – underestimated. His 'Golf Club' manner and reported views generated the long-running 'Dear Bill' letters in *Private Eye* and a stage play. A successful businessman, he always took great pride in his wife's achievements, and was never frightened of her. He used his influence primarily to reassure and protect her, but also to encourage her free market instincts. In the Thatchers' private life, he was boss. She informally sought his advice about trade and industry matters, and about people. His conduct as the Prime Minister's consort was impeccable, winning widespread affection and respect.

NIGEL VINSON Treasurer of the Centre for Policy Studies, 1974–80, he actually screwed the nameplate onto the Centre's Wilfred Street offices. A dynamic entrepreneur and inventor, he founded Plastic Coatings Ltd in 1952 in a Nissen hut (he keeps the photograph of the hut on his office wall). A Trustee of the Institute of Economic Affairs, he was an important connection to the world of business and finance for the Centre, for which he raised funds without competing with the IEA or the Party.

ALAN WALTERS The longest-serving of all Thatcher's advisers. Professor of Economics at Johns Hopkins University. He was instrumental in convincing Margaret Thatcher and Keith Joseph to adopt monetarist policies, and he effectively masterminded Thatcher's thinking about economics in Number Ten. He came from a working-class home in Leicester. His father was a Communist. He served as a private in the Army during World War II. For most of his career as a monetarist economist, he faced the animosity and – at times – ridicule of Keynesians, but always remained cheerful, enthusiastic and outspoken. His advice was proved magnificently correct after the 1981 Budget.

WILLIE WHITELAW 'Every Prime Minister needs a Willie,' said Thatcher of her – and Heath's – deputy leader. Willie's bluff and avuncular style masked an acute political mind and a deep dedication to the Conservative Party. He became truly committed to Thatcher as a result of working with her closely during the Falklands War, and he used his standing in the Party to support her leadership and to 'sell' Thatcherism. His popularity in Parliament and in the country was a tremendous asset to Thatcher until ill health forced his retirement from full-time politics in January 1988. He exercised tremendous influence on Thatcher who understood the nature of his loyalty and also that having contested the leadership with her in 1975, he would never do so again. Thatcher never found an adequate replacement for him, and in the opinion of many observers, his departure marked the beginning of her decline in popularity that culminated with her resignation in 1990.

DAVID WOLFSON A vital behind-the-scenes figure throughout Margaret Thatcher's time as Party leader, both in Opposition (he was secretary of the Shadow Cabinet in 1978–9) and in Number Ten. He gained extensive experience of management in Great Universal Stores, his family's firm. He was crucial in seeing that the Policy Unit and key advisers had access to the Prime Minister while he was her unpaid chief of staff in 1979–85. He was completely trusted by Thatcher.

DAVID YOUNG A stereotypical Thatcher Person. The son of immigrants from Lithuania, he became a successful solicitor-businessman. He was a Labour voter in the 1960s. He was involved in the Centre for Policy Studies in 1976 by Keith Joseph, becoming a director in 1979. After the 1979 general election, Joseph made him an adviser at the Department of Industry. In 1984, Thatcher put him in the House of Lords in order to bring him into her Cabinet. With the controversial Rover deal – whereby Rover cars was privatized and sold to British Aerospace with £44 million of Government 'sweeteners' thrown in – which he called 'the deal of the century', Young demonstrated the essentially pragmatic core of Thatcherism in Government. He was anything but an ideologue: a point he stressed in the title of his autobiography, *The Enterprise Years: A Businessman in the Cabinet*.

ONE

Thatcher herself

'I'd rather kiss Mrs Thatcher,' was the story in the sports pages of the popular press on Wednesday, 25 October 1989. Brian Clough, the impetuous and short-fused manager of Nottingham Forest Football Club, was saying that he had no intention of retiring.

Clough was, perhaps, saying more than he intended. He was appealing to an assumption that Thatcher and her policies were repugnant. At the time, the Conservative Party was behind in the polls, and Margaret Thatcher's personal popularity was low. The Party Conference season had just ended, and articles abounded about the third Thatcher Government's 'mid-term crisis'. With less accuracy, Clough was also appealing to a class consciousness, an 'Us and Them' view: that the sort of people who play football and go to football matches or watch them on television sets did not like or support Margaret Thatcher's Government or policies. Moreover, in a week when the *Daily Mail* was advertising a series of articles called 'The Gender Gap', Clough was acknowledging the obvious: Margaret Thatcher's sex. The fact that she had been an effective Prime Minister for over ten consecutive years, and leader of the Conservative Party for more than fourteen, had made people oblivious to another – that she was a woman. Indeed, one of her first Parliamentary supporters, John Biffen, who became her Leader of the House of Commons in 1982–7, said on one occasion, 'I never thought of her as a woman.'[1] Clough's insinuation was that Margaret Thatcher was too something – too strident, too dominant, perhaps? – for any football-thinking man to want to kiss her.

Margaret Thatcher was considered by most people to be formid-

[1] Interview, Rt Hon. John Biffen, MP, 6 June 1990.

able rather than likeable or admirable: there would have been plenty of Conservative as well as Labour voters who, no doubt, chuckled at Clough's remark. She was not taken to the heart of the Party or of the country in the way that Churchill was, although she was leader of the Party and Prime Minister for longer than he was – indeed, for longer than any other Conservative this century. Probably few people, if asked, would have wanted Mrs Thatcher as a next-door neighbour. She lacked the common touch, the ability to convey an impression of being at ease with people of all sorts. Alec Douglas-Home, perhaps surprisingly, had it. Harold Wilson, when everything else was stripped away, still had it. So did Jim Callaghan. People kept hoping that Edward Heath would develop it, but he never did. Like Heath, Margaret Thatcher was not a comfortable presence. People fully accepted her remarkable qualities – her courage and determination and grit – but retained a good deal of ambiguity about the frightening headmistress of the British school, apparently so confident and so certain.

She was a sign as well as an instrument of change. Her election as Party leader represented a major change in political assumptions – as a woman, as a politician who had never before held senior Cabinet office, and as a Conservative unidentified with any major Party grouping. Being self-made and a woman made her an outsider. 'Nobody could have fought through the spoken and unspoken prejudice of the Fifties,' observed Matthew Parris, who had worked for her in Opposition and who had been a Member of Parliament in the 1980s, 'the giggles and sneers of the Sixties, and the concealed male resentment and subtle male condescension of the Seventies and Eighties, without bearing the scars . . . An outsider to her party . . . cannot know what she has put up with.'[1] To some extent she profited by being a woman: no one thought of a female despot. There was a certain respect for her fundamental decency which meant that she was trusted.

Thatcher never really cut loose from her roots. She kept the faith with her father and his corner grocery shop in Grantham, Lincolnshire. 'A son is a son until he takes a wife, but a daughter

[1] Matthew Parris, 'One of Them?', review of Hugo Young, *One of Us* (London, Macmillan, 1989), in the *Spectator*, 15 April 1989.

is a daughter all her life.' She was always Miss Roberts to an extra-ordinary degree. The giants of twentieth-century British politics – Lloyd George and Churchill – saw further than she did. She was not a great intuitive person who handled affairs and events with endless resourcefulness. She operated on a set of rules. She was much closer to Attlee – a man of very strong will – than to Chur-chill. Her rules were important factors in the development of her policies in Opposition and in Government. They sustained her instincts and convictions, and gave her the personal strength to take on the trade unions, economists, civil servants, Brezhnev's USSR, the Falklands War, European politicians and bureaucrats, and her own colleagues.

Thatcher herself was unquestionably the central player in Thatcherism: without her, the policies named after her probably would not have come into being. She figures inescapably in any examintion of her people; she was the unifying factor that held them together. She is a formidable political operator. She liked being cheered. She saw to it that belief in dynamic entrepreneurism was substituted for the post-Second World War British belief in consensus. Only one parliamentary colleague, Sir Keith (now Lord) Joseph, was important in this development. Few of her people enjoyed the day-to-day life of democratic politics but they were carried by the locomotive of her liking for it. She was not so much intellectually energizing her people as nourishing them – the native bearer in the jungle of Westminster. David (now Lord) Young, who was Secretary of State for Trade and Industry, did not enjoy parliamentary interrogation. Sir Alfred Sherman would have erupted under severe questioning in the House. Keith Joseph, who with Alfred Sherman was the 'father' of Thatcherism, was genuinely upset because, as a scrupulously intellectual person, answering questions on the terms put in Parliament just was not his line of country.

The ideas of Thatcher's people were not synonymous with Mar-garet Thatcher's, and several of her intimate advisers left her in anger and frustration at her refusal to reform things as quickly as they would like, or at all. Thatcher's style was as important as substance when it came to disagreement. 'I criticized her policies,' said Norman Strauss, 'not from a spirit of opposition, but because

I thought they were wrong or could be improved. But she does not like criticism. I knew that from the start. In Flood Street [her London home in the 1970s] in 1976 she said about some MP, "I'm never going to give him anything!" So I knew right from the start that she was pettiness personified. She wants to be IT. I didn't vote for Margaret Thatcher to be Prime Minister to become a power dresser and have her teeth straightened.'[1] Sir Geoffrey Howe, her deputy, when he left her Government in November 1990, emphasized that style and substance were interwoven with Thatcher. Her style often dominated substance. 'Christopher Soames lost his place because of a clash with her over the civil service strike in 1981,' recalled a friend of his. 'He said that the strikers had a case and that it would be politic and would save money in the end to meet their demands. "No! No!" she said. "That's giving in to them! We can't do that!" So the strike, which affected the Customs and fairly huge sectors of public life, rumbled on. And finally she changed her mind. But she was so annoyed at having to do this, she sacked Christopher. He was right. I guess that was the most important element: right. It showed her up, and it cost the taxpayer millions, so he had to go. It was her at her worst: vindictive, ungrateful, pigheaded. Christopher told me later, and by that time he was very embittered, so you've got to allow for that. But nonetheless, the facts do stand up for themselves. Through sheer pigheadedness she refused to see the writing on the wall, cost the taxpayer millions, and then turned on the man who was right and shoved him out! He stood up for his side, and he was right, and it cost him his political life.'[2]

Any Prime Minister remaining in power as long as Margaret Thatcher did will lose supporters. 'Her technique, and it's true of ideas and it's true of people,' said a close adviser nine months before she resigned as Prime Minister, 'is that she does it as a full-time job, and she doesn't like pleasure: she doesn't want to be amused by much. She uses people and she spits them out when it suits her. Not in any nasty way, but she's not going to waste her time on somebody who is no longer of use. If somebody's got an idea of

[1] Interview, Norman Strauss, 25 May 1990.
[2] Interview, 20 January 1990.

use to her, she will want to see them. Those that have views about elections, she'll see at election time, and so on. She eats people.'[1] 'Her strengths are her weaknesses,' observed Nigel (now Lord) Vinson, who worked with her in establishing the Centre for Policy Studies in the 1970s. 'For a woman to get to the top and effect change, she can brook no argument, because she has to go battling through like a tank. That's why she leaves a trail behind her. And occasionally, tanks get it wrong.'[2] Norman Strauss left her Prime Minister's Policy Unit because he could not persuade her to more extensive reforms. John Hoskyns left the Unit, in part, because he felt that strategic clarity was being lost, and partly because he thought he had done the job he had come to do. Alfred Sherman, who was ousted as director of policy studies at the CPS in the early 1980s, indicated this division with the remark that 'Mrs Thatcher's political health and Thatcherism itself are not necessarily identical.'[3]

For Thatcher, the job of politics was pragmatism in the cause of her objectives. Not all her people accepted this, and they were frustrated as a result. An important consequence was that she became distant from her people and more dependent upon courtiers. 'She's lost the real, genuine Thatcherites like myself who would be glad to support her,' John Biffen tellingly observed in June 1990.[4] Alfred Sherman, John Hoskyns, and Norman Strauss in one way or another all moved away from her. They had specialized functions geared to the times, and provided services which were never substituted. 'The greatest disservice is done to her by Downing Street,' observed an adviser with feeling four months before her resignation. 'She is surrounded by civil servants and not by real political advisers. You never ever hear that she turned up late or was ill-equipped. She should have people who say "Bugger all that!" When she does things spontaneously, she's a real joy, but there's less and less of it all the time.'[5] 'What I thought at one time was the beginning of Glory,' one of her early people said with regret, 'was actually just an aberration between the decline

[1] Interview, 13 February 1990.
[2] Interview, Lord Vinson, 30 May 1990.
[3] Sir Alfred Sherman, 'The Thatcher Era in Perspective', *The World & I*, April 1989, p. 613.
[4] Interview, Rt Hon. John Biffen, MP, 6 June 1990.
[5] Interview, 5 June 1990.

19

started by Wilson, Heath and Callaghan, and the Prime Minister after her who will probably continue that decline. I don't see that she can take this culture by the scruff of the neck and change it. It's too difficult. We'll never go back to the Heath–Callaghan era, but we're not going to go forward. That's the tragedy of it. And she's surrounded by wimps.'[1]

Apart from presiding over the entry of a new generation and new groups of people into the Conservative Party (which goes with being at the top for so long), Thatcher encouraged entrepreneurs in the world of business, and sought to instil commercial attitudes in every sector of British life. Her conviction that business was good for Britain in every possible way was a mainspring of Thatcherism. She was less a creative figure than one who was convinced that Britain was badly run, from the shop floor to Whitehall. She was the Receiver in Bankruptcy of the British political order. She was the least Tory Prime Minister that the Conservative Party could produce. She had no attachments to the traditional political bases. She was not close to the Established Church, to organic Toryism, to the civil service, the Crown, the City, the House of Commons or the House of Lords. She was close to nineteenth-century liberalism – a point noted by the Institute of Economic Affairs. She insisted upon a rationalist view of the world which was simultaneously passionate, and in which the conflicts were not resolved. She had a deep and manifest impatience with the record and methods of UK Ltd, and this provided her strongest political drive. She had a great belief in responsibility and recrimination, which is why she pursued inefficiency and wrongdoing in the heartland of business and the civil service. If commerce and security – two of her objectives – were to thrive, she was determined that they should do so honourably and lawfully. She was no barrow-girl or merchant of quick profit.

Margaret Thatcher was brave. She was narrow. She was driven by certainties – usually of others being wrong. She was an uncomplicatedly middle-class person. She had a high degree of practical intelligence, shrewdness and acumen. She was not a reflective being. She was energized by the exercise of authority and of will. She was

[1] Interview, 5 June 1990.

20

unclubbable. She openly despised many people, and imputed worse motives to them than they might have possessed. 'She feels that most Government activity is full of wet little people who want to fix prices,' a Number Ten insider observed in early 1990.[1] She was of genuinely high moral character. She had a great appetite for power, but at the same time a deep impatience with the institutions upon which her power rested. She knew that courtesy, especially in a strong Prime Minister, is one of the few ways of fending off accusations of arrogance and ruthlessness. 'She believes in and seeks power,' said a close aide. 'She doesn't believe much in the apparatus of Government and she believes that a great deal of it ought to go.'[2] But she was wiser than many of her people, and recognized that an all-out attack on officialdom would smack of too much greed for power.

She demystified the Government, but she upheld a mystique of the State. When it came to the State and its heart of hearts, she was resolute. In economic policy, she was perfectly happy to reveal what Government was doing. But when it came to Britain's relationship to Europe, she saw Britain as a State, not just as a country. And that was because she felt that Britain was not just a society, but had a destiny of its own embodied in the State, not in the territory. 'She identifies very much with the national interest,' observed Lord Home.[3] She had no hesitation about tightening up on leaks when it suited her. She used Her Majesty's Government as a shield for the State – most notably when she argued that the sovereignty of the Crown would be jeopardized in a united Europe. A State has higher, transcendent purposes which made her risk her life when the IRA clearly had her on the top of their hit list. She felt she had a trust to rule. She did not merely persuade or administer: she ruled in the context of the State. She was not the Chairman of the Board. 'She is in that British political tradition that sees the Prime Minister as the unifying force in Britain, as the motive force in Britain,' considered John Biffen from his experience as one of her Cabinet Ministers, 'who alone is able to give authority and direction and shape and is prepared to use all the weapons to hand like the use

[1] Interview, 14 February 1990.
[2] Interview, 14 February 1990.
[3] Interview, Rt Hon. Lord Home, KT, 20 November 1988.

of the Cabinet Committees and more especially the use of the Ad Hoc Committees, the membership of which derives from her own judgement. And who has a small but effective back-up service in whatever think-tank happens to be in vogue. And is therefore the Chief Executive as well as the Managing Director, quite unlike many Prime Ministers in the past, particularly once you get pre-1939. Ted Heath was very much like that too. She wasn't that much interested in letting the "Finance Director" dribble on, and then the "Marketing Director" have his say, and then the "Production Director". She was much more there saying, "The strategy is we've got to get twenty per cent of the market in the next eighteen months. Get on with it!" It was not just the politics of conviction. I don't think she would recognize any virtues in the philosophy of creative tension. And I think that is quite important.'[1]

Margaret Thatcher was not an enactor of ideas. She was hospitable to ideas, but she always operated with a political agenda in mind, not an ideological one. For her, ideas were means to ends. She knew that practicalities were important. As a lawyer, she knew that power is often based upon the mastery of detail. She knew that there are people who are deserving but who do not receive, and she knew that there are whingers and spongers. She effectively geared her political appeal to this level of awareness. Anyone who has stood for Parliament in 1950, 1951, 1959, 1964, 1970, 1974 (twice), 1979, 1983 and 1987 has been exposed to a large number of the electorate, especially after campaigning around the country, and it is a salutary experience. Anyone who has canvassed has a different sense of what democracy is from those who have not knocked on doors. The reason that she changed her mind about the policies of Ted Heath in the early 1970s was because, for her, life meant the life of politics, and before most people she caught the mood of the moment and ideas whose time had come.

Samuel Brittan, possibly Britain's leading commentator on economic affairs, has said, 'Thatcher is no Thatcherite,'[2] playing on the differences between her, Thatcherism, and some of her people.

[1] Interview, Rt Hon. John Biffen, MP, 6 June 1990.
[2] *Financial Times*, 2 July 1990. Brittan is a born theorist and a very good one. He is a great stimulus to debate. He was arguing that 'Mrs Thatcher's utterances

Thatcherism was a consciously theoretical doctrine and she was not a consciously theoretical person, so it was no surprise that she was not a 'Thatcherite'. Karl Marx said he was not a 'Marxist' because he was always changing his mind and expanding. People with a given doctrine tend to be of closed mentality, and Thatcher was a practical, operating person, not very interested in conceptual analysis, convinced that certain things that were obvious to her should be done, even if others did not immediately grasp them.

She described her ideas as being 'born of the conviction which I learned in a small town from a father who had a conviction approach'.[1] 'The conviction was enigmatic often, and certainly inspirational,' remembered John Biffen. 'It was not that intellectual. She rather distrusted intellectual process. Coincidental with the inspirational there was also the great dedication to "Action This Day". So there was the motive, the theme, the great direction of the Government, and added to it the Executive ability to put into effect these various elements. They are two separate characteristics. That's the impression that I formed.'[2] The playwright, Ronald Millar, who had worked on speeches for Edward Heath in the early 1970s, became one of Thatcher's trusted helpers because – unlike most of her people who were more involved with business and economics and thus knew that very little is simple – he demonstrated a simplicity of conviction identical to her own. A Number Ten insider told Millar's tale: 'Ronnie has no influence on policy.

during the Dublin E[uropean] C[ommunity] summit have once more demonstrated that, whatever else she is, she is not a Thatcherite.' His rationale was that the reason she gave at the June 1990 summit for continuing to oppose European monetary union and the Exchange Rate Mechanism of the European Monetary System put her in agreement with the arguments of the Labour Left in 1976 that the requirements put upon the then Labour Government by the International Monetary Fund in exchange for financial assistance to Britain placed jobs and growth at risk. She argued against fixed exchange rates and 'conveniently forgets that the British espousal of floating rates in 1972 was part of the Heath dash for growth, in which a fixed sterling rate was seen as an obstacle to spending ourselves into prosperity through cheap money and higher public spending – the very things that Thatcherism is supposed to be against.' Brittan was a strong supporter of Nigel Lawson's policies as Chancellor, and an echo of this concluded his article: 'the political and economic cost [of Thatcher's position], unless Cabinet government is reasserted, could be huge' (cf. Chapter 13 below).

[1] Quoted in Chris Ogden, *Maggie* (New York, Simon & Schuster, 1990), p. 192.
[2] Interview, Rt Hon. John Biffen, MP, 6 June 1990.

He had been with Ted for two or three years. And after Ted went, she arrived, and she was elected leader, and she had a Party political broadcast to do in about four weeks, as the new leader. And she didn't really know quite what she wanted to say quite that quickly. And somebody said to her, "We've got this chap who does write for us called Ronnie Millar. He's worked for Ted." She said, "Well, ask him to do a draft and then I'll have a look." So Ronnie was asked to do a draft, and he sat and composed a statement of Conservative philosophy that she would give. It was going to finish with her speaking to the camera. And he thought of this quote by Abraham Lincoln, "You cannot enrich the poor by impoverishing the rich. You cannot strengthen the weak by weakening the strong." And he put it in as the final paragraph of her PPB. And he presented it to her. He'd never met her before, and she took it from him and read it, and didn't say a word. And at the end, when she'd finished it, she didn't speak. She laid it down and reached for her handbag and started pulling out bits of paper and finally, at the very bottom, she pulled out this crinkled piece of paper. She unfolded and handed it to him, and in her own hand was written: "You cannot enrich etc." And from that day, Ronnie could do nothing wrong and he's written every speech ever since.'[1]

Like many of her people, Thatcher was an outsider. Her generation did not accept women as equal to men. She had not been in a good regiment. Francis (now Lord) Pym, Secretary of State for Defence and then Secretary of State for Foreign Affairs in Thatcher's first administration, a leading 'wet' who had been at Eton and Cambridge, and had served in the 9th Lancers during the Second World War, being mentioned in dispatches and winning the Military Cross, once said to a backbencher: 'The trouble is, we've got a corporal at the top, not a cavalry officer.' 'Francis is just a snob,' Thatcher said when this was reported to her.[2] She had studied chemistry: not one of the 'right' subjects. She was not the kind of person who might have expected to be made a judge if she had stayed in the legal profession. A Lord Chancellor's Office, under the Conservatives or Labour, would probably not have thought

[1] Interview, 14 February 1990.
[2] Young, *One of Us*, p. 331.

that Margaret Thatcher was the kind of person to grace the bench in 1980 when she was 55 – the kind of age you make someone a High Court judge. She would probably never have been invited to chair a Royal Commission. She would probably have been seen as too partisan, as not being capable of detached judgement.

Thatcher's political desires and convictions owed a great deal to her background. She went through three of the great tradition-laden institutions of Britain – Oxford, the Bar, and Parliament – and they left hardly any mark on her. She was impatient with the House of Commons, and was deeply unimpressed with being a member of the Bar. She probably had little respect for the Church of England which she attended in wartime Oxford when there was emotional emphasis on aesthetic continuity and calls to the core of England. She apparently felt the pull of the moment, but it seems not to have meant much to her over the last thirty-five years: she was brought up as a Methodist and married a Methodist in a Methodist Chapel. No Prime Minister since Lloyd George has been so uncatchable by the fine nets of British assimilation.

Thatcher's academic and intellectual abilities were somewhat derided when she became leader of the Conservative Party and subsequently Prime Minister. 'Nobody thought anything of her,'[1] said Janet Vaughan, a distinguished medical expert on blood diseases who became principal of Somerville College, Oxford, in 1945 when young Margaret Roberts was an undergraduate there. 'She was a perfectly good second-class chemist,' the Nobel prize-winning chemist, Dorothy Hodgkin, remembered. 'None of us ever thought that she would go very far.'[2] But what her Oxford tutors were talking about was Margaret Roberts as a chemist, and she was not an exceptional chemist. Tutors do not mark general ability: they're there for specialization. Margaret Roberts's abilities were not those that Oxford Finals tend to reward: they do not put every quality through the examination system. There is no reason why ability in chemistry correlates with ability in politics and administration. 'One could always rely on her to produce a sensible, well-read essay,' said Hodgkin, 'and yet there was something that some people had that

[1] *Sunday Express*, 20 July 1975.
[2] Nicholas Wapshott and George Brock, *Thatcher* (London, Futura, 1983), p. 49.

she hadn't quite got. I don't believe she had a particularly profound interest in chemistry.'[1] She was simply not made to be a chemist. She has grown in ability – not personally, but in technical matters – from being regarded as 'ordinary' by her tutors. She is intensely interested in resolving practical problems. She is not someone who learned 150 rationalizations for market behaviour, but give her a practical consequence and she is an excellent student. It must have been something of a rebellion against what was expected of her for a sixteen-year-old girl to apply to read chemistry at Oxford from Kesteven and Grantham Girls School, despite her illustrious predecessor from the town, Isaac Newton. She had an argument with the headmistress of the school who felt she was reaching too far, too fast. She was not willing to do the Eng. Lit. crit. that smart girls were expected to do. Her drive and ambition came partly from her father who was a very direct person, and partly from her own temperament which is interested in results – that you go to do something and you prove you can do it so you go on to the next thing, and so on. You cannot prove you can do anything else by writing a dazzling review of *Middlemarch*. Chemistry was work; English Literature and History were play, and she was not interested in playing. It is noteworthy that so competitive a person as she is has no reputation in any sport. Her notion of competition comes from the work end of life.

As Prime Minister, she had an all or nothing attitude to Cabinet membership. Unlike Thorneycroft's resignation as Chancellor of the Exchequer in 1958, which was impersonal and clean (i.e., entirely about policy), and meant that there could be a genuine reconciliation later, the resignations of several of Thatcher's Ministers were acrimonious and highly personal: when Geoffrey Howe resigned from her Cabinet on 1 November 1990, he made a profoundly personal attack on her in his speech in the House of Commons explaining his action. She generally sought to keep men in Cabinet to make them complicit in her actions and her policies: Howe, for example, indicated that in his own judgement he should have resigned earlier. Thatcher let quarrels run on; the public learned about them, and the Ministers concerned looked exceed-

[1] Allan J. Meyer, *Madam Prime Minister* (New York, Newsweek, 1979), p. 49.

ingly awkward: they were troublemakers; they were not showing the nerve to quit. Such was the fate of Howe, Sir Ian Gilmour, her first Lord Privy Seal, Francis Pym, and John Biffen, who served in various posts in 1979–87. When Howe resigned, he was the thirty-fifth Cabinet Minister to do so since Thatcher came to power in 1979, and was the only person to have survived from her first Cabinet. Michael Heseltine, who resigned as Minister for Defence over the Westland affair in 1986, was an exception. He was the only Minister who got out from under: this was an important asset to him in his bid for the leadership of the Party in November 1990.

Thatcher kept her ascendancy. She had a limited range of response. 'She doesn't have friends,' said a Number Ten aide. 'If you were to say to her that there would be a dinner party for her and six friends, she wouldn't be able to fill the places.'[1] She was interested in encountering people, not in knowing them. 'If you look at the Ministers that she got on best with,' observed a senior advertising executive, five months before John Major succeeded her, 'they're all attractive figures. And the ones that she got on least well with are unattractive figures. There are obviously exceptions, but that's the general trend. She's a woman! If you think about it, it isn't a consideration for a man because they're all bloody men. They don't feel sexual about their Cabinets. What women they do get in there are normally ghastly. There's hardly been any women in the Cabinet. Barbara Castle was rather glamorous, but other than that there's been hardly any. So they're not faced with that dilemma. The thing that we're all getting is what, funnily enough, the British people accepted without consideration, which was having a woman Prime Minister. It wasn't an issue at all in 1979. It is an issue now.'[2]

Thatcher did not have the male attitude to conflict; there is a sticking point beyond which men will not normally go, largely because they realize that to go further means fighting to the death. Men understand this, and also seem to know instinctively where that point is. Thatcher was prepared to 'kill' opponents and rivals,

[1] Interview, 13 February 1990.
[2] Interview, 5 June 1990.

27

usually by letting them hang themselves. She sat there, unquestionably pre-eminent, patiently allowing the boys to get angry and impulsive – to kick up their heels. They waited for her to resolve matters, and she did not. She just went on, making no attempt to calm them down. And they could not yell at her. Tones of voice would rise with a male Prime Minister. Fifty-year-old men with a sixty-five-year-old woman boss feel very constrained. Looking at her Cabinet ministers sitting beside her as she made her final speech as Prime Minister to the House of Commons, it was obvious that she had worn them out.

Enoch Powell pinpointed her patience and her ability to indicate one view while actually possessing another. 'A characteristic of Mrs Thatcher is that she is a very patient person,' he observed. 'She can put up for a long time with being made to say what she doesn't believe. She can do it with extraordinary patience and tolerance. For ten years and more – more if you add in the years in Opposition – she talked about the European Economic Community in the language which the Conservative Party expected to hear talked, and she was surrounded by people who talked that talk. So time after time she got on the white horse of her instincts and armed with a lance she rode off to Strasburg or Milan on the right point, and came back with her lance broken, to general satisfaction, but without any deep feeling on her part. "Believing what you believe, you can't say what you've said!" is not something that upsets the Prime Minister because the consonance between thought and words is something in which she is basically not interested. This – as well as being a woman – enables her year after year to live with something, with a cross on a paper at the back of her mind saying, "I don't agree with that; I don't like it; it's rotten awful; but I can't do anything about it at the moment." It's not exactly the mood of a person who says, "I'm trapped"; it's more the mood of a person who says, "I don't like that. When I can settle accounts with that, I will settle accounts with it."[1]

This assessment makes her appear to be a stranger being than she was. The profession of politics includes agreeing with fifty-one per cent or more of what you are supposed to say. Margaret Thatcher

[1] Interview, Rt Hon. J. Enoch Powell, MBE, 1 November 1989.

28

compromised, and went along with policies and positions she did not like. What made her unusual was, as Powell pointed out, her patience and willingness to stick to her guns or to return to them when she thought she could win.

Many of Thatcher's attitudes – not least her encouragement of competitiveness – were American. Her background was Nonconformist and partly Welsh, both of which were terribly important to her.[1] If you were a Welsh Nonconformist small businessman in Lincolnshire in the 1920s and 1930s, and you heard about America as a place where they did not care who your father was, where they respected business enterprise, and where a great many Welsh people had done very well, being pro-American was almost natural. The Nonconformist idealization of the United States really only broke down with the penetration of socialism into the Nonconformist radical ideal. Thatcher's great-grandparents were probably enthusiastic defenders of the Union during the American Civil War, when the British aristocracy of both Parties was rubbing its hands at the bursting of 'the great Republican bubble'. In contrast, hard-working, chapel, lower-middle-class Welsh people were praying openly for the victory of the North. She was almost certainly an hereditary pro-American, this quality intensified by the experience of her lifetime. Just as in Irish villages you will hear about native sons who made good in America, so too in Welsh (and Cornish) villages.[2] In the 1950s, British elites were anti-American; in the 1990s they are pro-American. The business classes, the military, young people in Britain in the 1990s are all pro-American. In her own attitudes, Margaret Thatcher had much of what was natural to many of those who supported her.

When people said she was lower middle class, they meant the very obvious attachment to pieties: hard work, scrupulousness, loyalty.

[1] The Roberts family came from South Wales. Thatcher's father settled in Grantham, Lincolnshire, where she was born.

[2] Gaelic Scots went mostly to Canada, so there is much less of a tradition of pro-American sentiment in Scotland. The New York Yacht Club used to run up the Union Jack on Cowes Day, and in 1921 a mob of Irishmen tried to storm it. There was hand-to-hand fighting, and the President of the Club had both his eyes blacked. He later received a telegram from the Royal Yacht Club saying, 'Oh, say, can you see!' The American elite saw Britain sitting on the troublesome Irish, just as they were themselves doing, and only with the creation of the Irish Free State did American elite opinion shift behind Ireland.

They also meant that she was vulgar (which she was not) and narrow-minded. When she spoke of 'our people' concerning mortgage tax relief in the 1970s, she meant just that: the mortgage-owning middle class. She regarded large parts of the rest of Britain as neither her supporters nor potential supporters at all. She would have been happy to see quite a few millions of British people floating away to sea. She was not a One Nation Tory, and this was a clear attitude that coloured much of the opposition to her.

She could not be accused of being a reactionary when she was so obviously impatient with the trappings of traditional Conservatism. This impatience gave her a legitimacy in the eyes of the working and middle classes. Sir Robert Peel, the first 'radical' Conservative leader, was much more cautious about appealing to the middle classes against the old aristocracy. Bonar Law was uninterested in all that: he could not understand why people wanted to be peers and have the Garter and knighthoods and so on. He was a tough Scots-Canadian businessman whose imagination was fired by Ulster and Protection and other extremely down-to-earth matters. Thatcher, in a more attractive way, was like that, and this greatly enhanced her authority. You could not call her a 'Tory' woman, and this gave her a tremendous ideological position. Millions of people who did not think of themselves as Conservative voted for Thatcher. There were many people who knew that she did not want to dine at White's and did not refer to them behind their backs as 'grocers' or 'counter-jumpers'.

If Margaret Thatcher had become the Ramsay MacDonald of the Conservative Party and succumbed to the aristocratic embrace, she would have become waterlogged very soon. She did not do so, and this gave her a margin of victory each time round. One of the great strengths of democracy is that the experts and hereditary groupings should not have everything their own way, and this is one of the things politicians are there to articulate. But the politicians had better be right in what they choose to challenge. Thatcher chose correctly more often than not. 'Unlike most politicians, she has no desire to be trendy,' said one of her advisers in Number Ten. 'No desire to have new ideas, to be seduced by something that might catch the imagination. None at all. She just puts her head down and ploughs through, going on with the same themes repeatedly and identically.'[1]

'It was Charlie Pannell, my fellow Labour MP in Leeds, who first drew my attention to Margaret Thatcher in 1960,' Denis Healey wrote in his memoirs. 'She had just won her seat in Finchley at the age of thirty-four. For some reason Charlie had taken her under his wing. He told me to watch her, saying that she was exceptionally able, and also a very nice woman. This was quite a compliment coming from a Cockney engineer who was famous for his rough tongue.'[2] 'I first saw her in 1959,' recalled Peter Rawlinson. 'I noticed in the committee room a pretty girl. She had a creamy pink and white complexion, and beautifully, too beautifully, coiffed fair hair, not a single strand out of place. But there was a rather prim pursing about the lips. To look at, she was certainly far better than any other girl I had ever seen in the House . . . I watched the girl with the bright hair and I could see that she was winding herself up ready to join in . . . It was obvious that her "contribution" had been designed merely to attract attention. She had of course attracted notice from every man in the room before she had ever opened her mouth. But that was not the kind of notice which she sought.'[3]

Well, up to a point, Lord Copper! 'I love being at the centre of things,' she once said,[4] and on St Valentine's Day 1975, just after winning the Party leadership, she exploited the moment for a piece of political coquetry, acknowledging what Peter Rawlinson hinted at: 'I like to be made a fuss of by a lot of chaps!'[5] 'A characteristic about her advisers,' said a member of her Policy Unit, 'is that she has very tall, quite attractive men around her, which tends to support a sexual awareness on her part. But, equally, she's very dismissive about sex: the Parkinson thing did not matter in her eyes – that's what silly boys do, kind of thing.'[6]

She operated at the limits of politics, which was unusual. She

[1] Interview, 13 February 1990.
[2] Denis Healey, *The Time of My Life* (London, Michael Joseph, 1989), p. 487.
[3] Peter Rawlinson, *A Price Too High* (London, Weidenfeld & Nicolson, 1989), p. 246.
[4] *Reader's Digest*, January 1984.
[5] *Daily Mirror*, 14 February 1975.
[6] Interview, 25 May 1990. Cecil Parkinson had an affair with his secretary and fathered her child.

was prepared to press issues, despite interest groups and pressure groups, whenever she judged she could succeed politically. 'What has made her a Prime Minister whom so many of us admire,' said Nigel Vinson, 'is that she has a deep ideological sincerity. She believes. She is not there for herself at all. She is there because she believes we've got it wrong in terms of ideology in this country. And she's right.'[1] It took her a decade in Government to introduce poll tax – something she had first floated in 1974 – and she persevered with it, despite massive public anger, not only because she believed it to be right, but because she believed it would succeed politically. She knew that there is far more waiting to be done than politics allows for, and thus that there was always something else for her to turn her attention to. She was far more flexible than she was given credit for, as she demonstrated, for example, in her dealings with the Soviet Union. From being the 'Iron Lady' she became one of Mikhail Gorbachev's principal supporters in the West. All this separated her from the people who so many of the critics of Thatcherism assumed were identical with Thatcher.

She wanted continuous political power, not one specific victory. She would make sacrifices of dignity and consistency in order to keep power. Thus ministerial colleagues at times found themselves alone pursuing policies that she had ordered and then allowed to lapse because they proved unwinnable. For example, Cecil Parkinson – a man many considered she 'made' – as Secretary of State for Energy was isolated in his effort to include nuclear power stations in electricity privatization. In July 1990 the Parliamentary Energy Select Committee in a report whose title minced no words, *The Cost of Nuclear Power: What Went Wrong?*, held him to have been doctrinaire and incompetent on the issue. Colin Moynihan, when junior Minister for Sport, had to abandon an identity card scheme for football supporters because it was widely judged to be unworkable. In 1981, Michael Heseltine, then Environment Minister, in the face of political pressure had to withdraw a section of the Local Government Finance Bill proposing that councils seeking supplementary rates must conduct referenda first (an idea that Thatcher did not give up: her patience could be seen). Other ministers, who

[1] Interview, Lord Vinson, 30 May 1990.

32

had been less resolute in pursuing her wishes, had been sacked. Patrick Jenkin was dropped as Secretary of State for the Environment when he took too long to abolish the Greater London Council. John Moore was dropped as Health Minister when he failed to win the political debate over market principles being introduced to the National Health Service. A former minister said, 'There is a great deal of pressure on ministers to deliver. Those who say "no" get sacked. Those who don't deliver eventually get shopped by her. You have to be strong and say, "It can't be done." But few are.'[1]

Thatcher strongly desired technocratic and moral objectives of national improvement, but she had no obsessions. She had a general wish to make things more competitive, less cosy, more abrasive, recognizing that technical improvements are not enough without alterations of attitudes. She knew the sources of her support were impersonal, and that nationalism frequently confronted 'market' principles, resulting in inconsistencies. Bonaparte said, *'On s'engage, et puis on voit'* ('You give battle and then see how things turn out'), and that pragmatic view was her view too. The British public may have been angry with Margaret Thatcher at times, but they would have been really scared if she had started acquiring more power. She was eminently aware that her extraordinary power was as much based upon the failure of the Opposition as upon any desire to entrust power to her.

Under Thatcher, a very practical faith won the day, the essence of which was that hard work shall be rewarded, that restrictive practices from tariff protectionism to many professional monopolies were wrong, and that there are no soft rides. 'It's her own instinct,' said a close adviser. 'It comes from Councillor Roberts. That's what she's driven by. That's why she likes people who have the simple view: money in and money out. Subtract one from the other and if there's no figure you've been wasting your time. That's her whole view. She is very middle class, very proletariat, very ordinary. And she's not interested in all these tricksy, clever things. Whenever she goes wrong, it's when people start giving her all this complicated crap and she gets complicated about it.'[2] 'My policies are based not

[1] *Independent*, 29 June 1990.
[2] Interview, 5 June 1990.

on some economic theory,' she said in 1981, 'but on things I and millions like me were brought up with: an honest day's work for an honest day's pay; live within your means; put by a nest egg for a rainy day; pay your bills on time; support the police.'[1] 'She doesn't have an original idea in her head,' said Ralph (now Lord) Harris. 'That's not meant to be offensive: politicians aren't meant to have original ideas. But she has some instincts. And she brought to that superhuman courage that daily withstood the assault that was almost unremitting through the whole of the 1980s.'[2]

Intellectuals tend to put people in the wrong, and to insist on defining ideas in terms of their own thought. Enoch Powell, who saw individualism and the British nation in parallel, perhaps undervalued Margaret Thatcher's view of the United Kingdom as the ultimate corporation with absolute continuity from the village shop to British-owned multinational companies to UK Ltd. 'I have been guilty of saying that Ted Heath hated an idea, that if you showed him an idea he would go red in the face and lose his temper,' says Powell. 'There is a remarkable degree of similarity between Thatcher and Heath on this side of their personalities. But it wouldn't be true to say that Mrs Thatcher hates ideas. She's not comfortable with them. It's rather like her being in the company of people who are experts in Ming China, and the whole room is full of beautiful Ming porcelain, and they can see the difference between that vase and that vase, and you only wish you enjoyed Ming porcelain because obviously enjoying Ming porcelain is quite a thing. And Thatcher has tended to find herself in that kind of embarrassment: of being with people who actually enjoy ideas; who actually enjoy knocking them around; who actually enjoy playing with them and manipulating them; who enjoy thinking. Thatcher doesn't enjoy thinking. And she would be quite right if she were thoughtful enough to say, "But it would get in my way."'[3] In fact Ted Heath had a big idea of European cooperation, and he worked hard in its pursuit. Margaret Thatcher had a big idea of individual freedom and national resurgence, and also probably considered that the doubts

---

[1] *News of the World*, 20 September 1981.
[2] Interview, Lord Harris, 21 May 1990.
[3] Interview, Rt Hon. J. Enoch Powell, MBE, 1 November 1989.

and inexactitudes of intellectual pursuits would consume time and thus would get in her way.

The pride of possession that thinkers take in thinking, and seek to hold to themselves as a means of self-definition, was echoed by Alfred Sherman: 'Mrs Thatcher never "thunk" any thoughts,' he said, also making the point that the source of Thatcherism was linear and restricted. 'She took other people's ideas. She embodied them. The ideas were already there. They came from Bastiat, Sherman, Keith Joseph: fewer people than you would think.'[1] The intellectuals were simply saying that she does not think like them. It would be wrong to say that that means Margaret Thatcher does not think. She thinks 'to do'.

Thatcher's drive produced substantial changes in British post-war attitudes. She intensified debate enormously, not least in her own Party, and her resignation as Prime Minister and Party leader in November 1990 was a direct result of this. In the world of business and finance during the 1980s, restrictive practices were broken down. The arm of the law reached into boardrooms and into senior management to an unprecedented extent. Entrepreneurial activity was encouraged, some would say to the point of vulgarity. But every success in politics carries with it the seeds of defeat, and by the 1990s hedonism – a post-war British characteristic – looked as if it might submerge thrift. 'Old style thrift has gone out of fashion,' remarked the Governor of the Bank of England in the summer of 1990. 'The attitude is "I want it, and I want it now".'[2]

The demystification of business was a central element in the changes that took place under Thatcher. Government today is conducted without the overt support of the great traditional interest groups: the City, the trade unions, the professions. Indeed, each was attacked by her with varying degrees of success – not the action of a traditional Conservative Government.

Her people gathered behind her, but if they stepped beyond the shadow of her convictions, they were on their own. 'You cannot interest

[1] Interview, Sir Alfred Sherman, 30 April 1990. That's Alfred: the intellectual who fought very bravely with the International Brigade demanding that the Prime Minister should be a prophet. Walter Bagehot said that Prime Ministers should have 'the powers of a first-rate man; the creed of a second-rate man': that is Margaret Thatcher.

[2] Robin Leigh-Pemberton, *Sunday Times*, 17 June 1990.

her in really reforming any organization or institution,' said a close adviser. 'She's a woman and she doesn't trust them. The institutions are full of men. She now runs one, and she's not going to do anything other than order it about. Because if she does try reform, she'll be letting the men get ahead again, the Grandees and the Mandarins. So she's just going to order them about and let them stew.'[1] She did not believe that politics actually gets much done beyond a certain point, and she knew that political costs can be very high. National chauvinists, in effect saying, 'Who cares about market rationality? We must resolve matters through power and authority!', left her cold. Her scepticism about men and about male ways of solving problems was spot on in such cases. 'She is only radical insofar as her convictions go,' said Norman Strauss. 'She has radical convictions, but only radical convictions. If you want her to do something that's radical that's not in her convictions, you can just about forget it.'[2]

Her image, however, was not that of a practical – or a conviction – politician, but of a shrewish Attila the Hen. It was created essentially by commentators: literary people in politics and the media, universities, professions and civil service, both Right and Left, who have an agenda separate from the interests of their country. They are concerned with the enactment of certain principles, and range from libertarians who think that there should be no free public schooling for poor children to leftists who think that denationalization of coal is tantamount to a war crime.

Most commentators come from the 1960s cadre who are the heirs of the generation that provided the economic bases of the modern world. They assume that the people who make wealth will always be there, so wealth should and could be redistributed. Mrs Thatcher was cast as the family lawyer recalling people to first principles – which heirs traditionally dislike. She was a reminder that the world is a world of consequences, an awareness that has been suspended by the literary intellectual culture of the post-war years.

Politicians are not principally in business to enact principles: they are in business to keep society on the road, and to keep themselves in business. But the issues as put in the debate of the *literati* are

[1] Interview, 25 May 1990.
[2] Interview, Norman Strauss, 25 May 1990.

bloodless and wordy, concerned with principles and ideas and meanings rather than what is really happening. 'She really does dislike the left-wing intellectual chic world,' said one of her people. 'And, of course, they hate her, the chattering classes. She thinks they're silly, and they think she's vulgar – perhaps that's too strong – philistine. There's no love lost between them. The question is, does it really matter? It was inevitable, given her agenda.'[1]

It did matter. A key element in her departure from Number Ten in November 1990 was that she had been low in the opinion polls for over two years, and colleagues in Parliament and in the Conservative Party in consequence believed that she would lose the next election. 'Margaret Thatcher was destroyed by the opinion polls; and unjustly so,' said the commentator and psephologist Peter Kellner. 'For many MPs the clinching argument was the torrent of polling evidence which seemed to show that she could not win the Conservatives the next general election . . . The use of polls in Mrs Thatcher's downfall should cause some concern. Time may show that Tory MPs misread the evidence and that, far from sacking a vote-loser, they have abandoned a vote-winner.'[2] But, for good and ill, polls reflect images.

The most extraordinary event in Margaret Thatcher's political career was not the manner of her going, but her election as leader of the Conservative Party in February 1975. She grasped the moment in 1974–5 when people were more than fed up and when minds were changing in both Parties; when the Left was bankrupt and no longer possessed self-belief. In 1970–75, when the postwar consensus failed, it took several years for the fact to register through the political process. Thatcher's political antennae proved their excellence in 1974–5 when she ran against Ted Heath before that failure was manifest. Her antennae were always turned to the country rather than the Party (she calculated that her leadership of the Party depended upon her electoral success: what was new was it turned out that it depended upon opinion poll success, too), and the ruthlessness of Party colleagues in engineering her departure should not obscure the general accuracy of her political judgement.

---

[1] Interview, 16 August 1989.
[2] Peter Kellner, 'Polls That Should Have Been Taken, Not Inhaled', *Independent*, 30 November 1990.

TWO

The people: class and Party

Images played a major role in the motivation of Thatcher's people. They perceived the Establishment – a phrase publicized by Henry Fairlie to describe the alliance of institutions, attitudes and people involved in the maintenance of convention and the defence of each other[1] – as partisan, its ranks filled by the 'New Class' of commentators and administrators who thought the task of Government was to manage national decline, which the New Class welcomed, not least because it expected to be employed by the State as the managers. It was only this class itself which considered itself 'new'. It was preoccupied with trade union issues, social engineering and social liberalism and permissiveness, all to be mediated through 'representative' groups. It ascribed great importance to cultural events, and nervously despised energy. It deemed national resurgence to be impossible, greatly underestimated free market economics as an engine of radical social and political reform, and provided heartfelt opposition to Thatcher, her people, and Thatcherism.

Most of Thatcher's people were not the aristocrats or the professional captains of industry and the professions or the Mandarins of the civil service. Many had made or were making their own way in the post-war years without inherited wealth or family connec-

---

[1] Henry Fairlie first publicized the use of the word Establishment in his weekly articles in the *Spectator*. (Hugh Thomas, 'The Establishment and Society', in Hugh Thomas [ed.], *The Establishment* [London, Anthony Blond, 1959], p. 20.) 'The Establishment, briefly, is the English constitution,' wrote Thomas, 'and the group of institutions and outlying agencies built round it to assist in its protection; it naturally includes all those who stand like commissionaires before these protective institutions to protect *them*. The word derives, of course, from the ecclesiastical establishment of the Anglican church . . . (The word "Establishment" simply indicates the assumption of the attributes of a state church by certain powerful institutions and people; in general these may be supposed to be effectively beyond democratic control . . .)' (ibid, pp. 14, 20).

tions. They identified with the nine-to-five middle-aged; factory managers and foremen; clerks and matrons; people without posh accents and private school educations, sensing both social class discrimination and the New Class discrimination of being excluded from the 'common wisdom' on any subject. They appealed to young people full of enthusiasm for the possibilities of business and the professions. Their distance from fashion in every sense, in fact, was one of their most distinguishing marks. They watched as the wealth the country created was spent on no real change in the 1960s and 1970s, but on instituting a system of compulsory comprehensive secondary education or on organized labour wage demands to which there seemed to be little resistance because of social compacts between Government and the Trades Union Congress.

Susan Crosland captured something of the visceral dislike of the clannishness of the Establishment that built up in Thatcher's people in the 1970s and 1980s. In her novel, *Ruling Passions*, written after a decade of Thatcher as Prime Minister, Crosland portrays Benjamin Franwell, a ruthless, hard, amoral, self-made, young editor of a leading pro-Conservative Sunday newspaper, describing various members of his staff. His personal assistant, Rachel Fisher, is about to become a very 'dry' MP, and one of his columnists, Giles Alexander, is his token 'lefty'. 'Rachel stands for the decent, hardworking values that a lot of Conservatives in their hearts prefer to the la-dee-da of those upper class twits with all their garbage about compassion,' declares Crosland's Ben. 'Anybody can preach sodding compassion if he's never had to go out to work . . . You know what these left-wingers are like, shedding their tears for the underprivileged. So long as Giles Alexander has a handsome salary and the limelight, he'll manage to reassure his conscience.' He then turns his fury on a 'wet' Tory MP, Andrew Harwood, who will one day inherit a baronetcy. 'I can't stand those fucking aristocrats with their *noblesse oblige* – patronizing the rest of us just because they can afford to be magnanimous and "caring". Give me the guts of a Rachel Fisher who's had to make her own way.'[1]

Thatcher's people wanted to make their own way. They did not want to storm the bastions of society. They wanted to replace them.

[1] Susan Crosland, *Ruling Passions* (London, Futura, 1990), pp. 71–5.

'People worked at the Centre for Policy Studies because they believed in the policies,' said Norman Strauss about the 1974–9 period, 'but most importantly because they wanted to help to create a new order.'[1] In 1989, looking back over Margaret Thatcher's first decade in Number Ten, Alfred Sherman passed judgement on that early hope. 'As prime minister, Mrs Thatcher was never able to dominate the machinery of state – nor even that of her own party ... The outsiders at Mrs Thatcher's immediate disposal have generally numbered less than a dozen, with roughly the same number scattered among other departments, but by no means all of them are Mrs Thatcher's choice and, in some cases, are protégés of hostile ministers. They are swamped by several thousand senior policymakers whose main concern is to preserve their empires intact and, where possible, to expand them.'[2]

In addition to the bureaucratic obstacles, Thatcher and her people faced an intellectual inertia, which they dealt with more successfully. By 1979, one set of opinion in the country and in Parliament was committed to collectivism and trade union power; another was committed to compromise between Left and Right, and a third was fed up. The Labour Party was locked into a position where it could only go more to the Left or split and regroup (as it did). In either case it would exile itself from power for a considerable period. Thatcher and her people appealed to millions who wanted another way for Britain that included reducing union power, and they established new polarities in politics and in social affairs.

In the 1960s and early 1970s there had been steady inflation. But people had become accustomed to that. They could say that yes, inflation was going up, but for the really needy this was being compensated for by decent pensions systems. Governments could – and did – say, 'We are not letting little old ladies on fixed incomes starve and freeze in bed-sitting rooms.' Inflation appeared to be – and was said by economists to be – necessary for growth. But it was not seen as an ideal system. There was a general assumption until the mid-1970s that the system provided a net gain, and people were prepared to live with most of the consequences, cursing at

[1] Interview, Norman Strauss, 25 May 1990.
[2] Sir Alfred Sherman, 'The Thatcher Era in Perspective', *The World & I*, April 1989, p. 613.

times, but aware of the possible danger of stopping inflation and then seeing growth stopping too.

'For thirty years since the war, the whole of Britain's domestic politics had been centred on the promise of ever increasing growth, ever rising expectations,' said Christopher Booker in his epigrammatic book, *The Seventies*. 'The two great ideological driving forces of the age, Socialism and Consumer-Capitalism, were so allied on this matter that they were indistinguishable, except in the prescriptions of how best to arrive at the common goal.'[1] This alliance would have provided a workable compromise if Britain had been more economically adaptable. But the fact was that the country was simply falling more and more behind other developed countries and some developing countries, making it even less flexible. This made the alliance more and more dangerous.

In the period since 1979, changes were implemented in ways that broke the promise of ever-increasing growth by attacking the traditions of British political and administrative behaviour. Making the civil service more publicly accountable for its actions was one of the most important Thatcherite changes in the 1980s, because the civil service had been the harbinger of the alliance between socialism and consumer-capitalism. Thatcher reduced the status of the civil service, and made its Mandarins seem no longer indispensable. For the first time in British history a Cabinet Secretary appeared as a witness in court. Thatcher and her people brought into the open what had long been the hidden reality, from the actual role of the Cabinet to the lumbering inefficiency of institutions such as the National Health Service and the Bar. 'We brought implicit ideas into the open,' Alfred Sherman accurately stated about her and her people.[2] They were not concerned to live with the decent appearances.

Thatcher's people were not laterally connected: they really were just Thatcher's people. They were kept going as a political undertaking in the practical world by her presence. Most of them were not Cabinet material. Some of them were too idealistic, and felt that she owed them more than she felt she did. She clearly con-

---

[1] Christopher Booker, *The Seventies: Portrait of a Decade* (London, Penguin, 1980), p. 186.
[2] Sir Alfred Sherman, Letter, *Encounter*, June 1990.

41

sidered that their – and her – loyalty was to a set of self-evident truths. The people she felt a personal loyalty towards were the handful who backed her against Ted Heath in 1974–5 and then over the next four years in Opposition. With feeling, she called them 'The Long Marchers'. 'People who serve in Downing Street, as long as they're there, they have great influence,' said a Number Ten aide. 'And she will always retain great loyalty to them. But once they move on there is not the same opportunity for her to talk to them. Ian Gow, who was really close to her as her Parliamentary Private Secretary in the first four years, is somebody she had immense respect for, and he would come in for a late night drink after a vote. If you've been in the Thatcher Court, you'll always be close to her.'[1]

Thatcher's people were the closely-knit inside group of theorists and advisers who were at the heart of Thatcherism. They tended to be yesterday's outsiders, not only in terms of their views, but also – with some notable exceptions – in terms of class.

The British class system and the elite system are different, and they only partially overlap. Among the real British elites, background is far less important than it is with people who are class conscious. Thatcher's people had a great deal more to do with an elite than with the upper classes.

Americans, and indeed most other foreigners, think that the British elite institutions are highly hereditary. With exceptions, they are not and have not been for a long, long time. An exception was the quite conscious effort until recently to keep the Army in the hands of people with an hereditary stake in the country. The Royal Navy, by contrast, placed competence first, and so there is a strongly middle-class naval tradition from at least the eighteenth century, if not earlier: Admirals Hawke (1705–81) and Nelson (1758–1805) came from quite humble backgrounds. The higher civil service, since the introduction of the Northcote–Trevelyan reforms in the mid-nineteenth century, has been remarkably open. Shamefully late, Oxbridge has taken in people almost entirely on the basis of merit since 1940.

A class system of social consciousness and restraint exists which

[1] Interview, 20 August 1989.

42

is partly due to the homogeneity of the English people. The distinctions between Jew and Gentile, layman and cleric, which dominate Spanish or French or most other developed Western cultures, never really took root in England. So pecking orders of minor distinction developed instead.

Within the class system, a number of Thatcher's voters, but not many of her people, came from the working class; in particular, a core of her electoral support came from the skilled working class, the artisans. Thatcher herself, and a number of her people, are from the lower middle class. The middle class was the most ambivalent about Thatcherism: their delight in material prosperity is balanced by real concern for the less well-off. The upper middle class is the Establishment class: the senior ranks of the professions, Anglican clergy, the civil service and military. Denis Thatcher, the son of a successful businessman and a more successful businessman himself, was from within this class. Into the 1970s, a large proportion of Conservative Members of Parliament, and a dominant number of the Party's bosses, were also from this class. Most of the men Margaret Thatcher had most difficulty with were in the Establishment. The British upper class is strikingly stable, although not every peer is regarded as upper class. In the old days (before 1940) you became upper class by being made a peer, but this is no longer the case: some life peers are seen as irredeemably middle or working class. None of Thatcher's closest people came from the upper class. As one of her supporters who does have a country estate said, from his experience of her, 'She doesn't like country gents much. There's a natural suspicion there.'[1]

Salman Rushdie, in *The Satanic Verses*, makes one of his characters – Hal Valance, an advertising/television producer/Orson Wellesian/mid-Atlantic man – comment on class, Thatcher, and her people to Saladin Chamcha, one of the central figures in the novel: '"The thing that's so amazing about her is the size of what she's trying to do . . . I'm talking about you-know-who," Valance explained helpfully. "Torture. Maggie the Bitch." Oh. "She's radical all right. What she wants – what she actually thinks she can fucking *achieve* – is literally to invent a whole goddamn new middle class

---

[1] Interview, 30 May 1990.

in this country. Get rid of the old woolly incompetent buggers from fucking Surrey and Hampshire, and bring in the new. People without background. People without history. Hungry people. People who really *want*, and who know that with her, they can bloody well *get*. Nobody's ever tried to replace a whole fucking *class* before, and the amazing thing is that she might just do it if they don't get her first. The old class. The dead men. You follow what I'm saying." "I think so," Chamcha lied. "And it's not just the businessmen," Valance said slurrily. 'The intellectuals, too. Out with the whole faggoty crew. In with the hungry guys with the wrong education. New professions, new painters, the lot. It's a bloody revolution. Newness coming into this country that's stuffed full of fucking old *corpses*. It's going to be something to see. It already is."[1] Thatcher in fact did not try to invent a new middle class: she made it easier for new people to get ahead economically and thus enter the middle class. Julian Critchley, a Conservative MP of independent and acute mind, more accurately described this phenomenon as 'Essex Man': the children of East-Enders who moved to the new suburbs of Essex, around towns such as Billericay, Basildon, and Enfield, providing a heartland of support for Thatcherism. They were upwardly mobile socially and economically, wanting to buy council houses and shares in privatized companies.[2]

The unfashionableness of much of Thatcherism and the class snobbery that was attached to both Heath and Thatcher – the two Party leaders who came from the lower end of the social ladder – provided the ammunition that opponents used, whether over port at dinner, in the media, or in the House of Commons. Sir Peter Hall, director of the National Theatre, in January 1988 declared that 'well over ninety per cent of the people in the performing arts, education and the creative world are against her'.[3] A BBC documentary television producer in 1989 echoed this, saying, 'There is not one producer in the BBC who is for Margaret Thatcher.'[4] Mary Warnock, headmistress of Oxford High School for six years until 1972, Mistress of Girton College, Cambridge,

[1] Salman Rushdie, *The Satanic Verses* (New York, Viking, 1988), pp. 269–70.
[2] Julian Critchley, *The Palace of Varieties* (London, Faber & Faber, 1988).
[3] *Sunday Telegraph*, 10 January 1988.
[4] Private information.

and created a Life Peer in 1985, although denying the accuracy of the report, was quoted as making the sort of snobbish and rude remarks that are rarely pinned down publicly. Every time she thought about Mrs Thatcher, she was reported as saying, she 'felt a kind of rage'. She epitomized 'the worst of the lower middle classes'. Her clothes and hairstyle were 'packaged together in a way that's not exactly vulgar, just *low*'. Seeing Mrs Thatcher in a television programme choosing clothes at Marks and Spencer, she was reported as declaring that, 'There was something quite obscene about it, picking out yet another blouse with a tie at the neck.'[1] Jonathan Miller, one of the original *Beyond the Fringe* cast, and a distinguished theatrical producer, television performer, academic and medical doctor who was made CBE in 1983, said he found Margaret Thatcher 'loathsome, repulsive in almost every way', and decried 'her odious suburban gentility and sentimental, saccharine patriotism'.[2]

Such remarks actually reflected more accurately on the politics and snobberies of the people who made them than on Thatcher and her people who were, in fact, highly intelligent and resourceful and personally uninterested in gentility or in which shops they bought their clothes. They were not from deep within the political or the snob systems. Generally, they were self-made men. They tended to be Americanophile and suspicious of Europe. They flocked naturally to Margaret Thatcher (rather than the other way around), and none found it necessary to be indoctrinated. There were doctrinaires among them, but in general they were not looking for a systematized doctrine: they did not spend their time 'excommunicating' one another, for example, although they were not uniform in agreement on policy or about each other.[3]

Alan Walters, her personal economic adviser in 1980–83 and again in 1989, came from a working-class home in Leicester, and his economic thinking was formed at Birmingham University. His father had been a communist. Brian (now Lord) Griffiths, head of her Policy Unit, is a Welshman and maintains a strong Anglican

[1] *Sunday Telegraph*, 10 January 1988.
[2] Ibid.
[3] See, for example, Maurice Cowling, 'The Sources of the New Right', *Encounter*, November 1989; Sir Alfred Sherman's reply, Letter, *Encounter*, June 1990.

religious interest, untypical of the Nonconformist Protestantism of his compatriots who successfully disestablished the Anglican Church in 1920. In a Welsh context, one might say, Griffiths is a 'nonconformist'. Alfred Sherman is a journalist, was director of studies at the Centre for Policy Studies, and comes from the working-class East End suburb of Hackney in London. Denis Thatcher, one of her most important people, is a Londoner, but has a strong set of non-metropolitan (one might say Blimpish) attitudes.

John Hoskyns was a professional soldier and then started his own computer software and systems company. Nigel Vinson founded a remarkably successful manufacturing company. David Young was an effective solicitor and property developer. David (now Lord) Wolfson ran a mail-order firm. Tim Bell, the man who spearheaded the successful 1979 election advertising campaign and went on to become one of Thatcher's closest election advisers, is a very successful advertising executive. Friedrich von Hayek and Milton Friedman developed ideas that found expression in Thatcherism, but they were not British political figures.[1] Norman Strauss is a management consultant.

Some of Thatcher's people were from the world of politics, but they were the minority. Nigel Lawson, Chancellor of the Exchequer in 1983–9, was a parliamentarian; in 1988–9 he showed that he was no longer one of her people. Keith Joseph, Secretary of State for Education and Science in her first administration, the son of a Lord Mayor of London, was an MP for thirty-one years, but is actually more typical of well-meaning inherited wealth and academic distinction than a man of affairs or of the City. Angus Maude, Airey Neave, John Biffen and Norman Tebbit were all MPs who had not received much recognition before Thatcher became Party leader, and both Biffen and Tebbit grew away from her. Bernard Ingham, her press secretary, is a Yorkshireman through and through. Like Charles Powell, her private secretary, Ingham was a civil servant and as such was not involved with electoral politics. Ralph Harris, the guiding spirit at the Institute of Economic Affairs

[1] Hayek was naturalized as a British subject in 1938, and was made a Companion of Honour in 1984. Friedman is an American citizen.

for over thirty years, stood as a Conservative candidate in Scotland in 1951 and 1955, but then devoted himself to the Institute's cross-party objectives.

Her people were not the same as the Conservative Party. They appealed to a British anger about national decline. They formed a group that was not centred in the House of Commons or Oxbridge or the civil service. Some did, in fact, come from all these groupings, but they put themselves on the margins of each one. To an extraordinary extent they were men: there was no woman close to Margaret Thatcher professionally.

Under Thatcher, the Conservative Party in Parliament no longer embodied the traditional British ruling class: the landowners, financiers, and senior members of the professions. It was instead the embodiment of today's ruling interests. Unlike Heath's, Macmillan's, Eden's and Churchill's Party, which did not appeal to young people, Thatcher's Party appealed to young men in particular. In the 1987 general election, the majority of first-time voters voted Conservative (although more women in the 18–24 year-old age group voted Labour than for any other Party). Part of the reason why young women were not so attracted was because they were more libertarian in their attitudes and assumptions than Thatcher was. Many women felt betrayed by her advocacy of traditional female roles. 'I do not want to see a generation of creche children,' she declared.[1] Nevertheless, in May 1990 a survey by the accountancy firm, Kidsons Impey, revealed that more women than ever before were starting their own businesses and that ninety-five per cent of people starting new businesses borrowed the necessary money from banks rather than being able to take it from inherited capital. More than forty per cent of people launching new businesses were under the age of thirty, and fifty-five per cent were between thirty and forty. 'The Prime Minister is credited with playing a major part in motivating the new whizzkids,' a newspaper report of the survey said. 'Of those questioned, seventy-three per cent believed she had encouraged the spirit of enterprise, mainly by lowering personal taxation, and she was also praised for "making success socially acceptable".'[2] It appeared that Thatcher succeeded

[1] BBC Radio Four, 'Woman's Hour', 17 May 1990.
[2] *Daily Mail*, 29 May 1990.

in appealing to hope for the future rather than remorse for the past, and in making business fashionable once again.

In the last decade of the twentieth century, the Conservative Party is in a state of flux. Its traditional principal components are in a state of decline. The squire and his relations, though still firm supporters, are on the way out in terms of influence: there has been a great decline in deference. The parson is on the way out. The Synod of the Church of England is no longer the Tory Party at prayer, partly because of a Christian reaction against being connected to the modern, technological state, and partly because of the economic collapse of the Church. The fashionable regiments are on the way out. The military elite are the working (and up to a point classless) regiments, notably the Special Air Service, Special Boat Service, and the Parachute Regiment. The British military is no longer a very important institution, and this is reflected in the declining importance of military people in the Party. There were no generals or admirals or air-marshals on Thatcher's backbenches or in her Cabinet. The hereditary aristocracy has long been discounted, having failed to provide any significant leaders apart from Lords Home and Carrington.[1]

There are three elements in the Party: the Tories, the Unionists, and the Conservatives. Each element represents a principal strand of Party philosophy, quite separate from power groupings within the Party. In simple historical terms, a Tory believes in three out of a list of four: the hereditary element of the Crown and the House of Lords; the established Church of England; the State in the sixteenth-century 'Good of the State' sense, where ideologies fade out against great State interests and nations are not thought of as being friends (Enoch Powell, a leading nationalist, was very much a Tory in this sense); and an organic, non-mercantile, nationalistic society. A modern Tory thinker, the Presbyterian Iain Macleod, regarded himself as a Tory Democrat, admiring the glamour of the Crown, but felt that the organic aspect of British society enabled some people to call themselves Tory Socialists. Toryism genuinely tries to avoid rancour, although it does not always succeed. It greatly dwells upon the emotional qualities that bind a society. And

[1] Viscount Whitelaw was created an hereditary peer, but is the first of his line.

while in some forms it believes very definitely in an open society, it believes in a hierarchy, although not a closed hierarchy. It is delighted to welcome talent from below, but it must be recognized that there *is* an order and there *is* a below.

The Unionists believe in economically illiberal nationalism with a strong dash of municipal socialism. Illiberalism in the Conservative Party (whose official name is the Conservative and Unionist Party) springs from Unionist sensibilities. Unionism is committed to the integrity of the United Kingdom, and is strongest in Northern Ireland and Scotland. The Unionist Party in Northern Ireland, created to fight Irish nationalism, is however much more interested in this aspect than in empirical economic and social arrangements.

There is a conservatism that says that if it is not necessary to change, it is necessary not to change. But Conservatism overall, rather less in England than in Europe, is a soft form of classical liberalism. It is a non-Church, landed-interest, right of centre position that is also anti-socialist. In dynamic times, it is an unelevated creed of the energetic businessman; at other times the creed of a society that does not feel very adaptive. Willie Whitelaw was a Conservative.

A Conservative is different things at different times. Conservatives in 1845 were also the Tories, and they broke the Tory Party over the issue that agricultural protection came above any other interest, humanitarian or other. They let Ireland starve to death during the Famine of 1847–50 rather than force down the rentals of the English squirearchy. That was conserving an interest. What is thought of as Conservative by Americans, and for a while now in Britain, is a 'light' government doctrine involving free trade, minimum restrictions upon business enterprise, and the conscious reduction of State intervention. It is actually classical liberalism. There are many conservatisms because the world changes in so many ways. Although conservativism is hypothetically opposition to change, by a series of historic accidents in the English-speaking world it involves the defence of the free market, which is not a conserving force.

Separate from these elements, three distinct and unequal power groups with different views of the world compete for control of the Conservative Party, as the election of John Major as Party leader made plain. Each of these groups contains Tories, Unionists and Conservatives. The weakest of the three at present, the traditional ruling group – those with hereditary status and wealth, who own certain slices of Britain both literally and figuratively – and those who identify with them, have been displaced and find themselves being treated on a par with other interest groups. 'I think Margaret Thatcher regards a great many traditional Tories as being "wet" and unsound and guilt-ridden,' John Biffen reflected, 'and not really prepared to give the proper recognition to work because they've never had to practise it.'[1] Much of the sourness about Thatcher within the Conservative Party emanated from this group. They felt that she was too hard, too abrasive, too shrill, too nagging. At the start of her leadership of the Party, there were quite a few of this group in her Cabinets: Sir Ian Gilmour, who was her first Lord Privy Seal; Willie Whitelaw who, until illness forced his retirement in December 1987, was her deputy; Lord Carrington, her first Foreign Secretary; Lord Soames, her first Leader of the House of Lords; Paul Channon, Minister for Trade from 1983 to 1986; Douglas Hurd, her Foreign Secretary. Nicholas Ridley, her Minister for Trade and Industry until he resigned in July 1990 (following a 'Thatcherite' outburst when he compared the integration of Britain into a German-dominated, unified, political and economic EEC to surrendering to Adolf Hitler), was born within this group, but as a proto-Thatcherite did not represent it.

The second group, the Thatcherites – the lower middle class in politics reflecting certain very strong lower-middle-class values – strongly opposes the traditional ruling group, and has been leading the attack on the old political consensus. Norman Tebbit, who was Thatcher's Chairman of the Conservative Party from 1985 to 1987, has, perhaps, been the most effective spokesman for this group. When he entered the House of Commons as a new Member in 1970, he remembered with pleasure being elected to the 92 Group dining club of Conservative MPs. It was, he said, one of the 'less hidebound and snob-free groups'.[2] John Major, the son of a vaude-ville and circus performer, whose formal education ended when he

[1] Interview, Rt Hon. John Biffen, MP, 6 June 1990.
[2] Norman Tebbit, *Upwardly Mobile* (London, Futura, 1989), p. 122.

left school aged sixteen, was a Thatcherite, although never a leading spokesman of the group.

The Conservative Party has had people like Norman Tebbit for centuries. No Party has been able to do without such people in the last 250 years. He was interesting because he insisted, rightly, that he belonged to the new ruling class, and that he was an important articulator of the views of that class, and not just a manager of ruling class interests. He has no desire to make the transition to being the Earl of X. 'I carry no brief for people who just happen to have been born in the right bed,' he says.[1] He does not think that his children were born, in that sense, in the right bed: he loves them for what they are. He does not think that it lies within the power of the State to make them existentially different: making him Lord Tebbit is not going to transform them. He has hard elbows: he does not believe that having stormed the heights he can bestow upon his children a standing that is indelible. He feels his superior virtues would be greatly misused in his being just another inter-changeable member of the aristocracy. His is an echo of Harold Macmillan holding out to be 'Mr Macmillan' for so long, but more so. Macmillan felt that he had been at the top of the tree, and to be Mr Macmillan the former Prime Minister was to be very formidable. Tebbit is a sharp spokesman for the Thatcherite class. 'Tebbit is the worst symbol of Thatcherism ever produced,' said a Thatcher media adviser, 'because he's seen as nasty. Thatcherism is basically nice.'[2]

John Biffen describes himself as 'part of the new Thatcherite class. If you look at my background – rural, day school, grammar school, Cambridge – it's very typical,' and he places Margaret Thatcher herself as 'rather militantly lower middle class: make your own way by your own savings. Councillor Roberts [her father] was a great influence.'[3] Many of her advisers outside Parliament came from this class too.

The third group are the people whose political views have changed with the experience of Heath and then Thatcher. Sir Geof-frey Howe, her deputy in 1989–90 until his resignation, was of

---

[1] Interview by Muriel Gray, *Walkie Talkie*, Skyline Productions, Channel Four TV, 9 February 1990.
[2] Interview, 5 June 1990.
[3] Interview, Rt Hon. John Biffen, MP, 6 June 1990.

this group, which comprises a majority of the Party. Whatever his later disaffection, in the 1970s and early 1980s Howe was a free marketeer (although he was never particularly close to Thatcher). Tom King, her Minister for Defence, Chris Patten, her Minister for the Environment, and Kenneth Clarke, her Minister for Health, came from this group. They would describe themselves as taking the best of old Toryism and the best of Thatcherism to mould the Conservative Party of the future. They have a bridging function between the two other wings of the Party. It is from this group that John Major's successor is most likely to emerge.

What is not always remembered is that because the Conservative Party's leader is elected by the Conservative members of the House of Commons, it is in that forum that the essentially consensual nature of this third group most thrives. However, it is all very well to criticize Margaret Thatcher for confrontationalism and acting decisively and thus, at times, divisively, but she is a tough act to follow. The minute trade union leaders start going through the door at Number Ten, any Prime Minister is going to be depicted as a wimp and not even half the 'man' she was. 'I think what's going to happen is that they're going to say, "Woof! Thank God the punch-ups are over",' said one of her closest advisers prophetically in June 1990. 'Five years on or a year on, maybe, they'll be saying, "We're giving in to every dumb shit in the world." But at first they'll say, "It's such a relief to get rid of that ghastly tension the whole time."'[1]

In contrast to the traditional elements of the Conservative Party, Thatcher's people were from other traditions and were not metropolitan, landed, or Unionist. They were often not liked by many of those that they worked with in Government: the civil servants, the generals, the diplomats. They asked awkward questions. They were in a hurry to be effective. They wanted to solve problems. They had little ambition to be accepted by the civil service or the great professions. They were driven by an intellectual and programmatic discontent with their country. They were a radical, business-oriented grouping. They tended not to be public schoolboys, Anglican, or from the south of England. They were to a high degree

[1] Interview, 5 June 1990.

52

nonconformists, Jews, grammar school men, and impatient. They themselves represented major breakdowns in the British post-war consensus. They were competitive: it is notable that sportsmen and sportswomen were among Margaret Thatcher's most enthusiastic supporters.

The degree to which she was a politician first and foremost was demonstrated by David Young in his controversial management of the sale of the State-owned Rover Group to British Aerospace in July 1988. Young, the son of Jewish immigrants from what is now Lithuania, was without political experience, but was ennobled by Thatcher in 1984 so that he could enter her Cabinet as Minister without Portfolio, becoming Secretary of State for Trade and Industry the following year. He was perceived as being a Thatcher insider and, as a Minister, someone who could be depended upon to support her fully. He had come into government through Keith Joseph, who had involved him in the work of the Centre for Policy Studies in the later 1970s and had made him an adviser at the Department of Industry in 1979–82. Norman Tebbit, who as Minister of State for Industry in 1981 had worked with Young, appointed him to head the Manpower Services Commission in 1982. In 1985 his promotion to Secretary of State upset many Conservative MPs who resented an outsider entering the Lords and occupying one of the most important Ministries. He was emblematic of resourcefulness and of the people who flocked to Thatcher, having changed their minds about politics in the late 1960s and 1970s on pragmatic grounds. In the 1960s Young first considered that the Conservatives had failed and then that Labour had failed. He was a technocratic man looking for technical solutions.

Young was a tremendously practical man, representing a crucial practical element among Thatcher's people. He was not interested (in contrast to Keith Joseph) in demonstrating the rightness of things, from which spoon to use at lunch to the rotation of the solar system. He saw life as a set of operational issues. He thought that a shrewd, hard-working, resourceful, courageous approach was right. He was not ungentlemanly, but he was not haunted by a gentlemanly ideal. Money and success were to him immensely worthwhile, without his being crude and greedy, distinctly more interesting and intellectually demanding than politics or the social

53

circuit. He did not feel it necessary to apologize for seeking money and success, and he was a generous contributor to Jewish charities. He did not try to enact philosophy and was sceptical of philosophers. He operated in a world that was very definitely here and now. He had for years been a supporter of the classical liberal, market-oriented Institute of Economic Affairs, and he called his autobiography *The Enterprise Years: A Businessman in the Cabinet*,[1] emphasizing his practical bent.

As a Minister, he completed several functions for Thatcher. He got to the point very fast – noteworthy in Cabinets peopled by men best suited to be junior ministers (she did not nurture the world's best Cabinets). He was never a threat to her position. He was a great pacemaker. Few issues came his way where he did not make up his mind and come with a first recommendation that he was prepared to take back without panic if counter-evidence built up against it.

People like Young are very rarely tapped by politicians. He had to have the Prime Minister as patron to reach the level he did. He was somebody who would have remained generally unknown were it not for Thatcher. He was a problem-solver, and this was why Thatcher relied on him.[2] His approach to the privatization of Rover cars was a case in point.

On 27 June 1990, the European Commission declared that British Aerospace had to repay £44.4 million that it had received from the British Government as part of the deal whereby it bought Rover, and warned that a further £40 million might have to be repaid in 1991.[3] The sale itself was an apparently model Thatcherite affair: Britain's last indigenous car maker had been successfully privatized to a British buyer – British Aerospace – who undertook a £1.5 billion investment plan in the car manufacturer in the process.

[1] Published by Headline, London, 1990.
[2] Thatcher is famously quoted as saying, 'Others bring me problems, David brings me solutions' (e.g., *Observer*, 1 July 1990). However, although this is probably what she did think, she never actually uttered these words.
[3] The £44.4 million was comprised of £33.4 million British Aerospace saved in interest by a twenty-month deferment of payment of the £150 million purchase price, and £11 million paid by Young to cover costs of the sale incurred by Rover and BAe. The £40 million potential repayment related to debts in Rover's Truck Division not being as great as was envisaged at the time of the sale.

The problems came in the way the deal was done. 'The deal of the decade', as Young described it, was found by the Commission to have been too favourable for the buyer. Young had written off Rover's debts (about £572 million) and had approved financial 'sweeteners' – subsidies – amounting to about £44 million to induce British Aerospace to complete the deal, without telling the Commission (which under European Community law had to approve the transaction for it to be completed) and others about them. The Commission held that the sweeteners were illegal under European Community competition rules. 'What the Brussels ruling and various inquiries by select committees of MPs are going to leave beyond dispute,' *The Economist* judged, 'is that, along the way, Lord Young deceived the commission, misled the House of Commons and undervalued the group he was selling.'[1] It was a judgement the House of Commons endorsed in February 1991.

Young was a chief-of-staff type. His trouble over Rover was profoundly instructive. It showed him as a fixer. Thatcher and Young were getting a technical, nationalistic, political job done without recourse to theories and ideology, but rather violating market principles – and thus 'Thatcherism'. And if Thatcher was put in such a fix (Young might not have told Parliament, but he certainly told Thatcher and the Treasury) it showed her continuity with political life: he – and she – were acting like politicians, not doctrinaires. It showed how inadequate her – and her people's – image was.

To a noteworthy degree, Thatcher appointed Jews to her Cabinets and as advisers in Number Ten. Harold Macmillan was reported to have quipped that her Cabinet had 'more Estonians than Etonians'. Keith Joseph, Alfred Sherman, David Young, David Wolfson, Norman Strauss were all involved with the Centre for Policy Studies in the 1975–9 period, and as advisers in Number Ten after 1979. Stephen Sherbourne, who had been Ted Heath's political assistant for a period after 1975, became her political secretary after the 1983 election. She had more Jews in her Cabinets than any Prime Minister before in British history: Keith Joseph, David Young, Leon Brittan, Malcolm Rifkind, Nigel Lawson,

[1] *Economist*, 23 June 1990, p. 33.

55

Michael Howard.[1] 'I think it is because she's an outcast and Jews are too,' said Strauss. 'I think it's as simple as that. She's an outsider. She needed new people. Therefore she needed people who by definition had been excluded because she could trust them to be loyal. Her foundation was Keith and Alfred.'[2] 'She reaches for Jewish people because they do partly personify the Thatcherite virtues,' said one. 'They are entrepreneurial. They are successful people anywhere. They believe in family life. On the whole they have strong families: few are divorced. Much less drunkenness. They believe in thrift and savings and doing things by your own efforts: in self-help.'[3] 'It is difficult to talk about this: it puts people in a great tizz,' observed John Biffen. 'But it just happens that the intellectual thrust of the new liberal economics substantially came from the Jewish intellectual elite. The Jews she had in Government were all very much of the new radical Right. They may not have been so identified with it as Keith Joseph, but Leon Brittan and David Young were part of the new, thrusting meritocracy. The Jewish community that she would have known in Finchley represented, I suspect, the Methodist values of Grantham to a very great extent.'[4]

Nigel Lawson took a different view, making the point that the Jews Thatcher had in her Cabinets were all individually very different, with different backgrounds and track records. 'It is a coincidence that there were a large number of Jews,' he said about her Cabinet Ministers, 'and the only way in which Margaret Thatcher was different from other Prime Ministers in this respect was not actually that she was looking for outsiders (unless you say that by definition a Jew is an outsider), but unlike other Conservatives, she has no anti-semitism in her makeup at all.'[5]

In December 1988, the *Sunday Telegraph* published an article

[1] Respectively Secretary of State for Industry (1979–81) and then for Education and Science (1981–6); Secretary of State for Employment (1985–7) and then for Trade and Industry (1987–9); Chief Secretary to the Treasury (1981–3), then Secretary of State for the Home Department (1983–5) and then for Trade and Industry (1985–6); Secretary of State for Scotland (1986–90); Secretary of State for Energy (1981–3) and then Chancellor of the Exchequer (1983–9); Secretary of State for Employment (1990).
[2] Interview, Norman Strauss, 25 May 1990.
[3] Interview, 14 February 1990.
[4] Interview, Rt Hon. John Biffen, MP, 6 June 1990.
[5] Interview, Rt Hon. Nigel Lawson, MP, 21 November 1990.

about the Jews around Thatcher which caused concern in the Jewish community. One of her people recalled: 'It caused a huge amount of offence in the Jewish community. Huge. You have no idea! I thought on the whole it wasn't a particularly offensive article. But they really didn't like it. They don't like being thought to be like America. They don't like to be told there is a Jewish vote or a Jewish lobby. They hate it. They want to be integrated, even if they're Orthodox, even if they're observant, even if they have very strong Jewish identity and practices, they want to be integrated socially. They don't want to be thought of as a group, a lobby. They don't want to be thought of as a group with views. They're all individuals with all their own views, all of whom made their way by their own efforts.'[1]

Making one's way by one's own effort was a cardinal point in Thatcherism, as was the corollary: that effort should be rewarded. One of the great complaints about Britain in the 1960s and 1970s was that hard work and its reward were increasingly scorned and penalized. Reversing this was a feature of the appeal of Thatcher and Thatcherism.

[1] Interview, 24 August 1989.

THREE

Thatcherism: the background

Even more than when the Labour Party came into power in the 1920s and a new generation drawn essentially from the professional classes entered the British governing group, colouring the political system, Thatcher's people represented a distinct change in the system. Her governments contained more unelected advisers, and gave them greater prominence, than ever before. Most of the brouhaha of Nigel Lawson's resignation as Chancellor of the Exchequer in October 1989 had to do with the role of a Thatcher person – her personal economic adviser, Sir Alan Walters – and a particular perception of her mode of governmental management. Lawson, who until then was regarded as very much a Thatcherite, raised questions about the nature of her administration and the constitutional position of Ministers and the Cabinet *vis-à-vis* advisers.

Thatcher's people also represented a change in the system in another way. Unlike Labour's professional trade unionists, academics, teachers, journalists, who were happy with Harold Wilson's boast in 1975 that Labour was 'the natural Party of Government', her people were suspicious of Government, were anti-civil service, and were scornful of the traditional Establishment. The dominant factor determining Thatcher's administration, for example, in the somewhat disillusioned eyes of Sir Alfred Sherman, was 'the large and still growing power and influence of the civil service as an integral part of the establishment subculture, which includes nationalized industries, universities, professional institutions, the Anglican bishops and their secular equivalents, the broadcasters, and the "quangocracy" – all kinds of state-financed appointed bodies accountable to no one.'[1] This was an outsider-looking-in view.

[1] Sir Alfred Sherman, 'The Thatcher Era in Perspective', *The World & I*, April 1989, p. 612.

Talent now counts for more than birth in Britain, and this has been a central Thatcherite reform. Many of Thatcher's people had previously felt themselves to have been kept out of power and positions of influence because of their political and economic views, and because of race and class. The feeling persisted despite Thatcher being Prime Minister. They considered that the Establishment cards were stacked against them – and her – and that their views were not suited to British culture. 'Britain has only one major talent,' said one of her longest-standing people. 'It's called hypocrisy. In Britain we like hypocrisy. We think it's funny and clever and witty and elegant and British.'[1] 'British cultural mores, our genes, are just not built to succeed,' said Norman Strauss, 'so unless we intervene in our culture we cannot succeed, and if you want to change culture, you've got to change the ethos of society. It's not in our culture to succeed. It's in the Japanese, American, German cultures to succeed. The French and Italians and Spanish, because of their passion, have a better chance of succeeding than we have.'[2] Mrs Thatcher's people's ambition to change British social and political attitudes cannot be emphasized too strongly, hence their deep hostility to traditional institutions, which was reciprocated. 'In sector after sector she has outraged interest groups and lobbies,' observed Ralph Harris. 'The homosexual community, Militant Tendency, pressure groups, the professions, the trade unions, they just rage and roar. She's built up enormous hostility because she's outraged sacred cow to sacred cow. I see chaps in the House of Lords whom I know, who were contemporaries of mine at university. They won't talk to me, and I'm not even Thatcher. I didn't like Harold Wilson as Prime Minister, but I never felt the hatred and animus towards him that they have towards her. Itching to kill.'[3]

The denial in 1985 by the University of Oxford of an honorary degree to Margaret Thatcher – arguably their most distinguished woman graduate – was emblematic of this hostility. Attlee, Eden, Macmillan, Douglas-Home, Wilson and Heath – all, like Thatcher, Oxford graduates – had received honorary degrees either before they became Prime Minister (Eden and Home) or during their

[1] Interview, 5 June 1990.
[2] Interview, 25 May 1990.
[3] Interview, Lord Harris, 21 May 1990.

first year in office. The dons voted 738 to 319 against honouring Thatcher on the grounds that she had done deep and systematic damage to the public education system. 'Oxford not giving her the degree was the greatest insult to her,' said one of her early people. 'Rather like the 1933 "King and country" debate. There's a decadent institution. Brains, sinecures, locked away. Any thinking intelligent person must know that that university structure wasn't sound: cradle to the grave jobs. They must know it in their hearts – a lot of them do, of course. The social scientists and philosophers were behind it.'[1]

To many of Thatcher's people, envy was *the* Left-wing characteristic. 'Labour is a party full of envy,' declared Norman Tebbit, 'peopled with failures and richly tainted with smug hypocrisy . . . [It shows] malice towards business and personal success.'[2] They discounted the idealism of the Left or else saw it as being historical and no longer relevant. They regarded the Left as proclaiming its hatred of the class system while actually seeking to become its 'social engineers', aspiring to the professions and the civil service ranks which conferred upper-middle-class status; as parlour pinks and limousine liberals who, if they could count an aristo in their number, were quietly flattered and flocked to her parties. They saw the Left as arrogant, as knowing better about everything, and attempting to ordain everything: that the common wisdom on any subject was theirs.

Thatcher's people saw themselves as coming in to change a Conservative Party that had been infected by decades of statist/collectivist – 'Butskellite' – consensualism and Tory (i.e. the social elements of the Party) arrogance. They had some success, but nothing like as much as they had hoped for. 'Our point of departure was the perception that "Butskellism" had failed in terms of its own criteria and objectives;' said Alfred Sherman, 'we offered explanations and policy implications. We were not "New Right", however Right be defined. Those of us who had formerly been Socialists, Labour supporters, or Butskellites became "newly Right", joining forces with those who had held comparable views

[1] Interview, 30 May 1990.
[2] Norman Tebbit, 'Why Can't Labour Bear to See Success?', *Evening Standard*, 13 June 1990.

longer.'[1] 'They want to control society,' said one of her most intimate advisers, referring to the Party hierarchs still in place after fifteen years of her leadership, 'but they want to control it not through Statism, which at least means that you have a responsibility, but through patronage, which is disgraceful. Anti-semitism and class warfare are really the property of the Tory Party, not the Labour Party. All they're interested in is controlling people. They want to have a say in other people's lives. And that's exactly what she doesn't believe in. People believe that Prime Ministers make decisions and determine the course of events. She thinks that's absolutely wrong. But everybody else who wants to be Prime Minister wants to get in there in order to determine the course of other people's lives.'[2] 'The problem with the Tory Party has always been that it doesn't give a damn about its members,' said a media adviser, hinting at the source of discontent inside the Party with Thatcher's leadership that erupted in November 1990. 'It's a hierarchy and it doesn't like her because she's a woman, because she's from the lower middle class, because she's not an academic or a philosopher, and because she's shrill. They like slightly grand people, or people they think are slightly grand. The Tory Party is not a Thatcherite Party.'[3]

Deeper than their dismissal of the Left and their ambivalence about the Conservative Party was a practical, businesslike hardheadedness. In complete contradiction to traditional Tory principles, her people talked of the primacy of economics over politics. They were furious with Britain as a museum without walls, seeing the maintenance of traditions, protectionism, and a frequent harking back to the past as alibis for inefficiency, arrogance, and complacency.[4] They felt cheated by a generation wasted. They sensed that they, and Britain, would be far more important had things been different over the last forty years.

In these respects Thatcher's people were very close to Edward

[1] Sir Alfred Sherman, Letter, *Encounter*, June 1990.
[2] Interview, 5 June 1990.
[3] Interview, 5 June 1990.
[4] The *Spycatcher* affair, when a disgruntled retired Intelligence officer wrote an autobiographical exposé and was sued in an Australian court by the British Government for breaching the Official Secrets Act, needs to be seen from this perspective. See Chapter 12.

Heath, the other Conservative Prime Minister from the lower middle class, and both Thatcher and her people actually owed him a great deal both in a straightforward and in a backhanded way. With the 1970 Tory election platform, nicknamed Selsdon Man, he ushered in the prospects of circumscribing the unions and of operating market principles; with his U-turn in 1971–2 he gave Thatcher's people their *cause célèbre*. 'By the early 1970s it was quite clear, following the débâcle of Heath and even before, when we saw the disaster of the second Wilson and then Callaghan administrations, that the UK really was going down,' said John Hoskyns. 'I spent a lot of my time in the United States on business and I began to realize what a scruffy, second rate little economy we were. And there were Americans who were beginning to say "We're worried that we're going the same way as you are." I began to think I must somehow get involved. I was absolutely convinced that the only sensible thing to do was to get some systematic and systemic thinking – two quite different things – to bear on complicated inter-related problems. I found that most civil servants and politicians are linear thinkers, and there were very few people around who had any idea of the *totality* of what was going wrong with the country. And even if they had a theoretical grasp they would not know how to make it happen: how to put together the innovations and the applied thinking.'[1]

The post-war political and social consensus and the Establishment had failed to arrest national decline or to provide any solution to its continuing. So Thatcher's people determined that they not only had to ram through reforms, but also that much of the wisdom of the previous thirty-five years had been tried and had not worked, and that the Establishment had presided over this failure and was thus not to be seen as the repository of wisdom. 'It's a gross oversimplification, but I don't think it's so much the world of White's, Pratt's, and Brook's [the most prestigious London social men's clubs] that she feels she's let down by,' said Robert Blake, the leading historian of the Conservative Party, 'but the world of the Athenaeum [elite academic, senior profession and ecclesiastical] and the Reform [media, politics and civil service]: that's the Great and

[1] Interview, Sir John Hoskyns, 25 June 1990.

the Good. I think she does feel that a lot of the Great and the Good have let the country down. It is not accidental that she's never appointed a Royal Commission.'[1]

At the end of February 1990, the newly-appointed director general of the Institute of Directors, Peter Morgan, a former senior manager with IBM, delivered an outspoken attack on the Church of England, the Establishment, and the 'middle-class Salariat' of State employees, articulating much of what Thatcher's people think and feel about the 'Great and the Good'. He said that the economic revival seen since Thatcher came to power was being put at risk by 'Establishment attitudes, the middle-class Salariat and the lumpenproletariat . . . It is obvious that responsibility for the 100 years of decline of UK plc must be laid at the door of the Establishment which purported to guide the affairs of the nation. By its record, it has lost its authority, but it has not acknowledged its failure nor has it renounced its anti-enterprise attitudes. You don't have to be a political supporter of the Prime Minister to appreciate that the spiteful, petulant treatment of her in the case of the Oxford honorary degree was the action of dons caught in a timewarp . . . The enterprise culture is an alien concept for the established Church. It takes no pleasure in wealth creation. Unfortunately, these Establishment attitudes are also held by many of the middle-classes. They hope that the Eighties will prove to have been a nasty one-off experience which can be set aside in the Nineties . . . [They have used propaganda] in the classroom, pulpit, press, stage and the broadcasting channels to characterize the Eighties as a decade of greed, to brand the successful as materialistic, and to denigrate individualism . . . For them the distribution of wealth is a noble activity – creating wealth is mucky and squalid . . . The middle-class Salariat [which is] our vast body of state employees who do not have to worry where the next pay cheque is coming from – in nationalized industries, in central government, in schools and universities and in Health . . . [have] an enormous vested interest in the status quo [and are] a huge obstacle to enterprise . . . The lumpenproletariat [which is] the mass of the population we choose

[1] Interview, Lord Blake, 16 August 1989. The nearest she came to a Royal Commission was the committee of inquiry into the Falklands War under the chairmanship of Lord Franks, the epitome of the Great and the Good.

not to educate . . . because they cannot profit from enterprise, they are thrown into the dependency culture.'[1]

The post-war Establishment consensus had been given its chance by Thatcher's people: some of them – Young, Hoskyns, Ingham, Griffiths – had voted Labour in the 1960s. They had given National Plans a chance. Thatcher herself had gone along with the consensus and Heath's 1971–2 U-turn away from market principles and back to state intervention. These were not people who had been in permanent rank opposition. They were practical people who changed their minds, and Thatcher herself was above all else a masterly politician. It was why the ideologues amongst her people did not generally stay the course.

Ideologues always feel that more should be done, and that is the difference between them and politicians. 'Whenever I say, "Why don't you put me in charge of . . .", she says it's too difficult,' said a long-standing adviser somewhat ahistorically, and painting with a broad brush, not understanding that Thatcher did not want to fight his battles. Then he went on to pinpoint what was, for him and many of her people, her unexpected deference to the Establishment modes. 'She really is genuinely middle-class. Consequently she still actually has a sort of reverence for the Archbishop This and the Lord That and the Duke of Whatever. She really does. She actually still slightly bends the knee. It's not as if she thinks it: she was brought up to it. Councillor Roberts must have imbued in her a level of punctiliousness and politeness and courtesy that overwhelms thought. But the danger of it is that in the same breath that she disregards titles as being a complete nonsense, she doles them out and treats them with respect! The Bishop of Durham is a jerk! You can't pay any credence to what he says. She would say, "Nevertheless, he's a Bishop, and if you destroy the establishment of the Bishops, you will have done severe damage to Britain." I've always thought this is her greatest weakness. She has a passion for the institutions and establishment of our society, and she doesn't recognize that in the very process of wishing to destroy all that crap which she hates, i.e., socialism, these things are bastions of it. They're not there for freedom and individualism. They are bastions of socialism and State control. Watch the

[1] Quoted in the *Evening Standard*, 27 February 1990, and the *Independent*, 28 February 1990.

way they seek groupings. They don't want any individuals. They're only interested in using individuals as a micro example to make a macro point, which we all know is fallacious. There aren't people in their world. There are only groups of people: the poor; the rich; the averagely well-off; the ordinary folk. There are no human beings except as micro examples of a macro group.'[1]

She knew that people would have thought that power had gone to her head if she had done what some ideologues wanted her to do: politicize the civil service; privatize the National Health Service. It would have frightened people – and rightly so. She knew there was no public remit for such changes. By 1990, many voters considered that the changes (not least in attitudes) wrought by more than a decade of Thatcherism had gone far enough, and that it was time to stop and take stock.

Thatcherism was about some very simple principles, just as two generations earlier the Welfare State had been. 'It's a really nice idea,' said a close adviser. 'It's an idea that says "Everybody can prosper." It's the first time in modern political history, other than Disraeli if you call that modern, that any leader ever actually believed that everybody can prosper. The others say it. They don't mean it. What they want is, "Keep it the way it is." She actually believes it. There is no reason why everybody shouldn't prosper.'[2] The Welfare State held that the British people were living less well than they could, given the resources of the country. Thatcherism held that people should work harder; that they should look things in the face and decide whether what they've been told for thirty-five years is true. It considered that neither Europe nor the unions had the weight ascribed to them in the 1960s and early 1970s. It was nationalistic, and positive that Britain was not doomed to secular decline – that the country did not have to lose relatively and absolutely, and that even without North Sea oil Britain had tremendous opportunities. It was convinced of the need for light government and sound money for a healthy, productive and free society.

Thatcherism was characterized by opponents as greedy, selfish, casino capitalism, but its supporters saw it in a very different light.

---

[1] Interview, 5 June 1990.
[2] Interview, 5 June 1990.

'The basic morality is one of freedom, opportunity and mobility,' said Alan Walters. 'It is very important. I'm sure that we'll find that mobility in Thatcher's Britain is enormous. Vested interests of both the Left and Right oppose it.'[1] Thatcherites saw Thatcherism as the reassertion of old and ordinary ideas – not ideology. 'I think you could make a very interesting analysis as to how it has been that the spiritual values that would have been represented by her father have not been capable of sympathetic projection over this last decade,' said John Biffen, who as Leader of the House in 1982–7 had responsibility for presenting the Government's policies to Parliament. 'It is one of the areas where Thatcherism has not found an accurate projection. It was actually highly intellectual in its origins, and its policies were systematically researched: the universities were more trawled than in any post-war situation. But Thatcherism is thought of as selfish and shallow and all the rest of it. I believe that to be unfair. But that the situation exists to some extent is a failure on the part of those of us who were involved. It is a problem, in actual fact, of rhetoric.'[2] It was also a sign of the deeply emotive response Thatcherism generated amongst its opponents. Thatcherism was a shock to the descriptive cadres who saw politics, economic organization and society in terms of competing French or German or Marxist models. To them, Thatcherism was a real change. To Thatcher's people, the change was very much in the way their opponents had become steadily more doctrinaire and extreme.

Irving Kristol, who had been a socialist in the 1930s and early 1940s, remarked in 1963 that it had become apparent to him that while he wanted more and more democracy and less and less socialism following the experience of the Second World War and Stalin's last years, the socialist journal, *Tribune*, had 'decided that totalitarian socialism was generally better than none',[3] and that its fellow journal, the *New Statesman*, was not far behind in being prepared to accept socialism without democracy. Making his point, he quoted from a 1952 editorial where the editor of the *New States-*

---

[1] Interview, Sir Alan Walters, 25 May 1989.

[2] Interview, Rt Hon. John Biffen, MP, 6 June 1990.

[3] Irving Kristol, 'Learning to Live with the *N.S. & N.*', a review of Edward Hyams, *New Statesmanship* (London, Longmans, 1963) and *New Statesman* (London, Longmans, 1963), in *Encounter*, August 1963.

man, Kingsley Martin, wrote: 'Thirty-two lucky people, some Communists, some fellow-travellers, other sympathetic persons, have left by plane for Peking through Prague and Moscow. The opportunity is too good to miss and they will be able, we may be sure, to tell us about the feelings of liberation among common people now that the Kuomintang is gone, about an administrative honesty and efficiency never before known in China and about the great constructive work that is proceeding in industry and agriculture. But I hope they will not stop there. They must tell us what the Chinese say about the million and a half "enemies of the people" who, it is apparently admitted, have been executed since the revolution. Were these executions really necessary?'[1]

Ten years later in the 1970s it seemed as if Kristol's point was true about the attitude of a wide band of people. Democratic values were on the decline, and extra-Parliamentary political action was encouraged by Labour Cabinet Ministers. It was unfashionable to talk about the morality of capitalism. Instead, East Germany and Czechoslovakia were hailed in some quarters of the Labour Party, academia, and the press as providing economic models for Britain to learn from, if not copy.

In consequence, there were some very important resignations from the Labour Party, and some notable converts to Thatcherism in the mid-1970s. Christopher (now Lord) Mayhew, who had been a junior minister in the Attlee and Wilson Governments, left Labour for the Liberals in 1974. 'The Left has advanced sharply in the Party in recent years,' he said. 'The trend is shown plainly in the Party's changed attitudes towards nationalization, Europe, trade union power, the supremacy of Parliament, the media, the supremacy of law, the independence of the Parliamentary Party, membership of Communist Front organizations, Chilean Marxism, picketing, law and order and so on.'[2] Lord Chalfont, who had been a Labour Foreign Office Minister from 1964 to 1970, and in 1970–71 had been foreign editor of the *New Statesman*, resigned from the Labour Party in September 1974, citing. 'The growing influence of the Left-wing of the Party . . . the Party's industrial and economic

[1] Ibid.
[2] Letter, *The Times*, 18 July 1974.

policies ... [and] its approach to defence expenditure.'[1] Lord George-Brown, formerly deputy leader of the Labour Party and one of its most senior and experienced politicians (he had been Harold Wilson's principal opponent in the Labour leadership election in 1963), resigned from the Party in March 1976, saying that Labour 'no longer seems concerned with individuals. It has become another kind of machine.'[2] Sir Leonard Neal, formerly chairman of the Commission on Industrial Relations and a lifelong Labour voter, declared that he could not vote for Labour's October 1974 Manifesto. 'I think the Labour Party has departed from the ethical emphasis that motivated it in years gone by,' he said. 'Now it seems a selfish party, a party of sectional interests.'[3] Quietly, John Vaizey, Britain's leading educational economist, ennobled by Harold Wilson, gave important help to the Conservative opposition to Labour's 1976 Compulsory Comprehensive Secondary Education Bill.

Reg Prentice, Labour's Secretary of State for Education and Science in 1974–5, and then Minister for Overseas Development in 1975–6, resigned as a Cabinet Minister in December 1976, and in October 1977 crossed the floor of the House and joined the Conservative Party. He explained his move in terms of the growing extremism of the Left. 'The Labour Party,' he said in the statement announcing his decision, 'has been moving away from its traditional ideals. There has been a growing emphasis on class war and Marxist dogma. Some of us have tried to swim against the tide. But we have watched too many of our fellow moderates making deals and compromises with the Left. For ten out of the past thirteen years Britain has been under a Labour Government. These have been years in which our economic performance has been worse and our social progress slower than in other Western countries. Britain has paid a heavy price for all the surrenders by Labour Ministers to the militant elements of the so-called Labour movement.'[4] Labour, he said two months later, was moving 'away from free society, away from prosperity – towards East Germany rather than West Germany'.[5]

[1] *The Times*, 23 September 1974.
[2] *Guardian*, 3 March 1976.
[3] *Daily Express*, 26 September 1974.
[4] *Observer*, 9 October 1977.
[5] Press release, Petersfield, 9 December 1977.

Two of the most distinguished converts were Paul Johnson, the brilliant ex-editor of the pro-Labour *New Statesman*, and the historian Hugh Thomas, who had been a Labour parliamentary candidate in 1957–8. They gave important voice to the perception that the Left had a direct responsibility for Britain's decline.

Paul Johnson is a Roman Catholic, yet holds that Christianity was created by St Paul, demonstrating an independence of mind that is admirable and impressive. He was a Catholic intellectual when that was a very rare thing to be in Britain. Because of his religion, there was opposition from Leonard Woolf and other members of the *New Statesman* Board to appointing Johnson editor of the journal in 1965: afterwards, Woolf said to him that 'there was nothing personal' in this opposition. He came out with *The Suez War* which Hugh Thomas, writing ten years later, said fundamentally anticipated much of importance in his own book on the subject, *The Suez Affair*. He is an enterprising person and an impatient intellectual. Like Enoch Powell, he followed ideas where they took him, terrifying political associates. Announcing his resignation from the Labour Party in September 1976, he said: 'Why has the Party become a repository of destructive envy and militant failure, a Party of green-eyed monsters! The answer is that Labour has starved itself of intellectual nourishment and the stimulus of debate . . . It was inevitable that the Marxists should fill Labour's intellectual vacuum. Alas, Labour has never been able or willing to throw out Marxism bodily; it has always held that there must be *something* in it. Such feeble resistance as it once offered has been overwhelmed, and the crudest kind of Marxists now roam through the Party at all levels.'[1]

Hugh Thomas is a man of great application. He once stayed with the Aldrich family in Boston, and so that he could work undisturbed locked William Aldrich out of his own library. Thomas wrote a novel called *The Oxygen Age* about how depressing it was to be educated and bright in mid-1950s Britain. The novel ends with its most sympathetic figure sitting with a final glass of champagne as his friends beg him to leave a burning house, so sick of the world that he's willing to be burned to death. Thomas is a cat that walks by him-

---

[1] Paul Johnson, 'Farewell to the Labour Party', *New Statesman*, 9 September 1976.

self: he never sought to be a group person. He was a classically discontented very bright young man. He then became a classically discontented very bright middle-aged man who had seen Britain change more than he had. He became a Thatcherite, joining the Conservative Party in 1976. In 1979 he became chairman of the Centre for Policy Studies. He was ennobled by Thatcher in 1981. In the House of Lords he strikes at a great deal of the bad conscience of the old, moderate Left Establishment: 'Come on: by 1975 you were just committing *la trahison des clercs*,' is the drumbeat of his presence. There he is, visibly the same man he was thirty years ago, just a bit greyer at the temples. 'In the 1950s, there seemed a good chance that the jaded arguments of the class war would soon disappear,' he said, explaining his change of mind, 'that the Labour Party could cut the cord that bound it to the unions; and that the movement would mature into a broad national one, comparable, say, to the Democratic Party in the US . . . I see the Englishman of today as one walking on a ridge. On the left, the streams flow down eventually to a tranquil but rather grey sea of state socialism. On the right, they flow to the more turbulent but brighter waters of free enterprise.'[1]

There is a great continuity between Thomas's acid choppings at British society a generation ago, and his Thatcherism. He was never a socialist visionary. He was a radical. He supported Labour in the 1950s and 1960s because he thought Britain needed change and the nearest instrument to hand was the Labour Party. Paul Johnson and Hugh Thomas were ex-respectable Left: 'I was never on the extreme Left,' said Johnson. 'I was never a Marxist or anything like that.'[2] They just said, 'Enough! This is not what we were hoping and working for.' They were people who reacted strongly to the evidence that it was 'their' Labour Party – and they did feel a strong sense of possession – that had changed, rather than they themselves. In contrast, others who became Thatcherites in the 1970s, like David Young and John Hoskyns, did so by a process of elimination, driven by anger and frustration at seeing their country decline in almost every sense.

With union power growing, the ban-the-bomb movement gaining support at home and in Europe, and Jimmy Carter in the White

---

[1] *Daily Mail*, 23 November 1976.
[2] BBC Radio Four, 'In the Psychiatrist's Chair', 29 August 1990.

House, it was fashionable in left-wing and centre-left political and intellectual circles to speak with approval of collectivist solutions to social and economic problems, and it was unfashionable to be openly hostile towards the Soviet Union. Thatcher was hailed in condemnatory terms as 'The Iron Lady' first in Moscow and then in British media circles for making speeches supporting NATO and arguing for nuclear deterrence, and was disparaged in private. 'Ted with tits' is how Christopher Soames, Winston Churchill's son-in-law, described her, getting a good laugh each time.[1]

Thatcher, her people, and Thatcherism were very conscious of these strains, and of Labour's (and the post-1971 Heath Government's) political bankruptcy. 'Thatcherism began less as a doctrine than as a mood,' reflected Sir Alfred Sherman. 'From the outset, the mood, beliefs and values that underlie Thatcherism have been more identifiable than its ideas ... The mood that Margaret Thatcher seized and rode to power reflected not only a general disillusionment with the bipartisan post-war settlement but also with the hypocrisy of socialism and its self-seeking proletarian cant.'[2] 'She believes in people knowing better how to run their own lives than the State knows,' said one of her people, capturing the simple view of her supporters. 'There's no other version of it. The moment you fiddle with it, you start to lose it. That's the problem with it: nobody is satisfied with the simple explanation of it.'[3] 'What is now described as "Thatcherism" was more or less common ground between Conservatives and Liberals in the nineteenth century,' observed Ralph Harris. 'She has not invented anything new. It's a return to a stream that was there.'[4] Thatcher herself put it simply: 'I came to office with one deliberate intent,' she said in February 1984. 'To change Britain from a dependent to a self-reliant society – from a give-it-to-me to a do-it-yourself nation; to a get-up-and-go instead of a sit-back-and-wait Britain.'[5]

[1] Private information. Denis Healey described her as 'Ted Heath in drag'. Soames had been Secretary of State for War and Minister for Agriculture under Macmillan. In 1973 he was Britain's first appointee in Brussels as vice-chairman of the European Commission.
[2] Sherman, 'The Thatcher Era in Perspective', pp. 611, 618.
[3] Interview, 5 June 1990.
[4] Interview, Lord Harris, 21 May 1990.
[5] *The Times*, 9 February 1984.

FOUR

The breakdown of consensus

'The Tory Party does not like brains,' Willie Whitelaw once remarked to an aide as he walked down the committee room corridor of the House of Commons. Then he paused, shaking his head sadly, 'Thank God I don't have any!'[1] One of the great shocks delivered to the Conservative Party by Thatcher and her people was that they did like brains. Thatcher herself was not an intellectual, but she respected intellect and looked for it in her people. 'When people don't enjoy thinking,' said Enoch Powell, 'but have a feeling that a thought or two would come in handy, then they look for somebody who will supply them: "Here you! Give me a thought! There must be a theory behind this. Kindly explain to me what it is."'[2]

Margaret Thatcher looked for people who could sustain her instinctive convictions with the chapter and verse of theory and study. First and foremost was Keith Joseph. Theory and conviction were crucial characteristics of an important section of her people, notably of Alan Walters (who also brought practicality to his conclusions). But coming to the conclusions that State control of prices and incomes and State regulation of business were 'bad ideas' was the result of her own cogitations. When she came into office in 1979, she had determined on monetarism as the essential answer

---

[1] Private information. Of course, Whitelaw was very brainy: he was just very good at hiding the fact. 'To watch Willie at work,' said Norman Tebbit who, as Secretary of State for Trade and Industry, was a member of the 'Star Chamber' committee under Whitelaw's chairmanship which resolved differences between the Treasury and other Ministries, 'was a time-consuming task but . . . worth every bit of it. He is so subtle a master of his craft that really to appreciate his skill one has to be in his confidence and know in advance his objectives and his tactics. Despite his reputation as an old waffler, Willie has one of the sharpest political brains in Westminster.' (Norman Tebbit, *Upwardly Mobile* [London, Futura, 1989], p. 270.)

[2] Interview, Rt Hon. J. Enoch Powell, MBE, 1 November 1989.

to Britain's economic ills. Yet less than a decade earlier monetarist theories were still on the fringes of economic thinking, and had not been considered by the politicians.

'What are you going to do about the money supply?' asked a young Treasury civil servant in 1970 when an election was imminent. 'Where is it in the Manifesto?' He was speaking to a friend from Oxford days working for Edward Heath and the Conservative Party. The Manifesto did not address the question for two reasons: most politicians did not know what the money supply was all about, and in any event, operating the money supply is not the sort of thing that goes into Manifestos. Years later, as the money supply became a familiar subject, it became apparent that economists keep changing their minds about it so much that it was politically wise to leave it out.

'My generation had been indoctrinated in Keynesian theory,'[1] said the Party official looking back at this period, explaining the failure to consider the role of the money supply. It was perceived as arcane economics. Elections were about the pound in the pocket, not about the pound on an academic's graph.

Alan Walters had a similar experience in 1959. Then it was the civil servants who had been ignorant. He had returned to England after a spell as visiting professor of economics at Northwestern University, at Evanston, outside Chicago, convinced that the quantity of money in the economic system was vitally important. But the Radcliffe Report on the monetary and credit system had just been published. Radcliffe and his committee had, *inter alia*, determined that the supply of money was of no interest to economic management. 'I was convinced that the view prevalent among British economists,' said Walters, 'and confirmed by the Radcliffe Report – that the quantity of money was of little consequence because of the (Radcliffe) *infinite* variability of the velocity of circulation – was dangerously wrong.'[2]

The common wisdom amongst economists at the time – not just in Britain, but also in the United States – was that the speed at which money moved around was the key monetary element in

---

[1] Interview, 24 August 1989.
[2] Sir Alan Walters, 'My Deviationist Economics', *Independent*, 26 October 1989. This was the article that led to his resignation as the Prime Minister's personal economic adviser in 1989.

determining an economy. Thus, it was considered, in theory a single pound note could activate any number of transactions in a short space of time; the number of pound notes would make little difference: they would, in effect, simply denote transactions.

Alan Walters thought that each pound note in the system – the quantity of money – was important because each one could activate any number of transactions. Thus if there were 100 pound notes, the number of transactions would be fantastically greater than if there were just ten. This, in turn, would mean that the number of pound notes in the system would directly affect inflation, because with more money around there would be less resistance to rising prices. But in order to demonstrate his theory, he had to find out how much money was in the system. Together with a small team at the University of Birmingham, Walters began his investigation: 'We had the monumental job of preparing the historical series on money and credit supply, etc. I applied to the Bank of England for a modest research grant. The Bank refused to support such research since, it said, the quantity of money was of little consequence and there would be few people interested in such statistics. Such was the wisdom of the day.'[1]

Alan Walters is a man whose obvious decency, loyalty, commitment to his beliefs, and lack of arrogance made him a natural adviser and staff officer. He is a man who claims far too little for himself. He has had the courage to change his mind on important matters and make no secret of it, and then set about convincing people at the highest levels that they should change their minds and policies too. He was in the vanguard of monetarist economists in Britain, and had met Enoch Powell in the early 1950s when Powell was one of the bright young thinkers in the Conservative Research Department along with Iain Macleod. In 1951 Powell was elected to the House of Commons. He introduced Walters to Joseph and to Macleod. By the early 1960s, Walters was also associating with the economists in the Institute of Economic Affairs,[2] one of the

[1] Ibid.
[2] The IEA had, for example, established the Evan Durbin Prize for the resolution of problems through the price mechanism. Evan Durbin was a brilliant Labour MP who tragically drowned. He believed that social goals were better pursued if possible through market mechanisms. He was a firm democratic socialist who had no time for communism.

74

great breakers of the post-war consensus (that advocated a combination of direct State intervention in the economy and State management of markets). The IEA was a genuinely innovative place. It was the great rehabilitator of the price mechanism in the British economic debate. When the Radcliffe Report on the credit and money system came out in 1959, the Institute produced a set of essays entitled *Not Unanimous*, ripping into Radcliffe in a pioneering, quasi-monetarist assault. It endorsed general conservative propensities towards individual freedom while simultaneously attacking Keynesianism, making the case that State interference in the economy was worse than the dynamizing force of the free market.

Keynesianism required fundamentally that institutions – corporations, unions – should drive the economy, and that Government should appear as the great intervener. Keynes was chaplain to the assumption that central government is the creator and destroyer in economic matters. Confronted with certain very specific economic questions congregating around the Great Depression, he overgeneralized the notion of the central government's ability to manage demand and stimulate growth, and underestimated the complexity of economic structures. He did great work in two World Wars as a practical Treasury official, and his intellectual interest in economics focused very heavily on public policy. He argued that conscious public policy was the crucial factor in economic life. The counter-Keynesian revolution of the post-1945 period has been to emphasize the enormous number of variables in the constraints and creative sources of society. Keynes's great practical contribution was to overthrow the ideas that public debt was a disaster, and that you could not spend your way to growth. His success in this respect was such that British macroeconomics became sterile and extraordinarily statist after 1945.

Keynes died before his sixty-third birthday having been deeply preoccupied by nearly a decade of war and peace in the 1930s and 1940s. Had he lived longer, there is no telling how far he might have revised his doctrines. 'When inflation was what had to be fought, Keynes was the first to fight it,' said Thatcher, pointing to the difference between Keynes's own flexibility and the more rigid precepts of the Keynesians, echoing Keith Joseph's observation that the monetary bias in Keynes was often missed. 'When production was above the money supply, he brought the money supply up to production. That is monetarism. When the money supply was greater than production, he would bring the money supply down to the production, because he had to fight inflation. Keynes was most totally abused by those who spoke in his name.'[1] 'The dead body of Keynes was body-snatched by Labour,' was Noel Annan's view.[2]

Milton Friedman, the high priest of monetarism, has always taken the line that Keynes was a very great economist who simply did not have the necessary data at his disposal to be as certain of his judgements as his followers were – no one did – and would have thought very differently had he possessed the information now available. So Friedman has always made his students at Chicago read Keynes very carefully. Keynes made certain valuable contributions which were grossly over-systematized and overvalued. This has been recognized by his followers. Paul Samuelson, for example, perhaps the most influential Keynesian, in the later editions of his classic economics textbook, *Samuelson's Economics*, conceded limitations on central government effectiveness.

Keynes was always grossly overworked by his own choice. He was simply outdistanced by the overall development of the discipline of economics early in his life.[3] He really expected the genuine satisfaction of social needs at a very early stage of economic improvement, and simply did not see the almost infinite expandibility of demand. He did not imagine a world in which the mass of people, having got one car, would want two, and so on. He really did believe that society was moving to satisfaction that could be fulfilled, and he was not alone in that belief. He at least said there ·was inadequate demand; his diagnosis for the reasons for inadequate demand were· almost certainly wrong: that it was the result of over-saving (rather than in the 1930s bad central banking). Keynes saw the crucial tool as being that of demand-management.

[1] John Newhouse, 'The Gamefish', *New Yorker*, 10 February 1986.
[2] Noel Annan, *Our Age: Portrait of a Generation* (London, Weidenfeld & Nicolson, 1990), pp. 176–7.
[3] Hayek has made the point that after about 1920, Keynes did not keep up with the literature.

Plenty of economists had argued for counter-cyclical spending during recessions: Keynes produced a model in which this was systematic.

In many respects, the attack on Keynesian assumptions was led by Friedman at the University of Chicago in the 1950s and 1960s. Friedman is not a libertarian: he believes, for example, in government restrictions on the ownership of guns.[1] He argues that money is not just the veil through which the economy operates: it has a powerful autonomous existence. Money, to him, is not merely the way you record transactions in a society: it is an entity whose interactive relations are important. He says, in effect, that blood must be considered not just as the necessary nutrient that goes running around the body, but as its specific ingredients of iron and plasma, etc. So must money be considered. He has a strong streak of almost rabbinic pessimism.[2] He dislikes Government because he feels there is something like original sin in the human race, and he regards dispersing guns to the human race as foolish as granting enormous powers to central or any other government. He does not like power. His *Capitalism and Freedom* makes a strong case for the presumption in favour of freedom, which is as far as Friedman goes (as opposed to what a libertarian would say).

The charm of Friedman's monetarism is that broadly speaking he suggests that politicians do not have to get into a labyrinth of complicated taxation and budget policy: the necessary health and safeguarding of society can be achieved through control of the supply of money, the driving force in the economy. Enemies of statism find the use of the monetary tool infinitely more attractive than the more coercive tools of fiscal policy. Monetarism, Friedman once said, was being invoked 'to cover anything that Mrs Thatcher

---

[1] Economists tend to be great state interveners. Hayek, for example, believed in a properly managed central bank. Keynes said that the instrument of intervention should be fundamentally through fiscal policy rather than through monetary policy.

[2] Friedman can become very emotional about economics. When he was ready to go to university, his sister, whom he considered far more brilliant, could not: the Depression had come and there was only money enough for one of the two to go. Given the realities of the time, his parents decided that it had to be the boy, and his sister's career was stifled. Friedman feels that by doing his work he can help prevent that kind of human cost again.

at any time expressed as a desirable object of policy'.[1] 'I consider myself a person who believes in honest money,' said Thatcher, 'and that means, yes, I have to fight inflation by the only way I know how, and if you just print money you are debasing the coinage, and I think it is a totally dishonourable and immoral government which deliberately sets out to debase the value of pensioners' savings in order to have a temporary situation of employment which would not last longer than eighteen months or two years, and after that the great inflation you create would, in fact, have undermined your competitiveness and would start to affect the whole of your society.'[2]

Keynesian economics, however, dominated the British academic and professional landscape to the virtual exclusion of monetarism throughout the 1960s. The common wisdom was that government intervention was necessary to stimulate and to channel demand – and thus growth – in the economy. The Chancellor of the Exchequer, Peter Thorneycroft, and his two Ministers at the Treasury, Enoch Powell, the Financial Secretary, and Nigel Birch, the Chief Secretary, resigned in January 1958 in protest at Harold Macmillan's and the rest of the Cabinet's refusal to agree to their proposed monetarist application of cuts in expenditure. Peter Thorneycroft went to the House of Lords in 1967 as a life peer, effectively out of the policy debate. He had made it very clear after his resignation that he did not wish to be a challenger either to Macmillan's leadership or to the Conservative Party's slide towards statism. Enoch Powell turned his attention to immigration and opposition to the United Kingdom's membership of the European Community, and Nigel Birch made a career on the backbenches as the Conservatives' 'demolition expert', often turning his attention to his own Front Bench. On 17 July 1962, four days after Macmillan dismissed Selwyn Lloyd as Chancellor, a terse letter by Birch was published in *The Times*: 'For the second time the Prime Minister has got rid of a Chancellor of the Exchequer who tried to get expenditure under control. Once is more than enough.'[3] Such miss-

[1] Newhouse, 'The Gamefish'.
[2] Ibid.
[3] Nigel Birch, Letter, *The Times*, 17 July 1962.

ives made clear that Birch was happy on the backbenches and that Macmillan was unlikely to recall him to the Cabinet.

The three made it clear that they had resigned because their solutions to deficits, State spending and inflation differed radically from those of Macmillan and the rest of the Cabinet. Enoch Powell described how the three had come to hold similar monetarist views well before these became either current or generally accepted: 'I had very little contact with Nigel Birch. We sat in different rooms and did different things. Nor did I have a great deal of contact with the Chancellor of the Exchequer either. But, as the year 1957 progressed, a curious thing happened. In trying to answer the question, "How can all prices rise?" we all independently gravitated to the monetary explanation and simultaneously produced the same answer. I started to drop in on Nigel and he started to drop in on me, and we started dropping in on the Chancellor of the Exchequer. We discovered that we were all exploring the same causation.'[1] Thorneycroft set up the Radcliffe Committee in order to investigate the monetary system. 'They were certainly pioneers as far as the Conservative Party was concerned,' Lord Home considered. 'I don't think anybody had taken the point until they did so. Nigel Birch was really the most forceful speaker on their behalf at that time. Margaret certainly has understood. In a country that lives by its trade, costs matter and relative costs matter absolutely. And basically our costs are too high, have been for quite a number of years, and therefore we're falling behind even the Europeans. And unless we can get our costs under control, we're going to have a very bad time.'[2]

The resignations came to be seen as an important moment in political life, and they were: they foreshadowed the split over economic policy in the 1970s. Macmillan had talked of 'little local

---

[1] Interview, Rt Hon. J. Enoch Powell, MBE, 1 November 1989. Powell also described the effect of their discovery of the monetary causation inside the Treasury: 'That causation was understood and appreciated by the second and lower levels in the Treasury, but it was hated by the top levels. And I remember one Treasury official saying to me: "You know, after the line that the three of you have taken, it would have been a mortal blow to Treasury morale if you had not resigned!"' (Ibid.)

[2] Interview, Rt Hon. Lord Home, KT, 20 November 1988.

difficulties',[1] later saying presciently: 'I had a feeling that the strict puritanical application of deflation was in danger of being developed into a sort of creed.'[2] He had gone on to win the next general election, thus seeming to put Thorneycroft and his colleagues in their place. In 1959, Walters' interest in the money supply no doubt seemed equally odd to the civil servants in the Bank of England to whom he applied for a grant. 'Monetarists – and I was one,' said Walters, 'were looked on as being absurd in 1959.'[3]

That young Treasury official in 1970 who asked about Conservative plans for the money supply was emblematic of an extraordinary change not only in economic assumptions, but also in the professional civil service itself.

The proudest claim of the civil service is that it serves all masters equally. The civil service is a very manipulative body. This is often underestimated, partly because very few politicians will admit to being manipulated. The idea of a subversive Mandarin was, perhaps, not as unusual as purists may like to acknowledge ('if the top echelon in the Treasury had been monetarists,' said Enoch Powell about the 1958 resignations, 'the subtle briefing of Ministers would have been different'[4]), but it was still unusual. It is inevitable in any system or profession that there will be round pegs in square holes on occasion, and even the odd original thinker from time to time. But in the Administrative Class of the civil service such individuals had always existed as exceptions, few and far between. Instead, a self-conscious elite applied itself to practical problem-solving, and to its own regeneration.

In 1985 the Head of the Civil Service and Cabinet Secretary, Sir Robert Armstrong, testified to the nature – and the strength – of the civil service's track record with the remark: 'I'm not sure that the underlying requirements of civil servants have changed really in 400 years.'[5] He was referring to the Administrative Class, the elite,

[1] Robert Blake, *The Conservative Party from Peel to Thatcher* (London, Methuen, 1985), p. 281.
[2] Lord Butler, *The Art of the Possible* (London, Hamish Hamilton, 1971), p. 232.
[3] Interview, Sir Alan Walters, 25 May 1989.
[4] Interview, Rt Hon. J. Enoch Powell, MBE, 1 November 1989.
[5] Sir Robert Armstrong, BBC Radio Four, *Analysis*, 'The Vanishing Mandarins', 13 February 1985.

who fill all the top positions and people key ministries, notably the Treasury. Lord Zuckerman, chief scientific adviser for many years, numbered them at 'no more than some 3,000 highly intelligent men and women who decided to make non-electoral politics their professional career'.[1] They tended to come from Oxford (more so than Cambridge) and, by design, to be generalists with a good classical education in the Arts: Greats (Latin and Greek); Modern History; English. Scientific and engineering subjects were shunned. Pure economists were not liked either: preference was shown to those with a degree in Politics, Philosophy and Economics. Lord Balogh, a prominent socialist economist and adviser to Harold Wilson's Governments, called the Administrative Class 'non-specialist dabblers' in a 'Mandarins' Paradise'.[2]

The great civil service achievements over the centuries were, first, managing England's expansion to Empire and, secondly, managing and sustaining the transition from monarchic to democratic rule. Within this, the internal objectives of the civil service were to maintain Treasury supremacy within the service and over ministers and, ever more from the mid nineteenth century, to secure domestic reform. Empire was a significant entity, but no one from the Indian civil service or the Colonial Office ever became head of the civil service. Perhaps the most influential civil servant of the century, Sir Horace Wilson, who became *éminence grise* to Neville Chamberlain in the late 1930s, started his career in the Ministry of Labour but made his reputation in the Treasury and Number Ten. Civil servants established the essential nature of the United Kingdom: that the Crown is the State, and that they serve the Crown. They may work assiduously and loyally for each Minister of the Crown and each Government of the Crown, but they do not necessarily march to the tune being banged out by the House of Commons or Number Ten. They have a higher loyalty: to the Crown. Lord Bancroft, head of the civil service from 1978 to 1981, put this point directly:

[1] Lord Zuckerman, 'Scientists, Bureaucrats and Ministers', *The Maxwell-Pergamon Discourse Proceedings* (London, Royal Institution, 1984), Vol. 56, p. 207, and quoted in Peter Hennessy, *Whitehall* (London, Secker & Warburg, 1989), p. 507.
[2] Thomas Balogh, 'Apotheosis of the Dilettante', in Hugh Thomas (ed.), *The Establishment: A Symposium* (London, Anthony Blond, 1959), pp. 109–10, and quoted in Hennessy, *Whitehall*, p. 172.

'The Service belongs neither to politicians nor to officials but to the Crown and to the nation.'[1] Politicians come and go: the Crown is always there, and so are its civil servants. Over the centuries, this thought has consoled them.

And it has needed to. In 1960, George Kennedy Young took early retirement from the civil service as under-secretary at the Ministry of Defence.[2] Two years later he published a book, *Masters of Indecision*, containing a devastating discussion of the decay of Britain. The context was his decision to leave the civil service. He had been one of the principal organizers of the Suez invasion in 1956, and he felt deeply that its failure through humbug and indecision was the moment of disaster for Britain. The implication of Young's observations was that there was an inner purposelessness and hollowness in the British higher establishment: that when Harold Macmillan spoke (as he did in the 1930s) of the will at the centre having gone, he was really making a self-fulfilling prophecy. Young had a sense that administration had replaced government, and that just getting by – drifting – was the result and it was not good enough. He had put his finger on a feeling that was to grow, mushrooming with Thatcher: that at a time of increased risk in the world at large, authority in Britain had lowered its sights, and that there was an atmosphere of defeatism and failure of will that was rationalized by emphasis on social harmony.

In 1973 Sir William Armstrong, then head of the civil service, and inevitably closely involved with Ted Heath and Government policy, declared that the job of the civil service was 'the orderly management of decline',[3] effectively confirming George Young's

---

[1] Quoted in Hennessy, *Whitehall*, p. 346. Sir Robert (now Lord) Armstrong has made the point that the 'Crown' is effectively the Government of the day: 'Civil servants are servants of the Crown. For all practical purposes the Crown in this context means and is represented by the Government of the day . . . The Civil Service as such has no constitutional personality or responsibility separate from the duly elected Government of the day.' (Quoted, ibid., p. 346.) However, officers in the armed forces and in the secret service of the United Kingdom take an oath of allegiance to the Crown, not to the Government or Parliament, and at times as officers of the Crown act separately from Government wishes and directives. Bancroft was putting the technical case; Armstrong the functional case. Most civil servants, it should be said, are not like the military.
[2] Much of Young's career had been spent in the secret service.
[3] Hennessy, *Whitehall*, p. 76.

dark view of the attitude of the British governing elites. Armstrong could see social disorder mushrooming in Britain. In 1974 he was talking about actual social collapse. The matter-of-factness with which he did it was a Treasury manner clothing a very different matter: Thatcher saw him as panicking about social strife and union power, turning tail, and then helping to turn Ted Heath.

Every great change in Britain involves a considerable amount of political persuasion of the civil service. Lloyd George had his 'Garden Suburb' civil servants; Labour had civil servants who felt that the Welfare State and independence for India were necessary and overdue. Margaret Thatcher had a very important Thatcherite element in the civil service that antedated her. They tended to be younger people who, in relatively junior positions (thus not committed in the way that the senior levels of the civil service were to particular policies and attitudes) and from the vantage point of the inner workings of government, saw the acceleration of British decline in the 1960s and early 1970s. Thatcher did not pack the civil service: people there emerged as Thatcherites. 'Her reaction to papers was influenced by the civil servants who were seconded to work closely with her,' observed John Biffen. 'Robert Armstrong and now Robin Butler [both Cabinet secretaries and head of the civil service] and Charles Powell [her private secretary] played quite an important role. Powell knew a lot about foreign affairs. If you look among the "court favourites" [i.e., the Number Ten insiders] – and I do not use the term disparagingly – they tend to be her chosen people from the public sector.'[1] She could not have produced a cadre of permanent secretaries out of a hat. There were many people evolving parallel notions in the decades before 1979. She gathered together into one river streams that were already flowing down a mountain range. Clive Whitmore, Thatcher's principal private secretary from 1979 to 1982, had developed Thatcherite views before 1979. 'Clive had a view that was Thatcherite before she came in,' said one of her people who worked closely with him in Number Ten after 1979. 'He was one of the civil servants who thought Britain was in a mess and we'd better do something about it. He was terribly helpful. If there had been

[1] Interview, Rt Hon. John Biffen, MP, 6 June 1990.

another principal private secretary there who didn't want to be helpful, it would have been much harder work.'[1] Tim Lankester, private secretary to Jim Callaghan in 1978–9, and then to Thatcher in 1979–81, and Andrew Duguid, an assistant secretary at the Department of Industry who was seconded to the Prime Minister's Policy Unit in 1979, were others.

There were civil servants who did not agree with Thatcher, and that raised one of the big questions for many of her people: now that it would be possible, should she break into a civil service system of high morale and complexity and start systematically promoting the like-minded? It was one of the areas where her unwillingness to change the system highlighted a difference with her people, several of whom pressed for civil service reform. There may also have been genuine patriotic restraint in her not being prepared to re-engineer the watch. If it was not inherited, she would not have accepted it, but having inherited it, she was authentically dubious about reform. She flirted briefly with the idea of creating a Prime Minister's Department, 'which, had it happened,' said Peter Hennessy, the historian of the civil service, 'would have been an institutional and constitutional change of the first order comparable to Lloyd George's creation of the Cabinet Office in 1916.'[2] Her answer was to be tough with the civil service, and not to stand between it and criticism, as Hennessy pointed out: 'Mrs Thatcher's approach to Whitehall reform was a classic manifestation of conviction politics: icons were there for the toppling but very little was done to create something new from the fragments.'[3] 'It has changed quite a bit in many ways,' Sir Alan Walters observed about the service after ten years of Thatcher in Number Ten. 'One of the great things they now do in the Treasury and some of the other Departments is to have interchange with the City and with business. They never used to. It's a very good change indeed.'[4] She recognized that she would have a successor one day, and that that successor might not have the guts to keep things on track, and the result would be the worst of all possible worlds: a politicized French

[1] Interview, Rt Hon. John Biffen, MP, 21 December 1990.
[2] Hennessy, *Whitehall*, p. 682.
[3] Ibid.
[4] Interview, Sir Alan Walters, 25 May 1989.

Third Republic civil service. She felt herself to be a national trustee, more than most Prime Ministers do (and most Prime Ministers have a strong feeling of that). She probably said to herself, 'If I made Brian Griffiths Permanent Secretary at the Ministry of Employment, there'd be a state of civil war in Lincolnshire in a year or two, because he isn't sufficiently politically acute.' She made an assessment of resources, and was almost certainly right.

The idea of decline infuriated many people, not because they still thought that Britain was a great power (they did not), but because of the assumption that decline was a permanent feature of British life. Many young men and women in the Administrative Class of the civil service told themselves that they had not joined to help steer the State Coach downhill. The thought of managing decline displaced thoughts of transition to a new condition. A significant element of the idealism for joining the European Community was that Britain would be able to move from Empire to Europe and a worthwhile role as a major European power. Armstrong, by speaking of the management of decline, was implying that Europe was a life-raft rather than a new opportunity, and this also angered people who believed that Britain had better possibilities.[1]

The anger signalled a change within the civil service and – although not immediately apparent – in the politicians' view of civil servants. No longer would there be an operating consensus based on the common wisdom in major areas. Armstrong may well have been accurately voicing the common wisdom of his colleagues at the top of the civil service and of Ted Heath. But it would not be the common wisdom for long. Noel Annan, a representative Establishment figure,[2] later considered that 'The top civil servants

[1] Armstrong's implication was rather accurate at that point. Britain has not really found a happy home in the European Community, and Armstrong was astute enough to doubt that it would.

[2] Lord Annan, OBE. Military Intelligence during the Second World War; supervised the development of political parties in the British zone in Germany after the war; Provost of King's College, Cambridge, at the age of thirty-nine; Vice Chancellor of the University of London; chairman of the Trustees of the National Gallery; chairman of the Royal Commission on the Future of Broadcasting; ennobled by Harold Wilson in 1965; trustee of the British Museum for seventeen years and a director of the Royal Opera House for eleven; a distinguished biographer and intellectual historian.

were on the whole consensus men,'[1] that they were complicit in the failure to control trade union power, and were thus partly responsible for British decline. Decline was felt in Britain at many levels, most acutely in domestic terms. When social harmony started to go, voters began to say, 'If there's not going to be harmony in the trade-off with the unions and any other power group, what is the point of trading-off with them?'

Harold Macmillan carried a great deal of the political responsibility for British decline. Instead of reforming industrial relations and revitalizing British industry, he concentrated on seeking to append Britain to Europe. By the mid-1960s, Harold Macmillan's Butskellite policy of yielding at home in order to obtain flexibility abroad, as he disengaged Britain from Empire and applied for membership of the European Economic Community, had seen the steady enhancement of the presence and influence of the unions and of State enterprise. In 1962, Macmillan's Government established the National Economic Development Council ('Neddy'), chaired by the Chancellor of the Exchequer, with members drawn from industry and the trade unions, and a secretariat, the National Economic Development Office. The Council's purpose was to make plans for industry with employers, unions and Government working collectively. This was built upon by Harold Wilson with Pay Boards, a National Plan, and 'little Neddys' investigating specific industries' problems, all involving central government ever more in detailed economic transactions, and further enhancing the presence of the unions.[2] It was a classic Butskellite affair.

Butskellism was actually the Conservative Party's version of a philosophy of State intervention in the economy and in the management of people's lives. It was a gross misnomer: it was a combination of the names of R. A. Butler, the Conservative's leading welfare politician, and Hugh Gaitskell, Clement Attlee's successor as leader of the Labour Party in 1955 until his death in 1963. The fact that Butler was on the 'left' of his Party and Gaitskell was on the Labour 'right' did not mean that their hands touched (as the Social Democrats who split away from Labour in the 1980s

[1] Annan, *Our Age*, p. 347.
[2] The great damage to union standing was precisely because their presence was enhanced above their power in the long term.

discovered: there were no significant defections to them from the Conservatives). The main emphasis of Butskellism was on an increase in social services and the alleviation of the circumstances of unemployment, and it was assumed by commentators that in this respect the two Parties had found common ground. But while operationally this appeared to be so, it was not the case, and the suggestion that two doctrines overlapped was lazy.

Butler, from a distinguished academic and Indian civil service family, had a humane but highly inegalitarian approach – a kindly, paternalistic elitism. He was meritocratic and believed in differential rewards for merit. He was not at all unsympathetic to the aristocracy of wealth, especially old wealth. Gaitskell, a Wykehamist, believed that life was about co-operation and goodwill. He was a womanizer and a passionate dancer who found personal fulfilment in reaching out to the working class. Butler felt obligation, but very little sympathy. He would have been happy never talking to the aristocracy or the working class: he was the supreme upper-middle-class Briton. He felt it was dangerous to have high unemployment (a feeling that also dominated Heath, for example), while Gaitskell thought that society owed people jobs. Butler was concerned with the art of the possible combined with a view that the British people could not be expected to put up with economic decline and domestic disorder.[1] Gaitskell believed that genuine social benefits would flow from the dissolution of social distinctions. Butler identified with the top professional five per cent. The two men had common technical objectives, but they did not have common values.

Butskellism developed in a world in which Britain had made a remarkable recovery from the Second World War. The recovery was substantially due to US money and the Attlee Government. However, that Government's policies were fundamentally the product of the times, and no Labour Government since then has had policies of remotely the same quality. The Labour leadership after Attlée was never convinced that the creation of wealth was at least as important as its redistribution. 'What Butskellism was supposed to signify,' said the American commentator John Newhouse, 'was that there wasn't really much to choose between the

---

[1] Butler titled his autobiography *The Art of the Possible*.

domestic policies of Tory and Labour Governments in the post-war era, any more than there was between the policies of Republican and Democratic Administrations in Washington. The Labour benches were manned largely by sensible men who drank their pints in the evening, were home by ten o'clock, and forgot about socialism except at Party conferences, because, like the Tories, their main concern was giving people a quiet time.'[1]

Macmillan's famous remark that 'We've never had it so good' carried with it an implication of ease and quietude. Macmillan possessed a deep feeling that the colossal achievements of everyone in the developed world except the United Kingdom would go on and on. No one thought then that the steam would go out of the advance in the 1970s. The question people were asking in Britain in the 1960s was, how to get aboard? In the United States the Vietnam War was becoming more and more divisive. By 1968 in France, Charles de Gaulle was on the ropes. Japan was beginning to forge ahead. Germany was a recognized economic power. The enemies in the Second World War seemed to be the effective victors. Certainties and confidence across a wide range of issues in Britain had been dashed. People lost sympathy with power, and icons began to be questioned. In academic circles, monetarists began winning some of the debates: the economic mess and the humiliations of de Gaulle's 'Non!' to British membership of the Common Market all helped. The contrast between Britain on the one hand and France and Germany on the other, where a measure of monetarism was working, was increasingly apparent, although a high degree of State planning also appeared to be working, especially in France.[2]

The moment when the Butskellite consensus really began to split was in 1969 when *In Place of Strife*, the White Paper brought in by Barbara Castle, Labour Minister for Employment and Productivity, called for regulation of trade union power. It was a landmark last-gasp achievement of the common wisdom – this time on industrial

[1] Newhouse, 'The Gamefish'.
[2] The success of central planning in practically all continental European countries is connected to a broad range of popular consent because of the fear of social upheaval. Continental Europeans tend to see stability and social cohesion in statist arrangements.

relations. Castle's proposals had the support of the civil service, a good portion of the Labour Party, and of many on the Opposition benches.

But instead of seeing it through, Harold Wilson's Government ducked for cover when the unions flexed their muscle. The White Paper was scrapped, and the Industrial Relations Bill stemming from it was neutered. On 8 October 1969, Richard Crossman, Secretary of State for Social Services in the Wilson Government, recorded in his diary that despite having the core of her proposals rejected, Barbara Castle wanted to proceed with some legislation, 'even though this has the disadvantage of being wholly pro-trade union. All it has omitted from *In Place of Strife* are her three sanctions proposals, so the trade unions get everything they want. I accept her view that she can't afford to go without any Industrial Relations Bill and that it must please the trade unions and keep to the terms by having no sanctions. It may look like a sell-out but there is no choice.'[1]

From then on it was clear that Harold Wilson might hold office again, but would not hold power. *In Place of Strife* was the last time that there was a broad consensus on appeasing the unions: in the next few years, more and more people were prepared to jettison social harmony for radical action. If, instead, Wilson had forced the issue and the unions had brought him down in 1969, he would have been returned to power in 1974 with a great mandate. The country did not want the Conservatives to face the unions down: it wanted the Labour Party to do that. It did not want the conflict that it sensed a Conservative show-down would entail. A Conservative show-down would mean that Labour would have a residual commitment to the unions. Sooner or later Labour would be returned to Government, and then it would be back to square one.

Barbara Castle's *In Place of Strife* had been an initiative for an increase in community. The unions had established themselves two generations earlier as alternative centres of power within the national community in order to counterbalance certain other

<hr/>

[1] Richard Crossman, *The Diaries of a Cabinet Minister* (London, Hamish Hamilton & Jonathan Cape, 1977), Vol. III, p. 670.

powers. They had considerable justification when they were formed and later, and in the main had successfully operated to achieve sensible working arrangements and conditions. By 1969, the conditions that had created unions no longer existed, and Castle attempted to woo them into a more conciliatory and comprehensive system. Following her failure, a more aggressive Conservative approach was a natural reaction.

Heath was alive to the issue. In January 1970 he summoned the Conservative Shadow Cabinet to meet at the Selsdon Park Hotel at Sanderstead in the suburbs of south London to determine the Party's strategy at the next general election. They readily agreed to a manifesto commitment to introduce legislation for trade union reform. They also accepted the arguments of Iain Macleod and Keith Joseph for a more free market and monetarist approach to the economy.

Macleod and Joseph were two of the first politicians after Thorneycroft, Birch and Powell to consider the monetarist evidence and to draw monetarist conclusions from it. They had divined that greater and greater State direction of the economy was dangerous. They saw that it had not succeeded in Britain, which was falling behind so many other countries. They had been looking for alternatives.

Joseph sought out Alan Walters during the late 1960s for discussions about monetarist theories and applications, and he introduced Margaret Thatcher to the economist. On occasion, the two politicians would come to Walters's London apartment for what were, effectively, tutorials in economics. 'In Opposition from '64 to '70,' John Biffen recalled, 'Keith Joseph and Thatcher showed some signs of sympathy for Powell's economic view, but a great deal of the time she was Shadow Education and really not identified with the mainstream of the economic debate.'[1]

Iain Macleod led the argument for free market policies, rather than those of State intervention that had characterized the 1960s. He urged that Government intervention and Government expenditure should be kept to a minimum and that nationalization be forgotten and he also advocated that, where possible, industries

[1] Interview, Rt Hon. John Biffen, MP, 6 June 1990.

be returned to private enterprise. At Selsdon, his arguments were accepted.[1]

Macleod was a romantic and a gambler – neither of which was Selsdon Man (the platform of the Conservative 1970 general election victory that came out of the Selsdon Park meeting). When he came down from Cambridge, Macleod joined Bowaters as a trainee and made three times his salary playing bridge. But Selsdon Man was about risk-taking, which is subtly different from gambling, and its background theme was that the Conservatives, in emphasizing individual over collective enterprise, were prepared to break post-war custom: as Edward Heath put it, 'to break the mould of British politics'. Macleod would have been able to paint a human face on Selsdon in a way that Ted Heath was never able to. Heath came over as a self-satisfied, self-made man, and so did Selsdon. Instead of being seen to be about wealth-creation and greater opportunity, Selsdon Man – like Thatcher Man – was seen as successful and vulgar with a devil-take-the-hindmost attitude.

Selsdon Man sprang to life not only because of Macleod, but also in response to the growing feeling that trade unions were becoming too powerful. But after winning the election, in 1971–2 Edward Heath's Government turned away from the confrontations implicit in Selsdon, just over a year before the first oil shock by the Organization of Petroleum Exporting Countries (OPEC) when the economy and industrial relations really began spinning out of control. Each phase of Selsdon Man's life – birth, the beginning of implementation, caging and death – was a shock to the civil service; not because the civil service resisted it (it did not), but because each phase required preparation and administration and the use of ever scarcer resources of talent and finance.

Selsdon Man was very close to Thatcher Man. 'The 1970 Manifesto was in many ways indistinguishable from the 1979 Manifesto,' said Ian Gow, an opponent of Heath in 1974–5 and later a staunch supporter of Thatcher.[2] 'There was one addition to Selsdon that was uppermost in the Thatcher mind,' said John Biffen. '– when I

[1] Peter Walker, *The Ascent of Britain* (London, Sidgwick & Jackson, 1977), states that only three members of the Shadow Cabinet – himself, Reginald Maudling, and Sir Edward Boyle – opposed Macleod's arguments.
[2] Interview, Ian Gow, MP, 8 August 1989.

say "Thatcher" I am talking about all of us who were on the liberal wing of the Party – and that was the enormous extension of ownership. Council houses, and the idea of privatization of the great public utilities – that all that was going to be put out for mass ownership has become one of the most durable and to my mind one of the most significant parts of the programme.'[1]

Selsdon Man was a phrase of Harold Wilson's, not of the Conservative Party, and it caught on with the press. 'Selsdon was an invention of the press,' said Alfred Sherman, making the point with, perhaps, some exaggeration. 'There were no policy decisions. Selsdon was a myth.'[2] Wilson, not Heath, wanted to make the Conservative platform look revolutionary: he saw in Selsdon an opportunity to panic a very cautious electorate. Selsdon did not emphasize monetarism, and this was an important difference between it and Thatcherism. It emphasized 'light' government, law and order, tax cuts, restraint of the unions, and greater selectivity in the social services. There was widespread agreement in the country as a whole that change was needed, and Selsdon was, in part, an attempt to meet this. It proposed to produce change by intensifying competitiveness, as opposed to *In Place of Strife*'s emphasis on responsibility. 'No one should doubt that at the time of the election in 1970 Ted Heath was committed to the end of [the post-war Butskellite] consensus and to the new liberal economics,' Norman Tebbit recalled with feeling. 'Ted Heath's arguments at that time, and the 1970 manifesto with its commitments to the liberation of the economy from the web of Government controls, to denationalization and its absolute pledge against state controls of prices and wages, were music to the ears of radical Conservatives like myself ... I admired the courage and judgement which had led him to the commitment to tackle the abuse of trades union power which was the most damaging single poison in our economy.'[3] Fundamentally, the Conservatives were saying that the

[1] Interview, Rt Hon. John Biffen, MP, 6 June 1990.
[2] Interview, Sir Alfred Sherman, 30 April 1990. While Selsdon was overstated at the time by Wilson, and subsequently by Thatcher in her search for consistency, nevertheless it was a key conclusion for the Conservative Party on the eve of the 1970 general election, indicating that the post-war consensus on social harmony and the role of Government would be challenged by them.
[3] Tebbit, *Upwardly Mobile*, p. 120.

country was sufficiently well-off to maintain everyone, and therefore it could allow much greater differentials. It was not calling for a cut-back: it was calling for increased inequality within an increase in wealth.

Significantly, Macleod was one of Margaret Thatcher's principal supporters in the Conservative Party. 'This one is different,' he said of her when he was Shadow Chancellor and she was a junior member of his team in the 1966–70 Opposition years. 'Quite exceptionally able, a first-class brain.'[1] 'Iain always got the politics of any problem right,' Thatcher later recalled. 'He had an instinct for how the ordinary person would react to situations and proposals. He would look at a budget in political terms first and establish what the consequences would be of a certain course of action. He believed you had to bring human nature into your calculations. If you did not get it right politically, the economics would turn out to be wrong.'[2]

Peter Rawlinson, who became Attorney General in Heath's Government, remembered the reaction to the Selsdon communiqué: 'There was born into the world a creature whom the liberal establishment at once christened "Selsdon Man", a low-browed, hirsute creature, much mocked by their scribes for wanting to bash the unions and protect old ladies being mugged and even to lower taxes.'[3] Wilson and Labour seized upon this image of Selsdon Man to show the Conservatives as madly bent upon dismantling the Welfare State.

Keith Joseph, who was not at Selsdon Park, became a particular target for opponents of free marketry and was portrayed as a wild man determined to destroy the social fabric. Quite independently of Macleod, Joseph had adopted a free market approach, with speeches (often drafted by Alfred Sherman, then working on the *Daily Telegraph*) making the case for competition and the encouragement of private enterprise, arguing that before wealth could be spent it needed to be created and that the private – not the public – sector

---

[1] Nicholas Wapshot and George Brock, *Thatcher* (London, Macdonald, 1983), p. 85.
[2] Chris Ogden, *Maggie* (New York, Simon & Schuster, 1990), p. 102, from an unpublished interview by Geoffrey Parkhouse.
[3] Peter Rawlinson, *A Price Too High* (London, Weidenfeld & Nicolson, 1989), p. 140.

was the principal source of wealth creation. Edward Heath, however, successfully led the Conservatives into the June 1970 election on the Selsdon platform: the appeal to change and the strong hint of being willing to deal with the unions, embodied in the Conservative election campaign, had apparently worked. But Heath and Selsdon Man had won, not because either was so marvellous, or because everybody loved Selsdon, but because Harold Wilson had failed in Government.

FIVE

The Heath Government, 1970–74

Despite Wilson's failure to arrest growing union power and economic demands, in the run-up to the 1970 election all but one opinion poll gave him and Labour the lead. Four days before the election, Heath had been filming the last Conservative Party political broadcast of the campaign. He returned to his apartment in Albany with Willie Whitelaw, who made his excuses and left. Only afterwards did it emerge that a conclave of the Party's power-brokers had met that Sunday evening at Peter Carrington's country home to determine how to get rid of Heath and who his successor should be after the election they believed he was about to lose.

Heath discovered all this, and given his character it made it very difficult once he got into Number Ten for Whitelaw or anyone else to get him to listen or change his mind about anything. 'Ted always listened attentively in Cabinet, generally reserving his own position till he heard the discussion,' Jim Prior remembered. 'However, one could not always be sure about Ted's position even by the end of Cabinet: he would quite often go his own way afterwards.'[1] For a proud and self-sufficient man who had endured the social snobberies of the Party's Grandees, who had proved himself a loyal and effective Party man (he had served as Government Chief Whip, aged thirty-nine, and had fundamentally delivered the backbenches to Harold Macmillan in 1957), only to be deserted by the Party's power-men when all looked black, the 1970 election victory was a rare moment: it was his chance, at last, to do things his way. There were, perhaps, more similarities between Heath and Thatcher than either would care to acknowledge.

A close colleague of Ted Heath in Government and in Opposition later reflected: 'Heath was a loyal Chief Whip man. A loyalist

[1] Jim Prior, *A Balance of Power* (London, Hamish Hamilton, 1986), p. 66.

all the way through. He reacted to the end of the "Thirteen Years of Tory Misrule" [one of Labour's campaign cries in 1964], and the advent of Wilson – a dynamic man, with "The white heat of technology" and "Britain's looking for efficiency" and the end of Macmillan, Grouse Moors, Home the fourteenth Earl and so on – with a determination to be better at it all. I believe that Heath was part of that: that's how he saw himself. He was managerial, based upon how better to run our affairs. It wasn't about fundamental values with him. It was about how we can run our affairs better. And then there was the complication: moving into the free market and the market economy and no Prices and Incomes Policy, which is the monetarist textbook way to be efficient, to "Crikey! It isn't working! We'd better sit down with these chaps around the table and fix an Incomes Policy! That'll be more efficient!" All of which, of course, was entirely consistent with trying to be efficient. He tried one way that did not seem to be efficient, so he decided he'd try the other way and be efficient at it.'[1] John Biffen, looking back at the Heath period, commented: 'Ted Heath was very pragmatic in a management consultant way who would say, "Well, this isn't working, so we'll try that!" If the machine didn't seem to be doing the job properly, he'd change it.'[2]

Self-sufficiency characterizes Ted Heath. He is also a man of real rage. He undertakes his enthusiasms with the vigour of battle, becoming a fine musician, a remarkable international yachtsman (winning the Sydney to Hobart Ocean Race in 1969 and captaining Britain's winning Admiral's Cup team while Prime Minister in 1971), and a brave and able officer during the Second World War, rising to the rank of Major in 1945, being mentioned in dispatches and awarded the MBE.[3] His passions, while intense, are few, forming a narrow channel down which he runs. In a fundamental sense he keeps a great distance from everyone. He had no Minister in Government who was closely associated with him, and no particular

[1] Interview, 13 February 1990.
[2] Interview, Rt Hon. John Biffen, MP, 6 June 1990.
[3] Member of the Order of the British Empire. Heath's was a military honour, not a civilian one. MBE is the fifth (and lowest) rank of the Order of the British Empire. When the Beatles were all made MBE by Harold Wilson in 1965, several people who had the military honour protested that they felt their achievements had been devalued.

group of intimate private or political friends with whom he relaxed. He has a roomy and broad-gauged intelligence, but somehow has very little ability to communicate enthusiasm.

As a senior politician, he evoked no affection whatsoever. He never married. On the one hand, he is indelibly sensitive about his lower-middle-class background; on the other he took care not to polish the rough edges away: it was only after 1965 when he became leader of the Conservative Party that the Party managers insisted that he take elocution lessons in the belief that his Thanet vowels would be an electoral hindrance. The sense that the public (not the private) Heath was a grinding bore had much more to do with his voice than with the content of his speeches, which was usually rather good. Colleagues were always struck by the difference between Heath's private and public speaking manner. At a dinner for the Shadow Cabinet given by the Mayor of Brighton during the October 1969 Party Conference in the town, Heath made the speech of thanks in reply to the Mayor's toast. 'As he always did on such occasions, Ted made a particularly felicitous speech, as always without a single note,' remembered a member of the Shadow Cabinet. 'In the next few years I heard him make many such in Downing Street. To those who have heard only his "plummy", rather turgid official speeches, they would come as a surprise. These were always graceful, witty – and short.'[1] As Macmillan's chief European negotiator in the early 1960s, he left the great visions to his boss to articulate. Heath made Europe sound boring, even though he was privately enthused on the matter. He was no little clerk totting up figures.

Heath was not a visionary. He was a representative man allegedly of the technocratic New Class, typical of the type C. P. Snow was holding out as the coming lords in *The New Men* and in the later volumes of *Strangers and Brothers*. He was supposedly the Conservative Harold Wilson, which he was not: he was a much less ruthless politician than Wilson and much more intellectually consistent.

Such a man could be expected to manage a new Britain, and it was the subliminal understanding of the Conservative Party that

[1] Peter Rawlinson, *A Price Too High* (London, Weidenfeld & Nicolson, 1989), pp. 138–9.

Heath would do so. He had been elected leader because he was seen as the man who represented best the Party's claim to manage the future. He was managerial (the whole European negotiation business had been an exercise in bureaucracy), and could deal with appeals to 'the white heat of technological change' that Harold Wilson had collared for Labour in the mid-1960s. He was not from the Grouse Moors or the gentrified City. He was elected leader, in part, because he was from the same sort of background as many of the new faces on the Labour Front Bench.

Ted Heath was an outsider who worked and fought to make himself indispensable, bending every fibre of his being to the task. For him, the world was not just divided between insiders and outsiders: it was a triangle where there are insiders and outsiders, and people who do things, who talk policy independent of being inside or out. He sought the authority conferred by supreme competence. He was not seeking to be an insider. He took on some of the protective coloration of being on the Tory inside – membership of Buck's; weekends at country houses – but he yachted, he did not shoot. Yachting is a sport of the rich, but not of the hereditary rich. Just at the moment when he thought he really had made it, he found that he had all along been the *condottiere* of his Party's power brokers. And when a *condottiere* loses a battle, the brokers rub him out and hire another one.

The Party wanted a person to deal with the new and far more democratic age, and with the trade unions. When Heath stumbled, Thatcher's similarity to him was actually an important asset to her: parliamentary colleagues had supported Heath because of his personal qualities, and when he failed in Government they reached for someone else – Thatcher – who had similar qualities, only more so. She was Heath II.

Heath did not know how to change himself, and there was no reason why he should: there was no wistfulness about him. So he retreated even further into his already thick shell. Jim Prior reflected on this alienation: 'I am quite certain that the more Ted saw of the party establishment or for that matter the establishment in general, the more he became convinced he could beat them, as of course he did; and the more successful he became, the more he came to despise them as well. This is evidenced by his reactions when

Margaret Thatcher became Leader, and the establishment turned against him. He never liked them and this was reciprocated.'[1] He had a real sense that the day of the Grandee was past, and that their continuation in the Party was a case of historical inertia – of the conservatism of the Conservative Party. This was a sense he shared with Margaret Thatcher. Heath probably thought that the day of the Grandee was done at least by 1956; Margaret Thatcher probably did not have to think about it: to her it was entirely obvious.

Sir William Armstrong, the son of two Salvation Army officers, as head of the civil service acquired a personal ascendancy over Heath. He was another outsider. Along with Heath he felt – in a very different way because he was a gentle soul – that the structure upon which they had to rely was just not good enough. Groucho Marx once joked that he would not belong to any club that would have him as a member. By the same token, Heath and Armstrong probably both felt that if they could get to the top of their respective poles, there was something wrong with the poles. Armstrong committed himself beyond the call of duty to Heath's policies, and suffered a breakdown in consequence. For him, as, no doubt, for Heath, it was a matter of the utmost importance to achieve economic growth for his country. And as Heath's attempt foundered on Nixon's moves, OPEC's oil shock, and strike after strike at home, the pressure on Armstrong became unbearable. At Ditchley Park, a Government conference centre, in January 1974, Armstrong gave a lecture. The impression he gave was of a man on the ropes. Campbell Adamson, the director general of the Confederation of British Industry, was there and remembered, 'It was quite clear that the immense strain and overwork was taking its toll.'[2] In February 1974 Armstrong was led from a meeting into recuperation and retirement from the civil service.

By 1974, of Heath's two principal rivals in the Party, Iain Macleod was dead and Reginald Maudling had given up. Peter Rawlinson noted the effect: 'The administration had lost its two principal political heavyweights, with whom it had begun its life. The first had gone very soon indeed in the first weeks of the new

[1] Prior, *A Balance of Power*, p. 101.
[2] Quoted in Phillip Whitehead, *The Writing On The Wall* (London, Channel Four Books and Michael Joseph, 1985), p. 110.

Parliament, when the true heir apparent, Iain Macleod, had suddenly died one month after taking office. It was said, and it was true, that right from the start we had lost our trumpet. The government was badly maimed. Two years later Reggie Maudling was forced into resignation.'[1] With both Macleod and Maudling out of the game, and Enoch Powell on the backbenches, regarded by the Party as too controversial ever to lead it successfully, there did not seem to be anybody who could challenge Heath's supremacy.

Heath was surrounded by bewildered, not quite first-rate men, who when the most intelligent official (Armstrong) and the strongest-minded politician (Heath) were in retreat, just fell back on to more and more State intervention without really thinking through policies, objectives, and consequences.

Extraordinary tensions and bad luck characterized Heath's experience in Government. His first Budget cut income and corporation tax, raised prescription charges and sought to reduce Government expenditure in every area. A ten per cent rate of growth was set as the 1973 target. The bankrupt Mersey Docks were allowed to close. Plans were announced to abolish the Prices and Incomes Board and the Consumer Council. An industrial relations bill making unions legally accountable for breaking contracts (unless – a great loophole – both employers and unions agreed that they were not to be) was introduced. The unions applied their muscle. There were dock strikes, go-slows, demands for twenty per cent pay rises, and electricity blackouts during the 1970–71 winter. Before very long the Government moved away from the Selsdon outline plan. Keith Joseph, now Minister for Health and Social Services, yielded to the intellectual pressure of the time, and appeared to forget Selsdon Man. He endeavoured to improve the lot of those most in need and to use the Welfare State as an alternative insurance policy for

[1] Rawlinson, *A Price Too High*, p. 145. Maudling resigned because of a business involvement with a corrupt architect. When Macleod died, Rawlinson later says, 'the young administration seemed to judder like a ship suddenly struck by a giant wave. It had lost the leading debater in the House of Commons – and Enoch, there was no Enoch, the figure who ought to have succeeded him. He was glowering on the backbenches, alienated, resentful at what he took to be betrayal by his Party colleagues for whom, he claimed, he had personally delivered in the general election the vital West Midland vote. There was now only Reggie Maudling as an alternative Prime Minister.' Ibid, p. 152.

them. He argued for greater State funding for the social services and introduced a new benefit, the Family Income Supplement. He was, in effect, saying that as the country became more prosperous, the Government should focus on the poor and not on those who could afford (and should be encouraged) to make decisions about their futures. The point at issue was whether people who were perfectly capable of paying out sums for insurance and other services without mediating institutions should be made to do so, or whether laziness should operate and the State should make these decisions for them through taxation and a benefits industry.

One year later State intervention had returned. Heath and his Government conducted a U-turn and spoke no more about rolling back the frontiers of the State or of cutting expenditure. Instead there was the encouragement of inflation in a race for increased economic activity and, it was hoped, the realization of full employment: the elusive goal of the post-war political consensus. The miners secured a twenty-seven per cent pay rise, having deployed flying-pickets and fought the police at National Coal Board mines and depots.

What pushed Ted Heath around the U was a storm of bad news. There was the shock of Rolls-Royce, a great prestige, elite British operation, going bankrupt. The civil service was violently and intensely convinced that Britain was only just holding on economically. Armstrong was convinced that the country was on the brink of disintegration into frantic strikes and wage-push inflation. The Nixon 'shoku' of Sunday, 15 August 1971, when he cut the dollar from the gold standard, introduced wage and price controls, and broke the General Agreement on Tariffs and Trade by imposing import surcharges, was a major blow. Here was the United States, the last country expected to bring in anything as 'socialist' as wage and price controls, introducing them. The pressure on Britain to do the same in the face of union wage claims was enormous, particularly as it became clear that the country was still prepared to try to buy off the unions. The Palace made known its fear of greater social division, as did the senior levels of the civil service. Armstrong really felt that the country was living from month to month economically and that great disruption might mean that Britain would price itself out of the world market to such an extent that it would be consigned to perpetual poverty and unrest. And part of the U-turn was the implicit recognition by Heath of the fact that he had won in 1970 on a negative vote: that the heather was not on fire for Selsdon.

Heath also had a very hard ride over Britain's application to join the EEC, which actually did nothing for his political standing. The early 1960s idealism about the EEC had faded. It was seen as the only alternative to more rapid decline, as an index of bad news, not as a great and wonderful redeeming cause. 'We cannot live without it', was the underlying argument of the protagonists for membership.

Macleod had been appointed Chancellor, but, tragically, died within weeks. He represents one of the great 'Ifs' of recent times. Had he lived, would he have fought for Selsdon Man? Could he have persuaded Heath to stick to his guns? He was an independent thinker and not a yes-man. He was not overawed by Heath and he could have challenged him for the Party leadership. But he had refused to serve under the premiership of Sir Alec Douglas-Home in 1963–4, and it was unlikely that he would have resigned under Heath: a second time would have been too blatant an expression of ambition, and if the ploy proved unsuccessful would have meant the end of his hopes. So, had he lived, the likelihood is that he would have gone along with the U-turn.

Macleod was succeeded by Anthony Barber who was more than a loyalist: he was an extremely pleasant man with no doctrines of his own, which was probably precisely why Heath appointed him. Barber saw his job as being to facilitate what Heath wanted, not as being to argue with him. Heath himself had been a brilliant subordinate, and such people are often more jealous than most about being Number One. He did not want challenge from below when he was Prime Minister. By the second half of 1971, Barber was beginning a dash for growth, tripling the rate of monetary expansion. At the time it was called the 'Barber boom'.

There was little discipline over the employment policies of central and local government. Having spoken of 'getting government off people's backs', Heath and his Cabinet colleagues were faced at the end with a larger number of employees in non-productive public sector jobs than ever before.[1] There was capitulation to a sit-in

[1] Robert Blake and John Patten (eds.), *The Conservative Opportunity* (London, Macmillan, 1976).

against closure at Upper Clyde Shipbuilders; a draconian statutory incomes policy, developed to counter rising inflation, was attempted.

Union power had once again prevented any change in industrial relations. Many people in the professions, in business, and in the civil service began to doubt if the civil service management of the policymaking system was any longer in the best interests of the country. They considered that there should have been more resistance from the professional managers, the Mandarins; that the politicians had, once again, let the country down and that the civil service had helped them do it. It was a sense shared by many in the civil service, and when Sir William Armstrong spoke of the decline of Britain being inevitable, within the service there was an almost audible snap of elastic being stretched beyond its limits and breaking. There had been what the physicists call 'phase change' in Britain in the early 1970s. The trade unions had tasted their power; economic mismanagement was apparent, and OPEC's quadrupling of oil prices in 1973 made the country finally comprehend its relative insignificance in the scheme of world power and trade. It no longer had that sense of invulnerability that had carried it through other crises.

The atmosphere of the time was also a factor in the behaviour of Heath and his Government. In particular, violence, terrorism and murder in Northern Ireland were increasing every day. It seemed to betoken what could happen in mainland Britain if the Government's social and economic policies resulted in unemployment rising too high. It was the common wisdom of the period that the social fabric of the United Kingdom would be torn apart if unemployment much exceeded one million (which it was approaching in 1971). And nearly every one of Ted Heath's Cabinet meetings began with a grim and depressing report on Northern Ireland. Within the Cabinet, in such circumstances, despondency and despair coloured the psychology of most people there. The siren song of the U-turn was all the more seductive.

Beyond that, there was an awareness from the late 1960s on that the world was changing unpredictably. In the United States, 1968 had witnessed the forcing out of office of Lyndon Johnson. In France, de Gaulle was forced out by rioting students in 1969. There was an atmosphere of wildness and espionage and disorder. Northern Ireland translated that into British terms, although the feeling that the storm of the world was rattling every tree had a greater focus than the troubles in Ulster.

Jim Prior was at the heart of Heath's Government, and was closely involved with Heath's effort to halt decline. His experience in these years committed him to the view that the improvement of industrial relations and the nation's economic performance was best attempted in co-operation with the trade unions. Throughout the 1970s and 1980s, in Opposition and in Government, Prior argued for accommodation, fighting, in effect, for Butskellism. This was to make him a principal bogey-man for Thatcher and her people. He was as close to a technocrat as the Conservative Parliamentary Party had thrown up. He was a pragmatist in that he did not want to be tramelled by doctrine. He was a man who did not believe, broadly speaking, that we have the perception to see the long term, so he concentrated on dealing with things here and now and regarded theories as a nuisance. He had some basic ideas, notably that competition is preferable to fixed prices (because we are not smart enough to fix prices; if we could show that we are smart enough, then Prior would go along with fixing them). He explained about the Heath Government: 'We were strongly committed to the post-war economic and social consensus in which the basic goal of economic policy was full employment. We recognized the need for an improved Welfare State. We believed in a society in which the social services should be expanded and more done about housing.

'We were equally committed to working through the institutions which had been developed to implement this consensus approach . . . In January 1972, although the jobless total adjusted for seasonal factors remained below one million, the unadjusted overall total exceeded that . . . It was therefore no surprise in which way Ted decided our economic policy should go when he now had to choose between tolerating a continued high level of unemployment, in the hope that this would keep some control over wage claims and inflation – or trying to run the economy with a higher level of output and growth, and seeking some other means of control over wage and price increases.'[1] The Government was back to Butskell-

[1] Prior, *A Balance of Power*, p. 71.

ism and the 1960s' cycle of 'Stop/Go' (which would be better called 'Go/Stop'): slackening money controls and increasing public expenditure, then slapping on credit controls and pay ceilings to stop the economy from going more into debt through inflation, interest payments and trade imbalances, elevating the hope that 'Go' would outweigh 'Stop' to the status of faith. It was a disaster at several levels.

Within the Conservative Party – particularly on the backbenches – the spectacle of ever-increasing public expenditure and more powerful trade unions (more powerful because there was a higher percentage of union members within the State apparatus, and this apparatus was costing more and more money, effectively dominating Government policy) led to muted unrest. Enoch Powell, once more concentrating on the question of the money supply, influenced several MPs. Two backbenchers, both future Ministers in Thatcher's Governments, John Biffen and Jock Bruce-Gardyne, were especially active in consequence. 'I had an attitude which very much reflected an apprenticeship served with Enoch Powell,' said Biffen, carefully explaining his own view. 'So I was a balanced-budget, sound-money person, critical of statutory control of prices and incomes. I was not actually a low-taxation person, so therefore I was rather less convinced of supply side economics than some people. I accepted trade union reform because it was part of the liberalizing process. And, of course, I was hostile to membership of the European Community when that was being debated.'[1]

Within the political intellectual community, a different view existed. Most thought that the pace of 'Go' would beat the pace of inflation and that, as Sir Alan Walters later remembered, 'there would be such an expansion of employment and real output that there would be a *reduction* in the rate of inflation.'[2] Walters took yet another view. He had been in Israel when the 1970 election took place. There he was telephoned by Keith Joseph with the news of victory. He returned to London and became a part-time consultant both to Joseph at the Department of Health and Social Services, and with the Central Policy Review Staff.

[1] Interview, Rt. Hon. John Biffen, MP, 6 June 1990.
[2] Sir Alan Walters, 'My Deviationist Economics', *Independent*, 26 October 1989.

With great hopes he had accepted the consultancies, assuming that he would be helping to institute a new economic policy based on 'monetary stability, fiscal rectitude and free and unfettered markets', thinking that this policy had been endorsed by the Conservatives at Selsdon Park. By the end of 1970 he had worries on this score. A year later, he had had enough. He wrote a memorandum to Joseph and forwarded a copy to Ted Heath. 'Inflation, Devaluation and More Inflation' was a graphic piece, the title succinctly summarizing the content. He forecast that by 1974, given the continuation of Barber-boom Government policy, inflation would rise to over ten per cent and probably as high as fifteen per cent; that there would be a balance of payments deficit of as much as £1 billion, and that the Government would be forced to impose prices and incomes controls.[1]

Joseph accused Walters of being an alarmist and stated – correctly – that Walters was out of step with everyone else: Ministers, other Government advisers, and public commentators. Walters replied that he was giving his professional view. Joseph took faith from the fact that everyone else was convinced that 'boom' would overpower 'bust'. He was in the forefront of high-spending Ministers, and was once more in the ranks of those who argued for measures of State intervention and control. He rejected Walters' memorandum and told the economist that there was not much point in his coming in to give advice any more. The Prime Minister took the same view. Walters resigned from his job with the Think-Tank, but did stay on with Joseph.

He probably stayed on to struggle for Joseph's soul rather than in a belief that he could affect broad policy. Joseph is a man who lives by changing his mind. He is constantly wrestling with his soul, and is in need of company in the process. Walters was holding on. But there was a personal price to pay. In 1974, Joseph, having once again changed his mind and begun to proselytize about the monetarist policies that Walters had been arguing for in 1970–71, found: 'When I went back to pick up old friendships, I found that Alan Walters, for example, was very scornful, scarcely willing to talk to one because of what, from his understandable point of view,

[1] Ibid.

was a shameful failure to perceive error.'[1] 'I remember him snubbing me in 1974,' he said, 'and a very fruitful snub it was. He refused to shake my hand. And he was quite right.'[2] 'One particular friend, Alfred Sherman,' he said on another occasion, 'kept emphasizing to me that Keynes was dead and you can make more problems by trying to print your way out of difficulties than you solve.'[3] Alfred Sherman described Joseph as 'a lion in opposition', who, once back in office, allowed his civil servants to run all over him.[4] Joseph put it another way: 'I time and again became a prisoner of the philosophy which the civil service manifested: the good intentions of the Welfare State. But that is slightly different from being a prisoner of the civil servants.'[5]

The only Minister to protest about the Government's policy was Nicholas Ridley, parliamentary under-secretary at the Department of Trade and Industry. He had found that he disagreed so strongly with the amendments that were being proposed to the 1971 Industrial Relations Act that in April 1972 he resigned. He had worked on industrial relations policy before the election, and the Act had reflected Selsdon Man's determination to clip the unions' wings, much to the anger of the trade unions – especially the miners who went on strike in early 1972 against the Act and for more pay. In the interests of peaceful industrial relations, Heath decided that the Act should be changed to placate union opposition to it. By the end of the year, Heath had completed the U-turn with plans for the introduction of a statutory prices and incomes policy.

In his diary, the newspaperman Cecil King recorded: 'Tuesday, December 5th, 1972. Lunch yesterday for A.B. [a senior civil servant] . . . I asked him why Ted had been so very keen on an agreement with the [Trades Union Congress] and the [Confederation of British Industry]. If there had been an agreement it would not have been honoured. A.B. took part in these talks and said Ted showed all the enthusiasm of the convert. He had tried a rather

---

[1] Hugo Young and Anne Sloman, *The Thatcher Phenomenon* (London, BBC, 1986), p. 28.

[2] Interview, Rt Hon. Lord Joseph, CH, 26 June 1990.

[3] Young and Sloman, *The Thatcher Phenomenon*, p. 30.

[4] Sir Alfred Sherman, 'The Thatcher Era in Perspective', *The World & I*, April 1989, p. 616.

[5] Interview, Rt. Hon. Lord Joseph, CH, 26 June 1990.

muted form of confrontation, which had been defeated by the miners, and he then decided that conciliation was the only course.'[1]

The imposition of prices and incomes control was the 'other means' Jim Prior spoke about and Alan Walters had warned about. By February 1974, when Heath lost the general election which he had called to defeat another miners' strike, inflation was running at an annual rate of 14.7 per cent and the balance of payments deficit was over £3.3 billion. The three-day working week that was a consequence of the miners' strike, and power shortages, had bedevilled the early months of the year. Enoch Powell threw his considerable electoral weight into the ring against Heath and called upon voters to support Labour as the best hope of Britain pulling out of membership of the European Community. As many as forty Conservative-held seats, it was thought, may have changed to Labour in consequence. It was not surprising, in retrospect, that Labour won the February election, and the next one in October that year. It was as if the country hoped that Labour had learnt from Wilson's and the Conservatives' mistakes, and would now bring the unions to heel.

Heath had a healthy majority and over a year to go before he needed to call an election: people expect Governments to govern, and did not like it when Heath in effect said, 'Despite my majority, I cannot deal with the trade unions. I need a new vote before I feel safe enough to move.' Then, the economic record of the Government was dismal. Heath had adopted the measures to deal with the economy that were recommended by Labour. Why not have the people who really believed in what they were doing in Downing Street? And Labour might have learned the lesson of a Heath defeat and might tackle the unions. Finally, Heath and Selsdon Man had represented a new dawn in 1970, but in Government had disappointed everyone. 'It was the last two years of the Heath Government which filled the Conservative Party with the feeling, "We won't do that again! That was a blind alley. We won't be trapped in that again!",' Enoch Powell reflected. 'The disaster of prices and incomes statutory control from 1972 to 1974, and the disastrous failure of an Industrial Relations Bill which attempted,

[1] Cecil King, *The Cecil King Diary* (London, Collins, 1975), p. 245.

in addition to reforming industrial relations, to provide power for anti-inflationary control, I think were the crucial factors that swung the Conservative Party into a readiness to listen to a different approach.'[1]

What had happened? It was not just Ted Heath who had done a U-turn, but the whole Cabinet with him, including the Secretary of State for Education and Science, Margaret Thatcher. As a Minister, she was notorious for her refusal to compromise with the Treasury on her Department's expenditure plans and requirements. In the Cabinet committees where such negotiations take place, Margaret Thatcher would insist upon every penny of her request. Other Ministers understood that give-and-take was the order of the day and would go in asking for £40 million and come out having compromised on £32 million. Not Thatcher: the meetings with her went on and on. Colleagues looked for excuses not to attend. And her refusal to compromise meant that her case was often referred to the Cabinet to decide, much to the annoyance of the Prime Minister and other Cabinet members. She wanted money for comprehensive secondary schools, for nursery schools, for colleges of education and for teachers: everything that her Labour opposite number also wanted. Sir Keith Joseph was the same. He boasted in January 1974 that 'Over the last three years we have spent, on average, in real terms, thirty per cent more each year than the average of Labour's last three years.'[2] By the end of the Heath Government, there had been no permanent break in the post-war consensus, despite the backdrop of Selsdon Man.

Enoch Powell, had he been in the Cabinet, undoubtedly would have resigned in a cloud of sulphur in 1972: Margaret Thatcher and Keith Joseph did not. Joseph, by his own admission, had been caught up in the U-turn and had become an enthusiast for State spending.

Margaret Thatcher probably considered that a woman could not afford to appear shrill in Tory politics at that stage. If she had resigned, as a woman she would immediately have been cast as 'silly' and been made marginal. She would have been described as

[1] Interview, Rt Hon. J. Enoch Powell, MBE, 1 November 1989.
[2] *Hansard*, 28 January 1974.

'flouncing out of the Government', and all those other charming phrases that men might use against a woman. But she is also an enthusiast politician who needs to believe strongly in what she is doing in order to do it. So her state of mind between 1972 and 1974 needs to be considered.

She was not being cynical and accommodating in being a good, progressive Conservative in the 1960s and early 1970s: she believed in what she was doing then. How far that involved setting aside doubts is another matter. As doubts grew, she immediately started to reconceptualize, and her tutorials with Joseph – a man born to believe, who cannot live without deep and energetic belief – were where she began to hammer out an alternative framework of belief. She is not someone who generally sits around and says, 'Let's think all this out,' so this effort was particularly important to her. As a tremendous doer, she stuck to the Heath Government with all her might. Nor is she someone who wants to sit and worry. A mandate for comprehensive secondary education? Bingo! It was something big to do. Comprehensives, she said as Secretary of State for Education, 'have often been working best in Tory areas and for a very simple reason. It is not only because these are more homogeneous areas but because their parents are passionately concerned about their children's education.'[1] As a girl she would have known children who had been denied opportunities by secondary school selection.[2] The second half of the Heath Government was a period of almost frenetic activity on her part, filling her mind while at the same time she explored for deeper certainties.[3] Her caution came

[1] *Sunday Times*, 15 November 1970.

[2] In the late 1960s and early 1970s, education was seen more and more not merely as a means of social engineering (which was why the Labour Party favoured compulsory comprehensive secondary education), but as the way to achieve a bigger talent pool for Britain than had been envisioned in the past. Wilson's remarks about 'the white heat of technology' connected to people's awareness that Britain was lagging behind other countries. Thatcher had a technocratic as well as an ideological push to her.

[3] Sir William Pile, the permanent under-secretary at the Department of Education and Science while Thatcher was Education Secretary, said, 'She never seriously delegated anything. I asked her on several occasions, "You know, this is quite a trivial matter, one of us can do that for you, if we get it wrong you can kick us on the bottom." She said, "No, I'll do it myself." She worked all hours of the day and night . . . Every single bit of paper was attended to the next day. So she never delegated.' (John Newhouse, 'The Gamefish' *New Yorker*, 10 February 1986.)

through: she was prepared to take her time, and was not flustered into precipitate action. 'Her views really became apparent after the defeat in 1974,' John Biffen recalled. 'For the period 1970–74, she was identified with all the Government's economic policies. She didn't use any code means of telling people outside that she was going along with it because she felt it was better to stay in than to walk away, but that she'd got anxieties. It is a facility that most Cabinet Ministers use.'[1] She cannot be blamed for holding on in the Cabinet after she had lost a lot of her belief in the Government. It was an act of political self-preservation.

And it was an act of self-discipline. By 1974 she was probably deeply distressed at being complicit in Heath's Cabinet. Keith Joseph virtually had a nervous breakdown in 1974 from the strain of the inner conflict he experienced in Government. Margaret Thatcher, who is more robust, fought back instead. She recognized that any independent action on her part would be dismissed by her colleagues. She had no power base in the Party and was, as 'Thatcher – Milk Snatcher!' (she had abolished free school milk), an unpopular Minister in the country at large. She was consciously an outsider who, until the moment she stood against Heath for the leadership of the Tory Party, had been careful never to act like an outsider.

Another reason why there was no revolt was that the Cabinet as a whole seems to have been genuinely persuaded of the need for a U-turn and the Barber boom policy, which was sustained in the columns of *The Economist*, and abetted by the warnings of doom and despondency being spread at the centre by Sir William Armstrong, the Cabinet Secretary, whom Heath had elevated 'almost into the role of Deputy Prime Minister'.[2] There was little evidence of Cabinet division at any point, and little squeaking from the backbenches either. Powell, Ridley, Birch (from 1970 in the House of Lords as Lord Rhyl) and their friends were a small minority.

People were genuinely startled at how the United States, France, Germany and Italy had comparatively boomed during the 1960s, which was a period of stagnation in Britain. British parochialism

[1] Interview, Rt Hon. John Biffen, MP, 6 June 1990.
[2] Rawlinson, *A Price Too High*, p. 145.

had been at its height: Japan, for example, did not enter the general British consciousness until the 1980s, more than a decade after it had streaked ahead of the European nations.[1] Heath's Cabinet felt that Britain could not afford ten years of adjustment, and that it had better go for growth under almost any circumstances. This had been the policy of both Harold Macmillan and of Harold Wilson, and there was some comfort for Heath in being consistent with them. Also, Ministers probably thought that they could control a boom, go to the country in the spring of 1975, win the election, and then taper off slowly without bringing the economy to a screeching halt. The unanticipated events of 1973–4 blew that plan off course.

But there was a reasonable political calculation behind the Barber boom: that they should go for growth, putting Selsdon Man on the back burner. That they should do everything possible to maintain Britain's place in a roaring world economy. It was a constructive attitude, and although twenty years later it looks a failure, Heath and his colleagues deserve credit for it: neither Thatcher, Joseph, nor anyone else in the Cabinet spoke out against it, and only a handful of people – notably Alan Walters and Nicholas Ridley – disagreed. It took Thatcher eighteen years before in 1990 she directly condemned the change in policy that took place. 'I served in Ted's Government from 1970 to 1974,' she said in June 1990. 'We went back on a very similar manifesto to things I believe in. The difference is that after eighteen months to two years he did the biggest U-turn on policy of all time and started to go the wrong way. In the end, that cost us the next election.'[2] But from 1972 to 1974, to the overwhelming majority of senior people in the media, the Government, and the civil service, there seemed no alternative.

However, there was a great deal of retrospective wisdom in Margaret Thatcher's view. Selsdon Man and Heath's U-turn were – and are – overrated. In the late 1960s, there was prolonged discontent. Wilson's 'white heat of technology' had not arrived. There was increasing economic stagnation as Labour tried to maintain an unrealistic vision of Britain. People like David Young, who had

[1] In 1975 Patrick Uden produced the first television programme to look at the Japanese economic and industrial achievement for BBC TV's *Tomorrow's World*.
[2] BBC Radio 2, 'The Jimmy Young Show', 18 June 1990.

voted for Wilson in hope, were angry and looking for alternatives. Post-war and post-Depression institutional and cultural structures still abounded. Britain was not full of dazzling, young would-be entrepreneurs. Bright young people looked to large corporations like ICI and to the civil service and the BBC for employment. Selsdon came out of theory, not experience. Iain Macleod spoke of the 'salariat' (which is, by definition, not entrepreneurial) as the natural constituents of the Conservative Party, and Selsdon Man was fundamentally a manager, not an entrepreneur.[1]

The U-turn did not represent the evacuation of a philosophical position. It represented both a piece of very political economy about what to do with the unions after they had cut the guts out of Harold Wilson, and a collective loss of nerve. It should not be put down to Heath personally. The personal point is that he was able, in consequence, to reverse the whole ideological thrust of his revamped Conservative Party with less difficulty than Harold Macmillan had faced when he had extracted Britain from her colonies. By then, Heath had a dominance in his Cabinet so formidable that if the whole Cabinet had turned and he alone had remained on course, he could probably have faced the other Ministers down. 'What of course did happen was that we had said in the 1970 Manifesto, "We utterly reject the philosophy of compulsory wage control",' said Ian Gow, 'and then we introduced the Prices and Incomes Policy. It was the one thing we had specifically ruled out, and then we had it. And not one single person left the Government.'[2]

The actions of Margaret Thatcher when she became Party leader, and when she became Prime Minister, throw an important light on the Heath years. She did not start with a completely new set of Shadow Ministers in 1975, or Ministers in 1979. If she had thought that they were all total cowards, and not simply people who had, like her, felt that it was not opportune to challenge Heath in 1972–4, she would have found herself a new Cabinet. In 1979 she was

[1] Peter Walker, an emblematic Selsdon Man, and his subsequent career as a 'wet' was instructive in this respect. He had left business some years before Selsdon, and a decade later his business experience was dated. Walker (like Heath) saw himself as a manager. He was loyal to Heath. The general intention of Selsdon Man was close to Thatcher Man: the difference lay in the details and the time.
[2] Interview, Ian Gow, MP, 8 August 1989.

in a position to drop the entire Front Bench and bring in a new group. The country was so enraged at both Front Benches in the 1970s that if she had come in and appointed no one who had held Cabinet office before, the country would probably have clapped. But she did not: she stayed with men who had been in Heath's team. Clearly she felt that they had not been as possessed by apocalyptic panic as the top leadership was (although political tact had a part to play in her dispositions too: she was trying to heal wounds). The implication is that she considered there was something personal about Heath's actions in Government.

Selsdon Man had been a false start with the decade. The timing was wrong. Margaret Thatcher and Thatcherism could not have prevailed in 1970. The media, most politicians, and the Establishment did not want a nation of competitive entrepreneurs, or lower-middle-class people with aspirations. Heath himself lent substance to their worry. They just did not see him as a brave artillery officer. He was seen as the type to have been in the motor pool during the war. And a great deal of the attack on Heath and Selsdon was snobbish – the way that *Private Eye* called him 'Grocer', and not just because he had negotiated agricultural issues with the EEC. The snobbery was nurtured by a feeling that the 'new' managers and technocrats were going to be overbearing and not well-rounded types. The dislike of the self-made man is far less often expressed in a discussion of, 'Was his mother a housemaid?' than of, 'Isn't he a crashing bore, and – when he's not talking about the one thing he knows awfully well – aren't his views crude and dangerous?' It is always felt by the Establishment to be far easier to 'educate' such people than to do without them, and when they resist that 'education', no holds are barred in attempts to dismiss them.

Heath – notwithstanding the mid-term U-turn – also paid the price of the over-enthusiastic pioneer. Almost the entire Conservative Party, and the country at large, thought that the organized working class had superior power to the Government. And on Day One of any major confrontation, the unions did have superior power to any Government that was not prepared to use the Army. Then the question would be one of hard pounding and seeing who could pound longest. A Government with nerve could have won, and it would gain in authority as union behaviour deteriorated – as Margaret Thatcher knew by the time she became Prime Minister. The point in the late 1960s and early 1970s was that a determination to assert Government authority was grounded in policy – as with the resistance to the General Strike in 1926 – not in experience, and the fault was thus not in analysis, but in will. 'On the first leg of Ted's voyage he intended to remove the restrictive practices of the unions,' said Jim Prior, and then revealingly went on: 'But the unions and their members were not ready for it.'[1] Nor, in the end, were Heath or his Ministers.

The U-turn did not represent a vision of an economy authentically transformed by decentralization, initiative and enterprise. Anyone who had been through the Depression and the war had an entirely understandable bias towards large institutions and the idea that Governments should manage. The problem that Selsdon sought to address was what to do about the imbalance amongst large institutions upset by union conduct. When the view gained weight that all was not well with the capitalist model (and the Nixon 'shocku' reflected and fuelled this view), a U-turn seemed natural. Ted stayed within the confines of accepted governmental practices. He said, in effect, 'There's too much on our plate for the radical initiative of Selsdon.' He had not cut things loose in 1970–71, he simply stated a general intention in Selsdon. But like any other person who has reversed a nominally ideological position, Ted Heath suffered from the effective hiking of importance of Selsdon by Wilson. The positions of both Parties in 1970 were not that far apart ideologically. The debate between them was one of efficiency rather than doctrine: 'Anything you can do, I can do better.'

'Selsdon Man was important in the sense that he was there to remind Margaret Thatcher of what she must never do, which is to desert the principles on which you have been elected,' said John Biffen. 'She knew that Ted misread the electorate in 1974 and was thought to have reneged. You can renege if the new policy is successful. There is always a small clique baying for consistency at any cost, but Ted donned the rather tatty fabrics of socialism and

[1] Prior, *A Balance of Power*, p. 72.

they didn't look any more decorative on him than they had on Harold Wilson. So she had quite a determination of "The Lady's Not For Turning!" and all that. That was a very clear determination.'[1] In claiming that Heath had conducted 'the biggest U-turn on policy of all time', Thatcher was stressing this determination and addressing the background question of why she overthrew Heath. She had been promoted by him, and was explaining that she had not downed that Heath from whom she had accepted Office in 1970, but the Heath that changed the terms of the contract later on.

However, there is no evidence that at the time she thought it was a U-turn. She probably began to see it as such in 1973–4 when it did not ward off disaster. She was making the 'U-turn' a scapegoat for a general failure by Heath and before him by Macmillan, and as her justification to take a more radical initiative. She was saying, in effect, 'I went along with it because my boss, the Prime Minister, and the senior advisers in the civil service, all urged it and I knew no better. But when I found out how wrong it was, then I acted: and no one else did!' She also bid up the significance of the U-turn to claim consistency, to say that they had been on the right course in 1970–71 and she had merely returned to that course after 1979, and that she had turned against someone who had let the Party and the country down.[2]

Edward Heath and Harold Macmillan were the two men who hated Thatcher, and the two men she played off: Heath explicitly and Macmillan implicitly. Heath was the one unsuccessful outsider that the Conservative Party has had as leader. He hated her because she did what he thought he was going to do, and he let himself down after 1975 by bluntly making his feeling public. Macmillan was less straightforward, making his view of Thatcher known in asides and jokes. The historian and television interviewer Ludovic Kennedy was once interviewing Macmillan when, after a morning's filming, they were to drive to lunch. 'Which car are we going in?'

[1] Interview, Rt Hon. John Biffen, MP, 6 June 1990.
[2] Hidden behind this were reminders of the strength of consensus among opinion-formers (Heath and the Cabinet were not alone in 1971–2, as the columns of the *Economist* demonstrated), and of the spirit it took to resist the consensus: when Thatcher spoke of the 'greatest U-turn of all time' in June 1990, she was resisting similar consensus pressure on European political union.

Macmillan asked. 'Are we going in Mrs Thatcher?' Seeing Kennedy's expression, he explained, 'This car makes a noise if you don't fasten your seat-belt, and a light starts flashing if you haven't closed the door. It's a *very bossy* car.'[1] Macmillan thought that he had brought about a synthesis of Tory men and Whig measures; that he was being genuinely conservative, preserving free enterprise while ensuring that the poor prospered. But he presided over the progressive decline of British competitiveness without apparently noticing. He hated Thatcher because she effectively repudiated his record and his view of Britain, which, until she came to power, had not been seriously challenged. It never occurred to Thatcher that Britain was not one nation. She never felt the need to search for existential connections between the working class and the upper class, and she never thought that the hereditarily advantaged were distinguished. Unlike so many of her colleagues, and so many people in academia and the media, she did not regret the distinctions between the classes, and she had no romance about the working class.

The ultimately overriding feeling that unions should be appeased was buoyed by idealistic social engineers and by romance. In the thirty years after 1945, there was a general sense that the working class had borne the brunt of the killing in the First World War, of the Depression of the 1930s and of the distress of the Second World War, and deserved 'fair' treatment. This was very much Harold Macmillan's view. Public school men often seemed fearful of, or deferential to, the working classes. In 1970, soon after he became Prime Minister, and after he had announced plans to curb union power, Heath gave a dinner party at Chequers for Harold Macmillan. At the end of dinner, Macmillan spoke. 'The words of the speech flickered like the lights from the flames of the fire around our splendid young leader's prematurely silvered head,' recorded Peter Rawlinson, one of the few people present. 'We must remember, said the sage, that the men from Stockton and the Yorkshire coalfields had fought and died with him at Ypres and Passchendaele and he had seen their sons march past their Sovereign in triumph

[1] Ludovic Kennedy, *On My Way to the Club* (London, Fontana, 1990), p. 377.

in the great parade after victory in North Africa. Here the orator flicked away what appeared by the gesture to be the ghost of an inconvenient tear. Happily only temporarily overcome, he went on gravely to reflect that we had at last become as a nation truly one people. No one and indeed no organization of our people must be crushed. Caution, he counselled, staring into the fire, caution and, above all, restraint.'[1]

Macmillan was voicing the Old Guard's view that Heath, by attempting to 'break the mould of British politics' in challenging the unions, was breaking the post-war consensus. 'It was a stern, paternal warning,' reflected Rawlinson, 'against dividing the One Nation which the past quarter-century had at last created, and it demonstrated how in 1970 the mould of the "Butskellite" era was far tougher and harder to crack than it would be a decade later after the defeat of Ted and the second, raffish reign of Harold Wilson, when the unscrupulous exploitation of power by the trade-union bosses had finally brought the nation to the end of its toleration of their holding the nation to ransom.'[2]

There were plenty of Conservatives who were against the Butskellism of Macmillan and Heath. There was also a great degree of discontent within the Conservative Parliamentary Party at the way in which Heath managed it. For whatever reason, he came across to many of his backbenchers as arrogant and uncaring of their problems and their opinions. He had, said John Biffen who was a backbencher from 1961 to 1975, 'a glacial personality'.[3] An MP might find he had a problem with a policy proposal, and privately attempt to secure some changes. All too often he or she would be told by the political officials around Heath: 'We had a Policy Group on this issue some time ago. Why didn't you make your views known then? Now it's too late: the policy has been agreed.' It was a sign that Heath had really diminished: a Chief Whip type should be acutely aware of what is not said, and should have an exceptional sense of micro politics and backbench feeling. After losing two elections on the trot in 1974, Ted Heath could not escape the consequences.

[1] Rawlinson, *A Price Too High*, p. 249.
[2] Ibid., p. 250.
[3] Interview, Rt Hon. John Biffen, MP, 6 June 1990.

Heath had developed a number of enmities in the Party. Drawing a distinction between Tories and Conservatives, Tories never liked him; at most they found him useful. Conservatives – hard-headed business types who felt no organic Toryism in their bones – did not like him because he had betrayed Selsdon Man. The largest body of enmity towards him consisted of backbench MPs who would follow any leader who did not appear to be compromising the nation's interests. They were people who made a temperamental – not a class or an operational – critique of Ted. They were not like the Conservatives, angry about his U-turn, or like the Tories, pursing their lips about his rough self-presentation. They were simply in the ordinary field of politics observing that they might well be killed in an attack their general did not believe was coming.

SIX

Keith Joseph

There is a room you can go into in the William James Building at Harvard. You enter the building, and then go through a series of very formidable doors, and each door shuts with a soft, heavy thud. Finally, you find yourself in a completely empty windowless room deep in the building, with the door closed. As you stand there, you start to hear a hum that becomes louder and louder. The room is soundproof, so the hum does not come from outside. What you are hearing is the combined sounds of your heart beating, the blood passing through your arteries, and your muscles tightening and relaxing. It is the tone of your self.

Keith Joseph has lived his whole life, in effect, in a room like that. He lives in a state of hyper-awareness that burns him up. 'There was a time when he couldn't wear a watch,' a friend remembered. 'His internal electricity stopped it, so he said.'[1] He is constantly thinking about what he ought to be doing and thinking. He is passionately interested in the process of his own mind, a very self-referential person – which is not the same as self-centred, which Joseph is not.

He is of philosophical mind. He has been a guide, philosopher and friend to Margaret Thatcher. He genuinely liked her, which was more than could be said of most of her male contemporaries. At his own wish, he left full-time politics in 1987, and Thatcher put him in the House of Lords. He is a good-hearted man, generous, upright, decent and without side. Not for him the reactionary certainties of so many of his elders: he has always been open to the currents of the time, which is one of the reasons why he led the attack on the post-war political and social consensus. Like Denis Thatcher, he never made the assumption that so very many men of

---

[1] Interview, 30 April 1990.

his generation did: that a woman's place is in the home and certainly not challenging or competing with men in any serious professional sense. He always accepted Margaret Thatcher as an equal, recognizing her brightness and intellectual curiosity. He admired her obvious courage. He probably felt the proprietary interest of a tutor to the brilliant pupil in her. She was so eager to learn, and she learned so well. She, certainly, has always demonstrated a real affection and respect for him.

For all his having been to Harrow and to Oxford, there is still something of the outsider about Joseph. The average Conservative, confronted by this highly-strung, brilliant, Jewish millionaire Fellow of All Souls College, Oxford, doubtless finds him a bit rich for the diet. Joseph got on well with Reginald Maudling because Maudling was a very bright man who enjoyed a very wide – slightly too wide, it turned out – range of friendships. But in general, as Willie Whitelaw observed, Tories are suspicious of obviously brainy people, preferring the roast beef and Yorkshire pudding of the less able, unimaginative, steady types. There was something lamentably exotic about Sir Keith. Thus it is, one might argue, in a representative democracy.

His money and his ability saw him through to the top of parliamentary politics. Money gave him the opportunity to be his own man, and he took it. His ability as a manager made him an effective Minister. At the age of 44 he was one of the three brilliant promotions that followed Macmillan's Night of the Long Knives in 1962. There might have been four, but the 46-year-old Ted Heath was negotiating in Brussels and was not moved. Reginald Maudling, aged 45, became Chancellor of the Exchequer. Edward Boyle, aged 39, was put in charge of Education. Keith Joseph went to Housing.

The Ministry of Housing was something Joseph knew a lot about: his family business (Bovis) was in construction. All this carried him in the direction of consensus social policy, which was Macmillan's forte. As Minister of Housing in the early 1950s, Macmillan himself had 'built' 300,000 homes. Joseph was very much a Macmillan man, and presided over a policy that he inherited (and later regretted) of demolishing houses in favour of tower blocks. When the Conservatives were thrown out of office in 1964, he took it all very personally. His response was to go off and start cogitating, and that took him inexorably towards the free market.

He did not just talk about free enterprise and business practices: he actually knew a lot about them. He might not have known about how the world really turned on its axis, but he did know about construction costs and time lags and how you have to budget for the once-in-seven-times that snow stops building dead for two months. He had a strong sense of practicalities. He read law at Oxford, going down in 1939 just before war started. He became a captain in the Royal Artillery. He was wounded in the battle for Monte Cassino, and was mentioned in dispatches. Out of the Army in 1946, he qualified for a licence from the Institute of Building: this meant digging foundations, mixing cement, stacking and laying bricks. It was tough, physical work. At the same time, he also passed the All Souls examination and qualified for the Bar. He joined the family firm and worked on building sites, becoming a site foreman, a manager, a director, and later, for a time, chairman of the company. He entered the House of Commons in 1956 as a 'Tory': he insisted on differentiating between that and 'Conservative'. In the 1960s when many young Conservatives were accepting the idea of central planning, and when British business was not in such a state as to command deep respect, except in certain brilliant areas such as aviation and jet engines, Joseph was a rare link for the Party in the House of Commons to the world of business: he was an ambassador from the real world in the political one.

Since the war, there have been very few major businessmen in the House of Commons. The post-war Conservative Party simply did not attract such people to the benches. Before the war, when the House of Commons met almost entirely in the evenings so that squires could come up to town for a night or two away from their families, and a handful of barristers could earn their day in court, there were more businessmen. Stanley Baldwin was an eminent ironmaster. But once the House started meeting in the daytime (which became usual in the 1950s), businessmen tended to politick over lunch and dinner in the City and the clubs and at their London homes rather than in the House of Commons.

Britain was slow to respond effectively to the pace of technological change and of business efficiency that was happening in the outside world in the post-war decades. The principal British response came in the 1970s when in the upper middle class an excitement attached to business for the first time in two generations. This 'discovery' of business was very late: many of the upper middle class in France, Germany, Italy, Spain and the United States, from the 1940s on, automatically went to business schools. In his novel, *Nice Work*, published in 1988, David Lodge has one of his characters – Professor Swallow, the head of the English Department at the University of Rummidge, who is trying to deal with the effects of Thatcherism on the university – say, 'Isn't it extraordinary how interesting money has become lately? Do you know, I've suddenly started reading the business pages of *The Guardian* after thirty years of skipping straight from the arts page to the sports reports.'[1] Despite the pioneering 1960s successes of the Beatles, the Rolling Stones, The Who, Pink Floyd and 'Swinging London' (as *Time* magazine christened the capital), it was in the United States, Japan and continental Europe that the real business explosion took place.

After the February 1974 general election, Joseph – as he put it – 'converted' to being a 'Conservative', discovering the true faith of the free market and monetarism. In 1975 he was to write, in explanation, 'It was only in April 1974 that I was converted to Conservatism. I had thought I was a Conservative but I now see that I was not one at all.'[2] 'All the time I was in favour of short cuts to Utopia,' he said. 'I was in favour of the Government doing things because I was so impatient for good things to be done, and I didn't realize that the Government generally makes a mess . . . We invented the whole process [of the free enterprise economy] . . . yet we have allowed the rubber-stamp of collectivism . . . to dominate our lives.'[3]

Business was a subtext of Joseph's 'conversion' which showed (not least to Joseph himself) how much of a businessman he was. From 1974, being a Conservative meant to Joseph being in the Party of business, and in this respect being in the tradition of Joseph Chamberlain and really wanting enterprise to flourish. 'Joseph held

[1] David Lodge, *Nice Work* (Harmondsworth, Penguin, 1989), p. 326.
[2] Keith Joseph, *Reversing the Trend: A Critical Reappraisal of Conservative Economic and Social Policies* (Chichester, Rose, 1975).
[3] *Listener*, 26 June 1975.

Our Age responsible,' said Noel Annan, addressing the question of whether his generation, which he described as 'Our Age' – men and women who had come to power and authority in the 1940s and 1950s – was responsible for British decline. 'He accused the dons and intellectuals of not perceiving that the comfortable bough on which they rested was sustained by business.'[1]

The Conservative Joseph became a key player in the game of electing a leader. Enoch Powell was out of the running: in February 1974, he refused to stand for Parliament and endorsed the Labour Party. In October he came back to the House as an Ulster Unionist for a Co. Down constituency, no longer a man of power within the Conservative Party, which never forgave him for breaking ranks. For Powell, Heath's U-turn and UK membership of the EEC (Heath's great achievement) were too much.

Joseph represented a set of opinions, once identified with Powell, that were again gaining ground within the Party and outside, and he made it clear that Ted Heath had to go, not simply because he had failed to win the election, but because his policies were wrong. Margaret Thatcher was initially the only member of the Shadow Cabinet to side with him.

Joseph pursued his thoughts and his new mission of proselytizing for the free market and monetarism. After the February 1974 election, Harold Wilson led a minority Government and it was clear that another election would soon be held. This occurred in October, giving Wilson a slim parliamentary majority. Between February and October, therefore, whereas a leadership challenge was on the cards, it was muted. Conservatives did not want to reduce their chances of winning – or so it was generally thought – by having a contest in that period. After October, however, the gloves came off.

Heath's friends urged him to face the inevitable leadership election and to do so immediately as his best chance of holding on. But he refused on the grounds that he was determined to fight the right wing in the Party. He considered it best to force his opponents into the open, thinking that they would slink back into the shadows, away from the light. He, and most observers, believed that being

[1] Noel Annan, *Our Age: Portrait of a Generation* (London, Weidenfeld & Nicolson, 1990), p. 338.

'right-wing' – pro-hanging, anti-union; anti-welfare – was the kiss of death politically and that once exposed, right-wingers would be defeated by ridicule and political realities. He failed to recognize that he was now being seen as an electoral liability, having lost three of the four elections he had led the Party into (two in 1974; one in 1966), and that a leadership contest would be as much about this as about policy. He also failed to see that public opinion was far more right-wing (e.g. pro-hanging) than the views prevalent in the Mandarinate, the media, and the House of Commons. The 1922 Committee – the gathering of backbench Conservative MPs – made the seriousness of Heath's position plain when it ignored his wishes and called for an election for the leadership. Heath asked Lord Home to review election procedures. Home reported that there should be provision for annual leadership elections in the Parliamentary Party in the House of Commons, and that if there was no majority winner on the first ballot, new candidates could enter on the second (these provisions also applied in November 1990).

In the summer of 1974, between the two general elections that year, the Shadow Cabinet had conducted a post-mortem. Joseph had been instrumental in persuading Heath to do this. They met in the Leader of the Opposition's rooms in the House of Commons. Heath opened by saying that a review of his Government's record and policies was necessary, although he did not think that any serious mistake had been made, except that he had not persisted long enough. Sir Donald MacDougall, who had been chief economic adviser to the Treasury from 1969 to 1973, gave an analysis of the economic record and ended up saying that unless the growth in money supply was blown up from the then rate of 7.5–9 per cent to 25 per cent, he was afraid that unemployment might reach one million or more. He did not think that inflation was a consequence of money supply increases, but that it was a consequence of all sorts of other things – international trade movements, price hiking in raw materials, and so on.

Alan Walters was there too. Joseph and Thatcher had insisted that he be involved. He replied to MacDougall, arguing that money supply had a great deal to do with inflation, and that monetary stability, reduced public expenditure and free markets wherever possible – Selsdon Man, in effect – provided the best medium and long-term answer to the country's economic ills.

Walters was listened to in silence, Heath making plain his annoyance, although others present, including Airey Neave, a longtime opponent of Heath's and a free marketeer, who was now spokesman on Northern Ireland, and Angus Maude, another free marketeer who had been given a policy role within the Party, were more inclined to agree with Walters' argument. When Walters finished, Heath called upon Professor James Ball to speak, obviously expecting him to refute Walters. Ball was an expert on economic modelling and Principal of the London Graduate School of Business Studies. His models had played an important part in the Government's economic forecasting. 'Perhaps you'd like to give your side on this?' Heath said to Jim Ball, and then pointedly reminded everyone that Ball had been very much a part of the policy picture in 1973 and early 1974: 'Remember, you forecast that inflation was going down instead of up.'

This was a moment of great importance, and most people present knew it. Ball was being asked, in effect, to pass judgement on the Heath Government and in so doing was also passing judgement on Heath as the Party's leader. Heath had made it clear that he regarded the professor as his main witness, as the person who would justify his record. What Ball said would now influence a great many Tory insiders. 'Yes,' he said, 'we did forecast that inflation was going down, and we were completely wrong. Alan Walters was completely right! We made fundamental mistakes in our modelling. The best thing I can suggest that you do in terms of policy is what Alan suggests!'

Heath refused to accept Ball's view, and the meeting went on until close to midnight before Heath concluded as he had started. 'It's late, and it's time to sum up,' he said. 'I think I can sum up the proceedings adequately. The main conclusion, I think, is that our policies were right, but that we didn't persist in them long enough.' He was absolutely refusing to concede that his economic policy had been wrong. Of the key players in the policy fight that was now to unfold, Sir Keith Joseph's eyebrows shot up; Angus Maude shook his head and looked down; Sir Geoffrey Howe looked astonished, and Margaret Thatcher sat without expression with her back to the wall, away from the centre table.[1] Heath had lost his sense of objective reality. The division was forming between those who could not accept that the post-war consensus had got things wrong in a fundamental way, and those who were more convinced than ever that monetarist policies should be pursued.

Jim Prior, looking back at this period, was to identify the months after February 1974 as a time when sides were being taken in an ideological struggle that persists to the present day: 'The battle lines of the great ideological argument within the Party, which has raged ever since, were being drawn up. The months immediately after the February 1974 election were a period of "phoney war", with no more than skirmishes, but soon the monetarists would feel free to go on the attack. In our desire to break through the vicious cycle of "stop–go" after the winter of 1971–2, we had misjudged the level of demand and allowed the money supply to expand too fast. In his own rethinking in Opposition, Keith Joseph had latched on to "monetarism" as the panacea, and during 1974 was steadily building a denunciation of our entire approach.'[2] 'Joseph sparked off the Thatcher revolution in 1974,' said Alfred Sherman, who had a major role in the development of Joseph's thinking at this time, 'by his thoroughgoing criticism of his party's economic philosophy and policies since the Second World War. His views came to be regarded as the fountainhead of Thatcherism.'[3]

On 5 September 1974, what was seen at the time as the most serious skirmish took place. Joseph effectively raised the 'Drop Heath' standard with a speech in Preston arguing for monetarism and placing the blame for ineffective economic management on the post-war consensus, on the State spending more than it received in tax income, and on a loss of nerve:

> Our post-war boom began under the shadow of the 1930s. We were haunted by the fear of long-term mass unemployment, the grim, hopeless dole queues and towns which died.
>   So we talked ourselves into believing that these gaunt,

[1] Interview, 25 May 1989.
[2] Jim Prior, *A Balance of Power* (London, Hamish Hamilton, 1986), pp. 96–7.
[3] Sir Alfred Sherman, 'The Thatcher Era in Perspective', *The World & I*, April 1989, pp. 615–16.

tight-lipped men in caps and mufflers were round the corner, and tailored our policy to match these imaginary conditions. For imaginary is what they were.[1]

Joseph was expected to stand against Heath. After February, he had rapidly become disenchanted not only with the 1970–74 Government record, but also with Heath as leader. Joseph's views had crystallized with his post-February experience and 'conversion'. At Upminster and Preston he gave the first of a set of speeches about what he saw as the range of options available to Britain.[2] In the enthusiastic opinion of Alfred Sherman, 'Joseph first lent political respectability to rejection of the Keynesian myth in his 1974 Upminster and Preston speeches, whose side-effect was to undermine Edward Heath and thereby pave the way for the ascendancy of Mrs Thatcher.'[3] 'Inflation is Caused by Governments' was the title of the Preston speech. 'Incomes policy alone as a way to abate inflation caused by excessive money supply,' he declared, 'is like trying to stop water coming out of a leaky hose without turning off the tap; if you stop one hole, it will find two others . . . Why did successive governments for the last score years, led by well-intentioned and intelligent people advised by conscientious officials and economists, take a course which led inexorably and predictably to the present nightmare? . . . We, the Conservatives, are not without blemish, I freely admit; but how much of this derives from bi-partisanship, from middle-of-the-road policies, from confusing a distinctive Conservative approach with dogmatism?'[4]

A number of Shadow Cabinet members tried to dissuade Joseph from giving the speech. It was obvious that Harold Wilson was about to call an election, and many of Joseph's colleagues thought

[1] Press release, Sir Keith Joseph, Preston 5 September 1974.
[2] At Upminster on 22 June 1974, Joseph had announced the establishment of the Centre for Policy Studies, rocking the boat slightly with his speech. Compared with Germany, Sweden, Holland and France, he said, 'we have the longest working hours, the lowest pay and the lowest production per head. We have the highest taxes and the lowest investment. We have the least prosperity, the most poor and the lowest pensions.' Since the text of his speech was not circulated to journalists beforehand, it did not receive much coverage.
[3] Sir Alfred Sherman, 'Economic Doctrines, Political Dilemmas', *Encounter*, December 1988.
[4] Press release, Sir Keith Joseph, Preston, 5 September 1974.

that he would be playing into Labour's hands if he gave it then. Jim Prior 'even had a word with Margaret Thatcher, who by then seemed to have become one of Keith's followers: "You know this is a disastrous speech – can't you stop him giving it?" Margaret replied that it was the work of Alfred Sherman: she felt that Keith did not always understand the political impact of arguments, but that she did not have much influence over him.'[1]

In addition to Alan Walters, Alfred Sherman had a major hand in drafting the Preston speech.[2] Sherman saw some monetarist methods (he was never a full-blooded monetarist) and the operation of the free market as the key to a revived Britain. After the February election, Sherman sought out Joseph as the best hope for a new beginning in the Conservative leadership.

Joseph had hoped to be made Shadow Chancellor in 1974, but when that did not happen, at his own request he was given responsibility by Heath for developing Party policy. 'Shortly after the election,' Alfred Sherman remembered, 'he rang me up and asked me round. He said that he hadn't got the Shadow Chancellorship and therefore he wasn't going to take a Shadow portfolio. He'd be in the Shadow without a portfolio, and he wanted to set up a unit to show that we would be better off if we did what we eventually did do over trade unions. And I drew him forward to be much bolder and attack the whole corporate/Keynes economics. If he'd got the Shadow Chancellorship, there would have been no "Thatcher revolution", and Heath would still have been the leader of the Opposition, or at least leader of the second biggest Opposition Party.'[3] In order to search out new policies, Joseph had approached the Institute of Economic Affairs, a bastion of market economics under its director, Ralph Harris, and its editorial director, Arthur Seldon, and asked for – and was given – an education. 'He first came to see us in 1964 after the collapse of the Alec Douglas-Home Government,' recalled Harris. 'He said, "I gather you've been doing some work and have some ideas." And he took various publications that were laid out. He also said, "Who is the

[1] Prior, *A Balance of Power*, p. 97.
[2] Samuel Brittan, not a Conservative but a strong proponent of monetarism, also gave advice.
[3] Interview, Sir Alfred Sherman, 30 April 1990.

129

best man to put the other view? I want the other views, the strongest views. Who should I go and see?" We made some suggestions and gave him some names. He made endless notes. He came again in 1974 after Heath lost. "Look," he said, "I'll understand if you think it's a waste of time. I came to see you ten years ago, and we've been discredited in between."[1]

The awareness that the best Welfare State/Butskellite intentions had been discredited was the background to Joseph's declaration in April 1974 that he had been converted to Conservatism. It also convinced him that the Party needed a new policy centre, removed from the thinking and the personalities that had dominated policy-making so far. He went back to Heath with a proposal that came from Sherman: he would establish a new Think-Tank on policy, the Centre for Policy Studies (CPS), independent of the Party and funded privately, to examine how market economies worked, the role of the entrepreneur, and how socialism could be rolled back. Heath agreed, insisting only on the right to appoint one of the directors of the Centre.

In retrospect, this was to be the most serious move towards a new Conservative philosophy that developed over the next five years: the Centre was a vital step in enabling colleagues to distance themselves from the Heath policies without publicly tearing the Party apart. Heath was probably glad to see Joseph disappearing into what was still regarded as the loony fringe of economic thinking and away from Party leadership contests and the *realpolitik* of winning an election. He said that this was a way for Joseph and Thatcher (who had joined in the venture) to learn more about industry. It was a barbed remark: Bovis had experienced calamitous times and was taken over by P & O in January 1974;[2] Margaret Thatcher had been able to enter politics because her husband was wealthy and could support her career: she had no personal business experience.[3] Sir Geoffrey Howe had combined with Joseph and Thatcher in their determination to try to secure new thinking in

---

[1] Interview, Lord Harris, 21 May 1990.

[2] Joseph later persuaded the chairman of P & O, Sir Jeffrey Sterling, to be his industrial adviser at the Department of Trade and Industry. Sterling stayed on as an adviser in the Department throughout the 1980s.

[3] However, being a barrister is an entrepreneurial profession.

the Party. They all became directors of the Centre with Joseph as chairman and Sherman as director of studies.

'I want you to know that Geoffrey Howe and Margaret Thatcher and I are setting up an organization which will be more political than the Institute of Economic Affairs and attached to the Conservative Party,' Joseph told Ralph Harris, who welcomed the initiative.[1] 'We don't want to get involved in politics,' Harris replied. 'I've even got a name for you: "The Centre for Alternative Policies – CAP."'[2] 'I had always written letters to the papers,' said Nigel Vinson, who became co-director and treasurer of the Centre, 'and Ralph Harris liked the flavour of one and invited me to lunch and subsequently asked me to become a trustee of the IEA. So when Keith and Margaret were looking around for true believers to help them set up the CPS, Ralph Harris gave them my name. He knew me as an entrepreneur and a doer and said, "Nigel Vinson will help you set it up, help you raise money and put it in place for you." I actually walked the streets and found the premises and screwed up the nameplate with my own hands.'[3] Heath was happy to write letters asking for financial support for the Centre, which was established in Wilfred Street off Buckingham Gate, just outside the division bell area of Westminster. Doubtless he thought that this was a painless method of tucking Joseph away.

The chairman of Cavenham Foods, James Goldsmith, was an early donor along with other businessmen. They saw in it an opportunity not only to influence the Conservative Party, but also to proselytize for business and wealth-creation – for what Keith Joseph now saw as Conservatism. 'We had a deal with Central Office that we would approach nobody from whom they were getting money,' said Nigel Vinson. 'And that was rigidly stuck to for the first six years. After that, things eased up. But in my day we never poached at all, so Heath or Central Office could never say that we were stealing their clothes. We were very careful not to raise money in rivalry to the Conservative Party or the IEA.'[4] While never rich, the Centre was able to devote itself to its purposes and to acting as a

[1] Interview, Lord Harris, 21 May 1990.
[2] Ibid.
[3] Interview, Lord Vinson, 30 May 1990.
[4] Ibid.

131

research base for Joseph and later Margaret Thatcher, and for those who believed that it was essential to change Party policy.

It took time for the Centre's influence to be felt. When Wilson called a second election for October 1974, a commitment to an Incomes Policy was in the Conservative Manifesto. Heath still controlled the Party apparatus and its policymaking. Joseph was not immune to the pressure that was building up behind him to challenge for the Party leadership, if only to clear the air. Geoffrey Howe wanted him to stand and spoke to him about it. Ian Gow, a close friend of Howe, wrote to Joseph also asking him to stand. After Heath's general election defeat in October 1974, the two friends had determined that there must be a new leader, and had centred on Joseph as the obvious choice. The first day back in London immediately after the election, Howe and Gow dined together. 'We talked almost exclusively about the leader of our Party,' remembered Gow, 'and we both concluded that Ted would have to go. We thought that Ted's most grievous disadvantage was not the personality problem, but his policy. We both believed that inflation was a monetary phenomenon, and that inflation could only be caused by Government, and could only be cured by Government. It wasn't due to dry weather or oil prices or Harrods or anything else. We wanted a leader who shared our view about the cause of our economic ills, and who would not seek the abatement of inflation by means of Prices and Incomes policy, but by means of monetary policy. And also, of course, a far more free enterprise economy – we were both keen denationalizers. And Keith was the articulate voice. Howe and Gow both wanted Keith.'[1]

Airey Neave was in the group of MPs who, for one reason or another, also wanted to get rid of Ted Heath. Within days of the general election on 10 October, Neave asked Joseph to stand against Heath, and Joseph considered doing so. Later he was to say that he did not take the idea seriously, but at the time it looked as if he might. On 18 October, he wrote a letter to Ian Gow. 'If Ted does decide to resign,' he said, 'I shall certainly allow my name to go forward. But, of course, he has not yet made any decision.'[2] 'At

[1] Interview, Ian Gow, MP, 8 August 1989.
[2] Letter, Sir Keith Joseph to Ian Gow, 18 October 1974.

that time the so-called libertarian right, if you like, people like Nicholas Ridley,' Ian Gow recalled, 'we thought that Keith was the person in the former Cabinet and then in the Shadow Cabinet who most closely reflected our views about what should be done to the economy. So Keith was our man.'[1] 'Keith was determined to effect change,' said Nigel Vinson, looking back. 'I don't think that at that stage he thought Margaret Thatcher might have got it. Who did? Keith is a giver, a server, not a self-seeker in any sense. He's a *pro bono publico* to the top of his head.'[2]

The following day, Saturday, in Birmingham, Joseph blew his candidature out of the water with a second major speech – drafted in large part by Alfred Sherman, and quoting from an article in the Child Poverty Action Group's magazine, *Poverty* – arguing that people in socio-economic classes four and five should not have children: 'A high and rising proportion of children are being born to mothers least fitted to bring children into the world and bring them up . . . Some are of low intelligence, most of low educational attainment . . . They are producing problem children . . . These mothers, the under-20s in many cases, single parents, from classes four and five, are now producing a third of all births . . . Yet proposals to extend birth control facilities to these classes of people, particularly the young unmarried girls – the potential young unmarried mothers, evoke entirely understandable moral opposition. But which is the lesser evil?'[3]

There was an outcry, and Joseph compounded the mistake he had made by apologizing. 'I think I may have damaged things in which I rather deeply believed,' he said.[4] 'Behind his frantic re-thinks and apologias today,' said the *New Statesman* later, and accurately, 'can be discerned the figure of a man obsessed by lost and wasted time.'[5] 'He's one of the few politicians who can say that he's sorry, that he got it wrong,' said Vinson, 'which is, I think, the mark of a truly great man.'[6] 'The phrase which attracted hostile comment and deliberate misinterpretation was a quotation from a

[1] Interview, Ian Gow, MP, 8 August 1989.
[2] Interview, Lord Vinson, 30 May 1990.
[3] Press release, Sir Keith Joseph, Birmingham, 19 October 1974.
[4] *Daily Mail*, 21 October 1974.
[5] *New Statesman*, 29 October 1975.
[6] Interview, Lord Vinson, 30 May 1990.

Left-wing publication noting that most poverty was generated by "fatherless families" headed by mothers from "classes IV and V",' Alfred Sherman declared sixteen years later. 'Joseph had quoted this in previous articles and speeches without eliciting comment. When the *London Evening Standard* misrepresented him, he panicked instead of fighting back, though he received sackfuls of supporting letters. It was this incident which persuaded him that he lacked "a certain robustness" necessary for political leadership.'[1] But he did not take himself out of the running against Heath – yet.

Five days before the Birmingham speech, however, the process for a leadership election was set in motion by the 1922 Committee. Its chairman, Edward du Cann, held a meeting of the 1922's executive committee at his home on 14 October, four days after the general election. All sections of the Parliamentary Party had agreed that there should be a leadership election, if only to reaffirm Heath in the job. The 1922 Committee had formal responsibility for conducting it.

Other, informal groupings in the House of Commons also stirred. There were new Members from both the February and October elections, and their views and support for various candidates needed to be gathered. Heath stayed above the politicking, believing his position to be secure and trusting in the support of the Whips and the Shadow Cabinet, where most were behind him. A lot of the politicking inside the Conservative Party in 1974–5 was due to Heath's belief that there was no alternative as leader to him.

Airey Neave's was the single most influential informal group of Conservative MPs. Neave was a war hero – he had escaped from Colditz and had organized escape routes for MI-9 – and a distinguished author. He had been a junior barrister at the Nuremberg War Crimes Trials and had served the arrest warrants on Rudolf Hess and Albert Speer. He was a very intelligent, hard-headed man. He had a great deal of charm, and was capable of a high degree of personal loyalty. He was much tougher than he looked, and was often underestimated. He was in the Party's mainstream, and was not involved in the ideological battles that consumed Joseph. He

[1] Sir Alfred Sherman, Letter, *Encounter*, June 1990.

was loved by many, and liked by most who met him. But he had long been an enemy of Heath's who as Chief Whip, it was said, had been particularly brutal with Neave in 1959. Neave, then Parliamentary Under-Secretary for Air, had gone to tell him that he had heart trouble. Heath was reported to have said, 'Well, that's the end of your political career, then.'[1] Neave's heart trouble did not incapacitate him in any way – throughout the 1960s he took a leading role in science committees in Parliament – but he lost his Ministerial post and he was kept off the Front Bench for the next fifteen years. He never forgave Heath for that.

As the prospect of a leadership election became reality after October 1974, Neave was absolutely determined to do everything in his power to see Heath defeated. To this end, he worked tirelessly. He had a reputation for operating secretly, and he put this trait to full use. He understood that the more the Heath camp knew of his activities, the better prepared they would be to take counter-measures: they could bring pressure to bear on individual MPs through the Party apparatus and their constituency chairmen; they could offer dazzling prospects; they could make it clear that unless an MP did what was required by them, they would make it their business to blight his career, just as they had Airey Neave's. So Neave talked privately and to small groups of other MPs, quietly organizing a team that would campaign against Heath. He found many more MPs anxious to be rid of Heath than anyone thought likely: the 'anyone-but-Ted' alliance was his formation.

His problem was that he did not have a candidate. This was to be a crucial element in the nature of Thatcher's authority once she became leader. At first, Neave's group under the leadership of another backbencher, Nigel Fisher,[2] had been working for Edward du Cann's candidature, but it was early on apparent that the chairman of the 1922 Committee would only command a small number of votes from colleagues if he stood for the leadership. Some of his business interests were questioned, and his wife did not want him

[1] Nicholas Wapshott and George Brock, *Thatcher* (London, Futura, 1983), p. 126.
[2] Norman Tebbit, *Upwardly Mobile* (London, Futura, 1989), p. 178, gives Nigel Fisher's story. Fisher did not feel he could commit himself totally to Thatcher and resigned as leader of the group while proposing that Airey Neave take over from him to promote her candidature.

135

to run. Next Joseph was approached. He said he did not think he should stand. What was more, as a member of Ted Heath's Shadow Cabinet, he felt he had a duty to inform Heath of the approach and his response. This made Neave very anxious. He said to his friends that when Heath learned of the extent of the operation to find a replacement leader, 'He'll kill us! He'll kill us!'[1]

Margaret Thatcher had also pressed Joseph to stand, and to do so with conviction. She saw herself at first as his supporter rather than a candidate in her own right. She thought he could win if he put his heart as well as his head into doing so. To both of them, the ideological battle was what was important: neither had any personal animosity towards Ted Heath, although his lack of respect for Thatcher was well known. She had been as staunch a member of Heath's team as Keith Joseph, and the two had been in charge of big-spending Ministries. She had no reputation as an orator or as a parliamentarian. She was not a favourite of the House, or of the country: 'Milk Snatcher!' reverberated. She was not noted as a political thinker. She was seen as a makeweight: the necessary woman in a Tory Cabinet. She was derided and patronized by many of her colleagues. Peter Rawlinson, driving to the Selsdon Park conference in 1970, wondered if she – as 'the only woman among us' – would find a man other than her husband in her room by accident one night, but 'felt it unlikely' that she would suffer such a mishap.[2] 'She didn't make much of an impression as Minister for Education,' remembered one of her most senior colleagues in the 1970–74 Cabinet. 'Ted Heath used to get very annoyed with her in Cabinet. He used to begin tapping the table, because although she talked sense, she did talk too much.'[3] On one occasion when Thatcher, who made a practice of speaking about matters other than Education in Cabinet meetings, was thus engaged, Heath's patience snapped. Never the most receptive of men, Heath leaned forward (Thatcher was along the side of the table, out of his sight) and shouted down at her, 'Shut up! Shut up!'[4] That sort of experience leaves a lasting mark.

[1] Private information.
[2] Peter Rawlinson, *A Price Too High* (Lomdon, Weidenfeld & Nicolson, 1989), pp. 140–41.
[3] Interview, 20 November 1989.
[4] Interview, 10 November 1989.

All along, however, Joseph's heart was not in running, and never had been. 'I know my own capacities. Adequate for some jobs, but not for others,' he has said. 'Had I become party leader, it would have been a disaster for the party, country and for me.'[1] He always had a modest estimate of his own suitability, and it was this self-appraisal, rather than the unfavourable publicity that surrounded his Birmingham speech, that took him out of the leadership contest. 'It was never a sensible idea,' he later said. 'It was an illusion. I was only running out of despair. I was flattered by the idea and was willing to be swept along. But I was a joke, a useful joke.'[2] 'At the time when his cap was very nearly in the ring,' a friend recalled, 'a number of us who knew him well said to him, "We don't think that you are of this mould." We thought the job would kill him. He suffers from the great error of so many highly intellectual people: he sees so many sides of the coin that he cannot come down on one side or the other very easily. It takes him time to make decisions.'[3] 'I only came into anyone's mind because of the apparent poverty of choice,' he reflected, 'not because of my virtues. And vanity is an enormous stimulus. Ted had been very good to me. He was the man who promoted me because he was Chief Whip and Chief Whips make the junior appointments. But I did not have the dilemmas that Willie Whitelaw felt he had – that he was so close to Ted that he could not reconcile with his conscience to stand against him. I think I had a recognition of my own inadequacies and shortcomings for that job.'[4]

'Keith Joseph's fate was that of a butterfly broken on the wheel,' said Enoch Powell, who had also endured sharp criticism in his career. 'He always was a butterfly, not only in the sense that he had a mind which loved flitting from flower to flower, and sipping honey where honey could be sipped, but he was a butterfly, not a hawk. And the things that he wanted to say could only be said by a hawk if they were to have any effect. I remember very vividly – or I think I remember: that's usually a necessary correction – Keith

[1] Morrison Halcrow, *Keith Joseph: A Single Mind* (London, Macmillan, 1989), p. 77. It must be said that it is very doubtful if Joseph has ever enjoyed the restfulness of being of a single mind.
[2] Chris Ogden, *Maggie* (New York, Simon & Schuster, 1990), p. 118.
[3] Interview, 30 May 1990.
[4] Interview Rt. Hon. Lord Joseph, CH, 26 June 1990.

137

Joseph walking up the floor of the House just after the terrible row about his class 4/5 speech. It was a man who didn't like the heat in the kitchen. Keith Joseph has never enjoyed the kind of struggle which the triumph of one explanation over another brings with it.'[1] 'He's a man who doesn't like contentiousness,' said Alfred Sherman. 'It takes a lot out of him. He's full of contradictions. He did bring about a revolution, but he can't say "Boo!" to a goose.'[2]

Joseph had never brought his policy disagreements head-on to the Shadow Cabinet. He was, rather, making mutterings. So there was never a split inside the Shadow Cabinet. What was more, Keith Joseph was not a confrontational person. He was sitting there in obvious intellectual and emotional agony. He devoted himself to a campaign of public education, appealing – he hoped – above the fray of Party politics in an effort to make people understand that a new approach to the country's problems was essential. 'The horror was that good intentions so often did not work,' he said, describing the essence of his message. 'It was later that I came to realize that we were far too ambitious and far too destructive in our good intentions: the unintended bad consequences of the good intentions of the Welfare State.'[3] Getting this message across to people was Joseph's principal effort, and it was fairly apparent that he was not taking serious Party political initiatives. He did not try to develop a core of activists in the cause of his becoming leader of the Party. Policy groups and centres were the secondary level of politics. He saw himself as picking up the baton that Enoch Powell had dropped – as a less effective champion of the market than Enoch 'with that marvellous voice I can't hope to match'.[4] He never tried to overthrow Heath, although the common assumption was that he would try, and that is why Heath was so taken aback by the events of 1975 when he lost the leadership.

Additionally, Heath was supported in the serious press, notably by *The Economist* which derided Joseph. 'Sir Keith is recommending that Britain should parachute to safety with something closely

[1] Interview, Rt Hon. J. Enoch Powell, MBE, 1 November 1989.
[2] Interview, Sir Alfred Sherman, 30 April 1990. Benjamin Disraeli once remarked that the major quality of a political leader is the ability to say 'Boo!' to a goose.
[3] Interview, Rt Hon. Lord Joseph, CH, 26 June 1990.
[4] Lord Harris to author, 26 August 1990.

resembling a pocket handkerchief,' it declared in September 1974, just after his Preston speech, and then went on effectively to endorse Heath's 1972–4 approach. 'With an incomes policy, total real income will be kept up; but the power of the big unions then confronts the government. Sir Keith, like many thoughtful people, wants to escape from this confrontation but he has not yet shown the way out.'[1] After his Birmingham speech, the magazine declared: 'His has been the fatal innocence of the truly innocent.'[2]

The Economist had become the fount of common wisdom by the mid-1970s because people no longer had confidence in their own opinions. The magazine was hostile to monetary-market principles, and had egged on the go-go for growth in 1971–2. The business classes did not feel that being good businessmen made them good economists. They knew that business and finance were terribly complicated and world-wide, no longer activities that could be controlled in a British context. *The Economist* was in many respects an entity that recognized that it had been both too radical and not radical enough. Its great strength was that it did not seek a value system to impose on the British nation. Its role in forming opinion came about partly because other instruments of opinion-forming had fallen away. *The Times* (too much the prisoner of the increasingly distrusted Establishment), the *Spectator* (discredited by its Gaullism), the *New Statesman* (becoming too militantly Left), *Encounter* (suspect because it had received funding from the US Central Intelligence Agency), all had been found lacking in one way or another. By process of elimination, The *Economist* came through. Roy Jenkins in *Asquith* (1964) referred to *The Economist* as

[1] *Economist*, 7 September 1974.
[2] *Economist*, 26 October 1974. The editorial went on to say: 'The Tories should now indeed be sowing new policies, and they should be refraining from digging up the seeds too soon just to show there is something in the garden . . . Joseph . . . is too intelligent to miss the paradox of advocating moral discipline with economic permissiveness . . . The Tory Party draws its support traditionally and variably from agricultural England, from suburban England, from the middle class, the rural working class, from the self-employed, the skilled workers, the businessmen of Britain. It does not revitalise its appeal to them by beating its breast over Britain's moral decline. It may revitalise itself by a serious rehearsal of political philosophy.' There was an ambivalence in *The Economist*: it was saying that new thinking was needed, but that the country's power blocs, notably the unions, had to be accommodated, and so any new thinking that offered confrontation was *ipso facto* incorrect.

possessing radical rationalism: actually, it possessed sardonic pragmatism. Most politicians and commentators did not have confidence to override the radical centre, which is where *The Economist* was.

Thatcher did have that confidence. In November she brought the question of Joseph's candidacy to a head. She confronted him at the Centre for Policy Studies. Joseph said that he would not run, and she was heard to say to him, 'Well, if you won't stand, I will,'[1] and she announced her formal candidature. It was the moment when she broke all the rules and became a confrontationist Conservative leader and rode confrontation to victory. 'They broke Keith,' Thatcher said, speaking of the critics of his Birmingham speech, 'but they won't break me.'[2]

Thatcher was the only person with even the slightest hope of winning who was willing to challenge Heath at that stage. Neave proposed that his group of about fifteen MPs should back her. 'Airey wanted to be rid of Heath,' said Ian Gow, later a close colleague of Neave's. 'And Airey would use whatever was the best weapon that he thought was available. Originally Airey and Howe and Gow and Thatcher all believed that the best weapon they had to get rid of Heath, was Keith. When that one was unavailable, Airey had to find another one, and the best one that could get rid of Heath. And, let's face it, there was also a policy difference as well as a personality difference between Airey and Heath. It was then that Airey picked up the Thatcher weapon when the Keith weapon said, "My sword is blunt."'[3] Norman Tebbit was an early supporter of Thatcher, and he remembered the unfolding drama. 'It soon became clear that Margaret Thatcher was the only heavyweight candidate willing to challenge Ted Heath on the first ballot,' he said, 'the rest of the Shadow Cabinet feeling inhibited from doing so.'[4]

Keith Joseph was probably enormously relieved to be able to support Thatcher rather than to have to stand himself. He might

[1] Halcrow, *Keith Joseph*, p. 91.
[2] Ogden, *Maggie*, p. 122.
[3] Interview, Ian Gow, MP, 8 August 1989. Gow was not involved in Airey's campaign.
[4] Tebbit, *Upwardly Mobile*, p. 178.

have eventually stood if no other candidate had stepped forward, but his would have been a forlorn effort. His usefulness lay in his opening the prospect of a leadership challenge to Heath, and in setting the terms of the intellectual (as opposed to the emotional) debate that would surround the contest. 'In February 1974, the lost election shook Keith, and I made him go further,' said Sherman. 'And if it hadn't been for Keith, Heath's position would not have been shaken, and Margaret would not have become leader. Obviously, all these are contingent. So I was a link in the chain of cause and effect. So was Keith. So was Margaret. And so was Airey Neave because he said to her, "I'll run your campaign."'[1]

Neave had found a candidate. But Thatcher was beholden to no one.

---

[1] Interview, Sir Alfred Sherman, 30 April 1990.

SEVEN

Party leader

During the October 1974 general election, and afterwards on the floor of the House of Commons, Margaret Thatcher improved her Parliamentary standing. She had been an effective spokesman during the election. In Opposition Heath had moved her up from being Shadow Education Secretary (a second-level Cabinet post, ranking in the pecking order after the Ministry of Defence) to being the number two Treasury spokesman, and she shone. She was cheered by the Tory backbenches. She scored points off the Labour Chancellor, Denis Healey. She was the first MP to challenge publicly a sitting Conservative leader in peacetime, and it was soon apparent that her challenge was a serious one.

'Margaret's stature in the Party had been enhanced by her performance at the dispatch box,' observed Jim Prior, who was a firm Heath supporter. More, he saw her candidacy taking off. 'Up to that time, I do not believe that she had thought of herself as a candidate for the leadership. My conversations with her gave me no inkling to that effect, and, although she was ambitious, I do not think that she felt her time had come.'[1]

Despite what can be seen, in retrospect, as serious signs of disaffection with Heath's leadership, Heath himself – and his advisers and most of his Shadow Cabinet colleagues – did not realize how vulnerable he was. Heath seems to have thought – and he certainly acted as if this were the case – that a challenge to his leadership was an unnecessary formality: he would win.

The press agreed. Immediately before the leadership election *The Economist* declared itself 'For Heath' in lukewarm terms. 'There should be no doubt in sophisticated Tory minds what the best result on Tuesday would be – even if, in this age of fence-sitting, it is not

---

[1] Jim Prior, *A Balance of Power* (London, Hamish Hamilton, 1986), p. 99.

certain that it will. The Party should cease havering and give its most forceful man the backing he needs if Mr Wilson and the Labour Government are to be given a run for their money in what is a singularly decisive year for British and European politics. We say this as a newspaper which has held since the October election, and still holds, only lukewarm admiration for the leader of the Opposition.'[1]

Heath was caught with his planes on the ground. He was lulled. He knew Joseph for what he was, a nice man emotionally unfitted to seek the first place, who was having what amounted to a nervous breakdown in public. He also knew that the Parliamentary Party shared this view of Joseph: no doubt his Chief Whip had established that clearly. 'Any less likely leader of a party has seldom been seen,' one of the most senior men in the Party said. 'When Keith's name was mooted, we all roared with laughter. If that's the person who's going to challenge Ted, then we're all right.'[2]

Heath could not imagine Margaret Thatcher running against him except as a curiosity: when he first heard the news that she planned to do so, he probably laughed too. Sir Ian Gilmour was reported to be saying that if she won the leadership, the Party would be condemned to 'permanent opposition, a class-based rump'.[3] If the reality principle had been more present in Heath's and his supporters' thoughts, they might have been able to finesse it.

Airey Neave became Thatcher's acknowledged campaign manager, but few believed that hers would be a successful challenge to Heath's leadership. This, paradoxically, was a key to her success. There were several other MPs, not part of Neave's operation, who considered themselves to have been slighted by Heath and his officials, or who thought that Heath was too prepared to abandon political principles in pursuit of Government, and was unsuccessful at it to boot. Ian Gow was typical of many MPs who felt this way: 'I had never thought of Mrs Thatcher. She never entered my head. It was known among my friends – I made no secret of it – it was known in my constituency, that I was against Mr Heath. And I had become increasingly disillusioned during the Heath years. I wasn't

[1] *Economist*, 1 February 1975.
[2] Chris Ogden, *Maggie* (New York, Simon & Schuster, 1990), p. 118.
[3] *Economist*, 1 February 1975.

passionately keen on the folk in Brussels. I was totally opposed to the statutory Prices and Incomes policy, and I did not approve of Mr Heath. I thought it was pathetic that we only denationalized Thomas Cook and Carlisle Breweries despite what we said in the 1970 Manifesto.'[1]

Many Conservative MPs did not necessarily want to ditch Heath as leader: they did not think that the Party had an adequate alternative to Heath. But they wanted to teach him a lesson; to make sure that he would be more responsive to their concerns in the future. They began to go around saying, 'Ted is bound to win. No question about it. So we can vote for someone else and make sure that he gets a smaller majority than he thinks. That'll teach him!'

The enmities that Ted Heath had generated coalesced to oust him. 'Airey ran a brilliant campaign,' Jim Prior recalled. 'I was in a good position to judge because at that time Margaret had the little box of an office immediately opposite mine in the Shadow Cabinet corridor at the Commons, and this became Airey's headquarters. There was a constant flow of MPs to see them, and I began to realize that these were drawn from a wide cross-section of the Party.'[2]

Neave, instead of simply concentrating on those MPs who were definitely going to vote for Mrs Thatcher, canvassed the whole Parliamentary Party. He downplayed the support she was actually receiving, and implied that if MPs wanted either a new leader or to give Ted the shock so many of them wanted to deliver, they had better vote for her or else neither result would be achieved. The electoral arrangements dictated most of the tactics, just as was to happen fifteen years later when Michael Heseltine challenged Thatcher for the leadership.[3] In both cases, tactical voting secured surprising results. 'Those of us close to the centre of Margaret's

[1] Interview, Ian Gow, MP, 8 August 1989.
[2] Prior, *A Balance of Power*, p. 99.
[3] The election procedure established by Lord Home consisted of a three-ballot process, the first two ballots separated by a week, the third two days after the second. If, on the first ballot, a candidate obtained a majority of half the votes plus fifteen per cent, that candidate won and there was no second ballot. This was the case in 1989 when Sir Anthony Meyer, MP, challenged Margaret Thatcher for the leadership (he was the first person ever to challenge a Conservative Prime Minister), and Thatcher won with a majority of over eighty per cent. In November 1990, Thatcher polled just four votes short of the number she needed for outright

campaign never revealed how optimistic we were,' said Norman Tebbit of 1975. 'We knew that a good many colleagues might want to get rid of Ted Heath but not necessarily to elect Margaret, and we needed their votes on the first ballot. A difficult balancing trick was required. We had to imply that her campaign was strong enough to win and strong enough to deny Ted Heath victory on the first ballot, but not to achieve either outright victory herself nor such domination as to prevent others, such as Willie, from coming forward on the second ballot. I recollect John Nott [later Thatcher's Minister for Defence] and myself persuading Michael Heseltine, who was a Whitelaw man, that unless he voted for Margaret on the first ballot there would be no second ballot and no opportunity for Willie to stand.'[1] 'Her courage in opposing Ted went down well in the Party and in much of the press,' Prior reflected later. 'Other potential candidates, who were loyal to Ted but who it was known would come in on the second ballot if Ted were defeated, were quietly being accused of cowardice by the Neave camp. The fact that a vote for Margaret was the only way to secure a second ballot was also turned to advantage.'[2]

contd:

victory over Michael Heseltine. If no candidate obtained such a majority, then there was a second ballot, and additional candidates who had not been involved in the first ballot could enter the race. Thus an important element in Thatcher's campaign against Heath, and Heseltine's campaign against Thatcher, was to persuade a sufficient number of MPs to vote against the leader, or to abstain, thus opening up the race and possibly mortally wounding the leader: in both cases, this is what happened. By resigning in 1990, Margaret Thatcher opened the way for members of her Cabinet to enter the race (professional loyalty was held to prevent Ministers standing against their Prime Minister; part of Ted Heath's anger with Thatcher was that she was a member of his Shadow Cabinet). On the second ballot, the candidate obtaining a majority of the votes won; if no candidate obtained a majority, there would be a third ballot on a single transferable vote basis; the votes of the weakest candidate would be redistributed, and if this did not produce a winner, the votes of the next weakest candidate would be redistributed too, until there was an outright winner. In November 1990, this would have been the case had Michael Heseltine and Douglas Hurd (the other two candidates on the second ballot) not stood down in favour of John Major who came within two votes of a majority. In the run-up to the second ballot, however, the Hurd camp argued that their candidate would be the second choice of both Major and Heseltine supporters, and could win through on a third ballot.

[1] Norman Tebbit, *Upwardly Mobile* (London, Futura, 1989), p. 179.

[2] Prior, *A Balance of Power*, p. 100. Everyone on the first ballot. This suggests that was a third candidate, Sir Hugh Fraser, on the first ballot. This suggests that the success of Neave's campaign, although consciously muted, was nevertheless recognized sufficiently for everyone to understand that Thatcher was far and away the stronger of the two and that a vote for Fraser would be 'wasted'.

Gordon Reece, a producer of television light entertainment programmes, joined the Thatcher team as an adviser. He soon was to achieve 'an apparently unassailable place in Mrs Thatcher's affections', a senior Tory was quoted as saying. 'She likes him and admires him and so she's going to look after him. He's been successful in his own right and he makes her laugh; she likes that.'[1] He was also to become a stereotype Thatcher person. He came across as charming, with a bit of flash, smoking big cigars and being a natty dresser. His father was a car salesman from Liverpool who sent his son to Ratcliffe, a minor Roman Catholic public school. Norman St John-Stevas, a leading Roman Catholic in politics who was to become Thatcher's first Leader of the House and Minister for the Arts, was also at Ratcliffe and on one occasion, it is said, reported Reece for atheism, which was a trait not apparent in his later life when he developed a strong religious faith. He has a genuine enthusiasm for the homely virtues, although this was never reflected in his lifestyle.[2] After Cambridge, he entered journalism, developing a happy circle of friends and acquaintances in the media. He joined ATV as a religious affairs programme producer, but left the 'God slot' to join the team making *Emergency Ward 10*. In 1964 he took part in the election coverage of Independent Television News.

Reece first met Thatcher in the early 1970s when he was making Party political broadcasts, and he got on with her. When she stood for the leadership, he did not need to be called. He schooled her in her television presentation, advising her not to wear fussy clothes and jewellery or scooped necklines. The ideal outfit for her, he determined, was a tunic dress with a blouse underneath. He also helped organize lunches with journalists and newspaper editors.[3]

At one dinner she was asked by Frank Johnson, who was then writing a very witty daily column on Parliament for *The Daily Telegraph*, if she really expected to win: most people still believed Heath was a certainty. 'I would not be standing for the leadership,'

[1] *Sunday Times*, 18 November 1984.
[2] In 1979 Reece separated from his wife and six children and began a nomadic life, flitting between hotels and the homes of friends.
[3] *Sunday Times*, 18 November 1984.

she replied, 'if I was not certain that I shall win.'[1] It was the necessary claim of a serious candidate. How could a woman take on the Party leader and not put it in such terms? But that was not the way it really was. She knew Heath was through, rather than that she was going to win. She couched it in terms of personal certainty, and not in negative terms, because she was a good politician. The moment she said, 'I'm just the counter-candidate,' she went down. But it was far more important that Ted had switched and changed so much that he was lost. She had to put her candidacy in positive terms: but it was mostly as a negative candidate that she won. Not many people actively wanted her to be the Party leader when she stood: therefore she had to overstretch her position. She was considered even less of a threat than Keith Joseph by Heath and his circle, and the assumption amongst observers was that Heath's confidence was not misplaced. *The Economist* opined four days before the first ballot for the Party leadership that 'If Mr Heath wins 130 votes he should be home and dry for the second round with much pressure on Mrs Thatcher to stand down. Which she should be encouraged to do.'[2]

On the eve of the first ballot, 4 February 1975, Thatcher was interviewed on Granada Television's *World in Action* programme, and was considered to have done well by the MPs who crowded around sets in the House of Commons to watch. By Neave's count she was well ahead with 120 votes pledged to Heath's 84. In the actual vote, she had 130 to Heath's 119 and Sir Hugh Fraser's 16. There were 11 abstentions. Slightly more Conservative MPs had voted against her than for her, but she had beaten Heath. Fraser, a senior backbencher, had stood for those who wanted neither Heath nor Thatcher. Heath immediately announced his resignation as Party leader.

Since Thatcher had received the largest number, but not a majority of the Parliamentary Party votes, as was required for an outright win on the first ballot, there was a second ballot. New candidates now entered the lists, notably Willie Whitelaw who stood as a more acceptable Heath figure. Jim Prior and John Peyton (a junior Minister in Heath's Government), both of whom had supported Heath,

[1] Private information.
[2] *Economist*, 1 February 1975.

147

stood for the leadership too.[1] It was thought that they were running interference for Whitelaw and would siphon off votes from Thatcher. Ian Gow thought that Whitelaw would win in the second ballot.[2]

Geoffrey Howe, who had been Solicitor General in Heath's Government, also stood. Howe was able, well-liked, ambitious, and cherished hopes of becoming Party leader one day. He probably regretted that he had not run against Heath in the first place, and he now stood in order to put down a marker for the future. On 5 February 1975 he put his hat in the ring, issuing a statement carefully aimed at both right-wing and liberal Conservatives: 'It is clear that the Party must now unite under a new leader in presenting the country with the case for the free society. That society must be founded upon realistic economic policies. And it must be one that cares about every citizen.'[3] It was entirely safe ground to stake out, leaving him with a full range of options in the future.

The second ballot was held on 11 February. Margaret Thatcher won a majority with 146 votes. Willie Whitelaw came second with 79. Jim Prior and Geoffrey Howe had 19 votes each, and John Peyton had 11.

Whitelaw and other leading supporters of Ted Heath were to blame themselves for not being aware of the strong and widespread feeling against him that resulted in his defeat by Margaret Thatcher. 'It was certainly the worst time in my political life,' said Whitelaw. 'I remained Chairman of the Party and so observed the bitterness, dissension and general bad feeling in the Parliamentary Party. It was only then for the first time that I appreciated the strong feeling against Ted Heath. I considered it most unfair. But even at that

[1] Jim Prior recounts how Humphrey Atkins, the Chief Whip, told him 'in enthusiastic and forceful terms that I should stand for the leadership. This surprised me, as I had not thought of him as someone who would favour me, and in any case I presumed that he would support Willie Whitelaw.' Atkins also pressed Sir Geoffrey Howe to run (Prior, *A Balance of Power*, p. 100). There was clearly a calculation that if sufficient candidates stood in the second ballot, none would obtain a majority, and Thatcher would be seen as having been brave and tried hard, but as not having quite enough support to win outright. And then either Whitelaw would make his big push or possibly, even, Heath would be recalled having been taught his lesson.
[2] Interview, Ian Gow, MP, 8 August 1989.
[3] Press release, Sir Geoffrey Howe, 5 February 1975.

time I did not realize how widespread it was.'[1] 'I was quite sure Ted would win,' Whitelaw remembered. 'I ignored the warnings of my friends that all was not well. I was deeply dismayed when I heard the result of the ballot.'[2]

The Party[3] had taken a new path, and the size of Thatcher's vote showed that a majority of MPs, including many who had voted for Ted Heath on the first ballot, considered that she not only deserved to win the leadership, but that the Josephite policy direction she stood for was the one to take. The Parliamentary Party, surprised by what it had done on the first ballot, was carried away by the thrill of the new.

Naturally enough, Thatcher's political circle was not the same as Heath's. 'I had been at the centre of Tory Party politics for almost ten years,' said Prior, '. . . but once Margaret Thatcher took over it all altered . . . [I]n any Party, and in any Government, the Leader, or Prime Minister, inevitably relies on a very few trusted colleagues – usually a few Ministers and perhaps two or three aides. With Ted as Leader and Prime Minister, I was right on the inside. But, when Margaret became Leader, I became one of the outsiders, saying my piece, at times able to exert some influence, but all the time aware that the centre of decision-making and weight of the Party and Government machines lay with others.'[4] Thatcher's people were those who only weeks before had been dismissed as loonies by men like Prior. Campaigns of denigration flourished behind the scenes between Heathites and Thatcherites. Keith Joseph, as head of policy formation, had to work with both groups. 'In the end,' Alfred Sherman remembered, 'Keith avoided trouble by spending most of his time walking between the Centre for Policy Studies, the House of Commons, Bovis, and the Conservative Research Department with a large case of books so that he didn't have to spend much time reading or

[1] William Whitelaw, *The Whitelaw Memoirs* (London, Aurum Press, 1989), p. 141. See also Prior, *A Balance of Power*, pp. 101–2.

[2] Quoted in 'Whitelaw on Thatcher', *Sunday Times*, 23 April 1989.

[3] Thatcher's victory on the second ballot made her leader of the Parliamentary Party. Her leadership of the Party as a whole began some days later at the Europa Hotel in Mayfair. She was proposed as Party leader by Lord Hailsham and seconded by Willie Whitelaw.

[4] Prior, *A Balance of Power*, p. 103.

listening to arguments.'[1] Journeying in this way with his case of books actually gave Joseph trouble with his neck.

In 1974, perhaps as a safety measure, Heath had appointed a distinguished *Daily Express* journalist, Michael Wolff, to run Central Office and the Party machine as director-general of the Party organization, and Chris Patten to run the Conservative Research Department, the Party's own Think-Tank. Wolff had reported from Havana at the time when Fidel Castro came to power, and he had known Ernest Hemingway. He had a fund of fascinating anecdotes, and was a sought-after companion. One of Thatcher's first acts, however, was to dismiss Wolff.[2] It was rumoured that both Wolff and Patten had clauses in their contracts of employment that ensured that they would receive large pay-offs if they were dismissed early: that they had been put in place by Heath to ensure that the Party machinery would not fall into 'right-wing' hands if he were to lose the Party leadership, and that when Thatcher found that it would be too expensive to get rid of both of them, she chose Wolff for the chop because in the Centre for Policy Studies she had a rival to the Research Department and therefore did not have to worry about Patten so much.[3] She appointed Peter Thorneycroft as the new Party chairman in place of Willie Whitelaw, and did not replace Michael Wolff. Angus Maude, a founder member of the 'One

[1] Interview, Sir Alfred Sherman, 30 April 1990.

[2] Within months of his dismissal, Wolff died while cycling. Sir Geoffrey Howe and some other friends, including Lord Carrington and William (now Lord) Rees-Mogg, then editor of *The Times*, established a trust fund for his widow and two children.

[3] Maurice Cowling, 'The Sources of the New Right' in *Encounter*, November 1989, argued that the Centre 'was invented by Lord Joseph (and Mrs Thatcher) as a makeweight to the Conservative Research Department'. Sir Alfred Sherman takes issue with this contention and maintains that the Centre was established for other purposes entirely: 'At no time did we even consider acting as a "makeweight" to the Conservative Research Department, whose functions were totally different from our proposed organization's, and rarely overlapped with them. The CRD serviced Shadow Ministers, committees, and other Party bodies. Our aim was to change the climate of opinion. They had several dozen executives; we intended to have at most three.' (Letter, *Encounter*, June 1990.) David Wolfson had been called in by Thatcher to help reorganize Central Office, and on purely administrative and managerial grounds he had recommended that the Research Department be moved from Old Queen Street and into Central Office. This happened in 1980. However, people not immediately involved at the time did think that part of the purpose of the CPS was to balance out the Research Department, and this was certainly a media view.

Nation Group' of MPs,[1] a contributor to the *Black Paper* (which challenged accepted wisdom on educational policy while Margaret Thatcher was Education Secretary), and a highly experienced journalist, was made deputy chairman. At the Centre for Policy Studies, Sherman seized the opportunity to develop a new policy with Keith Joseph. 'We started out to change the Conservative Party's approach,' said Sherman about the Centre, 'hence our primary aim was not to wean Socialists away from socialism but to wean Conservatives and other non-Socialists away from the corporate state and Keynesian panaceas, which had helped bring about the Heath debacle . . . Our second major aim was trade-union reform.'[2]

Joseph became even closer to Thatcher than before, and was the acknowledged policy supremo. 'I think that, intellectually, Keith has been a great influence on her,' Ian Gow reflected. 'They really became friends because they were both anxious about the economic and industrial policies of the Heath Government, and out of that their friendship grew. And then after the 28 February 1974 defeat they became very much closer.'[3] 'Margaret, from the first day of leading the party,' said Peter Carrington, 'made clear that she thought and felt that we needed to take a new direction, and there was no hope for the country unless inflation was destroyed by strict monetarist measures . . . no hope unless the possibility and the will for individual effort and reward were revived among the British, no hope unless the power of the state were sharply diminished, particularly in economic affairs, and unless the function of the trades unions was restored to representing their members' interests (as opposed to dictating to Governments which economic policies the TUC found acceptable) . . . In all this – or in the specific policies her philosophy indicated – she was particularly supported and inspired by the studies led by Keith Joseph.'[4]

[1] The 'One Nation Group' included Heath, Macleod, Maudling and Enoch Powell among its members. It had a progressive view of Conservatism and was seen as being to the left of the mainstream of the Party.

[2] Sir Alfred Sherman, Letter, *Encounter*, June 1990.

[3] Interview, Ian Gow, MP, 8 August 1989.

[4] Lord Carrington, *Reflect On Things Past* (London, Collins, 1988), p. 275. This is the only mention of Joseph in Carrington's memoirs. In Whitelaw's memoirs, Joseph is not mentioned at all. Whether or not they had a high opinion of Joseph, it really is amazing that neither man seems to have appreciated Joseph's central role in the battle that was being fought between the Thatcherites/monetarists/free marketeers/classical liberals and the Heathites/Keynesians/establishmentarians.

Joseph based himself at the Centre in Wilfred Street, and energized the selling to the intellectual community of what came to be called 'Thatcherism'. '[A]t that time we just had beliefs, faith in what could be done,' Thatcher said, looking back thirteen years later. 'Keith made that faith into something that intelligent people were willing to share. And their acceptance spread the message through the press and other media to everybody. If Keith hadn't been doing all that work with the intellectuals, all the rest of our work would probably never have resulted in success . . . It was Keith who really began to turn the intellectual tide back against socialism. He got our fundamental intellectual message across, to students, professors, journalists, the "intelligentsia" generally.'[1]

One of Joseph's most interesting speeches in this effort came at the 1975 Party Conference in Blackpool. In it he argued that the language of politics had become (dangerously) misleading. The 'middle ground' was being generally defined as that area of overlap between Left and Right, so 'the trouble with the middle ground is that we do not choose it. We do not shape it. It is shaped for us by extremists. The more extreme the Left, the more to the Left is the middle ground.' Instead, he said, the 'common ground' – those areas of agreement between the Parties, such as the need to defeat inflation – should be sought out.[2] It was an intellectual, academic point, aimed at commentators, attempting to change the assumptions that so many of them had when it came to discussing the developing policies. The 'middle ground' should be seen for what it was, he was saying, and not proclaimed as the proper basis for agreed action. At Patten's Research Department and elsewhere, the reaction was to wonder aloud if Keith Joseph was losing his mind. 'What does he mean?' Butskellites said. 'What is he talking about?' Soon, he was christened 'The Mad Monk' in Heathite Tory circles. Peter Walker said that having changed his views so radically once, it might well be that Joseph would change them again.[3]

The following year, Joseph delivered the Stockton Lecture to the London Business School. His title was 'Monetarism Is Not

[1] Morrison Halcrow, *Keith Joseph: A Single Mind* (London, Macmillan, 1989), p. 97.
[2] Ibid., pp. 102–3.
[3] *Listener*, 26 June 1975.

Enough'. He argued that money needs to be treated as a link between the movement of real resources and the effects of such movement, and that consequently controlling money alone should not be the be-all and end-all of policy. All monetary squeezes, he pointed out, weaken the private sector, and so each consecutive squeeze runs the risk of being even more lethal. This was a point that was to be central to the debates preceding the 1981 Budget when, as a result of several years of money squeezes in an attempt to reduce inflation, the private sector was screaming and unemployment was climbing towards the three million mark. In 1976, Joseph unfortunately (given what was to happen over the next five years) did not pursue his argument: most professional economists strongly disagreed with him and many Conservatives were becoming nervous that he might be stampeding them into a disastrous set of policies.

Over sixty per cent of the constituency associations had backed Heath for the leadership in February. This, too, was probably an element in Joseph's hesitation over pursuing his arguments. Heath's supporters provided the bulk of Party workers and officials – not least because he had made a point of controlling Party appointments. The Candidates' List had been vetted by Heath, for example, and men and women with 'right-wing' views – which included support for Enoch Powell and support for purist free market principles – were weeded out and taken off the List, thus ensuring that they would be most unlikely to be selected to fight a Parliamentary seat. Thatcher's move against Wolff was, in part, a signal that the Party would be more open in future.

In the Shadow Cabinet, she kept her changes to a minimum. She probably recognized that her election was the result of a series of surprises rather than the consequence of a determined and considered shift on the part of the Parliamentary Party, and that she had to convince the Party as a whole that she was competent to be leader and capable of winning elections. She immediately offered Heath an unspecified position in her Shadow Cabinet, but he refused to join her team, preferring the freedom of the backbenches, it turned out, for the rest of his career. Reginald Maudling was named spokesman on Foreign Affairs. Willie Whitelaw, who had made a point of pledging his loyalty to Thatcher right after the election, was named deputy leader. Keith Joseph, however, was effectively number two with responsibility for policy and research. If he was not to be Shadow Chancellor, this was the role he wanted. Geoffrey Howe was made Shadow Chancellor. This was a big step up for him, but he and Joseph were the only two people with Cabinet experience who accepted monetarist analysis and remedies. Airey Neave retained Northern Ireland responsibility.

Thatcher also probably realized that her victory had – despite her avowed effort to make it a policy victory – more to do with personalities. The widespread dislike of Heath coupled with admiration for her guts in standing up to – and against – him, had given her victory. Policy had played a part, but in the event a subordinate one. She had a very long way to go before the Party would be convinced of her policies. The Party would always be formally loyal to its leader, but Heath had captured its common wisdom and it would take some time to change. 'You can't have people who voted for a certain policy suddenly turning back and rending their garments like Old Testament prophets and pouring ash on their heads and saying: "I have sinned, I have sinned,"' Michael Wolff pointed out, in a thinly veiled attack on Joseph. 'This is incredible, not only in a political sense, but also in a purely human sense.'[1] 'The Conservative Party has never been the Party of unrestricted laissez-faire,' said Robert Carr (who had been Heath's Shadow Chancellor). 'All I am worried about is the danger of an over-obsession with one instrument of policy, namely monetary policy.' There was, he went on to say, an opposition-in-exile waiting for Heath's ideas to be proved right.[2] Peter Walker hoped that Joseph would realize that he had to modify his views,[3] and gained a substantial amount of support from within the Party for his 'Tory Reform Group', the 'Reform' implicitly applying to Thatcherism.

The grouping of Whitelaw, Joseph, Howe, Neave and Angus Maude became Thatcher's Shadow Cabinet inner circle, but the majority of her Shadow had been supporters of Ted Heath. She was seeking to demonstrate that she was trying to unify the Party and would not carry grudges. Inner circles were to become a feature of her leadership, both in Opposition and in Number Ten. Rather

[1] Ibid.
[2] Ibid.
[3] Ibid.

than distrust of colleagues on her part, it signified the fact that she never did have many close supporters in Parliament. Peter Walker (who refused to serve in her Shadow team) pointed out that three of Heath's most able and effective supporters, Willie Whitelaw, Jim Prior and Ian Gilmour, were Thatcher Shadow Ministers and would have 'considerable influence' on policy,[1] the implication being that there was an opposition within that was watching her closely. 'The Heathites at first believed that if they stuck together they could control her wilder excesses until, like Heath, she finally made the U-turn they were certain would come,' remembered Denis Healey. 'In December 1980 Michael Heseltine told me that there was a group in Cabinet, with Christopher Soames, Peter Carrington, Peter Thorneycroft and Quintin Hailsham as its core, which could always impose an effective veto on her wilfulness.'[2] Later on, her continued operation through an inner circle signalled that the resistance to her style of leadership and to her determinedly monetarist policy approach was strong enough to keep her from being able to operate through a genuinely unified Cabinet.

Whitelaw was to prove one of the most important and long-serving members of her Cabinet. He was an uncomplicated fellow, ambitious, but not dry-in-the-mouth ambitious. He was a man who felt an intense sense of loyalty and a sense that almost any purpose was better than no purpose. After 1972 he probably felt that Ted Heath was purposeless, following civil service rather than political rationales. But he remained utterly loyal: Willie would never stab a man in the back unless he felt the man was about to betray his country. Yet it was probably a rather hang-dog Willie who frequented the lobbies between 1972 and 1975. And while his assertion of loyalty was always true, the quality of his loyalty is what changed. He became disillusioned with Heath, and when Heath was replaced by someone who had attachments which Willie did not possess and did not like in a woman, he was hard-pressed to remain loyal. Margaret Thatcher was an individualist; Willie was a Conservative collectivist: the good Company officer from the squirearchy, not the peerage (the Whitelaws were minor landed

[1] Ibid.
[2] Denis Healey, *The Time of My Life* (London, Michael Joseph, 1989), p. 488.

gentry). He was distrusted by Neave who at first could not reconcile the deputy leader's previous opposition to Thatcher with his new-found loyalty. 'We were a divided Party under an unknown Leader who was also the first woman in British politics to hold such a position,' said Whitelaw. 'I have to admit that I was among those who at the time still had reservations about the capacity of women to stand the immense physical and mental strains of leadership . . . She was also surrounded at the top of the Conservative Party by those who had served under Ted Heath and were dismayed by his defeat. In turn the divisions of the Party were underlined by the distrust which Margaret Thatcher's supporters still felt for those of us who had served with Ted Heath. I know that many of them were suspicious of me and my motives. My only hope was to show that I was determined to put the interests of our Conservative Party above all personal feelings. In this I was greatly assisted by Airey Neave . . . and by the time of his tragic assassination just before the 1979 Election I believe that we had become great friends.'[1]

Whitelaw believed that there ought to be a strong and decisive leader and that that leader should command the loyalty and respect of the chaps. He acted as he did for elevated reasons. But it was not really until the Falklands War in 1982 that Whitelaw became a firm supporter of Thatcher. Until then, in private, he was sceptical of her abilities and policies. The war made him genuinely impressed by her. 'Willie was a source of strength to her,' said Ian Gow who, during Thatcher's first four years as Prime Minister, had a ringside seat as her Parliamentary Private Secretary. 'She respected Willie's experience of politics – and at the highest levels: remember, Willie was Deputy Leader under Heath.'[2]

Peter Carrington,[3] who had been Heath's chairman of the Party

[1] Whitelaw, *The Whitelaw Memoirs*, p. 144.
[2] Interview, Ian Gow, MP, 8 August 1989.
[3] Carrington had been a Party senior for a long time: 1963–4 – Leader of the House of Lords; 1964–70 – Leader of the Opposition in the House of Lords; 1970–74 – Minister for Defence; 1972–4 – Chairman of the Conservative Party; 1974 – Minister for Energy. The Carringtons are a banking family, not a family of great landed acres from before the Glorious Revolution. His family name is Smith, and is from the second rank of nobility. Mr Smith was Pitt the Younger's banker and asked to be allowed to drive his carriage across Horse Guards Parade. Pitt said, 'I can't do that, but I can make you an Irish peer.' And, in 1796, did. A year later, Baron Carrington banked more money in Pitt's cause and received an English barony too.

(before Whitelaw) and leader in the House of Lords (in which post he was kept on by Thatcher), and Francis Pym,[1] who had been Heath's Chief Whip from 1970 to 1973 and then Northern Ireland Secretary until February 1974, took the same view as Whitelaw. Carrington was heard to utter a favourite refrain, 'She'll be out by Christmas!' in tones of hope, and to speak scornfully of her in private. 'She says that the first few years – 1979–82 – were the most difficult,' said a Number Ten aide. 'And when she became Leader in 1975, people said, "They don't really want this woman. They'll get rid of her. She'll be gone by Christmas, and after Christmas sanity will return and we'll have Willie Whitelaw, and all will be well." She was very conscious of that. And the people who actually came to her after 1975 and said, "You are right. We want to help," and, "Is there anything we can do?" have enormous affection from her.'[2]

Whether people liked it or not, Margaret Thatcher was the leader of the Party and had the authority – and the right – to appoint and dismiss people, and to make policy. Whitelaw in particular, therefore, saw the duty of all Party loyalists as being to keep the Party together. The more divided the Party appeared to be, the less likely it was to win elections. To many people in the Party and outside it, Thatcher's leadership might be seen as an aberration, but while she was leader she should be supported. He employed his influence with Carrington and Pym effectively. The three were enormously influential within the Party as a whole, and they lent their positions in an impersonal way to sustain her authority. This occurred, most importantly, in March 1981 when the three combined to throw their influence against a Cabinet revolt by the 'wets' against the 1981 Budget.[3]

---

[1] Pym was made chief Opposition spokesman on Agriculture by Heath in 1974, and was kept in that post by Thatcher until 1976 when she made him spokesman on House of Commons affairs and devolution.

[2] Interview, 20 February 1990.

[3] Hugo Young, *One of Us* (London, Macmillan, 1989), p. 216.

EIGHT

Thatcherism: the mood

Winning the leadership still did not mean that Margaret Thatcher controlled the Conservative Party. 'I think for brief periods she did control it,' an adviser reflected, revealing the frustration so many of her people felt and ignoring the fact that she did actually have ultimate control through her power of appointment. 'For the simplest of reasons: she did things that they didn't think were possible. I think when she fought the Falklands War she got them all on her side because that's a tradition in the Tory Party. I think she had control of them when she came in. I think she had control of them in 1983 because it was so bad there wasn't any choice. But I think for very large periods she had no control of them whatever. Mind you, the rank and file love and adore her. At the Party Conferences there's a passion that aroused. The problem with the Tory Party has always been that it doesn't give a damn about it's membership. It's a hierarchy and the hierarchy didn't like her. The hierarchy didn't like her because she's a woman, because she's lower middle class, because she's not an academic or a philosopher, and because she's shrill. They don't like those things. What they like is Michael Heseltine-type people. Slightly grand. Think they're grand. And he discovered poverty! He spotted poverty on the road to Toxteth! Big amazing thing. The Tory Party is not a Thatcherite Party, that's the tragedy.'[1]

At the 1975 Party Conference, eight months after the leadership election, Ted Heath was given a rapturous reception by the Party faithful, and was widely reported, both in private and in the press,

[1] Interview, 5 December 1990. Michael Heseltine was Secretary of State for the Environment at the time of the 1983 race riots in various cities, including the Toxteth suburb of Liverpool. He went to Toxteth and spent three weeks there, supervising projects intended to create better community relations. But in the end his colleagues did not like him enough to elect him leader in Thatcher's place.

to have described Thatcher and Joseph as traitors and as crazy, with right-wing views that would, if implemented, destroy the Party and the country. Heath denied that he had spoken in this way, but the credibility of such sentiments indicated the weakness of Thatcher's position within the Party. Pointedly, Heath left the Conference before she gave her speech.

Thatcher was quite shrewd enough to know that in 1975 she was being used by the Party. She knew that she had been elected by people who did not know her or believe in her. She was not a member of the principal social institutions of the Tory Party – the private dining clubs; the St James's clubs. Very few people were optimistic about her. In the 1980s she was seen as a popular optimist: in 1975 she was seen as a hard woman from a hard time. She was also seen as deniable, 'just a woman', by the people who elected her. 'We had to get rid of Ted with somebody, and we didn't have anybody else,' was the background thought. Few people believed that they would serve under her as Prime Minister, or that she was more than a battering ram. In the middle of the leadership election, the *Economist* reported a Labour Cabinet Minister (unnamed) saying that if Thatcher was elected, Labour would be in power for twenty-five years.[1] She knew all this, and it gave her – remarkably – an unromantic confidence. She identified with the task in hand so strongly that she was able to brush all doubts aside. She felt that what she had to do was so obvious, so desired by the country as a whole, that she would win. The fact that most of her Party were distanced from her certainties was something that she recognized, and so she also looked for advice to outsiders, much of it from the Centre for Policy Studies in Wilfred Street. 'What the CPS did for Margaret was to give her intellectual backing and help, and Keith too,' said Nigel Vinson. 'It gave Keith an office, and it mailed pamphlets. Keith's speeches were a turning point in Tory philosophy. It gave them a base. Everybody needs a base to operate from. It gave them an operating centre.'[2]

It is, perhaps, difficult today to appreciate the degree to which Thatcher and her people were ridiculed and cast as an aberration

[1] *Economist*, 8 February 1975.
[2] Interview, Lord Vinson, 30 May 1990.

on the part of the Tory Party by commentators and political opponents. Jock Bruce-Gardyne, a fervent monetarist who lost his seat in October 1974, worked as a consultant at the Centre for Policy Studies and then re-entered the House of Commons in a by-election in early 1979, noted during these years how quickly Thatcher was derided 'in the better class of political dining room' and now members of her Shadow Cabinet 'indulged in analyses of her character as the port was circulating which occasionally induced the bystander to wonder why they agreed to serve under her leadership'.[1] Frank Giles, then deputy editor of the *Sunday Times*, remembered an editorial lunch with Thatcher soon after her election as Leader of the Opposition: 'I think that very few people on the *Sunday Times* were, by disposition or condition, pro her. We all thought she was a rather bossy, hand-baggy sort of lady. Already, that's the way we felt. But by the end of lunch, she had argued so well, was so much in control of her facts, never lost her cool, and never let anybody get away with anything without pinning it down, and carried it off so well, that everyone around the table in their different ways was impressed. And after lunch we would stand around and have a quick post-mortem, and I remember very well everyone saying, "Ouf! She's quite something."'[2] Still, she faced derision and disdain into the late 1980s. Thatcher and her people and their ideas may generate strong opposition – and strong emotions – but they are still taken seriously, not least because Thatcher and Thatcherism won so many elections with thumping majorities, gradually denying opponents the plea that special circumstances (notably the 1982 Falklands War) had swung electoral victory each time.

Thatcher stood to the right of the Party before she challenged for the leadership. Since entering the House of Commons in 1959, she had supported corporal punishment in schools and the death penalty (which, although an individual and not a Party matter, has always been associated with being 'right wing'). In 1975 she put a large section of her past behind her, and made it clear – not least by keeping so many of Heath's men in her Shadow Cabinet and, ultimately, her Cabinets – that she valued Party unity and was

[1] Samuel Brittan reviewing Jock Bruce-Gardyne, *Mrs Thatcher's First Administration: The Prophets Confounded*, in *Encounter*, April 1985.
[2] Interview, Frank Giles, 28 January 1990.

prepared to lead with a broad base. It was only when she was convinced that her continued leadership would divide the Party that she resigned. She had beaten Michael Heseltine on the first ballot in the November 1990 leadership election with a majority just four short of the number needed for outright victory, but her Cabinet colleagues told her that even if she won the second ballot, she would be leading a seriously divided Party, and four Cabinet Ministers also told her that she could no longer count on their support. It was this that made her resign.

The value she placed on Party unity and on loyalty was very important, because she struck at powerful instincts for social harmony that were the products of decades of accommodation. In the week after her election, the *Economist* began to change its view of her and declared that Labour was being too sanguine in the belief that she was good news for them. Her election had 'dramatically changed the political landscape,' said the magazine, and confidently predicted that 'after a decent interval, during which she pays off debts to her more right-wing supporters, Mrs Thatcher is likely to head for the centre where elections are won.'[1] What was missed by practically everyone was that Thatcher was a politician with convictions. She meant what she said, and that meant she would, in her own eyes, be hypocritical if she trimmed very much. She was prepared to trim far more than many of her people were, but she never lost sight of her guiding principles. Her expediency was to pursue policies that she believed to be correct, but to do so in ways that did not directly challenge her political colleagues. She took her time, and took advantage of her position to win her way. 'She tended to make policy very much by shooting from the hip,' said Jim Prior. 'The reason was that she did not find it easy to get her own way round the Shadow Cabinet table, so she tended to make policy – usually of the more extreme kind – on television, or at Prime Minister's Question Time in the Commons. She was afraid of being pushed off what she wanted to do if there was much consultation with her colleagues beforehand, so she reckoned it was better to make the policy and argue about it afterwards.'[2]

[1] *Economist*, 15 February 1975.
[2] Prior, *A Balance of Power* (London, Hamish Hamilton, 1986) p. 107.

Before 1975, it would have been emotionally impossible for her to do what she did after she became leader. She would have sounded like a troublemaker and been hailed as irresponsible if she had pressed for a hard line in 1972. As leader, she benefited from the pressure in Opposition to oppose. She also benefited from the increasingly evident bankruptcy of the post-war consensus. It was only after she became Prime Minister that many of her Cabinet colleagues began to realize that she had meant what she said in Opposition, and then they had to look to their own careers and either hang on for the ride, or leave because they disagreed. In the latter case, the onus would then be on them to explain their reasons which would involve advancing a counter philosophy to Thatcherism. Geoffrey Howe was the only one who did advance a counter argument, not to Thatcherism, but to her attitude towards Europe over which he resigned.[1]

The 1970s saw the blowing away of the genial quality that had coloured the previous thirty years. To the present day, many people resent most what they see as Thatcher's attack on civility. But civility had fallen from other causes before Thatcher became leader of the Conservative Party, let alone Prime Minister. William Clark, who had been Anthony Eden's public relations adviser in Number Ten in 1955–6, wrote a novel in the early 1970s, before the 1973 oil shock, that was not published. He called it *Black Blockade*, and in it had an extraordinary premonition of how Britain would close down to two- and three-day working weeks; how critically ill people would not be brought to hospital – one of his characters loses his wife in such circumstances – and how the primary producers of oil would cut off supplies. In 1960, Constantine Fitzgibbon had published *When The Kissing Had To Stop*, about the collapse of nerve in a hedonist society. Clark took Fitzgibbon a step farther, prefiguring a Britain that was to come as a result of desires and

[1] In 1975, several members of Heath's team preferred not to work with Thatcher. Geoffrey Rippon, Shadow Foreign Secretary, decided that he would return to the backbenches. So did Peter Walker, Shadow Defence Minister, and Robert Carr, Heath's Shadow Chancellor. She dropped Paul Channon (Environment), Nicholas Scott (Housing), and Peter Thomas (Wales), from her team. Walker became Minister for Agriculture in Thatcher's first Cabinet, and served continuously in various posts until 1990. Anthony Barber, who had been Chancellor of the Exchequer under Heath, retired from politics after the February 1974 general election.

instincts for social harmony being exploited by special interests.

From the late 1950s, Enoch Powell began to provide an alternative view in the political arena that did much to make Thatcher and Thatcherism seem less radical in the 1970s. He argued that – in terms of money supply – it was responses at the centre to economic developments that dominated results, and that by operating under rules, not laws, it was possible to have a stable economy whatever the role of the unions – which, Powell considered, was in its way quite positive. He did not consider that unions were responsible for inflation, nor did he share the popular view that they were responsible for raising workers' real wages. He did not believe in breaking up unions: he felt that they were an appropriate force in a large, impersonal society.

Margaret Thatcher did not believe in breaking up unions either. Edward Heath, in contrast, might well have thought of doing just that. He believed that everything conjoined at the centre, and he saw unions as rivals to democratic political authority. Thatcher also saw the threat to democracy implicit in protected union power, but she felt that unions had to be reined into their proper sphere rather than smashed. She probably welcomed the acceptance by the Electricians' Union of no-strike agreements and strictly enforced wage deals (resulting in the union being drummed out of the Trades Union Congress) that occurred in the 1980s, seeing it as properly run and as actually increasing predictability and ease of administration in society. In June 1975, Keith Joseph took issue with Paul Johnson (then still a leading socialist intellectual) who had criticized Labour's alliance with the trade unions and had blamed the unions, in Joseph's view too easily, for ills for which they were only partly responsible and had thus excused the lack of will of successive Governments. The unions, said Joseph, should be made to realize that rehabilitating the market economy was their best salvation.[1] 'There is no problem about my getting on with trade unions or trade unions getting on with me,' Thatcher emphasized a year later, 'provided we are both interested in getting a flourishing Britain.'[2]

In 1972 people were terrified of deep social conflict because of

---

[1] Sir Keith Joseph, 'The Unions We Deserve', *New Statesman*, 13 June 1975.
[2] BBC TV, *Panorama*, 23 February 1976.

the attitudes and activities of organized labour. There was a keen awareness of the dangers of unemployment and social distress, but it was not thought that conflict with the trade unions was inevitable, as long as steps were taken to deflect it. This was the vital element in Heath's U-turn, coupled with a depressed world economy. Then, in the mid-1970s as inflation bit deeply and taxation rose, the real possibility was seen of the 'Argentine Solution': everybody understood that the United Kingdom could actually roll back downhill. Lord Rothschild, head of the Central Policy Review Staff (the civil service Think-Tank set up by Ted Heath), warned in 1973 that the country was living in a cloud cuckoo land. 'From the vantage point of the Cabinet Office,' he declared in a speech, 'it seems to me that unless we take a very strong pull at ourselves and give up the idea that we are one of the wealthiest, most influential and important countries in the world – in other words that Queen Victoria is still reigning – we are likely to find ourselves in increasingly serious trouble. To give just one unpalatable example, in 1985 we shall have half the economic weight of France or Germany, and about equal to that of Italy.'[1] By 1975, public expenditure was running at sixty per cent of the country's gross domestic product (partly because of the deficits of nationalized industries), and Rothschild's prediction was coming to pass a decade earlier than he had thought.

The trade unions contributed enormously to the atmosphere of conflict and decline. 'The whole exercise of union power has been in the hands of a tiny number of left-wing activists,' said a leading union leader in 1988, reviewing his experience of more than three decades in the Trades Union Congress. 'The trade union leadership knew that they held their positions because of corruption and control by minorities who still mistakenly assume that within the trade union movement are ardent bands of class warriors. It is a reversion to the attitudes of the 1920s ... And [referring to the formal connection between the TUC and the Labour Party] people do not like to see political Parties subject to the whips of unemployment.'[2] Eric Varley, Labour's Energy Secretary in 1974, told his Cabinet colleagues that when he told a miners' meeting 'that the Govern-

[1] Lord Rothschild, *Meditations on a Broomstick* (London, Collins, 1977), pp. 90–91.
[2] Talk, Eric Hammond, 15 November 1988.

164

ment could have used more oil at the power stations this summer and so built up coal stocks for the winter against a possible strike, but hadn't, they had merely retorted, "More fool you", and thanked him for letting them know how strong their position was.'[1]

In response, the Conservative Party developed a strong desire for confrontation – even more than in 1970 – signalling the end of the post-war consensus. 'Do you think you would ever have heard of Christianity if the Apostles had gone out and said, "I believe in consensus"?' is how Thatcher put it.[2] She and her Party were not alone: many men and women broke with the Labour Party after 1974. Monetarism provided a rationale for doing so. For every MP who understood monetarism, there were ten who invoked it as a way of dealing with other matters. It also provided a rationale for making a systematic repudiation of the Heath period. These changed awarenesses and attitudes made it possible for Thatcher to win the 1979 general election. The inner doubt about the quality of the British economy and anger with the unions did the trick. The questions of union power and of the country's economic condition and structure was what Thatcher addressed herself to, and dynamized.

By then, the country was in a mess, with accelerating inflation and domineering trade unions. Noel Annan acknowledged that his generation had a responsibility: 'Our Age prescribed two medicines to cure the British disease. The first was conciliation [of the trade unions]. The second was to reform trade union law. Victor Rothschild at the think-tank told Heath we were the only country that had no effective laws to control unions. But . . . the political will to restore power to management did not exist until Margaret Thatcher became prime minister.'[3]

Within the civil service, a great change took place between 1969 and 1979: many Mandarins kicked over the traces in that period. They had seen Wilson and the post-war consensus that they had been instrumental in forming fail from the inside. In 1969, the civil service took pride in its performance. By 1979, it had split. For

[1] Barbara Castle, *The Castle Diaries, 1974–76* (London, Weidenfeld & Nicolson, 1980), p. 221.

[2] John Newhouse, 'The Gamefish', *New Yorker*, 10 February 1986.

[3] Noel Annan, *Our Age: Portrait of a Generation*, (London, Weidenfeld & Nicolson, 1990) pp. 351–2.

fifteen years it had been thrown around by Governments' changing policies – not merely changes brought on by electoral swings, but changes brought on by loss of nerve by politicians, by indecision, by political compromises, and by outside agencies such as the European Commission and the International Monetary Fund.

In the levels below the Mandarins in the civil service, a great many men and women had come to scorn 'Our Age'. They were no longer content simply to perform: they wanted to change the country. It was a British version of a Latin American phenomenon 'Tenientismo' – 'Lieutenantism'; junior officers who overthrow generals, feeling that the generals, by obeying the policy, are selling out and are without honour. There was a lot of 'Tenientismo' in the civil service by the time Edward Heath left Number Ten in February 1974. There was even more by 1979. Jim Callaghan, Labour's Foreign Secretary in 1974–7, on one occasion in 1974 declared that Britain would go on sliding downhill. 'I haven't got any solution,' he said. 'If I were a young man, I should emigrate.'[1] Many younger civil servants regarded themselves as having enlisted in the public service, and as having then been betrayed. They were being told by their bosses to roll over, and over, and over.

Most Treasury officials knew in 1975 that Government policies of expanding public sector spending and massive and increasing borrowing were heading the country for disaster. The poor performance of the British economy relative to its competitors meant that debts would pile up and interest payments would increase, becoming too much for the country to afford, especially since so much public spending was on social services and subsidizing uneconomic nationalized industries. At one point, for example, British Steel was losing money annually at the rate of £1 per second. And then to have the IMF come in and do their job for them! That was what happened in banana republics. The Treasury, the most distinguished historic civil service in the Western world, was enraged.

Within the Conservative Party, the new awarenesses hit home more effectively than anywhere else. Conservatives had had a preview of a new approach to the country's problems in 1970. They knew there *was* an alternative to Butskellism and Barber booms. It

[1] Castle, *The Castle Diaries*, p. 221.

might have been rejected, but it was still there. This knowledge was an essential element in Margaret Thatcher's election as Party leader in 1975. 'The Selsdon Declaration, in a sense, was an attempt before the election of 1970,' observed Enoch Powell, 'to get the Conservative Party committed to the alternative-to-socialism approach to control of the economy and to relations with the unions. But it was swept aside in the revolution or counter-revolution of 1972, and it was the disaster to which that led in 1974–6 which, I think, sickened the Conservative Party of it, and made them amenable to an alternative interpretation.'[1]

A combination of desperation and possibility is the essence of Thatcherism, and it appealed to the same combination of intense feeling in millions of individuals who saw that Britain was in danger of going downhill in a terrifying way – becoming poorer and poorer, more and more inefficient, counting for less and less internationally, aspiring to an East German condition. In 1959, Britain was the strongest military and economic power in Western Europe; by 1979 it was well down the list of second-ranking world powers, leading Europe and most of the developed world only in days lost by strikes. Between 1974 and 1979, public expenditure rose by 9 per cent while gross domestic product rose by only 2.5 per cent. This meant that the public sector – the State – was taking 'a much bigger share of the national cake,' Bernard Donoughue was to point out. 'Within these general figures was a redistribution of resources ... Expenditure on defence was reduced by 10 per cent, while there was increased provision on housing of 56 per cent, on social security of 25 per cent and on support for industry of 75 per cent. Unemployment, which rose inevitably as the Western world slipped into the post-oil-shock recession, was deliberately kept out of the public sector and left to be inflicted almost wholly on private industry.'[2] British management was inefficient, and punitive rates of taxation penalized incentives.

Britain had been losing relative ground for decades, but did not want to be harnessed by the past. Simultaneously, millions of people were waking up to the computer revolution, and to the revolution

[1] Interview, Rt Hon. J. Enoch Powell, MBE, 1 November 1989.
[2] Bernard Donoughue, *Prime Minister: The Conduct of Policy under Harold Wilson & James Callaghan* (London, Jonathan Cape, 1987), p. 188.

in the division of international labour, where manufacturing and service industries on the large scale have become transnational as the international economy has increasingly swamped national economies. The assets of modernity were eating away at blanket claims. There existed a technological preparation for Thatcher's moment in that the world was decentralizing itself: there were more and more financial centres developing, and more economies moving from the 'third' into the 'first' world. By 1970, and certainly by 1974, Japan, unnoticed by most of Europe and America, was surging forward as a major world economic power. Taiwan, Singapore, South Korea were all on the move.

People sensed very clearly that Britain was in a world of progression or regression: that there was no in-between, and that traditional economic, social, cultural and industrial relations' attitudes were acting like an anchor, holding them and their country back. Thatcherism appealed to this sense. It came from being in tune with the time, rather than from being immersed in economic and social theory and academic debate. It owed most to Thatcher herself: her political acumen, her convictions, and her drive, all of which were remarkably in harmony with the popular mood.

This mood, in retrospect, can be discerned in the politicians and intellectuals who changed sides in the mid-1970s. People who were Conservatives all along also changed. When Keith Joseph late in the day said that he had discovered what it was to be a Conservative, he was voicing what others were also beginning to think. Many Conservatives, encouraged by Butskellism, had thought in the 1950s and 1960s that what we may loosely call the business perspective of Conservativism (as opposed to the organic perspective of Toryism) meant preventing foreign competition, and doling out Government subsidies to flagging companies and industries. Many Conservatives did not believe in the market as a creative force. There were a lot of people who had once thought of themselves as Tories, such as Iain Macleod and Keith Joseph, who supported PEST (Pressure for Economic and Social Toryism), a ginger group with a paternalist, social liberal view of society, which thought the social perspective of Macmillanism was excellent: the best of Toryism and the best of social democracy. Many Conservatives who had been of that mind in the 1960s and early 1970s, thinking it was the way to the future, suddenly started rethinking their view and realized that a serious business perspective was the one thing left untried in British life. It was these people, as things started getting worse and worse in the 1970s, who began looking closely at their position and saying, 'You know, we just took the truths of what we were told about the business world altogether too much for granted.' And so they began to examine business and its world.

Thatcher's willingness to look at alternative approaches to the country's problems, rather than at the blueprints of academic thinkers and theoretical economists, carried the day with the converts, as did her simplicity. As Hugh Thomas put it in 1976: 'New ideas have a much greater chance of being heard among [the Conservatives] than they had in the past, and at the very least the Party is committed to the preservation of the open society.'[1] Thatcher's own sense of business, enterprise and patriotism gave her a vital intellectual security in developing alternative approaches, and appealed to Conservatives.

However, it was not until Labour failed for a second time in 1974–9 that the country was prepared to accept the social strain that Thatcherism entailed. Only when domestic economic conflict had been ratcheted up to a level where the aggressor was obviously the unions and what was being demanded was no longer 'fair' were the British going to accept the dislocations inherent in defeating them. And by the time the unions were dealt with by Thatcher, the working men and women of the 1920s and 1930s were dead or retired: the people who had been sacrificed in the harsh decades and in the wars were not, in the 1980s, once again taking the punishment. Had they been, the country's hand would surely still have been palsied in dealing with them. Thatcher instead benefited from a feeling that 'These are people who have not paid their dues, so now we can have at them.' Heath was not so fortunate: the cards were stacked against him in 1970.

The effect of Heath's failure was compounded by the lack of new thinking in the Labour Party, which was becoming dangerously left-wing as far as Harold Wilson and Jim Callaghan and most of their Cabinet Ministers were concerned. At the 1975 and 1976 Labour Party Conferences, both Prime Ministers had publicly

[1] *Daily Mail*, 23 November 1976.

warned of the danger of left-wing infiltration of the Party. In the Conservative Party, new thinking had a false dawn with Selsdon, and was squashed in the U-turn. Nothing, it seemed, had been learned by the politicians from the 1964–74 experience.

In fact, a sea-change was occurring in the Conservative Party and in the country, although at the time few people anywhere realized it. Bernard Donoughue, who was an adviser to Jim Callaghan, was travelling with the Prime Minister in the official Rover car towards the end of the 1979 general election campaign. He gave his view that the opinion polls were showing an improvement in Labour's favour and that 'with a little luck, and a few policy initiatives here and there, we might just squeak through'. Callaghan turned to him and said quietly: 'I should not be too sure. You know there are times, perhaps once every thirty years, when there is a sea-change in politics. It then does not matter what you say or what you do. There is a shift in what the public wants and what it approves of. I suspect that there is now such a sea-change – and it is for Mrs Thatcher.'[1]

Callaghan was right. His was a shrewd judgement from a major author of union power. 'Callaghan was defeated by the forces of the unions despite the fact that cabinet papers on the home front were being sent to the TUC for their approval,' Lord Annan judged. 'His last words to the unions when the TUC General Council met the cabinet at No. 10 were of abject subservience. "We are prostrate before you – but don't ask us to put it in writing."'[2] The country was recognizing that the 1945 settlement was not so much over – it was still in force – but was steadily more out of date. The social agenda inherent in union power had begun to make even the people who agreed with it feel economically unsafe. It had moved into becoming a political agenda, and that meant 'Unions Rule, OK!' It was too off-putting to the democracy. While the unions were seen as fundamentally economic organizations, they could be quarrelled with and agreed with and conceded a high degree of legitimacy. But once it became apparent that they were being ridden as political warhorses, then the country – and a majority of union members – cried 'Enough!' This change involved what Rab Butler

[1] Donoughue, *Prime Minister*, p. 191.
[2] Annan, *Our Age*, p. 351.

called 'the patience of politics': things always take longer to happen than you wish or expect. If a confrontation had been undertaken in the first half of the 1970s, the country would have been less united about it than it was when Thatcher took on the unions a decade later, but it might have been undertaken successfully if Heath had been prepared for hard pounding. By the late 1970s the unions had disarmed themselves because their membership was by no means certain that their leaders, by calling upon them to become ever more political, were doing the right thing, even in their terms. A very large part of the British working class were disappointed with the unions after the three-day week in 1974, and furious with them after the strikes and distress of the later 1970s and the 1978–9 Winter of Discontent, marking a great decline in national civility. By 1979, there were other forces working in people's minds besides Margaret Thatcher, and there was a strong awareness that Britain either had to get out of its industrial relations mess or go down. The 1970s had begun with labour in one mind, and ended with Labour in two minds.

The political sea-change was, as is usual in Britain, an atmospheric affair. Its foreground was deep anger and despair about the state of Britain and trade union power. The arrival of the International Monetary Fund officials in Whitehall in 1976 had demoted Britain to the status of a Third World country in terms of economic management. Inflation and unemployment seemed to rise whatever was done by Government, and the desire of Wilson and Callaghan to reach deals with the unions seemed to many people – including many trade unionists – to be a surrender of democratic authority.

The background was the free market/libertarian set of ideas whose time had come, and disillusion with the post-war consensus. Huge institutions, both public and private, were seen as inefficient and fairly odious. Most able people did not want to work for them, in contrast to a generation earlier when the creation of the Welfare State attracted many of the best and the brightest, and when the civil service was perceived as the permanent government through which real changes could be made.

Hard on the heels of this change in attitude, there was the growing dispersal of initiative to the fringes. A young woman from Grantham, Lincolnshire, born in 1955, a generation after Thatcher, who had been to Oxford and was about to enter a career, was less likely to seek to qualify for the Bar than to start an enterprise or join a new concern like a computer software company. Margaret Thatcher had gone to Oxford; was called to the Bar; entered politics as a Conservative, and was a great enabler of comprehensive secondary schools. By the time she became Prime Minister, young people had career ambitions that did not involve politics or the State as central factors. Her ability to sense the sea-change, the popular mood, the growing intellectual reaction against Keynesianism (which was the core of the post-war consensus), and to adjust herself accordingly, was a mark of an exceptional politician.

Other factors converged to provide Thatcher's moment. In Britain, not until the 1970s did young people start taking degree courses in Business Administration. Entrepreneurs, notably in the fashion and pop culture worlds, only began multiplying in the 1970s. The pop and fashion worlds provided nearly all of Britain's success stories in that decade. British industry, with some exceptions (notably the City), became more and more sluggish and uncompetitive, all too often depending upon State subsidies. Nationalization (which meant more State spending and, ultimately, more taxation) became a safety net for unemployment. In the 1970s, if any major firm was going bankrupt, the Government was almost guaranteed to step in. 'Labour isn't working' was the poster campaign slogan the Conservatives used in the 1979 election, and it was effective. But the real strength of the message was the widespread agreement that Britain wasn't working, and that the country needed a dose of the salts.

Alfred Sherman was certain that radical changes were necessary in Britain. He felt that class resentments, insecurity and defensiveness played far too large a part in British life and in British dispositions. He grew up in Hackney in the East End of London between the wars. His father was a Labour councillor, and Alfred was a socialist. He joined the International Brigade in 1937 and served in Spain as a machine-gunner. He came back to England a Marxist in 1938. During the Second World War he served in field security and occupied territory administration. He helped organize the police in Libya, where he taught himself shorthand and Arabic to interpreter standard. After the war he attended the London School of Economics. He next entered journalism and went to Yugoslavia, writing for the *Observer*. In 1952 he moved to Israel, becoming foreign editor of the *Jerusalem Post*, while continuing to write for the *Observer* in England. He left the *Post* after six months and wrote for the main Hebrew daily newspaper, *Haaretz*. After this he was temporarily economic adviser in the Ministry of Finance and then to the General Zionists Party, the main Opposition Party in Israel. He returned to London, eventually joining the *Daily Telegraph* in 1965, as their first local government affairs correspondent, later becoming a leader writer.

The type of comment that infuriated Sherman, and demonstrated the anti-semitism that he considered all too widespread, was made by Harold Macmillan in 1976 about Keith Joseph. He was, he said, 'the only boring Jew I've ever met'.[1] The arrogant and patronizing quality of such a remark was something that Sherman – a poor Jew from the East End who was constantly marginalized and dismissed for holding unfashionable views, whether of the Left or the Right – had had to face himself.

At LSE a big change took place in Sherman's political views. 'I realized that socialism and communism were not the answer. At LSE that was rather unusual. You have to get back to the people all the time.'[2] In British journalism, Sherman carved himself out a niche in municipal political coverage. 'I had an interest in local government since 1964. I saw its spending and its growth and that it was going to be a menace and that something ought to be done about it, so I wrote about it.'[3] He wrote on aspects of local government for a wider public. By then, he accepted the market, but in his own words, 'eschewed market worship and utopianism'.[4] In 1971 he joined the Conservative Party so as to stand for Kensington and Chelsea Council in order to buttress his knowledge of local government. His principal connection with the national Party, apart from journalism, was through personal friendships, notably with Keith Joseph and Arthur Jones, a Conservative local government specialist. In 1962 when Joseph was Minister for Housing, Sherman had met him for the first time when he interviewed him about his policies. In spring 1974, Joseph introduced Sherman to Margaret

[1] *New Statesman*, 29 October 1976. Macmillan was not named.
[2] Interview, Sir Alfred Sherman, 30 April 1990.
[3] Ibid.
[4] Interview, Sir Alfred Sherman, 10 December 1990.

Thatcher, who was already familiar with his writings. They used to come to Sherman's house in the late 1970s for discussions about monetary policy and the operation of the free market, just as they did with his friend Alan Walters.

For Sherman, policies that accepted the validity of market forces were part of the way to revive Britian, sweep away socialism (which, by this time, he saw as a principal force for stagnation in British society and politics), and to regenerate the Conservative Party as the only hope for the time being for introducing economic reform.

Sherman's physical and intellectual energy sent him bustling in print and in private during the early 1970s. In 1973 he told Joseph that Heath had got it wrong, and immediately after the February 1974 election the two men joined forces in Joseph's 'conversion'. Indeed, it was to Sherman more than anyone else that Joseph attributed his new thinking, according to his biographer. 'Sherman's fecund mind was the "prism", he said, through which he now saw clearly the political reality that had eluded him in the previous twenty years.'[1] 'You know who was central to me?' he asked, speaking about the change in his thinking during and after 1974. 'Alfred Sherman. He was very important.'[2] Sherman could shame Joseph, which was why he was central to him. 'You weren't on the Ebro in 1937: you were having a nice time at Oxford,' was a subtext of their relationship, as was: 'I fought my way out of the East End. I've made my way. There are you, always with a connexion that makes things easy.' 'I remember one lunch,' said a friend of both men, 'and I heard him say in his gravelly voice, "Keith, the trouble is that you agree with me but you haven't got the backbone to say so!"'[3] Sherman put a burr under Joseph's saddle. His deeper importance is that he focused the issue by using his purchase with Joseph and saying to him: 'You have to do something about the state of the country.' For Sherman, argument was a means to an end, not an end in itself. Joseph, left to himself, is contemplative. Sherman forced Joseph to take on the struggle. 'Un homme d'esprit est ordinairement difficile dans les sociétés' ('Sociétiés usually find

[1] Morrison Halcrow, *Keith Joseph: A Single Mind* (London, Macmillan, 1989), p. 62.
[2] Interview, Rt Hon. Lord Joseph, CH, 26 June 1990.
[3] Interview, 21 May 1990.

a man of spirit difficult to accommodate')[1] Montesquieu remarked, and this was very much Sherman's situation. 'From 1974,' said Joseph, 'Margaret Thatcher's instincts and Alfred Sherman's economic education of me led the three of us together to establish the Centre for Policy Studies.'[2] The Centre was Sherman's idea, and his appointment by Joseph as director of studies two years after its creation was natural.

Sherman tried to involve Alan Walters in the Centre, but the economist had determined to go to the United States, and by 1978 was committed to a career there. He was bitterly disappointed by the last two years of the Heath Government. 'I think I can say that I was utterly ineffective,' he said, looking back. 'In 1974 the electorate, in two elections, threw out Edward Heath and elected Harold Wilson and his curious band of expropriating socialists. In the words of one of Wilson's ministers, Douglas Jay, "the man from Whitehall really does know best". Then I decided that Britain, facing the alternatives of Wilson and Heath, had a choice between the devil and the shallow blue sea. Whatever the political outcome, Britain was in for a pronounced decline into the absurdities of controls, planning and *dirigisme*. In 1974, I decided to leave Britain and, after a year at the World Bank, to join the department of political economy of Johns Hopkins.'[3] 'One of the most alarming features of the current state of opinion in Britain is the sense of hopelessness,' he wrote in November 1974, presaging his move to the United States. 'We may all at last agree that the power of governments to do good is severely limited. But that is not the point. The government's power to do *harm* is still frighteningly great . . . Barber, the money-printer, put a stop to all that sense of fiscal responsibility. Heath and his minions were determined to do good even if the country went bankrupt in the process.'[4] 'His wife

[1] Charles-Louis de Secondat, Baron de La Brède et de Montesquieu, *Les Lettres persanes* (Paris, Hachette, 1913), p. 260. I am indebted to Alfred Sherman for this reference and self-appraisal.
[2] Lord Joseph, 'Stepping Stones to Power', in *The First 10 Years: A Perspective of the Conservative Era that Began in 1979* (London, Conservative Central Office, 1989), p. 18.
[3] Sir Alan Walters, 'My Deviationist Economics', *Independent*, 26 October 1989. The World Bank is based in Washington DC, and Johns Hopkins University is in Baltimore, Maryland, about thirty miles north of the capital.
[4] Alan Walters, 'Moderation in Monetarism', *Spectator*, 2 November 1974.

wanted to go back to the States,' said Alfred Sherman. 'She's York-shire Irish and she felt the social scene.'[1] Nevertheless, Walters remained in close touch with his friends in Britain, and in 1980 Sherman was instrumental in securing his return as personal economic adviser to the Prime Minister.

From 1974, however, monetarist ideas began to take root in Wilfred Street, and from 1975 these ideas flourished in the private office of the Leader of the Opposition, and on occasion in Prime Minister's Questions in the House of Commons and Thatcher's television interviews. One of the most notable features of the early years of Thatcher's leadership was that very few publications appeared that could be attributed directly to her and to Joseph. Cyclostyled sheets were the main output from Sherman's Centre, but then Wilfred Street was an operating base for Thatcher's inner circle – especially Keith Joseph – and a great deal of time and energy was spent on researching and preparing speeches for him and for her,[2] and on organizing lunches and dinners, meetings and drinks, during which anti-Keynesian principles and market philosophy were propounded to journalists, businessmen, City types and Conservatives outside Parliament. Thatcherism was spun in this period in less tangible ways than print. Alfred Sherman's influence on Keith Joseph and, through him, on Margaret Thatcher, was crucial in the formulation of Thatcherism, but there were also other channels[3] and the

[1] Interview, Sir Alfred Sherman, 30 April 1990.
[2] In the three and a half years to the May 1979 general election, Joseph made 150 speeches at universities and polytechnics (Halcrow, *Keith Joseph*, p. 103). There were many more speeches to other audiences.
[3] There was, for example, a vitally important briefing team of MPs. 'We were comprehensively denounced by Miss Julia Langdon, a journalist writing in *Labour Weekly*,' remembered Norman Tebbit. 'Picking up from the trial of Madam Mao in China she dubbed Margaret, Airey Neave, George Gardiner, the Member for Reigate, and me as the Gang of Four, the hard reactionary plotters of the Party. We were all highly amused and certainly George and I were immensely flattered. At first Airey enjoyed the joke immensely and exaggerating his naturally somewhat conspiratorial air greeted me as a fellow conspirator. "Good morning, Three," Airey would say as we met, receiving the reply, "Good morning, Two." . . . Others, notably Nigel Lawson, joined the group whilst Geoffrey Pattie and Peter Rees were occasional members, too; but we, the original members of the Gang of Four, stayed together until Airey was murdered in 1979.' (Norman Tebbit, *Upwardly Mobile* [London, Futura, 1989], p. 186.)

background awareness of the time that the post-war consensus had not worked.

There were several reasons for the failure of the consensus, according to Sherman. In the first place, there was 'a growing disillusionment with the post-war settlement'. Then there was 'a lack of conviction about Conservative ideals, derived from the fact that in 1945 the Conservative Party chose to adopt the Labour Party version of state-socialism, not out of conviction but out of panic that followed the Conservative electoral defeat. In 1945 Winston Churchill went down to defeat despite his inspiring leadership during the war. The Conservative old guard, who never were at one with Churchill, believed that the people wanted socialism whether it worked or not, and that the essence of leadership was to follow them.' Responding to this, Margaret Thatcher (said Sherman), 'like most British politicians, feels constrained to speak in homilies rather than in concepts', and most of her speeches were written by speechwriters 'and would have been used as long as their views did not seem too contentious'. Her policies and objectives were 'determined less by ideas than by feelings, and more than either by circumstances'.[1]

This view carries echoes of the animus felt by Sherman against the Conservative Establishment and the established ways of doing things. Others (for example Jim Prior) felt that Thatcher's ideas and policies were all too clear. And Sherman lets Churchill off the hook completely, when in fact Churchill shared much of Harold Macmillan's sense that the Party had to accommodate a collectivist sensibility not simply out of electoral necessity, but also out of a sense of fairness.

In these Opposition years there were, of course, publications on policy. *The Right Approach, The Right Approach To The Economy, The 1977 Campaign Guide* and its 1978 supplement, and the 1979 Election *Manifesto*, all set out both the practicalities and the philosophy of much of what Thatcher planned to do in Government. But all of these were Party publications, each one essentially emanating from the Research Department, not from Wilfred Street. *The Right Approach* (1976) and *The Right Approach To The Economy* (1977)

---

[1] Sir Alfred Sherman, 'The Thatcher Era in Perspective', *The World & I*, April 1989, pp. 611–12.

owed most to the superb drafting skills of Angus Maude, who was a Thatcherite, and Chris Patten, who was not, and were consciously framed to provide Party unity and gain intellectual respectability rather than to set out daring new initiatives. The *Campaign Guide* and the *Manifesto* were also very careful to give as few hostages to fortune as possible, seeking the felicitous phrase rather than ideological hammer blows. Keith Joseph, for example, despite his formal responsibility for policy and research, and the fact that he had delivered hundreds of speeches in the period 1975–9, was mentioned only five times in the 789 pages of the *Campaign Guide*.[1] Jim Prior, one of the leading Heathites in Thatcher's Shadow Cabinet, was mentioned nearly twenty times. Sherman and the Centre were not mentioned at all.

Perhaps these were small points in themselves (and it should be remembered that Joseph had no Shadow portfolio, which meant that unlike Jim Prior and others who did, he was not directly shadowing any particular area of policy or Government operation), but they indicated very clearly that Thatcher and her people were considered by the Party insiders as outsiders who were just visiting and who would soon go away following electoral defeat. They saw Thatcherism – which was being enunciated in speeches by Keith Joseph and in behind-the-scenes policy work – as an embarrassing interlude. A profile of Joseph in the *New Statesman* in October 1976 touched on a central element in the mix: the British dislike of intellectuals and intellectualism. 'To be the intellectual gadfly at the side of the leader, but to be free of painful necessities like decision-taking – this is the stuff of life for him,' said the journal. The 'contempt and derision which British politics reserves for the man of ideas' was to be his lot.[2]

The irony of the view of Party insiders and most commentators was that Thatcherism was effectively the same as 1970 Heathism. The difference was that she not only really believed in her approach, but also was determined to carry out her promises when she formed a Government. 'She made up her mind really quite a long time ago that this country's future was damaged, really, by the trade unions,' Lord

[1] In the 236-page 1978 *Campaign Guide Supplement*, Joseph was mentioned another five times.
[2] *New Statesman*, 29 October 1976.

Home considered, identifying the two central elements of Thatcherism, 'and she made up her mind to deal with that. And she made up her mind that inflation was the worst enemy of progress. And the two things, of course, were connected because trade union activities led to an increase in costs. And she did them both . . . I think she felt her instincts were right and made up her mind to follow them, and in the course of that has done on the whole very well.'[1]

Thatcherism, like 1970 Heathism, emphasized a strong belief in individual responsibility and self-help. A belief in the morality of capitalism was an important element. It also stressed the need to enforce law and order, and to support the police. This is what she meant when she spoke of 'Victorian values' in the 1980s. 'I was brought up by a Victorian grandmother,' said Thatcher. 'We were taught to work jolly hard. We were taught to prove yourself; we were taught self-reliance; we were taught to live within our income. You were taught that cleanliness is next to godliness. You were taught self-respect. You were taught always to give a hand to your neighbour. You were taught tremendous pride in your country. All of these things are Victorian values. They are also perennial values. You don't hear so much about these things these days, but they were good values and they led to tremendous improvements in the standard of living.'[2]

'I think her attitude towards the leadership of Britain,' reflected Sir Alan Walters, '– the absence of a thrusting middle class; there's a lot of thrust in the lower middle class – and in the reference to Victorian values, I think she's thinking of Trollopian characters who were middle class, who were devoted not merely to making money – they did make money – but also to what they regarded as morally the right system. Moral courage says "This is the right thing to do," and she has great respect for that.'[3] Harold (now Lord) Lever was one of the Labour Party's most respected spokesmen on international economics in the 1960s and 1970s, and for him the question of Victorian values was worrying. 'When she talks of Victorian values, she is talking of ethics that were taken for granted in her youth – like telling the

[1] Interview, Rt Hon. Lord Home, KT, 20 November 1988.
[2] LBC Radio, 15 April 1983.
[3] Interview, Sir Alan Walters, 25 May 1989.

truth,' he said. 'I'm with her, but wish she would believe in more things. For too long, the British people weren't sure their leaders believed in what they were doing. Ordinary people know she at least believes that what she is doing is right. But that's not enough for me. It is a refreshing change to have someone who believes in copybook maxims. What is worrying is her interpretation of them when she applies them to modern economic conditions: it is too narrow. She thinks that any borrowing is hateful. She ignores the fact that the free enterprise she so admires is built around borrowing.'[1]

Thatcherism also spoke a great deal about individual freedom, and saw the job of government in minimalist terms: to get off people's backs. It was committed to securing financial stablility and a non-inflationary economic environment, coupled with a belief that freed of restrictions and controls, the natural entrepreneurial drive of the country would restore prosperity. It took a nationalistic view of membership of the EEC, rather than the more idealistic approach of Ted Heath, and it was firm in the conviction that communism was abhorrent, that the Soviet Union, given the chance, would not do good, that defence should be improved and that Britain should play a full part in NATO and the Atlantic alliance. 'She had three ideas,' said a close Number Ten political aide. 'Sound finance; strong defence, and little naughty bits should be hidden.'[2]

'Thatcherism is what you make of it,' said Alfred Sherman when asked for a definition. 'It was a knowledge that Butskellism did not work, but that one could not adopt market economics and patriotism without having a clear idea of what they entail. Thatcherism's mood was one of impatience with what was going on, the feeling that there were too many Old Etonians around. "In the beginning was the mood, and the mood became Thatcher." It was, essentially, beliefs, not ideas.'[3]

[1] Newhouse, 'The Gamefish'.
[2] Interview, 13 December 1990.
[3] Interview, Sir Alfred Sherman, 30 April 1990.

NINE

The thinkers

Most of Thatcher's people were in place when she won the leadership election in 1975. Some, like David Young and Airey Neave, who had rapidly become a most loyal supporter, she 'made' by promoting and preferring; others, like Alan Walters, John Hoskyns and Alfred Sherman, had adopted her rather than the other way around. Keith Joseph had put himself wholeheartedly behind her. Sherman and Joseph were the 'gatekeepers' who brought people into her circle in the early years and – notwithstanding Sherman's later view that Thatcherism had more to do with belief and a mood – introduced her to ideas. The consequence of her winning the leadership very much on her own terms was that she did not have an array of people – and of debts (despite what *The Economist* thought) – to pay off. There was no one who could look her in the eye and say, 'Margaret, I made you, and I can break you.'

This was another quality she shared with Lloyd George. Many Conservative Members of Parliament were reluctant about having her as leader. The fact that despite this, she was elected, gave her enormous authority; quite as much as her personality did, formidable as it is. No one could withdraw support from her and thus bring her down. Keith Joseph was not a king-maker. Nor was Neave.

Airey Neave challenged power and authority and orthodoxy. He zoomed in like an enormous bumble-bee and helped her to take power, but he was not an intimate usher of Margaret Thatcher. The consequence of Thatcher's being elected almost by surprise and then having to force colleagues away from the so very deeply held attitudes and assumptions of the Heath period, acted to keep her inner circle small and circumspect. 'You and I and Nigel must stick together,' she once said to Norman Tebbit, referring to the need for Tebbit at the Department of Trade and Industry to avoid clashing with Nigel Lawson at the Treasury.[1] She did not want 'her' people to fight among themselves: there were enough clashes with other Ministers and Departments.

She achieved the change to Thatcherism in the Conservative Party in large part because she was the leader of the Party. The Party has an extremely strong tradition of follow-the-leader. But the change also came in part because, through Keith Joseph, she was able to tap into an intellectually coherent and passionate group of thinkers who had business, monetarist and free-market alternatives to the British post-war consensus.

Thinkers were most unusual in the schema of British politics, let alone in the Conservative Party that prided itself on pragmatism rather than ideology. Karl Marx might be referred to by Labour politicians and trade unionists, but few are likely to have read *Das Kapital* (and certainly not in the original German) and even fewer would understand it. In both Parties, few are likely to have read John Maynard Keynes's *The General Theory of Employment, Interest and Money*, let alone understand it: Keith Joseph in 1975 made the point, for example, that 'vulgar Keynesians' missed the monetarist bias in Keynes's theories.[2] And until Thatcher came along, there was no particular text or empirical thinker directly associated with Conservative Party philosophy. The writings of Friedrich von Hayek and Milton Friedman (a schematic thinker) had greatly impressed Keith Joseph and Margaret Thatcher, but they never became Party dogma. Under Thatcher, as with every Conservative leader, policy was formed from a mood about Britain and the future, and not from a set of texts. 'It is very difficult to say that Hayek was a guru for Keith and Margaret,' said Alfred Sherman. 'I would say not. People like Keith and Margaret turned to Hayek and Friedman to justify what they already thought.'[3]

Enoch Powell came closest to being the Conservative 'thinker', and he influenced an important body of opinion in the Party. Ian Gow was to recall Powell's effect: 'I probably have every one of his speeches in my bookshelves,' he said. 'I studied them. It was his influence, his very clear, very great lucidity. What he was saying

[1] Norman Tebbit, *Upwardly Mobile* (London, Futura 1989), p. 277.
[2] *New Statesman*, 21 March 1975.
[3] Interview, Sir Alfred Sherman, 30 April 1990.

long before 1974 is said by everybody now. He was a monetarist, right back.'[1] Powell himself came to his economic conclusions not through studying Hayek or Friedman, but by thinking it out for himself. 'It didn't result from the study of the works of the Chicago School,' he said. 'Indeed, there was some irritation on the part of Thorneycroft, Birch and Powell when Friedman was given the Nobel Prize that we had not been cut in on it. Because we invented monetarism too, there in the Treasury. Monetarism is a comprehensive theory which you can go around applying. You can insert it as a key into a succession of locks. But comprehensive theories are antipathetic to the Conservative mentality which doesn't regard – and rightly so – human society and Governments as theoretical. It is suspicious of theory.'[2]

Powell was a very unusual figure in the House of Commons. He was a genuine intellectual, interested in and excited by ideas, and very well-educated to boot. In debate, he was formidable. He was a difficult man from the lower middle class. He had force because he had a constituency of people who believed in ideas and he was at home with ideas. He describes himself as a politician, not an academic or an intellectual. He could, if he redeployed his time, have produced works of real intellectual quality. He finally opted for the backbenches, and was a Burkean figure. He could not choose between being a very intellectual politician or a very politicized intellectual. But at least he had that choice, while few people in politics have. Powell's story, in many respects, is that of the brilliant outsider utterly taken prisoner by the Establishment, and then rising up to assault Establishment views, running a jagged course, never ceasing to learn or to air his opinions, more often right than wrong on economics, perhaps more often wrong than right on Ulster. On top of this, he had a strong practical ability: he could get things done. Many colleagues saw him as destined for the leadership of the Party until he jumped the tracks of political *politesse* and campaigned against further immigration to Britain (being sacked by Heath from the Shadow Cabinet in 1968 in consequence), and then in February 1974 supported the Labour Party as the best hope of the United Kingdom leaving the European Community.

[1] Interview, Ian Gow, MP, 8 August 1989.
[2] Interview, Rt Hon. J. Enoch Powell, MBE, 1 November 1989.

Powell was also a very complicated person. He was an atheist who became an Anglo-Catholic; a Birmingham Welshman who did dazzlingly well: a Fellow of Trinity College, Cambridge, at the age of 22; a professor in Australia at 25. Isaiah Berlin once remarked that Powell was so certain of being killed in the Second World War that he just had to undertake existentially meaningful commitments. Life, for him, was constantly to look down the barrel of a gun. He was a Nietzschean individualist who started discovering affirmations and had to internalize great truths.

He was a trail-blazer for Margaret Thatcher, but the wrong trail-blazer because his ideas were made to sound extreme. He realized, on the other hand, that he was unlikely ever to occupy the first place. 'I think it has something to do with my personality,' he said. 'I can't help being interested in how things work, how things "really" work.'[1] He was interested in all things all ways. Margaret Thatcher was not. She was a technician. Powell wanted the romance of Empire, the romance of the hereditary aristocracy, the romance of the market economy, the romance of social Toryism. He never said, 'Let the weak go to the wall.' For Margaret Thatcher, not letting the weak go to the wall was a subtext of what she said, but she placed the emphasis elsewhere: 'Protect the weak, but don't make a thing about it,' opening herself to the suspicion that she would let them go to the wall. Powell could always speak of 'a national Health Service'. She would say, 'The better the market economy you have, the better a Health Service you can afford.' Powell constantly saw a bigger picture. 'A society for survival needs a spread of types,' he has pointed out. 'I have a favourite saying about a battalion, that in every battalion there's one man who deserves the VC, and one man who ought to be shot for cowardice. The battalion depends upon a spectrum connecting those two. People have met me in the street for many years and said, "Ah, if they were all like you!" And I haven't had the heart to tell them that such a country would be ungovernable. A battalion in which fifty per cent deserve the VC is a battalion that destroys itself; and a battalion in which fifty per cent ought to be shot for cowardice is no use. Still, you have to have somebody within the ranks who says, "I'll charge

[1] Ibid.

184

that machine-gun!"[1] Powell always expected disaster and vindication, and the disaster never came.

Enoch Powell had too many notions for a Party that did not like intellectuals, and after February 1974 when he backed the Labour Party, Margaret Thatcher was careful to avoid any identification with him. This was both politically and intellectually shrewd of her. Before then, however, she acknowledged his trail-blazing qualities. Two days after the Selsdon conference started in 1970, Powell was speaking at a dinner in her constituency in Finchley. He, his wife, and the others present were very surprised to see Margaret and Denis Thatcher turn up before the dinner was over. They had gone to immense trouble to get back from Selsdon in time to show their approval of one of the architects of what Ted Heath and the Shadow Cabinet had been made to accept there.

The Conservative Party was never an enthusiastic European Party. It had in its number enthusiastic Europeans – notably Ted Heath. The fact that Powell could not do much more than very slightly raise the level of discontent on the issue is very significant. He had two tremendous hands to play: the economic foul-up of the Wilson–Heath years, and the grave suspicion of the EEC in the mind of the average voter. But despite the view in some quarters that Powell was a potential Prime Minister, there was no call from the Conservative Party after 1974 of 'Enoch, come back: all is forgiven.' Margaret Thatcher, passing as doctrinaire, won the leadership; Powell, who is really doctrinaire, was not in the race. The Party made a very subtle choice: it knew that Margaret Thatcher was above all a politician – with doctrinal interests; it knew that Powell was a doctrinaire who played politics.

Being so much brighter than the people he dealt with, Powell could fall into the trap of thinking that because he made the intellectual going with them, he was making the intellectual going in the world as a whole. Being a brilliant man in the House of Commons did not make him an authority on race relations, on economics, on international relations, on Ireland. He said many astute things on all these matters, but Margaret Thatcher was quite smart enough to know that she was dealing with a rogue intellectual – not a

[1] Ibid.

185

philosophical statesman – and one who has a way of taking up positions that are politically unviable and offensive.

Nevertheless, Powell played a vital role in making Thatcherism possible, even though he created difficulties for her. Without him, the task of convincing the Party of her policies would have been far more problematic. 'I used to have talks with her in the 1960s,' Powell recalled, 'in which she showed how strongly sympathetic she was to me over the consequences of immigration. There were those in Opposition under Ted who thought that there was a world elsewhere. They were not in the business of exploring that world: that was left to fools like me! But it formed part of the explanation of how the pushover eventually occurred, because once Ted had put his head in the noose, and once the Conservative Party had said "Not again!", the world elsewhere opened up like the Kingdom of Heaven.'[1] Powell was never a go-between, never a broker. Enoch was Enoch, and people rallied to him. That was his charm: he came out with what was on his mind, and people listened, or did not listen, as the case might be. Powell cast himself in terms of the last lines of Matthew Arnold's *The Last Word*:

> Charge once more, and then be dumb!
> Let the victors, when they come,
> When the forts of folly fall,
> Find thy body by the wall.

Powell was not alone in fighting folly as he saw it. The historians Correlli Barnett and Martin Wiener provided twentieth-century ammunition to attack the post-war consensus, arguing *inter alia* that British culture with its ideal of the country gentleman and its class divisions encouraged laziness, acted against business, and did not understand or value engineering and technology. Keith Joseph thrust Barnett's books on his colleagues in the 1970s and on civil servants in the 1980s; Nicholas Henderson, retiring as ambassador to France in 1979, quoted Wiener in his valedictory despatch which was leaked to the *Economist* and so impressed Thatcher that she

[1] Ibid. The phrase, 'There is a world elsewhere,' was uttered by Coriolanus as he went into exile and eventual death. Powell implies that Coriolanus, who first saw the 'world elsewhere', lost his 'life', but others returned to conquer 'Rome'.

recalled Henderson and appointed him ambassador to the United States.

The Conservative Philosophy Group also provided intellectual backing for Thatcherism. The Group was formed in 1975 immediately after Thatcher's election as Party leader, and she was a member from the start, along with Conservative academics, notably Roger Scruton from London University, John Casey from Cambridge, Anthony (now Lord) Quinton from Oxford, Hugh Thomas, and some MPs.[1] 'We must have an ideology,' Thatcher said. 'The other side have got an ideology they can test their policies against. We must have one as well.'[2] The Group helped provide one, debating and discussing ideas with the Party leader.

Milton Friedman and Friedrich von Hayek were very active in trying to change the post-war consensus as it developed in the 1940s and 1950s. Behind Hayek and Friedman were the doctrines of the Austrian and Chicago Schools, reaching back to the founding fathers of classical liberalism: David Hume (1711–76), Adam Smith (1723–90), David Ricardo (1772–1823) and Frederic Bastiat (1801–50).

Adam Smith's works provided the consolidation of classical liberal economics, and many Thatcherites regarded him as their foundation. The Adam Smith Institute, named in his honour, complemented the work of the Institute of Economic Affairs in arguing for the application of market principles to secure greater individual freedom. Over time, Smith's ideas have been folded into the general currency of economic thought and debate. Nationalization would not have had his approval; privatization would. A limitation of government and its intervention in the economy only for overriding public necessity was the groundwork of his argument. He saw the division of labour as the crucial power force in the economy, which had to be offset by general education, otherwise there would appear a nation of machine-minders and toolers who cease to be good citizens. He considered that a healthy society required effective levels of general education; that the quality of life

[1] Sir Hugh Fraser, MP, was the chairman. Jonathan Aitken, MP, was a member. People would be invited to attend a meeting and present a paper which would then be discussed.
[2] Hugo Young, *One of Us* (London, Macmillan, 1989), p. 406.

was central; that while prosperity is a splendid goal, money is not everything; that people reduced to one function – even if they are well paid for it – are less likely to be good supports of a free society; that if you have too undiluted a division of labour, you get the Morlocks in the time machine – the underground creatures toiling away in the dark, reduced to sub-humanity. Education would keep people as good citizens and members of the larger society, so that if their job should die, they have a flexibility and largeness of mind that enables them to go on, and that this imparts a countervailing pressure against their being made mere instruments of the market-place. Smith would say that given the choice of pulling a lever for £100 per annum and being in a Japanese quality circle for £50 per annum, you should choose the quality circle (where a group of people in a factory combine to maximize quality by exchanging jobs and circulating and discussing experience and ideas and innovations so that no one does the same job for twenty years). The society as a whole may most reward you for doing the most repetitive things, Smith held: it is the citizen's task to maintain a larger spirit as a full member of society. He sought to promote a concept of citizenship where there is a powerful and enduring tension between individuals and the collectives.

Smith was a great friend of the market economy. The idea of the market economy had been forming in a dispersed way during the eighteenth century. Hume, Smith's fellow Scot, was as vital a thinker about the market economy as Smith. His great original argument was that economic liberty was essential to political liberty. But Smith drew the thinking of many together. He was a political economist, regarding economics as a force shaping a society and the State, as an instrument in the formation of combinations of men, and not as the science either of scarcity or of wealth.

David Ricardo stressed the international division of labour and developed a theory of rent (which captured both classical economists and Marxists) as a return on capital. Frederic Bastiat was a super-optimistic Ricardian French economic philosopher who carried certain economic principles for good and ill to their highest level. He believed completely in the liberal order of economics: that the free market would deliver everything – peace, health, social harmony, productivity. He once typified his view with the remark,

'The state is the great engine by which everyone seeks to live at the expense of everyone else.'

The ideas of these economists had often been submerged after the First World War by Keynesian emphasis upon government operations. Through Alan Walters, Keith Joseph and Alfred Sherman, they were introduced to Margaret Thatcher. Even if they were called upon only after she had reached conclusions that she was seeking to justify, once she became Party leader and then Prime Minister classical liberal ideas began to energize the atmosphere of political investigation.

Hayek was once described by Thatcher as one of the three great intellects of the twentieth century.[1] It is an eminence that the man himself would probably contest. His book *The Road To Serfdom* published in London in 1944 was, however, a seminal work. It was read by Churchill on the eve of the 1945 election. Hayek provided a philosophical basis for the advocacy of a free and competitive economy: the principle upon which the Conservatives fought that election. Alan Walters, an intellectually hungry man, as a private in the Army during the Second World War, was turned around by *The Road To Serfdom*. Margaret Thatcher read it as an undergraduate.

Hayek was born in Vienna in 1899. His family were minor aristocrats, possessing a strong academic tradition (his father was professor of Botany at the University of Vienna), and probably partly Jewish: Ludwig Wittgenstein was a cousin. Hayek served in the Austrian army in the First World War. At the University of Vienna in the early 1920s he proved to be a brilliant student of philosophy and economics, and he espoused mild socialist views. One of his teachers was Ludwig von Mises, one of the great developers of the Austrian school of economics and one of the most formidable figures in the intellectual history of the twentieth century. Mises was *the* radical free-market economist, and at the University of Vienna the young Hayek found that he could not parry his arguments for the decentralization of initiative and the impossibility of

[1] Private information. The other two were Albert Einstein and (at the time that she made the remark) Sir Ian Gilmour! Gilmour's book, *Inside Right: A Study of Conservatism* (London, Hutchinson, 1977), had just been published; Thatcher, still feeling her way as Party leader, went over the top in an effort to win over one of her most adamant Tory opponents.

securing centralized control without gigantic waste and inefficiency. Mises' *Socialism*, published in 1922, convinced Hayek who became a classical liberal in his outlook and thinking (he always resisted being termed a 'conservative'). His change was a result of genuine yielding to intellectual defeat.

The Austrian school of Mises and Hayek saw the free market and the price mechanism as the sources of individual freedom, wealth and opportunity. Unlike socialists who saw society as being fundamentally concerned with the shaping and channelling of people to achieve the common good, the Austrians saw society's function as being to facilitate individual activity and to protect diversity. Hayek took this approach and sought to expand it by articulating a systematic view embracing many sciences in which diversity is the bedrock of development. His system was more successful than most. He was anti-religious, and his system traced its implications in economics, in the psychology and sociology of the individual, and in philosophy. He concluded that liberty under a minimalist state is the happiest and most productive form of human association.

In *The Road to Serfdom*, he argued that communism and fascism were both totalitarian, and their apparent differences should not be allowed to disguise this fact. He felt that the circumstances of war were blinding people to the dangers of communism, and that under the umbrella of war a socializing process had started that would steadily erode individual liberties in the West. His book looked back over the political history of the twentieth century: its warning for the present and the future came from its analysis of the past. It was, he said, his first 'political' book.

Hayek, who had left Austria and taken out British naturalization papers in 1938, was derided by most critics at the time. He was, after all, attacking the consensus that took shape during the war and that was to dominate the politics of the next thirty-five years. The consequences of the extent of mass mobilization in Britain, and of the central control of the economy that the Second World War brought in, was what Hayek was warning against and what the consensus-builders were basing their hopes for the future upon.

There was also an atmospheric element in the wake of wartime mass mobilization, hard to grasp, but real nonetheless. The 1920s and 1930s had seen the steady march of totalitarianism. Soviet

Russia and Nazi Germany projected an image of the future that was more efficient, technological, and scientific than the image of democracy. Nazi and Soviet art and design enjoyed cult followings. Their prowess at sport suggested energy, youth and virility. Many people in Britain were deeply influenced by this. During the war, especially after the Soviet Union joined the Allies, there was a strong feeling that totalitarian methods were necessary to smash a totalitarian enemy; that Stalin was not so bad after all, and that the future was collectivist. The authoritarianism required by the mobilization for war was reflected in the immediate post-war electoral appeal of socialist and communist Parties in Europe, all implying that victory had come from effective socialist and communist principles of organization, which now could be applied to peacetime conditions. It was abetted by the emotional sense that the people of the Soviet Union had suffered great losses and hardships and it was now the turn of those who had made blood sacrifices – both the countries and the classes.

In the Britain which Hayek observed, there was also a disquiet with and revulsion from Empire (reflected in the attitudes of both Oswald Mosley and Kim Philby, for example), and a loss of confidence in the ruling elite. In 1933 in a famous university debate, Oxford students had voted against fighting for 'King and Country'. In 1940 George Orwell, who viewed totalitarianism with loathing, wrote that 'The English intelligentsia . . . take their crockery from Paris and their opinions from Moscow. In the general patriotism of the country they form a sort of island of dissident thought. England is perhaps the only great country whose intellectuals are ashamed of their own nationality. In left-wing circles it is always felt that there is something disgraceful in being an Englishman and that it is a duty to snigger at every English institution from horse racing to suet puddings. It is a strange fact, but unquestionably true that almost any English intellectual would feel more ashamed of standing to attention during "God save the King" than of stealing from a poor box.'[1]

Four years later Orwell reviewed *The Road to Serfdom*. He was

[1] George Orwell, *The Lion and the Unicorn* (London, Secker & Warburg, 1941), p. 95.

one of the few critics to take Hayek seriously. 'By bringing the whole of life under the control of the State,' Orwell said, noting the central thrust of Hayek's argument and prefiguring the post-war 'New Class' Establishment, 'socialism necessarily gives power to an inner ring of bureaucrats, who in almost every case will be men who want power for its own sake and will stick at nothing in order to retain it.'[1] Margaret Thatcher and Keith Joseph could not have put it better themselves.

In 1990, on the bicentenary of Adam Smith's death, Thatcher acknowledged that the philosophy of Smith and Hayek had been most influential on her at Oxford when she had been working out her own basic ideas. 'The market is not a theory,' she declared. 'It is a natural part of society. The market enables you to be self-reliant. The market naturally fulfils natural ambitions. It enables people to use their talents and their humanity. How can you make up a community except of individuals? The community must be built up of responsible individuals.' Looking back to Selsdon Man, she said that the 1970–74 Heath Government had started off by being based upon Smith's and Hayek's principles, but then, 'Certain artificial ideas gained currency . . . This would be unthinkable now. All of a sudden a few of us said, "Look, we didn't get into politics for this." After the defeat of 1974 Keith Joseph and I asked how did it happen? We went back over fundamental philosophy again.'[2]

After the war Hayek followed *The Road to Serfdom* by starting an organization. Ludwig von Mises, the Oxford economist John Jewkes, and Milton Friedman helped him. The philosopher Karl Popper supported him. It came to be called the Mont Pelerin Society after the site of its first meeting in Switzerland in 1947. It was formed by Hayek so that like-minded and – given the pervasive collectivist attitudes in politics, the media and academia at the time – somewhat isolated people could gather in mutual intellectual support. Milton Friedman said of the society: 'For people who, in their home bases, were isolated, who were in a minority, who were always having to look behind to see if they were going to be stabbed

---

[1] Sonia Orwell and Ian Angus (eds.), *The Collected Essays, Journalism and Letters of George Orwell* (London, Penguin, 1970), Vol. 3, p. 143.
[2] BBC Radio Four, 8 July 1990.

in the back, there was a week in which they might have all sorts of disagreements, where they could be open and above board.'[1] Enoch Powell, Keith Joseph, and Geoffrey Howe all became members of the Society (although none attended more than one or two meetings). 'It was a mutual protection society against being caught being politicians,' said Powell,[2] who took the view that the Society was more academic and social than political. At one meeting, just after the murder of Israeli athletes at the Munich Olympics, the presiding chairman, a German, Professor Schmolders, called for a minute of silence for the dead. Powell argued against this, on the wholly logical grounds that deaths in Germany were no more their business than repeated murders in Northern Ireland or South Africa. While everyone else present then stood in silence, Powell sat, arms crossed, isolated.[3]

Hayek's principal effort was to articulate a systematic view embracing many sciences and intellectual disciplines. But he did so in an intellectual atmosphere, not a political one: Powell was right about Mont Pelerin people not liking to be thought to be politicians.

Politicians do not have time for, and are not habituated to concentrated reflection and theorizing. They are concerned with compromise and the right timing necessary to stay at the top in politics. Thinkers such as Hayek are concerned with facts and logic in a perennial effort to establish objective truth. Gladstone once remarked, 'I do not go to Church because the bell tells me to. I go because the bell tells me it is time.' There is right timing in politics, and Thatcher had it. She crystallized a whole set of discontents. She always recognized that the life of politics is not the life of ideological purity: it is a business like any other in which you get done what you can. She was happy that more intellectually disposed – which is not to say brighter – people had worked out a philosophy of business and freedom. Her commitment to theory in the practical world was rather modest. She was always a politician who believed that politics is an honourable profession which draws upon the

[1] David Graham and Peter Clarke, *The New Enlightenment* (London, Macmillan/Channel Four, 1986), p. 16.
[2] Interview, Rt Hon. J. Enoch Powell, MBE, 1 November 1989.
[3] Private information.

world of ideas to clarify and formulate policy, but that the voice of practicality and experience must override pure doctrine.

The world of ideas that Thatcher drew upon came in part from her own reading and thinking. Apart from Hayek, she once stated that *A Time for Greatness* by Herbert Agar, an American commentator, written to support US intervention in the Second World War, calling for a return to morality and a resurgence of courage in the face of Nazism, was one of the most important books she had ever read.[1] She was also impressed and influenced by the writings of Karl Popper, one of the greatest twentieth-century conservative thinkers.[2]

However, the liberal economic thinking that was to influence her most of all was the province of the Institute of Economic Affairs, and was something Thatcher was taken to. She had read Hayek and Popper in the 1940s, but thirty years later their ideas had been overlaid in her mind by the experience of politics. In the 1970s, she consciously re-educated herself, relying on IEA publications, ideas, and people to a great extent.

The IEA was started by a businessman, Antony Fisher, in 1957. He had read Hayek's arguments from *The Road to Serfdom* in the *Reader's Digest* in 1944 when he had been a fighter pilot in the RAF. So impressed was he that he sought out Hayek in the London School of Economics. A liberal, the professor said to him, has to abandon politics and make an 'intellectual case amongst intellectuals for what you believe in'.[3] 'Hayek is our great man,' said Ralph Harris, the first general director of the Institute. 'He always spoke of the spontaneous nature of so many things, and about the atmosphere of things, and about how outcomes are given from intentions.'[4] After the war, Fisher had been involved in Conservative politics, and he now set about creating an organization that would make the intellectual case and would aim itself at converting intellectual opinion exemplified by teachers, students, academics and leading journalists. He asked Ralph Harris, later a prospective Conservative candidate in Scotland and a lecturer in political

[1] Young, *One of Us*, p. 405.
[2] Ibid, pp. 401–2.
[3] Graham and Clarke, *The New Enlightenment*, p. 18.
[4] Interview, Lord Harris, 21 May 1990.

economy at St Andrews University, to speak to the Lewes Conservative Association. After the talk, Fisher outlined his plans for establishing a policy institute to Harris who volunteered his support should anything develop. In the 1950s the Buxted Chicken Company – Fisher's Sussex farm business – took off, and he had the money to set up the IEA. 'His idea was political,' said Harris. 'It was an anti-Fabian idea. We were set up as an educational charity, but he was inspired by the idea that it was an attempt to capture the Conservative Party. He saw the Labour Party as the enemy and the Conservative Party as the natural ally.'[1]

University dons in Britain and overseas were mobilized to support the IEA's work. Typical of the talent mobilized by the Institute in its early years was John Jewkes,[2] who had held chairs at Manchester, and from 1948 to 1969 was Professor of Economic Organization at Oxford. 'He chaired a fund-raising dinner once with about eighty businessmen,' Ralph Harris recalled. 'He was a mild, modest, even shy man. He spoke about the need to help these "mettlesome steeds" and "the whole thing is run on shoelaces. But we need stronger shoelaces!" An academic of that kind, who was totally unworldly in many ways, did that for us.'[3] In 1948 Jewkes had published a rare (because it flew in the face of the Keynesian/collectivist consensus of the time) attack on central planning, *Ordeal By Planning*. He played a central role in the revival of liberal economics in Britain; his influence and that of a number of like-minded supporters at the LSE made the IEA a place of real authority on the price mechanism. Jewkes imparted a strong sense that political manipulation was replacing government and that this process should be resisted in the interests of nationality and individual freedom and opportunity. Karl Marx, after all, had set as a communist goal the substitution of the administration of things for the government of men.

Ralph Harris remained general director of the IEA until 1987

[1] Ibid.
[2] Jewkes was also a Visiting Professor at the University of Chicago in 1953–4. During the war he was director of the economic section of the War Cabinet Secretariat in 1941; director-general of statistics and programmes, Ministry of Aircraft Production, 1943, and principal assistant secretary, Office of the Minister of Reconstruction, 1944. He was made CBE in 1943.
[3] Interview, Lord Harris, 21 May 1990.

when he became chairman. His hobbies he described as 'conjuring and devising spells against over-government.'[1] He modified Antony Fisher's original idea, seeking to ensure that the Institute did not become identified with any particular political Party: 'We started in 1957 and genuinely we told each other each week that we were now going straight and that you don't put your trust in principalities and power and politics and Parties and these frail characters. It was a marvellous period. We had no allies anywhere. The Liberal Party had stopped being liberal; the Tory Party was captured by Macmillan; the Labour Party was with Wilson and the "Budapest twins", [the Keynesian economists] Kaldor and Balogh. It wasn't difficult to be totally disembodied as far as politics went. We were academics. We recruited people – Graham Hutton, Colin Clark. I discovered afterwards that they were all Fabians, they were all active socialists before the war. They got fed up with the Tory Party and all that Baldwinism and protectionism. And we built up in the 1950s a group that was driven not from Conservative-type leaders, but from a liberal, awkward squad, renegade, former socialists like Colin Clark. We built up a network. In the same way that Sherman gave Keith Joseph reassurance, we had people like Lionel Robbins and Colin Clark and John Jewkes and Basil Yamey and Frank Paish and Harry Johnson and Sydney Caine, a dozen or more really powerful academics.'[2] 'The Institute of Economic Affairs,' runs the note in each of its publications, 'was set up as a research and educational trust under a trust deed signed in 1955. It began regular publication in 1957 with specialized studies of markets and prices. It is a company, limited by guarantee, controlled by Managing Trustees, and independent of any political party.' When Harris was ennobled in 1979, he sat in the House of Lords as an independent.

In 1959 a Liberal Party supporter, Arthur Seldon, became editorial director. He was born in the East End of London during the First World War and lost both his parents before he was three years old. Later, despite this, he won a scholarship to the London School of Economics. He became a dedicated exponent of the virtues of

[1] *Who's Who* (London, A & C Black, 1991), p. 760.
[2] Interview, Lord Harris, 21 May 1990.

capitalism and the market, and a thoughtful opponent of collectivist theories. At the IEA for almost thirty years he presided over texts aimed at students, not pamphlets on ephemeral topics, arguing the case for less statism and more trust in the individual. In his major book written in retirement, *Capitalism*, he engaged upon the same intellectual debate he had at the Institute. He argued that the quality of service in education, health, old-age pensions and housing would be much improved if they were to be made entirely private. Since most people are not particularly interested in the political life, he considered, politics in all Parties tends to be dominated by pressure groups, including bureaucrats who have vested interests in continuing to spend vast proportions of their countries' gross national products. In place of Abraham Lincoln's ideal of democracy of, by and for the people, we have government of the busy, by the bossy, for the bully. Britain, in his view, had been hit hard by this development. Since the outbreak of the Second World War, he held, most of the British 'bossy' had been educated privately but operated a system in which ninety-three per cent of children were in state schools. When state education failed to equip children for a competitive world, the 'bossy' decided that more state intervention – in housing, nationalization, pensions, the health industry – was necessary. This was the collectivist consensus that operated from 1939 to 1979, and despite more than a decade of Margaret Thatcher in Number Ten, Seldon believed, it had not been transformed.[1]

Arthur Seldon's view was representative of the IEA, and until Keith Joseph and Margaret Thatcher turned towards the Institute, it was either ignored or derided by most politicians and commentators. Being independent of Party in the first twenty years was therefore to a large extent making a virtue of a necessity. It was Conservatives who proved most open to the Institute's arguments. Enoch Powell wrote an early IEA pamphlet, *Saving in a Free Society*, in 1960; after the 1964 general election, Keith Joseph began to read the Institute's publications and to discuss economic theory with Harris, Seldon and others there. In 1974 Joseph asked the IEA to provide him with the course of tuition in what Harris

[1] Arthur Seldon, *Capitalism* (Oxford, Basil Blackwell, 1990).

termed classical liberalism which helped bring him to his 'conversion' to Conservatism.

Aside from being a repository of unfashionable ideas in the 1950s and 1960s, the IEA acted as a catalyst to business. 'There is no question that it was timely, it was well-poised, it was independent,' said Harris, looking back at the foundation period. 'Antony Fisher put up some cash, enough to keep us going for the first six months or a year while we tried our hand. We had an advisory council. There were teachers, students, conferences, our lunches were all seminars around the table with non-Keynesians: we would bring in some Keynesians, of course. We didn't have a rigid compartmentalism. But we tried to cement a strong band of market thinkers. It worked extremely well.'[1] 'Had it not been for the Institute of Economic Affairs,' said Alfred Sherman, testifying to the work of the Institute, 'there would have been no Thatcher Revolution. They prepared the ground. They were the John the Baptist of the 1950s and 1960s – *pace* Enoch Powell – the voice crying in the wilderness.'[2]

Antony Fisher was a businessman, and the essential focus of the IEA was with the efficiency (or otherwise) of the market. The ordeal of planning was suffered not only by individuals, but by the community of business. Enterprising businessmen supported the IEA financially and personally. Nigel Vinson, chairman of the trustees, summarized his philosophy: 'My whole philosophical motivations are to diffuse and spread wealth. I believe in the market as a means and mechanism to a free society; I don't believe in the market *per se*. I think the market is the least worst mechanism we have for achieving the free society we want, but markets are not in themselves perfect. Nor are human beings. But the markets will naturally oligopolize given half a chance, and so you must consciously make your market diffuse wealth the whole time so that it renews itself and starts again. The free society comes first, not the market.'[3]

Hayek, Friedman, Powell, Alfred Sherman, Keith Joseph, Ralph Harris (who was also an active member of the Mont Pelerin Society)

[1] Interview, Lord Harris, 21 May 1990.
[2] Interview, Sir Alfred Sherman, 30 April 1990.
[3] Interview, Lord Vinson, 30 May 1990.

and the thinkers at the Institute of Economic Affairs variously provided a cogent, comprehensive alternative to Keynesianism and Butskellism, and a base for Margaret Thatcher to pin her instincts and convictions to. The Institute of Economic Affairs played a vital part in keeping flying the flags of classical liberal economics and of monetarism against the prevailing winds of professional economic and political opinion. By the later 1970s, its tenacity began to pay off.

During the 1979 general election, Jim Callaghan, who felt in his bones that a political sea-change was occurring in Britain, did not have it in his heart to take advantage of the change because to do so would mean hammering the trade unions to which he, personally, owed so much of his career.[1] So confident was he of his assessment that six hours before the voting booths closed Callaghan telephoned Number Ten from his constituency in Cardiff to say that he was certain that Margaret Thatcher would take over as Prime Minister the next day, Friday, 4 May, and that his personal staff should prepare to leave Number Ten by 3.30 in the afternoon.[2] Thatcher won the 1979 general election on a platform of reducing public expenditure, strong defence and law and order, and dealing with trade union power. It was not much different from Heath's 1970 platform. There was a swing of seven per cent to the Conservatives, giving her sixty-nine seats more than Labour, and an overall parliamentary majority of forty-one.

[1] Denis Healey, *The Time of My Life* (London, Michael Joseph, 1989), p. 467: 'Jim Callaghan belonged to the generation of Labour leaders which had come to depend on the trade union block vote for protection against extremism in the constituencies; moreover, the trade unions had provided his main political base' in the 1960s. Bernard Donoughue, *Prime Minister* (London, Jonathan Cape, 1987), p. 189: Jim Callaghan 'was accustomed to working in comradeship with traditional trade union leaders. He had for a lifetime dealt on the basis that if he made a settlement with the top half dozen union leaders he had made a deal which would stick. He had made many such deals during 1978–9 but the union leaders were unable to deliver.'

[2] Donoughue, *Prime Minister*, p. 186.

TEN

Denis Thatcher

As the first woman Prime Minister in Number Ten, Margaret Thatcher might have posed a problem for her husband, Denis. He was a successful businessman and a member of the Second World War generation: if he had been true to type, he might have been nonplussed by his wife's achievement, and by her formal precedence. Instead, he fully supported her career and the realization of her professional ambitions. 'I do not have to worry about money,'[1] she said as an MP early on. Twenty years later as Prime Minister she acknowledged: 'Denis's money got me on my way.'[2] As the Prime Minister's consort, he was always correct and self-effacing.

Denis Thatcher was the first of her people. It was his money and common sense (insiders describe him as her 'bell-wether') that provided much of his wife's base. Her changes are called 'The Thatcher Revolution', not 'The Roberts Revolution', and carry an implicit acknowledgement to him. He was a shrewd, effective financial and industrial trouble-shooter who successfully slimmed down companies and made more productive use of their assets. He was also an unusually liberal husband for his generation. As a model, he has had an enormous influence on his wife's views and way of thinking. 'Denis has his own life and work and that's been very important to both of us,' said his wife. 'He's not my second fiddle. He's first fiddle in his own orchestra. In fact, he's his own conductor.'[3]

The *Private Eye* portrait of Denis as a gin-swigging, golf-obsessed ninny has an element of truth, but is substantially wide of the mark. He does like a drink – sometimes more than one – and his opinions

[1] *Guardian*, 23 March 1962.
[2] Penny Junor, *Margaret Thatcher* (London, Sidgwick & Jackson, 1983), p. 35.
[3] *Daily Express*, 20 February 1986.

are those of an unintellectual business type. To this degree John Wells (the author of the 'Dear Bill' letters in *Private Eye*) provided a distillation of the man. 'I once asked John Wells where he got his copy from for the "Dear Bill" letters,' Frank Giles recalled. 'He said, "Well, every so often – about once a month – I need to recharge my batteries. So I go to the Home Counties, Godalming or somewhere like that, and I go into the snug of a large pub and I listen to the talk. And that's it!" Super Tory talk of "Hang the buggers!" and "Bunch of Reds!" That kind of talk.'[1] 'Downing Street drinks are infrequent, and very weak,' an MP remembered. 'I was standing talking to Denis, both of us holding a glass, and at that point the Prime Minister was called away from the room. She came over to Denis and said, "I've got to take the call. I'll be back," and she left. Whereupon Denis crooked his finger at the waiter, took my glass out of my hand and put it and his down on the waiter's tray, and said, "Now, bring us two proper ones!" So we had two proper ones, and then two more proper ones! And when we were in the middle of the second ones, the Prime Minister returned, and she walked straight over to Denis – and they were gin and tonics, and you can't tell – and she said, "I know what you're doing: you're having proper ones! Put them back at once!"'[2] In this, her *official* world, she is the boss and Denis is clearly expected to support her. In their private life, he is in charge.

'Denis Thatcher is very important,' observed a Number Ten insider. 'She has no chums in the Cabinet. Denis provides that for her: she can talk to him without worrying, in ways and about people and events that she cannot talk to anyone else about. He is quite unlike the "Dear Bill" image. He is no intellectual. His opinions are straightforward and black and white. He is the only person who can tell her off, and he does. At the Party Conference when everyone is helping on the speech, and it is three o'clock in the morning and you are desperate to end and everything that's being said is making the speech worse, not better, and you'll agree to almost anything just to end it, he comes in and says "Margaret, that's enough! Go to bed. You'll just look tired in the morning,

[1] Interview, Frank Giles, 28 January 1990.
[2] Interview, 20 January 1990.

and you know how important it is to look well." And she'll do it.'[1]
'Come to bed, woman!' he said late one night in the Prime Minister's apartment in Number Ten when she was working with some
of her advisers on a speech. 'You're not writing the bloody Bible!'[2]
'Denis does boss her about,' said a member of the Number Ten
Policy Unit. 'I caught a glimpse of this once. We were all up in the
flat, and they were discussing their diaries, changing dates and
appointments. Her diary changes at a rate of knots during the day,
and they were discussing her diary, and I heard a snippet, "What
about Wednesday?" she asked him. "No, it can't be that!" he said
definitely. And that, to me, set the relationship: that simple little
phrase.'[3]

On one occasion in a London club with an acquaintance, Denis
encountered the new chairman of the Board of Governors of the
BBC, Marmaduke ('Duke') Hussey. 'Duke hadn't taken up the
appointment yet, but his name was common knowledge,' said
the acquaintance. 'Denis Thatcher came in and started talking to
him. "You've got to do something about that place!" Duke
Hussey didn't open his mouth. "You've got to do something
about that place. It's a nest of vipers! A lot of bloody Reds!
You've got to get it back under control!" I was pig in the middle
of this, and I said, "Oh, come on! Every Government says that
about the BBC. Labour used to say that too. Must mean they've
got it about right." This infuriated him. "How can you talk such
rubbish? It's well-known that they're a nest of Reds!" That was
Denis Thatcher. He believes it. And he's got these phrases.
Hussey didn't say a word.'[4]

'He's terribly clubby,' said a friend. 'He's a self-caricature. Before
the war, gentlemen carried silver cigarette cases: they did not carry
paper packs. He still carries a silver case. Then they would produce
a cigarette from it – everyone smoked much more then than they
do now. Denis puffs away like a chimney. And he produces this
thing, and tap, tap, tap, tap, tap, on and on and on and on, tapping
the end of the cigarette against the case, which was done much

[1] Interview, 13 February 1990.
[2] Interview, 21 May 1990.
[3] Interview, 30 May 1990.
[4] Interview, 28 January 1990.

more when cigarettes were more loosely packed than they are today. And this tapping personifies him to me as someone in the snug of the Dorking Golf Club circa 1935.'[1] 'I don't pretend I'm anything but an honest-to-God right-winger,' he once admitted.[2] Like most of us, he has also become more stereotypical with age.

That was one side of Denis, and his wife holds similar views too: old-fashioned, hang 'em, flog 'em conservative. The other side of Denis is far more interesting and, given the Home Counties Golf Club opinions, unpredictable. 'He's not in the least like the "Dear Bill" portrait in *Private Eye*,' said Robert Blake, making the point that Denis's business experience has weight to it. 'It's very funny, and he laughs at it himself, but he doesn't really talk like that at all.'[3] He has many admirable qualities – most of the qualities of Alfred Roberts, Margaret's father – and good judgement. His social ability has been very important, much more so than that of a wife of a Head of Government. It cannot be easy for a successful and opinionated man to play not even second fiddle (*pace* Mrs Thatcher), but *n*th fiddle in the political band, but he does it without remark. One guest at Number Ten noted about Denis: 'He's marvellous socially. She can drop tactless remarks and ignore people, and he always counterbalances that. In general, she hasn't got much time for women, and when we were being received my wife went first. And, of course, Margaret shook hands, and she looked past her at me and said, "Oh, how lovely to see you!" ignoring my wife completely. But Denis, standing next to her, moved in and said to my wife "How lovely to see you!" and kissed her hand. That's typical. He instinctively picks those things up.'[4]

As a woman of enormous ambition, Margaret Roberts needed an anchor to swing at, and Denis provided that with grace. 'Somebody with her enormous energy wants something comfortable and non-combative to return to, I would think,' said one of her people. 'He gives her the sort of moral and physical support she needs. He's always nice and polite and kind, and I think his country owes him

---

[1] Interview, 28 January 1990.
[2] *The Times*, 5 October 1970.
[3] Interview, Lord Blake, 16 August 1989.
[4] Interview, 16 August 1989.

a lot behind the scenes for what he's done for her.'[1] In the later 1940s, the young men of enormous ambition and of romantic quality were not looking for Miss Roberts: they were looking for dowries or Lady Mary X or The Hon. Susan Y. The men most like her did not want girls like her. But had Lord Edward Aristocrat, a war hero or a promising something, asked for her hand, she would have found it difficult to control her beating heart: indeed, she did have a fling with an Earl's son at Oxford. Above all else, Margaret Roberts wanted a man who was going somewhere, and although it took a bit of time for her to see it, Denis was going somewhere – in business. She would probably have loved to marry a major in the Green Jackets, but he would have had to treat her as an equal in the way that Denis did, and that was asking too much of most men in the 1940s and 1950s. There has never been 'Be quiet, little girl! Don't worry your head about that!' about Denis, even in the earliest stages of the marriage. He recognized that (in his terms) he had a live one on his hands. 'What caught my eye were the same qualities as now,' he said in an interview when she became Party leader in 1975. 'She was beautiful, very kind and thoughtful. Who could meet Margaret without being completely slain by her personality and intellectual brilliance?'[2] 'Denis does like a bit of glitter,' Margaret remarked.[3] 'I was just lucky with [him]. Absolutely marvellous. He's always encouraged me to use one's talents.'[4]

Denis Thatcher, over the two years he knew Margaret before they married, accurately saw her range, drive and resourcefulness. By then, she was working as a chemist developing adhesives for British Xylonite Plastics, or researching ice cream and cake fillings for J. Lyons & Co., standing as a Conservative candidate in hopeless seats in the traditional way of starting as a Tory MP, and studying for the Bar.

Denis is hardworking and upright. As a boy, he played golf with his father, and continued to be a keen golfer, but never reached more than a twenty-two handicap. He is an avid rugby fan, and enjoys television sports coverage. 'He has his rugger cronies,' said

[1] Interview, 30 May 1990.
[2] Ibid.
[3] *The Times*, 17 November 1986.
[4] Chris Ogden, *Maggie* (New York, Simon & Schuster, 1990), p. 339.

Margaret, 'and I have a circle of political friends. We have a life together and a life apart and I think that is very important.'[1] He is a man of mettle, with very few close friends. At the age of eight he was sent to Mill Hill preparatory school as a boarder. He went straight from school into the Royal Artillery, becoming a professional soldier. During the war he served in Sicily and France, rising to the rank of major and being mentioned in dispatches and made MBE. He married in 1942, but was divorced in 1946.[2] In 1945 his father died and Denis left the Army to run the family business, Atlas Preservatives, founded by his grandfather, a farmer, who had invented a sheep-dip and a weedkiller.

In the 1920s and 1930s, the firm had expanded further into chemicals and paints, and by the time Denis took over as managing director it was a sizeable concern. He made it even more successful, and he was sufficiently prosperous to court (and marry in December 1951) Margaret Roberts in a Jaguar motor car at a time when rationing of food, clothes, and fuel was still a fact of British life. In 1965 Burmah Oil bought out the family business, making Denis a millionaire. He stayed on as a director of Burmah until 1975, and then, aged sixty, left the company. He did not retire from business, however, and undertook a number of different directorships.

Denis Thatcher's great skill was in doing nothing that could have embarrassed his wife's political career. He has been her greatest and most constant supporter, and has always tried to give her good advice, even when she has not liked what he has to say. 'Sometimes she does not like what he tells her, but she knows he is totally on her side,' said Willie Whitelaw.[3] She trusts his instincts about people and his judgement of situations. During the 1987 general election campaign, as the Labour Party campaign kicked-off with a ritzy Party Political Broadcast by Hugh Hudson who had directed the film, *Chariots of Fire*, and as some opinion polls suggested she might lose the election, nerves in Number Ten were taut. David Young went with Tim Bell to the Prime Minister's apartment in Number Ten to outline an election strategy, and noted afterwards that 'Denis

<hr>

[1] *Daily Mail*, 3 May 1980.
[2] His first wife was also a Margaret.
[3] *Time*, 14 August 1989, quoted in Ogden, *Maggie*, p. 66.

kept on encouraging her to listen to us.'[1] She had a weakness for charming and well turned-out men, mistaking style for ability; he was good at seeing through charm and assessing people and talent accurately.

He encouraged and paid for what he must have seen as his wife's hobby in the first decades of their marriage, and then gave up in the 1970s, without apparent complaint, any chance for a regular and private life. 'The criticism has been vicious,' Margaret said in 1972 when her ending of free school milk was being attacked, 'but in the end you have to build an armour round yourself, knowing the things they say aren't true. I think it's worse for my husband, having to sit back and listen to it all. When he sees me tired, of course he says "Why don't you give this job up?"'[2] 'She'd give it up for him,' said a long-standing political colleague. 'She knows what he's given up for her.'[3]

Denis takes vicarious pleasure from her achievement. He is proud of her and happy for her. He did not dream of all her success, but he could see when he married her that she would be a first-class barrister and that when she got into Parliament she would probably get into the Cabinet. In business terms, he was backing a winner. He was the kind of businessman who marries an actress and is thrilled then to be taken into a world which he had previously only viewed through a glass with his nose pressed up against it. Also, for him, the marriage was the second time around and to a woman ten years younger: part of his gentleness and support to her derives from these factors. He had his generation's deference to the liberal professions, too, and Margaret as a barrister achieved a degree of superiority to him in his own estimation. He knew she was something special, that she was bright, hardworking, articulate, good-looking – not your average girl – and he has treasured her ever since.

It is easy to forget the simple human needs of people in positions of power and authority, to treat Prime Ministers as if they are

[1] Lord Young, 'Diary of a Near Disaster', *Sunday Times*, 2 September 1990, extracted from Lord Young, *The Enterprise Years: A Businessman in the Cabinet* (London, Headline, 1990), diary entry for Saturday, 23 May 1987.
[2] *Daily Mail*, 8 February 1972.
[3] Ogden, *Maggie*, p. 62.

unemotional automatons of office, functioning all the time as clear-headed assessors of risks, moods, policies and people. This was not something that Denis Thatcher ever forgot, and he was never frightened by or in awe of his wife either. 'He fully supports her,' said one of her close advisers about being in Number Ten with the Thatchers. 'I don't see him at all during the normal course of the day. If I am doing a normal day until about eight o'clock, there'll never be a sign of him. But if I am having to do work that involves weekends or late nights or suppers, he's almost always there. He'll come to lunch or dinner and then let us get on with it. But if it's late nights, and it's going on until midnight or one o'clock, then he'll come in and say, "Are you still at it?! God! You can't be doing anything constructive at this hour!"'[1]

In October 1989 when the Chancellor of the Exchequer, Nigel Lawson, rocked the Government by resigning either over an article by her personal economic adviser, Sir Alan Walters, or over the question of British membership of the European Monetary System (it was never clear which of the two issues was central to his resignation), the Prime Minister became most dispirited. Her colleagues and officials worried that she might throw in the towel, and in one interview she said that she did not intend to stay on as Prime Minister very much longer. Denis was vital to her personal recovery. 'He came up to us when Nigel and everything was breaking,' said a Downing Street official, 'and said, "Well, are we still in power?!" He would be quite happy to go home. He treats it light-heartedly. He manages to defuse tension. I think that she could not do the job without him.'[2] 'If she says she should go, which she does from time to time,' an aide said at that period, 'he'll say, "Right! As far as I'm concerned we can pop off on Tuesday! I'll be overjoyed!" She quite enjoys that. She says, "Denis always says to me 'It's got to be Tuesday!' Whatever it is, it's always next Tuesday that we're going to give up."'[3] Ironically, it was on a Tuesday – 20 November 1990 – that Michael Heseltine effectively torpedoed her stay in Number Ten when he polled 152 votes to her 204 in the leadership election.

[1] Interview, 20 February 1990.
[2] Interview, 20 February 1990.
[3] Interview, 20 February 1990.

Denis probably really was glad when she resigned the Premiership, although he was concerned and unhappy at her obvious distress. Just before midnight on Christmas Eve, 1970, some months after her father's death, she was deeply upset. She missed her father very much. She had always been close to him, and she revered him in a simple way. It was late and the children were in bed. She was crying. 'Why don't you chuck it all in?' asked Denis. 'You don't have to put up with this. Why go on?' But the steely determination to win in a man's world that was the strongest characteristic of her life, from her becoming a chemist to a barrister to a Cabinet Minister, was never far away. 'I'll see them in hell first,' she replied.[1]

Margaret Thatcher admits to crying from time to time, but it is not a sensitive reaction: it is an emotional one. She is saying that instead of screaming and raging, she cries her heart out because she does not like the people she works with in the world of politics. Indeed, she does not like many people. She is an instinctively discontented person, and regards energy as by-passing discontent. Denis is a contented man, but he does not like many people either.

In contrast to his public performance, in private Denis expressed his views to her without hesitation, and offered advice in robust soldier-speak. Once when John Hoskyns, Ian Gow, Ronnie Millar and the Prime Minister were talking together, one said to the other, 'Why can't you stop being so fucking obstinate?!' Then, a minute or two later the speaker, realizing his gaffe, said, 'Margaret, I do apologize for my language.' 'Don't worry,' she said. 'I'm used to it.'[2] And she was reportedly prepared to use earthy language herself. When Michael Heseltine angrily walked out of a Cabinet meeting during the Westland affair, and announced his resignation outside, still indoors and not sure exactly what Heseltine was doing, the Prime Minister allegedly asked, 'Has he resigned, or has he gone for a pee?'[3]

Her husband's opinions – and experience – did impress other

[1] Ogden, *Maggie*, pp. 111–12.
[2] Interview, 21 May 1990.
[3] Michael Mates, MP, in *World In Action*, Granada Television, 25 November 1990.

people at times. At a dining club evening, a member recalled discussing industrial relations and training policies with Denis. 'Someone started up the question of whether the relations between the workforce and the boardrooms are adequate. Are they suitably geared to what we need? Should there be, perhaps, worker representation on Boards? He wouldn't have any of this. "It's a mistake, a great mistake," he said. "It will never work." He spoke as an industrialist and as a director of companies himself. He wouldn't admit that it's a good idea not to have a directors' dining room as is the case in Japanese companies where in everyday life the directors go down to the canteen and take their places with the workers. That absolutely wouldn't be a good thing here, he said. "The workforce wouldn't like it, anyway." Those were his views. 'But I wouldn't think that she would be against worker participation or directors' mucking-in in the canteen.'[1] 'He's no fool at all,' said another dining friend. 'He's very interesting about the problems of British industry and the lack of proper training for people. He knows his stuff about all that. He's very much an encourager of the entrepreneurial economy.'[2]

Inside Number Ten, Denis Thatcher did not intrude, but his presence was felt. He was careful to avoid the limelight or intruding on her working day, but he did speak out. One official in Number Ten observed: 'Denis will express very, very strong views on policy. He will express strong views on anything where he has knowledge – which is usually business. So something like the bid for Jaguar Motors, on anything like that he knows a great deal and he will have spoken. He had strong views about the brewers' monopoly of public houses. He is very much a businessman: he still sits on some Boards. He's very good at reading a balance sheet and summing up whether or not a business is a properly-run affair or not. I don't say that she consults him, but she takes him very seriously. I don't think he has ever asked to see briefing papers: all the opinions he expresses will be based upon public information.'[3] 'He's a terribly genuine person,' said John Biffen. 'He's quite unselfconscious about holding views that were down-the-line Golf Club views. I don't

[1] Interview, 28 January 1990.
[2] Interview, 16 August 1989.
[3] Interview, 20 February 1990.

know how successful he'd been in business, and I had very little personal dealing with him, but I always thought that he was a decided plus in the court, not least because he was one person who could exercise very clear authority with her. And I think that he discussed quite a lot of the great issues with her, particularly in the economic field, but he'd bring to it the fairly brisk approach of the accountant rather than that of business-philosopher, management-consultant. I think he is like a Finance Director. He'd be there saying, "What Britain needs is more production engineers," and so on.'[1]

His wife has, in fact, acknowledged a professional debt to him. 'I discuss a number of political things with him,' she told an interviewer in 1980. 'He's absolutely marvellous on industry. We discuss the nationalized industries. He's great at looking through the balance sheets. I can say to him: "Look, is this firm in difficulties or isn't it? Tell me. Look at the figures. Do you think they'll need to borrow, and how much?" I really can draw on his experience . . . And then on broad issues he'll sometimes say: "Look, you've gone too far this time. Don't get too intense about this problem."'[2] Through his directorship of the British international waste-disposal company, Atwoods, he has company interests in the United States, one of them being a municipal cleaning firm in Florida. At a dinner party once he talked about the Florida company. 'He talked about it not just as a business venture, but what it can mean for municipal government,' remembered another guest at the dinner. 'I didn't get the impression of a razor intellect. But I did have the impression of a businessman talking business: a businessman who, if he has a wife, simply by pointing out to her certain basic facts of economic life, is likely to have a considerable influence on her. There's nothing like being married to a businessman to understand the actual facts of the market economy. He was a good expositor. His language was very emphatic. He waved his drink in front of me and leant forward and was very enthusiastic.'[3]

But his business acumen does not mean that his wife takes on his opinions as her own. 'Denis's influence in terms of direct policy is

[1] Interview, Rt Hon. John Biffen, MP, 6 June 1990.
[2] *Daily Mail*, 5 March 1980.
[3] Interview, Charles Mosley, 25 May 1990.

pretty small, but his influence in terms of her stability is far greater than one might think,' is the view of one of her closest campaign advisers. 'He is one rock that is always there for her. Everybody has to have that. All human beings need comfort and one point of certainty, and he keeps her down to earth as best he can.'[1]

His business experience played a direct part in his wife's economic thinking: Alan Walters and Keith Joseph were not the only ones to whom she listened. Free market principles were always close to Denis's heart, and he was never slow to enunciate them. He would frequently denounce Government intervention, let alone nationalization, and was extremely critical (in private) of Heath's U-turn. Monetarist theories meant little to him, but he was a strong advocate of controlling the supply of money in the economy rather than having prices and incomes policies. In the view of Willie Whitelaw, Denis made a 'great contribution' to his wife's 'incredible achievements'.[2] Within a week of Margaret Thatcher's resignation as Prime Minister, this contribution was rewarded by her with a baronetcy.[3]

---

[1] Interview, 5 June 1990.

[2] William Whitelaw, *The Whitelaw Memoirs* (London, Aurum Press, 1989), p. 265. This is the only mention of Denis Thatcher in the autobiography. In Whitelaw's view, 'the country as a whole has increasingly recognized' the importance of Denis in the Thatcher revolution.

[3] Technically, the Queen awards honours. In the case of Denis Thatcher's baronetcy (an hereditary knighthood), however, the hand of his wife is clear. A consequence of the honour was that their son, Mark, would one day be Sir Mark, and that their grandson, Michael, would one day be Sir Michael. 'Isn't my mother wonderful,' Mark Thatcher said. 'Doing this for me and my son.' (*Mail on Sunday*, 20 January 1991).

ELEVEN

Inside Number Ten

Unlike Denis, Margaret Thatcher has a theoretical mind. But like Denis, she was not in search of new beliefs and truths – quite the reverse, in fact. She wanted a series of hard, practical achievements that would stand the test of time and, she and her people hoped, would become the common ground of political debate. She did not want endless exploration. She wanted certainty. When she came into Number Ten first in 1979, she wanted trade union reform, wider share and home ownership in the interests of greater individual liberty, and to deal with inflation by keeping money 'honest' through monetarism.

Alan Walters, Keith Joseph and Alfred Sherman – and behind them Enoch Powell and the thinkers in Vienna, Chicago and at the Institute of Economic Affairs – were instrumental in bringing her around to monetarist principles. However, every complex system inherently contains contradictions, and it was not long before her monetarism was in trouble. The political columnist Adam Raphael, writing three months before the 1979 general election, noted: 'Mrs T has a knack of making policy, as it were, on the wing . . . [I]t is one of the things that make her an exciting politician. Instead of expecting the usual bland defensive stream of known and agreed party positions, one is on the edge of one's seat waiting for a new leap into the unknown. But political excitement has its price.'[1]

Thatcherism was always wider than a set of economic principles, but in 1979 in the area of economics she focused on monetary policy. The determination that the Government's main economic activity should be restricted to adjustments in the money supply was a dogma that was too limited: Keith Joseph's warning in 1976 that 'monetarism is not enough' had not been heeded. She had

[1] *Observer*, 14 January 1979.

inherited in 1979 nationalized industries such as railways, mines, shipbuilding, automobiles, aircraft, steel, as well as State monopolies in a host of areas – broadcasting, telecommunications, gas, electricity, power generation, water – and an economy in recession. However, the problem was that the insistence on 'pure' monetarist methods for dealing with the economy was coming from the politicians (in this case the Prime Minister and her Chancellor, Geoffrey Howe) rather than the Treasury. Thatcher and her people were suspicious of the civil servants, although Thatcher less so: 'I said to her that the day the advisers got into Government,' Alfred Sherman recalled, 'they'd be appointed as temporary civil servants even before the Ministers were appointed. Civil servants: circumstances determine their consciousness; they cannot act in any other way. She said "They're honourable men." I said, "So are they all, all honourable men."'[1]

Thatcher was adamant that there should be no civil servant with the influence and power that William Armstrong had wielded under Heath, and in any event believed that the upper echelons of the service were tainted by the Governmental experience of the 1960s and 1970s. She was also clear in her own mind that she first had to stop the leaks in the *SS Great Britain* and get it a bit further off the rocks, and that there would be real – but necessary – hardship for the country along the way. In this respect, her determination plugged into the country's own awareness: people were willing to make sacrifices as long as they saw that their sacrifices would purchase a better future.

Given these attitudes and the early commitment to monetarist principles (notably involving a toleration of high levels of unemployment), the people with most real influence on her were a few close political colleagues (Joseph; Howe; David Howell (Secretary of State for Transport, 1981–3), who drafted several of Thatcher's key speeches in the 1979–81 period; John Nott (Secretary of State for Trade, 1979–81; Secretary of State for Defence, 1981–3); Nigel Lawson (Financial Secretary in 1979–81, Howe's No. 3 at the Treasury)) and the advisers inside Number Ten (John Hoskyns; David Wolfson; Norman Strauss; and in 1980-82 Alan

[1] Interview, Sir Alfred Sherman, 30 April 1990.

213

Walters). 'I think if you ask Mrs Thatcher to whom she owes the greatest debt of gratitude, I think she'd say Keith,' said Ian Gow. 'At the start there were breakfasts in the flat. Keith always went, and John Nott and Geoffrey, I think, always went too. These were trusted friends who were regarded as being "One of Us". Then these breakfasts were discontinued because their existence leaked out.'[1] Joseph and the advisers were very much her people, chosen by her to be by her side rather than there because of departmental imperatives. Geoffrey Howe was Chancellor because he had demonstrated his commitment to monetarism in the Opposition years.

Outside Number Ten, Alfred Sherman at the CPS played an important advisory and facilitating role, chasing down people and ideas and feeding the ideas into the inner policymakers. Gordon Reece made important connections for Thatcher in the media world, notably with the advertising agency Saatchi & Saatchi, which acted as a lightning rod for ideas and provided analysis and information. 'Gordon said that we needed an advertising agency because adverts are very important,' remembered another adviser, 'so we asked him who was best. And he asked people, and they said Saatchi & Saatchi. There was no relationship with them before that. She didn't meet them until after they were appointed: they met Thorneycroft first.'[2] When she did meet the Saatchi team, she spoke bluntly. 'If by any chance you have the skills to dupe the people,' she said to them, 'please do not use them on my behalf. If they don't want me, I don't want to be elected, because if they don't want me, it won't work!'[3] 'You're now going to work for politicians,' she warned them, 'and I want you to remember that they have very large fingers and very large toes and you can tread on them remarkably easily. I, however, have stubs!'[4] From this introduction came some memorable – and effective – advertising campaigns, notably the 1979 slogan and poster showing a winding queue of people approaching an unemployment office, 'Labour Isn't Working'. 'It was one of those happy coincidences,' said a member of the Saatchi

---

[1] Interview, Ian Gow, 8 August 1989. David Wolfson and Ian Gow would also usually be present so as to be able to co-ordinate decisions that might be made.
[2] Interview, 5 June 1990.
[3] Ibid.
[4] Interview, 5 June 1990.

team. 'We all came together at the right time. It so happened that she ended up with people who believed in her and her policies, and that's why we did such good work.'[1]

The relationship with the Saatchis lasted until 1987 when, after the general election that year, the agency resigned the account. It was seen as an emblematic relationship. The agency, started in 1970, rose rapidly in the esteem of adland, mirroring Margaret Thatcher's own rise in the political world. After winning the 1979 election, Thatcher proceeded to encompass a decade of achievement. So did the Saatchis. And then, by the end of the 1980s, they both seemed to falter. Saatchi & Saatchi, having rapidly expanded to become one of the biggest agencies in the world, had to sell off acquisitions to secure liquidity. The firm entered 1990 as one of the UK's top 500 companies; by the end of the year it was no longer in that list. Margaret Thatcher, by the spring of 1990, enjoyed the lowest opinion poll ratings of any Prime Minister, ever, and by the end of the year had resigned.

Out of the connection with Saatchi & Saatchi came a Thatcher insider: Tim Bell. He was young – born in 1941 – and a grammar school boy from Barnet, Hertfordshire. After school, he went into television briefly, but in 1961 joined Colman, Prentis & Varley, famous as the Conservative Party's advertising agency. By 1970, when he joined the Saatchis as media director with 2.5 per cent of the ordinary shares in the new company, he was regarded as one of the best in the business. He had a ready smile and was charming, witty, very able, and politically astute. He was respected in the advertising industry, and admired for promoting women to senior positions. He became the public face of the agency, and the point man on the Conservative party account. Salman Rushdie (who had worked in advertising himself) in his novel, *The Satanic Verses*, was reputed to have used Bell as the basis of one of his characters, John Maslama, who made 'his first pile' by writing musical jingles for advertisements. Bell worked closely with Gordon Reece, and rapidly became a favourite of Margaret Thatcher. 'He makes her laugh,' said one of her people in Number Ten, remarking on his ability to cheer her up.[2] His success with the Conservative account

1 Interview, 5 June 1990.
2 Interview, 14 February 1990.

was a central factor in the City's support for the international expansion of the agency. In 1985 Bell left, starting his own agency with new partners. In the 1987 general election campaign, he was called in by David Young to second-guess Saatchi & Saatchi, the official Conservative Party campaign publicists, thus providing one of the main causes for Norman Tebbit's falling out with Thatcher. At the start of the campaign, Young arranged for Bell secretly to advise the Prime Minister. 'I asked her if she had had a good meeting with Tim Bell,' Young recorded in his diary. 'She looked startled, and said "Shh" – evidently it had been a very good meeting with Tim – but she didn't want Norman to hear.'[1] Tebbit, the Party Chairman, felt that Young's and Bell's activities with Thatcher's support were an implicit criticism of his campaign team and of his election strategy:

'Norman, I must see you – there have been one or two developments,' said Young, about to break the news to him that Bell had been shadowing the Saatchi campaign. 'Come on, I want to show you. She's asked for some other things to be done.'

'Who did this?' asked Tebbit, looking at the rough boards Bell had prepared to illustrate his ideas for the way the election campaign should go.

'Look at the programme,' Young urged, hoping that Tebbit would be won over to Bell's ideas.

'No, no, tell me who did it.'

'Tim Bell.'

'Well, that's it then, that's it.'

'Norman, listen to me,' said Young, grabbing Tebbit by the shoulders, 'we're going to lose this f----- election! You're going to go, I'm going to go, the whole thing is going to go. The entire election depends upon her doing fine performances for the next five days – she has to be happy, we have got to do this. Now look at this campaign, look at it!'

'It looks very good!' Tebbit admitted.

'Yes,' said Young, 'it's very simple – we'll look and see what they've got from Saatchis. If that is better, we'll use that and if this is better, we'll use this. One way or the other we will get it done.'

---

[1] Lord Young, *The Enterprise Years* (London, Headline, 1990), p. 200.

'All right,' said Tebbit unenthusiastically.

'But you've got to!' Young replied. 'It's your future and my future and all our futures, and the future of this flaming country.'

They then looked at the Saatchi programme which, in comparison to Bell's, was judged inadequate by Tebbit.

'This won't do, this won't do at all, it really won't,' he said. 'I don't know . . . she'll go mad when she sees it,' and with Young he went back to look at Bell's plans.

'We've got to use this one, haven't we?' Young said to him.

'Yes,' said Tebbit, 'we have; I can't possibly show her the Saatchi programme.'[1]

Bell represented service industry in Thatcher's inner circle, and something else. Advertising, to an extraordinary degree, is a profession learned through apprenticeship, and one in which people can still go anywhere without qualifications: you prove yourself as you do the job. Thatcher is impatient with qualifications, preferring an American 'can do' approach, and Bell was an example of American-style – rather than traditional British – success. During the 1980s he became a frequent visitor to Number Ten, and a trusted assessor of public opinion and moods. He was central to each of her general election campaigns. In her resignation honours, he received a knighthood.

Her determination to choose her own people had been made very explicit in the first days of her premiership. Adam Ridley, the very able economic adviser to the Shadow Cabinet and assistant director of the Research Department, moved into Number Ten even before she did, and began to set up a political office for her. But he was not one of her people. He was viewed as being a Heathite and a Keynesian, although by 1979 he had moved a fair distance from the views he held in 1974. 'Adam was on the other side,' said Alfred Sherman, on whose Board at the Centre for Policy Studies Ridley had been placed by Heath in 1974 to act as a bridge between it and the Research Department. 'Adam and Chris Patten were trying to stop her being a Thatcherite.'[2] Originally, it had been planned that the Prime Minister's Policy Unit would be

---

[1] Ibid., p. 222.
[2] Interview, Sir Alfred Sherman, 30 April 1990.

headed jointly by Ridley and John Hoskyns, but it soon became clear that Ridley and Howe, who had developed a close relationship in the Opposition years, worked effectively together. It was agreed between them all that Ridley should move next door to work in the Chancellor's office in Number Eleven Downing Street, leaving Hoskyns as head of the Unit.

John Hoskyns came from a military family. His father had been killed in 1940, when commanding one of the three Green Jacket battalions defending Calais. He went to Winchester, leaving in 1945 for a career in the Army, entering the Rifle Brigade and rising to the rank of captain. He left the Army in 1957 to join IBM. In 1964 he started his own computer company, John Hoskyns & Co., later the Hoskyns Group, which he sold in 1975. By then he had developed firm ideas about the needs of British industry, and was convinced that Britain was rapidly declining as an economic power. He cast around for a political voice, at first attracted to Dick Taverne's Democratic Labour group which had split from the Labour Party in 1972. Through Sherman, he met Keith Joseph in 1975, and the next year, through Joseph, he met Margaret Thatcher.

The nub of Hoskyns's practical political interest was not doctrinaire, but was that of a businessman seeking to apply business principles to policy-making and to secure business principles in the policies themselves, all in the interest of a competitive British economy.

Norman Strauss, a management expert with Unilever, became a close colleague and friend of Hoskyns in the later 1970s. Strauss was an intellectually tough and impatient man who gave no quarter when discussing ideas and their applications, and so could be abrasive. Strauss met Joseph at a lunch in 1976. 'Do a paper on profit for me,' Joseph said to him.[1] Joseph introduced Strauss to Alfred Sherman who introduced him to John Hoskyns. 'I polished up a paper that came out of a dinner with Alfred at the CPS,' said Strauss, describing the course of events in 1976–7 that led to his involvement in policymaking. 'I gave it to Alfred. He gave it to her. She demanded to see me. Alfred said, "You'd better take an officer

[1] Interview, Norman Strauss, 30 May 1990.

and a gentleman with you because you'll upset her too much!" That was John, and that's how the team was formed.' Strauss's paper was called 'The Need for New Data' and in it he argued that the Conservatives had to influence the nature of public debate by providing people with more information so as to make them think in a different way and thus be receptive to, and vote for, Thatcher's policies. 'I didn't know it,' said Strauss, 'but the values I was putting into the paper were overlapping her convictions about individual responsibility and sound finance. So the paper hit her value system.'[1] The reception accorded 'The Need for New Data' successfully established the credentials of both Strauss and Hoskyns.

The two had worked together on another paper on election issues for the Shadow Cabinet that came out of Hoskyns's fear that the politicians simply had no grasp of the practical complexity of implementing reform. Joseph had agreed, saying, 'It's very much a second eleven,' about the Shadow Cabinet. 'It seems to me that we might call it "Stepping Stones",' he said, and gave the paper its name.[2] It was written by Hoskyns and Strauss, and presented to Thatcher on 17 November 1977. 'John has a way of taking complexity and structure and making it all manageable, which is quite magnificent,' Strauss said about the paper.[3] It was followed by a small dinner in Margaret Thatcher's rooms in the House of Commons. Present were Thatcher, Joseph, Angus Maude, John Hoskyns and Norman Strauss. After dinner, Willie Whitelaw joined the group.

Hoskyns and Strauss argued that the trade unions stood in the way of the changes that were necessary if socialism was to be eliminated and if an economic infrastructure was to be developed, capable of sustaining the country after North Sea oil. The first section of the paper was entitled 'The Size of the Job', and the first paragraph declared: 'The task of the next Tory Government – national recovery – will be of a different order from that facing any other post-war Government. Recovery requires a sea-change in Britain's political economy. There is one major obstacle: the negative role of the

[1] Ibid.
[2] Interview, Sir John Hoskyns, 25 June 1990.
[3] Interview, Norman Strauss, 25 May 1990.

219

trades unions.'[1] This was emphasized in the paper: 'The one precondition for success will be a complete change in the role of the trades union movement.'[2] They warned in direct terms that there was a real danger of the Conservative Party, in Government, once again trying to reach a deal with the unions instead of confronting them, since confrontation and the severe reduction of union power were essential to economic recovery. 'Any strategy which does not address this problem of the trades union role from the outset ensures failure in office, even though it might, at first sight, appear to make electoral success more likely ... We cannot say "Win the election first, with a low profile on the union problem; then implement a high profile strategy when in power." The countdown for both has already begun.'[3]

In order to achieve this strategy, said Hoskyns and Strauss, it was necessary to change the common wisdom on economic and industrial relations. The unions should be seen as Labour's greatest electoral liability and as the single greatest impediment to a revitalized Britain. A major public relations exercise was necessary to secure the required change in public perceptions. 'Drag every skeleton out of the union cupboard, linking it to Labour,' advised Hoskyns.[4] '"Stepping Stones" became her trade union power secret weapon,' said Strauss. 'I'm sure of that. It was more than that, but in my view that was what she wanted from it.'[5] 'It's the best thing we've had in years,' Thatcher said of the paper.[6]

Jim Prior, responsible in the Opposition years as Shadow Employment Secretary for policy towards the unions, was very much opposed to the 'Stepping Stones' proposals. He wanted a 'softly, softly, catchee monkey' approach, and was a fully paid up member of the school that believed the unions had to be wooed, not confronted. He was proud of being on first-name terms with union leaders. He represented the view prevailing in the Shadow Cabinet that it would be a mistake for the Party to go into the next general election pledged to union reform of any kind, other-

[1] John Hoskyns and Norman Strauss, 'Stepping Stones', 17 November 1977.
[2] Ibid.
[3] Ibid.
[4] Ibid.
[5] Interview, Norman Strauss, 25 May 1990.
[6] Interview, Sir John Hoskyns, 25 June 1990.

wise there would be a replay of 1973–4 with U-turns and panic, and that the electorate would foresee this and so turn against the Party at the polls. *The Right Approach to the Economy*, published in 1977, had contained enough of Prior's view for him to endorse it, and he tried to secure formal sanction of the document as the basis of the Party's election stand: significantly Margaret Thatcher had refused to allow it to be published as a statement of Shadow Cabinet policy. 'Stepping Stones' had encapsulated her conflicting view.

The resulting clash was effectively resolved by Thatcher, who in public stuck with Prior and in private with Hoskyns. From the very first, ambivalence was her *modus operandi*. Surrounded by men, most of whom had supported Ted Heath against her leadership bid and who did not share her fundamentalism, she kept her thoughts to herself and to her inner circle of advisers and supporters. As a Minister under Macmillan, Home and Heath, she had kept her head down, never pursuing disagreement and reining in any desire to distance herself from policies which at the least she must have wondered about. She managed her Shadow Cabinet and then her Cabinets by temperament and attitude, not by procedure. She concentrated the emotions and sense of occasion of a very large number of people into channels of action (her use of Hoskyns typified this trait). Both Churchill and Lloyd George may be regarded as acting similarly. Her assumption throughout was that to act was the absolutely crucial thing, and she did this through her inner circle.

The view of the Shadow Cabinet changed towards the 'Stepping Stones' approach in the autumn of 1978. Hoskyns and Strauss argued that the unions were a central part of the British economic problem, and that if the unions were not reined in then public spending would not be controlled because the unions would not accept it. The nettle of union reform simply had to be grasped, they maintained. John Biffen, who was involved in a key economic policy group, became convinced by their arguments. He had been supporting Jim Prior's position, but came to the conclusion as the Winter of Discontent began that not to make a Manifesto commitment to union reform would be a major electoral mistake. This change of mind in a man highly regarded by colleagues had a marked effect on Shadow Ministers, and before the 1979 general election Prior agreed to the principal elements of trade union reform that were to become the basis of later legislation in 1980.

After 'Stepping Stones', John Hoskyns joined Thatcher's inner circle. He became a full-time member of her private office, advising on policies and speeches, and when she became Prime Minister he joined her in Number Ten, where Norman Strauss joined him. Shortly afterwards, at the suggestion of Sir Peter Carey, the permanent secretary at the Department of Trade and Industry, and following careful inquiries by Hoskyns, Andrew Duguid, an assistant secretary at the DTI, was transferred to the Policy Unit. 'Peter Carey did me a great service,' said Hoskyns. 'Andrew was the most clear headed, determined and tough minded young official I met in Whitehall. He was absolutely crucial to whatever the Policy Unit managed to achieve.'[1] Hoskyns matched the monetarist and free market principles of Keith Joseph and Alfred Sherman (Alan Walters was in the United States, not yet recalled as an adviser) with practical business sense. It was a vital matching, because Margaret Thatcher – apart from being far more isolated than appearances ever suggested – has always needed to find harmony between a need to have an overall political and moral philosophy, and a need to act politically and effectively. Hoskyns played a central part in the development of effective action. 'John Hoskyns had a marvellous influence in those early days as an anchor-man,' said Ralph Harris. 'He is a most impressive, technocratic, modern man. On managerial problems, he spells it all out, and it all fits and there's a strategy and a consistency internally.'[2]

Part of Margaret Thatcher's operational ambivalence lay in her need to reconcile morality and politics. The moment she fell into doubt, she searched for an alternative set of beliefs. She did not want to be without substance, drifting down the stream of history, fending off here, pushing off there, not trying to impose a pattern. In her own view, she became leader of the Party and Prime Minister to prevent just such aimlessness. 'I hang on until I believe there are people who can take the banner forward with the same commit-

[1] Interview, Sir John Hoskyns, 25 June 1990.
[2] Interview, Lord Harris, 21 May 1990.

ment, belief, vision, strength and singleness of purpose,' she declared.[1] And she meant it.

By the time she became Prime Minister in 1979, Thatcher's people (as opposed to Ministers) had become absolutely central to the implementation of Thatcherism. 'Stepping Stones' and the ensuing battle inside the Shadow Cabinet to ensure trade union reform had demonstrated this. When Thatcher came into Government, she and her people knew what they had to do to tackle the unions. A stepping stone approach was adopted. Labour's incomes policy was abandoned. Cash limits were imposed on departments in the public sector. Firms were allowed to go bankrupt. Rising unemployment was firmly accepted, thus dampening enthusiasm for strikes and wage demands. Employment Acts in 1980 and 1982 restricted picketing to pickets' places of work, removed unions' immunity from legal action for damages in the case of illegal industrial action, and required that four-fifths of a workforce approve in a secret ballot new closed-shop agreements. Strikes at the nationalized companies, British Steel, British Leyland, and British Rail, and by civil servants and National Health Service workers were all taken on and defeated by the Government in its first term.

In Thatcher's second term, the 1984 Trade Union Act provided State funding for union elections and required a ballot before strike action if a union was to be protected from claims for damages by employers. The 1984–5 miners' strike with its regular violence, invective and clashes with the police was broken. 'The finest body of men I've ever known,' said Harold Macmillan about the miners in his maiden speech as Earl of Stockton during the strike: the shadows of the Kaiser and Hitler and Tojo were always close to him. Thatcher, in contrast, never once indicated any sympathy with the miners and their families, or any recognition of the contribution mining men had made in two world wars. For her, what was at stake was the undemocratic nature of union power (the miners went on strike without a national ballot) and the rule of law. The defeat of the miners was, in effect, the culmination of the plans that had been made by her people in the Opposition years, and fought for against many of her parliamentary colleagues who feared both

[1] *Independent*, 9 May 1988.

223

a breakdown in the social order (like Macmillan), and a disastrous climb-down in the face of such disorder. Instead, Thatcher's intransigent determination won the day. Court-imposed fines were paid by unions; the number of days lost by strikes declined enormously, and union membership which was over 13 million in 1979 fell to 10 million in 1986 (from 54 per cent to 46 per cent of the workforce).

The 1981 Budget was the culmination of the first battle Thatcher and her people had inside Government. 'In the 1981 Budget, everyone was out to get her,' remembered Alan Walters. 'I mean those behind her: those in front didn't matter. They were all saying, "The woman is finished now!" For the weeks I was there beforehand, they were all laughing at her.'[1] The Budget also represented the convergence of Government control with Government spending.

The background to the Budget was that by June 1980, as a consequence of strict monetary policy (in particular trying to control the M3 measurement of money[2] through high interest rates and issuing a class of Government Bonds at 16 per cent – tying the taxpayer down to paying that rate on Government debt for the next twenty-five years), the rate of inflation had begun to fall. North Sea oil was beginning to make Britain a net oil exporter. Interest rates had risen to over 20 per cent, and foreign investment in Britain was rising. However, also as a consequence of monetary policy, unemployment was still going up (it reached 2.7 million in March 1981) and the value of the pound was high, making British exports expensive and imports cheaper. Gross domestic product fell by 5.5 per cent in the two years to 1981. And despite Government policy, M3 was proving impossible to control: it was increasing at nearly 20 per cent per annum as banks, taking advantage of interest rates, vastly increased their lending. Conventional (Keynesian) wisdom was that in such circumstances reflation – increasing the money

[1] Interview, Sir Alan Walters, 25 May 1989.
[2] There are a multitude of money measurements, and they vary with changing definitions and with financial innovations. Essentially, M0 is cash circulating in the economy; M1 is M0 plus demand deposits and chequing accounts; M2 is M1 plus short-term deposit accounts and certain forms of credit (e.g. credit cards); M3 is M2 plus remaining deposit accounts and other forms of short-term credit and commercial paper (e.g. debentures – company debts floated on the market as bonds).

supply and spending – was necessary to prevent a worse recession.

With this backdrop, by the end of 1980 the Prime Minister had come to the conclusion, not surprisingly, that she needed to promote more Thatcherites into the Cabinet in order to pursue her policies more effectively. 'Margaret Thatcher inherited a Shadow Cabinet that in Tory radical terms was largly agnostic,' said John Biffen. 'That position persisted even after the 1979 general election victory. Gradually, however, the balance of the Cabinet tilted as grandees like Soames and Carrington departed and the younger radicals such as Parkinson and Tebbit arrived.'[1] In January 1981 Thatcher had her first shuffle. John Biffen became Trade Secretary. 'When Margaret Thatcher and I were talking on our own,' Norman Tebbit recalled of this time, 'or with her close friends such as Keith Joseph, she had made it plain that she wanted to begin the reconstruction of the Government to bring forward more of those who believed in the policies on which we had been elected rather than those who still hankered after those on which Ted Heath had been defeated.'[2]

She also brought in people on a personal basis at the advisory level. David Wolfson, the nephew of the founder of Great Universal Stores, where he had worked running a large-scale mail-order business, came into Number Ten as Thatcher's chief of staff. He had been secretary of the Shadow Cabinet in 1978–9. In Downing Street he refused to take a salary. He was introduced to Thatcher by Alastair McAlpine, the treasurer of the Conservative Party, soon after she became Party Leader. The vast increase in the number of letters Thatcher received after February 1975 meant that her private office needed to be reorganized, and Wolfson's experience of dealing with 200,000 letters a week was valuable. He also made recommendations for the reorganization of Conservative Central Office and the Research Department, leading to the Department being moved from its long-established separate home in Old Queen Street and into Central Office in Smith Square. His discretion and modesty were appreciated by all who worked with him. In Number Ten his actual role was to co-ordinate and arrange the Prime Minis-

[1] John Biffen, 'The Prime Minister's Rubber-Stamping Ground', *Independent on Sunday*, 22 July 1990.
[2] Norman Tebbit, *Upwardly Mobile* (London, Futura, 1989), p. 218.

ter's diary, and to ensure that the work of the Policy Unit was taken aboard by the civil service. He became, in effect, Thatcher's gatekeeper, and he used his position to secure the Policy Unit's and advisers' input to her. 'Well,' he would say to advisers, 'if you think this is important, then you must go to this meeting, and you must tell the Prime Minister what you think directly because that's what she really wants you to do.'[1] Apart from his own experience of business, he had a degree in business administration and took a keen and informed interest in the economic policies and strategy of the Government. 'I tried to ensure the Prime Minister had adequate time in her diary to deal with the critical things for the economy that we were trying to do – in particular that she had the time for the Policy Unit – and that too much time was not spent on things we might like to do but that were not critical, so that we did not have to jump two hurdles at once,' he explained. 'But of course the critical issues came through John Hoskyns.'[2]

Thatcher had, in fact, inherited a neo-Keynesian (i.e. not derived from Keynes's own writings, but from the work of those who regarded themselves as his intellectual successors) squeeze. 'One should never forget that Callaghan and Healey between them were changing economic and social policy quite markedly,' observed Robert Blake. 'It suited both sides subsequently to play this down. Margaret Thatcher doesn't want to be beholden to them, and they, of course, do not want it implied that they were doing these things earlier. There's more continuity than one might appreciate between the Callaghan administration after the IMF and all that happened in 1976, and Margaret Thatcher's administration than either side wishes to admit.'[3] She and her first Chancellor, Geoffrey Howe, had ratcheted up the squeeze. 'It was very inefficiently done by the Treasury,' Alfred Sherman considered, 'and so there simply wasn't enough money around, and the pound was too expensive.'[4] But Thatcher was convinced that controlling M3 was the central policy target, and it took some time to shift her from this view.

Alan Walters played a crucial part in changing Thatcher's mind.

[1] Interview, Sir David Wolfson, 18 July 1990.
[2] Ibid.
[3] Interview, Lord Blake, 16 August 1989.
[4] Interview, Sir Alfred Sherman, 30 April 1990.

He agreed to take a sabbatical from his professorship at Johns Hopkins University in Baltimore, and return to London as the Prime Minister's personal economic adviser. Having been one of the principal 'salesmen' of monetarism to Thatcher, he was now being asked to provide remedies for some of the effects of tight control of the money supply. A *Financial Times* journalist, learning that Walters was in London, telephoned him:

'Hello, Alan. What advice are you going to give Mrs Thatcher?' he inquired.

'I'll tell her that the money supply is far too tight,' said Walters.

'But Alan, M3 is completely out of control.'

'Oh, bugger M3!' said Walters. 'Sterling is obviously far too high. That can only mean that sterling is scarce.'[1]

'It was so sensible,' said Anthony Harris, a colleague on the *Financial Times* of the journalist who had spoken to Walters. 'I nearly fell off my desk. And he gave this advice and the policy was reversed fairly quickly and everything started coming all right. Thank God he's not doctrinaire.'[2] Behind the scenes, however, Walters' arguments met stiff resistance. 'Alan was the guru figure with the ideas,' recalled Norman Strauss from the vantage point of the Number Ten Policy Unit. 'And because our relations with Geoffrey Howe were excellent, and because we didn't play politics with Alan – quite the reverse: we brought him into the team instantly – he was able to get all the Treasury papers and he was brought into the centre of things.'[3]

At the Centre for Policy Studies, Alfred Sherman – like Walters, Wolfson and Hoskyns in Number Ten – was concerned by the M3 target and its consequences. 'I decided in 1970,' said Sherman, 'that the reason generally given – North Sea oil – could not be right since petrocurrencies were generally weak, for example the Mexican Peso; the Venezuelan Bolivar; the Saudi Arabian Rejale. So at the annual Confederation of British Industry conference, I persuaded

[1] Interview, Anthony Harris, 3 April 1990.
[2] Ibid.
[3] Interview, Norman Strauss, 25 May 1990.

the chairman of Taylor Woodrow to finance a study by the CPS. I asked Alan for the names of people who might do it. He gave me three names.'[1] At Walters' recommendation, towards the end of 1980 he commissioned a study of the Government's monetary policy from Professor Jurg Niehans at the University of Berne. Niehans reported that monetarism had not been properly understood or administered within the Government, and that the M3 target was wrong. The pound sterling was too high as a result of the monetary squeeze, said Niehans, and the economy was heading for a deep slump.

Monetary policy is all technique: there is no simple principle. There is no such activity as 'controlling the money supply'. What can be controlled are various measures of banking mediation. The trouble was that Thatcher and Howe thought that there was a simple principle: that inflation (to which they ascribed all evil) could be reduced by reducing M3. They were recent converts to monetarism, with the corresponding rigidity of view. They were also avoiding Enoch Powell's spoor – not wishing to be identified with him and not wishing to endorse some of the doctrines which he had propounded (notably, that trade unions were 'as innocent as the babe unborn' of responsibility for inflation). The conclusion of Walters and Niehans was that in the midst of a recession the proper policy was to cut borrowing and raise taxes, thus reducing spending and accelerating the rate at which firms that did not adapt would go out of business. Sherman's view, in contrast, was that Government expenditure should be reduced.[2]

A policy battle of the utmost importance, in which the relationships between politicians and advisers and between politicians and the civil service were central, raged fiercely for several months. On one side was the Prime Minister, her advisers (including some civil servants in Number Ten), and Howe, Lawson, Nott and Howell; on the other, the Treasury knights and the Bank of England. A vital meeting was held by Thatcher at Chequers towards the end of 1980 as a result of a blunt note to her by Hoskyns in which he said that lack of intellectual clarity and lack of political will had already 'lost'

[1] Interview, Sir Alfred Sherman, 10 December 1990.
[2] Ibid.

two years and was jeopardizing the Government's central economic task.[1] The Policy Unit had warned at the time of both the 1979 and 1980 Budgets that fiscal policy was too loose: now Hoskyns was determined to make a last push to have it tightened and monetary policy relaxed. Keith Joseph and Geoffrey Howe were the two Cabinet Ministers present. Howe brought Terry Burns, chief economic adviser to the Treasury and head of the Government Economic Service, so that Treasury fears would be heard.[2] Burns revealed that one of the most worrying elements in determining what to do was that every time a forecast of the public sector borrowing requirement (PSBR) was made, it looked more horrendous. The Treasury was clearly beginning to panic. Keith Joseph was very firm in the view that however difficult, PSBR had to be reduced: 'If we don't do something,' he said, 'in two or three years' time we're just going to start slipping over the cliff.'[3] Suddenly, instead of fiscal and monetary policy, PSBR was at the centre of everyone's thoughts.

A week later, Wolfson, Strauss, Hoskyns and Walters met in Number Ten to devise a strategy for dealing with PSBR. Wolfson said that from what Geoffrey Howe and Terry Burns had said, there was a real danger of a funding crisis. Following the Niehans study, interest rates were coming down but the borrowing requirement was growing larger and larger in order to fund the gap between the tax take and obviously out-of-control public spending. Within an hour they all agreed that the only effective solution was to take a great deal of money out of the economy in a fiscal squeeze: they were back to fiscal policy. Walters said that PSBR should be reduced by £4 billion. This would take real courage on the part of Thatcher and Howe. The big question was: would they do it?

A year earlier, in the spring of 1980, a central element in enabling a real reduction in PSBR had been put in place. A low – 6 per cent – assumption for an increase in public sector pay was made at that time because otherwise the whole medium-term financial strategy that had been developed would be blown to shreds since all other

[1] Interview, Sir John Hoskyns, 25 June 1990.
[2] Also present were David Young, special adviser at the Department of Industry; Robin Ibbs, head of 'The Tank' – the Central Policy Review Staff; Lawson; Howell; Wolfson; Strauss; Hoskyns; and Walters.
[3] Interview, Sir John Hoskyns, 25 June 1990.

pay claims would start at the point that the Government pegged for its own employees. It would be impossible for the Government to argue for low pay awards if it was seen paying civil servants large amounts. By setting a low level of pay increase, the Government signalled its determination to control public spending. Doing this broke the civil service pay comparability system (by which pay was calculated in relation to pay in other professions) and resulted in a strike and an eventual 7.5 per cent pay rise in July 1981.[1] So the behind-closed-doors debates over the 1981 Budget took place in an atmosphere of great civil service discontent, making the job of convincing the Treasury and the Bank of England of the Government's economic strategy even more difficult.

Alan Walters carried the technical argument with the Treasury and the Bank, although at the Treasury, Douglas Wass, the permanent under-secretary, was adamantly opposed to Walters and Hoskyns, and argued for a 'Go' Budget. Margaret Thatcher and Geoffrey Howe were at first horrified by the idea of having a fiscal squeeze (i.e., increasing taxation) on top of the monetary squeeze (i.e., high interest rates and reduced money supply), and looked as if they might side with Wass. 'If you get this wrong,' Hoskyns said to Howe, 'and you under-insure in terms of putting up the tax take and reducing the borrowing requirement, the consequence could be the end of you and probably the end of Margaret, too.' 'It's all right for you,' Thatcher had said at the first meeting in Number Ten to discuss the proposal from the advisers. 'You don't have to stand up in the House.'[2] 'Alan Walters was probably the key figure,'

[1] Following on from the successful opposition in 1981 by the National Union of Mineworkers to the Coal Board's plans to close pits and cut 13,000 jobs, the civil service unions campaigned for a 15 per cent pay rise. They were offered a 7 per cent rise. For twenty-one weeks the strike went on before a 7.5 per cent settlement was agreed. Lord Soames, the minister responsible, fourteen weeks into the strike had judged that a 7.5 per cent settlement would be accepted, but Thatcher had refused to budge that half per cent more. The cost of the strike was estimated to be in the region of £1,700 million, with the last seven weeks accounting for about £500 million of this. Soames was accused of 'mishandling' the strike when, in fact, he had made the mistake of getting it right. Bernard Ingham, the Prime Minister's press secretary, told journalists that the point of the exercise was not the cost but to prove that 'we meant business'.
[2] Interview, Sir John Hoskyns, 25 June 1990. Present at this first meeting were the Prime Minister, Douglas Wass, Terry Burns, Alan Walters, David Wolfson and John Hoskyns.

said Wolfson, 'although he hadn't been there very long. Hoskyns in turn said that if you're going to err, err on the side of caution, of reducing PSBR rather than increasing it. PSBR was what the world looked at to see if Britain was recovering from its malaise, and if they saw that it was going up, and the Budget wasn't tight enough to hold it down, then we might face even worse problems.'[1] John Hoskyns made the point that the danger of more severe problems ahead was greater if the monetary squeeze was maintained while fiscal policy remained relatively relaxed: if it turned out later that fiscal policy had to be tightened, that might easily be seen as a panic measure and could lead to a run on the pound, whereas if it turned out that policy was too tight, it would be easy to loosen it without panic buttons being pressed in world markets. Early in 1981, Thatcher was convinced by such arguments. At the Treasury, Howe came around even quicker. 'David Wolfson set the processes in hand to get the Treasury view challenged,' said Norman Strauss. 'Geoffrey Howe, to his credit, made sure the challenge was effective. Another Chancellor would have stayed with the Treasury. Geoffrey was totally praiseworthy in this. It wasn't his idea, but once it got through to him, he shifted and brought his team on board.'[2] In the same way, in early 1980, Howe had resolutely grasped the nettle of civil service pay, knowing that a strike would probably be the consequence, and having to face the ridicule and opposition of Cabinet colleagues. He refused to take the line of least resistance, which almost everyone else in the Cabinet preferred to do rather than think about the long-term consequences of surrendering the assumptions behind the medium-term financial strategy. In the event, during the summer of 1981 the Government faced a twenty-two week civil service strike.

Geoffrey Howe was never close to Margaret Thatcher personally: she always saw him as a rival. Separately from her, he had been convinced of the need for monetarist policies in 1974, before Thatcher had thought of contesting the Party leadership. As Chancellor from 1979 to 1983, he abolished exchange controls – possibly the greatest single measure of freedom for individuals and corpor-

[1] Interview, Sir David Wolfson, 18 July 1990.
[2] Interview, Norman Strauss, 25 May 1990.

ations in the Thatcher years. He had done this against the advice of the Treasury and the Bank of England, and with the Prime Minister offering no more than permission; while no doubt accepting its intellectual harmony with the rest of her programme, she refused to invest her personal political capital in the initiative. She said that he would have to shoulder total responsibility for his action.[1] 'I remember the civil service objection to abolition,' said a Number Ten insider. 'They sent a letter saying the reason it shouldn't be abolished was because X number – I think it was thirty – of skilled people's talents would be wasted. That was one of their arguments.'[2]

The Cabinet had refused to agree public spending cuts in the summer of 1980, with the consequence that the PSBR was running out of control in 1981. Cutting Government spending plans would have taken time as the Treasury negotiated cuts with the big spending departments (what were called the 'Star Chamber' negotiations), and this time was not available if PSBR was to be reined in. Howe, by flouting all the conventional wisdom by raising taxes, produced a £3.5 billion reduction in the PSBR, which Walters said was sufficient. Despite his cuddly image, Geoffrey Howe had a steely quality: his decision (backed by Thatcher) to raise taxes in the middle of a recession was very brave. At the Treasury and the Bank of England the senior civil servants would not agree that a fiscal squeeze was appropriate, but they bowed to the Prime Minister's and Chancellor's decision. As John Biffen, Howe's Number Two at the Treasury put it, 'In my experience, Douglas Wass was clearly not sympathetic to the new policies, but he carried out his duties with dignity.'[3]

It was significant that the Cabinet was not the forum of the debate. Thatcher found that she could never depend upon her Cabinets to back her up fully, partly because she found it difficult to find sufficient parliamentarians of Cabinet calibre who agreed with her, and partly because she was always very conscious of the need to placate the broad range of Party feeling in her Cabinet appoint-

[1] Judy Hillman and Peter Clarke, *Geoffrey Howe: A Quiet Revolutionary* (London, Weidenfeld & Nicolson, 1988), p. 150.
[2] Interview, 25 May 1990.
[3] Interview, Rt Hon. John Biffen, MP, 6 June 1990.

ments. In November 1990, it was not Michael Heseltine who defeated her, but the two-thirds of her Cabinet who pressed her to resign in order to make way for a candidate – Hurd or Major – who, it was considered, would more easily defeat Heseltine's challenge. As early as 1981, the straws were in the wind for such an occurrence as Thatcher found it necessary to retreat from her Cabinet into a small circle of trusted Ministers and advisers as she planned her revolutionary monetary and fiscal strategy. 'The modern Cabinet spends more time confirming decisions that have been taken elsewhere than initiating policy itself,' John Biffen observed. 'That was particularly true in the 1979–83 Parliament, when the Chancellor of the Exchequer brought about substantial cuts in planned public spending, notwithstanding domestic recession and rising unemployment.'[1] This, in Biffen's view, did not mean that Cabinet Ministers were entirely excluded: the Cabinet Committee system was also a central part of the process. 'There were a number of people who were of great influence, outside the structure,' said Biffen. 'Alan Walters certainly did carry a lot of weight. But I think it's easy to exaggerate that. If I had to put my money on it, I'd say decisions were and are still made by working through the Cabinet Committee structure.'[2] This was where Lawson, Nott, and Howell were most effective. They had all been closely involved in developing economic policy with Howe and Thatcher in the Opposition years, and were frequent visitors to Number Ten in the 1979–81 period. They played an important part in mapping out the Government's economic strategy and in formulating the 1981 Budget. They provided the nucleus of political support for Thatcher and Howe that could not be found in the Cabinet.

Ian Gow, who had acted as campaign manager for Geoffrey Howe in 1975 in his bid for the Party leadership, had been chosen by Thatcher as her Parliamentary Private Secretary. He was her eyes and ears in the Parliamentary Party, reporting to her the feeling of MPs on various issues. He had a good understanding of the economic principles involved in Walters' proposals, and did his utmost

[1] Biffen, 'The Prime Minister's Rubber-Stamping Ground',
[2] Interview, Rt Hon. John Biffen, MP, 6 June 1990.

to secure their acceptance by the Prime Minister and the Parliamentary Party. What was, perhaps, surprising at the time was that the civil service private secretaries in Number Ten – her press secretary, Bernard Ingham, her principal private secretary, Clive Whitmore, and her economics private secretary, Tim Lankester (who had also been Callaghan's private secretary and was the Treasury's man in the Private Office)[1] – also supported Walters and Hoskyns. As the argument progressed, Whitmore would exhort Walters, 'Go in there! Give them hell!'[2] 'They were completely with me and her,' remembered Walters. 'They knew the stakes were very high indeed – that they were the whole caboose. I've never seen anything like her moral courage at that time.'[3]

On 11 March 1981, Howe introduced the Budget in the House of Commons. A day earlier he had told his Cabinet colleagues his plans, horrifying several of them. 'I couldn't say anything bad enough about it,' said Prior.[4] 'That morning when they had the Budget meeting in Cabinet,' Walters recalled, 'nearly everyone who left that meeting was convinced that she would be finished, perhaps in a matter of days.'[5] On the morning of the Budget, Prior had breakfast with Peter Walker and Ian Gilmour and discussed resigning in protest, but in the event did nothing. 'I think that during those four years when I was very close,' Ian Gow recalled, 'there was a certainty that the policies she was following were right. And she never wavered. And I will never forget the 1981 Budget, and Pym and Prior. Prior, in his book, says he almost resigned. I remember Pym came in to see me after Geoffrey had seen him to tell him, and Pym was very gloomy.'[6]

After Howe had completed his speech, announcing increases in personal and indirect taxation and in petrol tax, and forecasting that manufacturing output would decline by a further 1 per cent and that unemployment would rise to over 3 million in 1982, a senior

[1] The Private Office co-ordinates Number Ten activities and policy with Government Departments, and acts as the Prime Minister's lightning rod in the civil service.
[2] Interview, Sir Alan Walters, 25 May 1989.
[3] Ibid.
[4] Jim Prior, *A Balance of Power* (London, Hamish Hamilton, 1986), p. 140.
[5] Interview, Sir Alan Walters, 25 May 1989.
[6] Interview, Ian Gow, MP, 8 August 1989.

backbench MP, Peter Tapsell, influential in City circles, called for the Chancellor's resignation. Thatcher, going in to hear Howe's speech, ran into Alan Walters outside the chamber of the House of Commons and said, 'You know, Alan, they may get rid of me for this . . . At least I shall have gone knowing I did the right thing.'[1]

'The budget of 1981 must be reckoned as the biggest fiscal squeeze of peacetime,' Walters later considered. 'But it did convince the markets that the Government was going to stick to its policies. And, at first gradually, then much more rapidly, expectations adjusted to the reduced rates of inflation. Along this hard and rocky road, however, we were treated to an avalanche of protests by the massed ranks of the economics profession led by its most distinguished luminaries. It would have been so easy for the Government to ease up. But it would have been disastrous.'[2] 'The Budget was a terrific shock to the people who were saying that her days were numbered,' said Hoskyns, looking back. 'Her enemies in the Cabinet and elsewhere began to understand that if she and Geoffrey had the guts to do what they had done, then they were far tougher and stronger than people had thought.'[3]

At the end of March, 365 economists sent a letter to *The Times* declaring that there was 'no basis in economic theory or supporting evidence for the Government's belief that by deflating demand they will bring inflation permanently under control.'[4]

Six months later in a Cabinet shuffle, Thatcher began to Thatcherize her Cabinet even more. Jim Prior was moved from the Department of Employment and made Secretary of State for Northern Ireland. Norman Tebbit came in to replace Prior at Employment. Nigel Lawson became Secretary of State for Energy. 'I had always thought him a kindred spirit,' said Alan Walters, pointing to Lawson's role in developing economic policy since 1975. 'After the fall of the Heath government, Mr Lawson was an important discussant in developing a new economic policy.'[5]

[1] Hugo Young, *One of Us* (London, Macmillan, 1989), p. 215.
[2] Interview, Sir Alan Walters, 25 May 1989.
[3] Interview, Sir John Hoskyns, 25 June 1990.
[4] Letter, *The Times*, 31 March 1981. The letter was signed by Frank Hahn, supported by 364 other economists.
[5] Alan Walters, *Sterling In Danger: The Economic Consequences of Pegged Exchange Rates* (London, Fontana/Collins/Institute of Economic Affairs, 1990), p. 136.

Christopher Soames was sacked. So was Ian Gilmour who left Number Ten and told the assembled reporters that the Government was 'heading for the rocks'. A year later, the rate of inflation had halved from about 15 per cent to about 7 per cent. Less than six years later, the underlying rate of inflation was below 3 per cent.

Apart from the economic background in early 1981, a spate of riots reflecting racial tensions and rising unemployment helped fuel an atmosphere of crisis. In April there was disorder in Brixton, followed by very serious outbreaks in June, and in July equally grave riots in Toxteth, Manchester, Brixton (again), Southall, Reading, Hull and Preston. The pressure on Thatcher and the Government to reverse their policies was enormous. 'It was the time when everyone else would have U-turned,' said Strauss. 'John Hoskyns, David Wolfson and I in late 1980 in fact went in to check whether she wanted to. "Are you really going to stick to your guns or are you going to U-turn?" we asked. "Because if you're going to U-turn, this is when you've got to do it." And she said, "I couldn't. I've got to see this one through. That's what I've come to do. I couldn't possibly not do it. I'd rather resign!" It was great. We knew that Thatcher meant it.'[1] Her people played a crucial part in Thatcher's resolution. They had changed both her mind and that of Geoffrey Howe; they had successfully challenged the Treasury and Bank of England view, and the common wisdom of the economics profession; and they had built up a vital level – considering the lukewarm opinion of most of the Cabinet – of personal, emotional and intellectual support for Howe and Thatcher. The role of the civil servants inside Number Ten was also instructive, not least to Thatcher's people: it indicated the degree to which permanent officials were sympathetic to her arguments, and susceptible to the force of her personality.

And not just officials. Journalists and commentators had been impressed by her personally during the Opposition years. In Government as Prime Minister for the first time she impressed new cadres. Ian Gow remembered the general feeling at the start: 'At the beginning, I'm sure many people, including members of the new Cabinet, thought she'd got through four years as Leader of

[1] Interview, Norman Strauss, 25 May 1990.

the Opposition and presiding over the Shadow Cabinet; that she hadn't won the election: Callaghan had lost it, and that when she was presiding over a real Cabinet and not just the Shadow Cabinet, when she actually came face to face with people, not when she was Leader of the Opposition with no power to take decisions, but when she met all these other folk with the power to make decisions, they thought it wouldn't work. There were many people who thought it wouldn't work. When they came to the first Cabinet meeting, they were curious to see how it would be when shadow had become substance. And I think that the first weeks were really very tense. And then, of course, the unemployment started to rise and rise and rise. And the interest rates were high. And then the 1981 Budget. And I think it was all very tense, and there were doubters in the Parliamentary Party. And her confidence never wavered that the policies were correct, that in the long run new jobs would come, and that the abatement of inflation was of the highest importance, and that trade union reform was of the highest importance. She was absolutely convinced. She never wavered at all.'[1]

When Ian Gow started as her Parliamentary Private Secretary in 1979, he also had serious misgivings. But his experience of working with her, and observing her at close hand, transformed his view: 'When I started doing the job, it was for a person whom I didn't know, and to be perfectly honest, I hadn't been as impressed as perhaps I should have been with her performances in the House of Commons as Leader of the Opposition. I am sure I should have been more approving, but I wasn't. I was an agnostic, really, about Mrs Thatcher. And it lasted until the Monday after the next general election. I thought it wouldn't last more than about a fortnight: I shall get the sack! But it did last, and over those four years grew a bond of affection that will last until my death.'[2]

[1] Interview, Ian Gow, MP, 8 August 1989.
[2] Ibid.

TWELVE

Political and civil servants

A notable Thatcher characteristic was the way she put her head ahead of her heart. She had done it in Opposition when she saw that it was politically easier to work with colleagues in the Shadow Cabinet supporting Prior's approach to the unions than to announce her real intention of confronting them. Early in 1981 she did it with the miners who threatened strike action over the Coal Board's plans to close twenty-three pits and lose 13,000 jobs. She made a completely political decision to concentrate first on the 1981 Budget and to leave the fight with the unions until the Government was better prepared for real confrontation. So she decided to give in to the union pressure because the anti-union power legislation was not in place and there were not sufficient coal stocks at the power stations to ease the effects of a protracted strike.

The Policy Unit had first tried to get her to start thinking about the miners in December 1979 when they were awarded a twenty per cent pay rise, and the Unit successfully used the bad press following the 1981 climb-down in the face of miners' power to make Thatcher and the Cabinet think seriously about the problem. At first, Thatcher required considerable convincing that the plans could be successful and that the miners could be beaten. 'It was her manner and technique to take up a devil's advocate role,' said David Wolfson, 'and this probably made some people think that she did not believe that the miners could be beaten.'[1] Wolfson ensured that the Unit's arguments were heard and its plans studied. 'I shared her view in 1979 that trade union reform was absolutely critical because business was becoming unmanageable,' said David Wolfson. 'We had developed a national attitude that the object of trade unions was to prevent things happening, and I knew that if this did not

[1] Interview, Lord Wolfson, 21 December 1990.

change, we were going to go down the tubes at a rate of knots.'[1] 'David Wolfson was really doing strategic leadership for her,' remembered Norman Strauss, 'and trying to find the big issues, just a few things that matter, and make sure they happened.'[2] Tim Lankester supported and helped Hoskyns and his team. They convinced the Prime Minister that with planning and determination a miners' strike could be taken on and won. With the autumn 1981 Cabinet shuffle, Thatcher was able to commit herself with Cabinet support to the Unit's plan, and preparations for a showdown with the miners then began. The Civil Contingencies Unit in the Cabinet Office undertook studies of the movement of coal stocks, the dual firing of power stations, and questions establishing the logistical problems that would be involved if a coal strike were to be defeated. Three years later the miners were to find that coal stocks had been methodically moved from pit-heads to power stations, and a nearly year-long strike only speeded up mine closures and resulted in the National Union of Mineworkers splitting apart. 'People will probably remember her for her trade union reform rather than for monetary economics,' David Wolfson reflected. 'They were the two big issues. John Hoskyns and Norman Strauss did a large part of the thinking on trade unions, right through from "Stepping Stones". In monetary reform, Alan Walters was crucial, and his influence went on longer.'[3]

John Hoskyns was becoming more and more concerned about securing political and economic change, the decision-making process, and the strategic clarity of the Government. Eventually he decided to leave Number Ten in 1982. Part of the reason for his departure was that by November 1981, together with Alan Walters and David Wolfson, he thought that he had done the job he had been brought in to do. The crucial tasks for the first term had been achieved and the prognosis looked good: monetary discipline was tight (it turned out to be too tight) and inflation was thus set to come down much further and faster than the Treasury was forecasting; public expenditure plans had been brought into line with the realities of cash – real money – rather than assumptions of inflation being built in; the civil service pay comparability system had

[1] Interview, Sir David Wolfson, 18 July 1990.
[2] Interview, Norman Strauss, 25 May 1990.
[3] Interview, Sir David Wolfson, 18 July 1990.

been broken, and the resulting strike taken on and won – although at a price, it turned out; union reform had started: James Prior had been moved from the key Employment Ministry to Northern Ireland and his replacement, Norman Tebbit, was planning to remove immunity for union funds in the event of union action that broke the law; public sector strikes, the inevitable concomitant of the changes in union law and in pay comparability, had been or would be taken on and won (steel; the National Health Service); the two-year build-up of coal stocks at the right places to take on the miners had been started; the 1981 Budget had demonstrated resolution and had grasped the nettle of runaway public borrowing; the 'wet' Cabinet had been reconstructed in September with several Thatcherites being brought in for the first time, and a new and supportive Party chairman – Cecil Parkinson – appointed in good time for the next election. These actions had almost precisely constituted the Policy Unit's objectives for the first term, which, taken together, could be summarized as ending the economic civil war of the 1970s and stabilizing the Government's finances.

The work of the Unit was understood and appreciated by very few in the first (1979–81) Cabinet: Margaret Thatcher, Keith Joseph and Geoffrey Howe were the exceptions who supported the Unit and its objectives. At several points the programme was almost abandoned as Ministers, from Thatcher down, became more and more tired under pressure and increasingly confused about the various plans and the overall objective by early to mid-1980. The lack of Ministerial comprehension and resolution was a vital backdrop to the 1981 Budget.

Another reason for Hoskyns's decision to leave was that he did not think there would be similar strategic clarity in the second term which, in his view, required the complete overhaul and redesign of the Welfare State, and the stabilizing of the economy as a whole (and not just the Government's finances). It would be a ten to fifteen year task of enormous administrative complexity requiring great political delicacy. 'Ministers will, as usual, be engrossed in tackling immediate problems,' he said. '"Never mind about the strategy and all that stuff", they will be saying, "what are we going to do and, more important, what are we going to *say*, about unemployment, about the miners' strike?" Yet these immediate problems are merely symptoms of an unstable system. Governments, especially democratic governments, are in the business of system design. That is why coherent policy-making is so difficult and the "departmental view" so inadequate.[1] Thatcher herself, and most politicians, did not appreciate or understand the detailed groundwork necessary to achieve such reform. Without Hoskyns and other advisers, key issues would probably not have been addressed so thoroughly because so few Ministers had a complete grasp of what was really involved in terms of cross-departmental and interdependent arrangements, plans, and co-ordination of activity. So in 1982, somewhat disillusioned, Hoskyns left. 'John Hoskyns had a mind that was far too analytical,' said Nigel Vinson. 'He would present analytical solutions. But politics isn't like that. I think he felt that he was knocking his head against a wall in terms of getting done the things he felt he was doing there. She didn't like his almost over-numerical, over-analytical, computerized approach to problems.'[2] 'John was putting forward more radical suggestions than Mrs Thatcher felt able to agree – which was unlike her,' said Ian Gow. 'She's not afraid of radical ideas, but that's what happened.'[3] 'The politicians listened to us just about as much as any adviser has a right to hope,' said Hoskyns.[4]

Thatcher put her head ahead of her heart when she let Hoskyns go. She was prepared to declare all-out war on the miners but, despite her suspicions and feelings, not on the Welfare State and the civil service. Hoskyns had not argued for wars against the Welfare State and the civil service; he had a larger goal – the reform and redesign of British managerial and work habits as a step towards a stable and efficient economy – but Thatcher probably thought that Hoskyns's goals would involve wars. As a politician, she considered that such wars were unwinnable, although her conviction was that the civil service was in the way of her reforms.

A year after becoming Prime Minister she attended a dinner with all the permanent secretaries, organized by Sir Ian Bancroft, head

[1] Sir John Hoskyns, 'Needed Now: A Tory National Plan', *The Times*, 9 October 1984.
[2] Interview, Lord Vinson, 30 May 1990.
[3] Interview, Ian Gow, MP, 8 August 1989.
[4] Interview, Sir John Hoskyns, 25 June 1990.

of the civil service, in an effort to reassure her that the service would work diligently for her. Instead of the mutual reassurance the dinner was intended to provide, she had a furious argument with the permanent secretary at the Ministry of Defence, Sir Frank Cooper, and when she said that she hoped that by working together, she and they could beat 'the system', Bancroft spontaneously replied, 'But we are the system!'[1]

In 1983, speaking about the nature of the civil service and her thought processes when she was a junior Minister in the 1959–63 Macmillan government, she said in an interview: 'I used to sit there sometimes and say "That's not what you said to my last Minister. You are giving him totally different advice. Why?" And gradually they said, "Well, the last one wouldn't have accepted that advice." I said, "Well, you're now trying it on with my present one."'[2] Sir William Pile, the permanent under-secretary at the Department of Education and Science when Margaret Thatcher was there, described her as 'decidedly abrasive' to work with: 'I would call it an innate wariness of the civil service, quite possibly even a distrust,' he said.[3]

John Hoskyns, who had not been interested in civil service reform in the Policy Unit, turned his attention to it after he resigned. 'The strategic stepping stones [to arresting national decline and generating economic growth and financial and social stability],' he wrote, 'cannot be culled from a typical manifesto shopping list. To have any meaning they will have to be set out in network form (which at present only the younger and brighter civil servants will understand and would never dare to try on their superiors) . . . Fundamental questions are seldom asked inside Whitehall, because they often appear naïve. They are dismissed, not by reasoned argument, but by massed *knowledge* about the status quo before they can start anyone thinking. We therefore have to ask them outside.'[4] He began to wonder whether the civil service was a central roadblock to the long-term structural transformation of the economy. He wondered out loud whether, if civil servants were not able to

[1] Peter Hennessy, *Whitehall* (London, Secker & Warburg, 1989), p. 229.
[2] Ibid, p. 625.
[3] John Newhouse, 'The Gamefish', *New Yorker*, 10 February 1986.
[4] Hoskyns, 'Needed Now'.

implement Thatcherism wholeheartedly, they would blunt policies to some extent, because their effective loyalties were principally to themselves as the permanent government, and to the ideal of serving all Governments of the Crown equally, whatever their political hue. Accordingly, in Hoskyns's view, civil servants functioned by being bloodless. For Thatcher to be effective, she had to have Thatcherite officials personally committed to her policies. The service functioned, he considered, 'by cultivating a passionless detachment, as if the process they were engaged in were happening in a faraway country which they service only on a retainer basis.'[1]

Two elections later, apart from questions about the appointment of senior civil servants (it was inevitably alleged, but effectively refuted, that having been in power so long Thatcher was promoting civil servants on a political rather than a merit basis), the Prime Minister had manifested a perhaps surprising reluctance to reform the civil service. 'She has these blind spots,' one of her advisers noted in 1990. 'There are certain areas that she does not take a personal interest in, like Central Office and the civil service. The Honours system is another one. It continues to reward people who are hostile to what she actually stands for. She very rarely personally intervenes in it. She could have turned the whole intellectual establishment upside down with judicious use of it. One of her people gets something once every two years as opposed to the thirty, forty, fifty of the conventional, hostile, chattering class breed. But she's not interested. It was the same with Central Office. I don't understand why, repeatedly, she allows people who do not agree with her to maintain positions of power over the Candidates' List. It was only last year that one began to acquire some influence over the candidates' selection process to prevent all the wets who have been through the Young Conservatives, the Peter Walker brigade, getting all the plum seats. She doesn't seem to realize what's been done.'[2]

John Hoskyns's successors as heads of the Policy Unit – Ferdinand Mount, John Redwood, and Brian Griffiths – were part of the second wave of Thatcher's people who fleshed out Thatcherism as they concentrated on translating principles that had already been devised into

[1] Hugo Young, *One of Us* (London, Macmillan, 1989), p. 339.
[2] Interview, 23 March 1990.

policies. They were less staff officers, in effect, than supply officers. Ferdinand Mount, heir to a baronetcy, an old Etonian and graduate of Christ Church, Oxford, was a journalist, but had also worked at the Conservative Research Department. He was intelligent and creative rather than managerial. Immediately before coming to Number Ten in 1982, he had spent over five years as political columnist on the *Spectator*. He was very different from Hoskyns, much less concerned with detailed planning and much more concerned with an unsuccessful effort to place the family at the centre of social policy. He was in Downing Street during the 1983 general election, and spent a great deal of his time working on speeches for the Prime Minister: something Hoskyns had tried to avoid doing. After the election, Mount decided to return to journalism.

In November 1983, John Redwood became Thatcher's third head of the Policy Unit. Redwood was from a different generation to Hoskyns and Mount, and was the youngest person to hold the job: in 1983 he was 32 years old. He had had a distinguished academic career as an historian at Oxford, becoming a Fellow of All Souls when he was 21, before entering the City where, in 1977, he became an investment manager and director of N. M. Rothschild & Sons. In Number Ten he sought to energize and expand the Policy Unit, and concentrated on economic rather than social policy. He was influenced by John Hoskyns's views on the civil service, and determined – in the words of the historian of the civil service, Peter Hennessy – that the Unit should become 'a Whitehall in miniature with each member shadowing a cluster of policies and departments'.[1] He was the creator of the modern Unit. The miners' strike of 1984–5 was his baptism of fire, and he operated effectively to co-ordinate policy between Thatcher, the National Coal Board and its chairman, Ian MacGregor, and the Ministers involved.

From 1987 to the end of Thatcher's premiership, Brian Griffiths, an economist and dean of the London Business School, was head of her Policy Unit. Ten years older than Redwood, he was an enthusiast, taking vicarious pleasure from the achievements of others, and from certain transformations and entrepreneurial activities. 'Whenever you go into Brian's office,' said a member of the Policy Unit, 'there is

[1] Hennessy, *Whitehall*, p. 653.

a character from the United States who has started a new company in a ghetto, or some kids who rioted in 1981 but are now starting a company in the north of London.[1] Griffiths was born and grew up near Swansea where his father was a National Coal Board chauffeur. He is a native Welsh speaker. Dynevor Grammar School was his ladder of opportunity to the London School of Economics. In Number Ten, his concerns were not the same as Hoskyns's. He was principally interested in monetary policy (not surprisingly, since he is a monetary economist), and had been considered for the post of economic adviser to Geoffrey Howe after the 1979 election. He was not worried about the shift in Britain from manufacturing to service industries, which brought him into a certain amount of debate with Howe and Thatcher who were not sanguine about the change.

Griffiths' strong religious convictions fuelled an interest in family policy, echoing Ferdinand Mount's policy emphasis, and in religious matters. In the 1985 Patrick Hutber Lecture he publicly argued with the Bishop of Durham's relaxed interpretations of the Resurrection and the divinity of Christ. He substantially drafted the Prime Minister's moralistic, Old Testament, and only religious speech (to the Church of Scotland in 1988). 'Brian Griffiths is the same as her,' said a Number Ten insider. 'He can't stand criticism. When they brought him in to head the Unit, what they were doing was quite cleverly switching the styles and background of the head of the Unit. They'd had John Hoskyns, a businessman and a number-cruncher. Then they had Ferdy Mount, who was philosophical, and John Redwood, a powerful academic thinker. Then Brian: he's a salvationist nutter!'[2]

Griffiths was also personally interested in reforming television broadcasting law and arrangements to break down monopoly practices and introduce much greater competition in television programme production, marketing and transmission. He is a hyper-earnest person; the kind of person used by governments of all hues without ever being entrusted with any final say. In 1987, Margaret Thatcher considered making him a life peer and a junior Education Minister, but the idea was scotched by Willie Whitelaw and the then Education Secretary, Kenneth Baker. Griffiths left Number Ten with Thatcher in November

[1] Interview, 10 June 1988.
[2] Interview, 25 May 1990.

245

1990 and entered the House of Lords, ennobled in her resignation honours: she made no secret that she wanted him in the Lords as a young (he was 48) spokesman for the morality of Thatcherism who would keep the flame alive for years to come.

Because of the small number of her people, at times Thatcher was like the captain of a wagon train drawn up in a circle to repel an Indian attack, having to carry out parts of every aspect of the defence herself becuse she did not have enough people whom she could trust to load the guns, fire them, tend the wounded, mind the horses, protect the children. Robert Armstrong was like the wagon train master hired for the journey, and he did his job.

Her Cabinet Secretary for her first eight years in Downing Street, Armstrong was never quite a Thatcher person. He was loyal – extremely loyal, in fact – but always saw his role in traditional civil service terms. Had she lost the 1987 general election, he would have been at the door of Number Ten smiling a greeting to Neil Kinnock, and he would have been as loyal to the Labour leader as he had been to her. However, on two very public occasions he served her in ways that highlighted her continuing isolation within her own Government, and her tough attitude to the civil service.

The first big occasion was during the Westland affair. In the summer of 1985, Westland Helicopters was facing financial difficulties: the helicopter market was not buoyant. The US Sikorsky Helicopter company wanted to buy Westland. Free market principles – and Government policy – dictated that Westland management and shareholders should be free to determine their company's future. Michael Heseltine, Minister for Defence, took a different view. A politician very much in the Heath tradition, he saw the Cabinet as the Board of UK Ltd, and Ministers as Executive Directors. Against the backdrop of the Austin-Rover group being sold to an American buyer (a sale that did not, in the end, go through), Heseltine took the position that Westland should remain, at the least, European owned, in the interests of strategic defence requirements. He intervened to try to find a European partner to replace Sikorsky. At the Department of Trade and Industry, the Minister, Leon Brittan, tried to maintain Government policy and allow Westland to make its own choices.

Brittan was a Thatcher loyalist, not least because he was personally convinced of Thatcherite principles and had played an important part in the 1974–9 period in developing policy. He is highly intelligent and a decent and kind man. Combined with his loyalty, this was to be his undoing: he allowed his heart to overrule his head. Thatcher supported Brittan as Heseltine became increasingly active, actually putting together a European consortium himself to bid for Westland, much to the anger of the helicopter company which wanted the Sikorsky deal.[1] Leak piled upon leak as the affair progressed, coming to a head in January 1986. A letter to Heseltine from the Solicitor General was leaked on instructions from Brittan and with the approval of the Number Ten Press Office. Since the Law Officers – the Attorney General and the Solicitor General – while being Party people are charged with serving the Crown before Party and with upholding the law impartially, the letter was extremely damaging to Heseltine since it formally stated that he had been guilty of factual inaccuracies in his presentation of the affair. The next day the *Sun* on its front page carried the headline: 'You Liar!' with a picture of Heseltine.

The leaking of this letter, in Margaret Thatcher's own opinion, almost brought her down. 'I may not be Prime Minister by six o'clock tonight,' she said to an associate on 27 January 1986.[2] The Solicitor General, Sir Patrick Mayhew, was furious. Law Officers' letters and dealings are, by tradition, generally regarded as sacrosanct, and in addition his relationship with Heseltine was that of lawyer–client. He pressed for clarification of what had happened and who had authorized the leaking of his letter. So did Heseltine and the Opposition. Heseltine walked out of a Cabinet Meeting in fury over the matter, and announced his resignation as Minister in the street outside. Leon Brittan followed a week later when his part in the leak became public. He maintained a loyal silence, never saying what most people assumed to be the case: that he had leaked the letter because the Prime Minister had approved. 'It was a matter of duty that it should be made known publicly that there were thought to be material inaccuracies which needed to be corrected,' she said in the House of Commons. 'It was to get that accurate

---

[1] Heseltine was not part of the consortium and did not stand to benefit financially from it. He was simply organizing it.
[2] Thatcher quoting herself, TV-am, 7 May 1987.

information to the public domain that I gave my consent.'[1]

Bernard Ingham, her press secretary, moved in immediately to say that 'I gave my consent' was a slip of the tongue on the part of the Prime Minister. It was certainly the only time that she came close to admitting complicity in Brittan's actions. What she probably should have done was either fire Heseltine or tell him to stop his anti-Sikorsky campaign. Instead she had sought to keep him in her tent by not being officially explicit. It was her style of management, to be revealed again in 1989 with the resignation of Nigel Lawson as Chancellor of the Exchequer, and in 1990 when Geoffrey Howe resigned as Deputy Prime Minister and Leader of the House of Commons, citing Thatcher's style as one of his reasons for going.

An inquiry was demanded by the Attorney General, Sir Michael Havers, into Mayhew's leaked letter. He told the Prime Minister that unless she acceded to his demand, he would call in the police with the possibility of criminal proceedings following. The inquiry was set up and was conducted by Robert Armstrong. Thatcher claimed that when she had spoken of 'consent' in the House, she was referring to this inquiry. Armstrong found that the Prime Minister did not know the details of the affair and had not been involved in the leak: officials and Leon Brittan were responsible. Charles Powell, her private secretary, dealing with defence and foreign affairs on secondment from the Foreign Office, knew about Brittan's leaking of the letter; so did Bernard Ingham. Both Powell and Ingham saw the Prime Minister frequently on a daily basis and would be expected to keep her informed. Armstrong himself had been told about the leak by Sir Brian Hayes, the permanent secretary in Brittan's Department of Trade and Industry. Consequently, Armstrong's findings stretched credulity. In the separate inquiry conducted by the Parliamentary Select Committee on Defence, Armstrong stuck to his guns and refused to speculate about how it was that the Prime Minister's officials had not informed her properly. 'Robert Armstrong saved her and saved the government,' said a Cabinet Minister.[2] 'Robert got her off the hook,' said one permanent under-secretary, going on to give an echo of

[1] *Hansard*, 23 January 1986.
[2] Peter Jenkins, *Mrs Thatcher's Revolution: The Ending of the Socialist Era* (London, Jonathan Cape, 1987), p. 202.

Thomas Becket. 'Everybody knows what happened but nobody can prove it. They were out to get Heseltine. Brittan was fitted up, made the fall guy. She did not want to know and their game was not to tell her.'[1]

Behind the affair lay not only a great deal of resentment about the role of non-elected officials, but also about the number of Jews close to Thatcher. In her Cabinet at the time were Malcolm Rifkind, Brittan and Nigel Lawson. Replacing Brittan was David Young. Her closest parliamentary colleague was Keith Joseph. Inside Number Ten were David Wolfson and Stephen Sherbourne. Anti-Semitism was a factor that Leon Brittan had to deal with, and it was considered to be a strong element in his scalping. The political journalist, Peter Jenkins, who followed the affair closely at the time, observed, 'There was a nasty tone of anti-Semitism as the Westland affair closed in on Leon Brittan. He came from an Orthodox Jewish family of Lithuanian origin. His father had studied medicine and came to England in 1927. There had been unpleasant ripples of anti-Semitism in 1983 when he had been obliged by the redrawing of constituency boundaries to find himself a new seat. Now, with the future of the Prime Minister at stake, the poison reached the surface. Very senior Conservatives were guilty of quite disgraceful remarks – one described Brittan as "behaving like a cornered rat".'[2]

Brittan, by remaining silent about the details of the affair and accepting responsibility for the actions of his officials (the Department of Trade and Industry press officer, Colette Bowe, had at his instruction actually conducted the leaking of the letter), in effect walked the plank for Thatcher. If he had confirmed what many suspected, that she had authorized the leaking of Mayhew's letter and had been actively waging war against one of her own Cabinet colleagues, she might well have been forced to resign, not least because she would have been effectively refusing – in contrast to Brittan – to accept responsibility for the actions of her officials. 'It was an episode when she behaved like other politicians,' said Ralph Harris. 'She brought into question that which has marked her out

[1] Ibid., pp. 202–3.
[2] Ibid., p. 201.

249

from other politicians, namely that she does not dissemble and that she makes it clear where she stands.'[1]

Hard on the heels of Westland came another public outing for Armstrong. Peter Wright, a retired MI-5 officer, disgruntled by the smallness of his pension, had emigrated to Australia and, with a Granada television producer, had written a rather lurid book, *Spycatcher*, exposing various secret operations and alleging that a former director-general of MI-5, Sir Roger Hollis, had been a Soviet spy. Thatcher instituted proceedings in an Australian court against Wright for breaking the Official Secrets Act.

Peter Wright descending and Margaret Thatcher ascending came from the same class. They both went to Oxford, although in Wright's case it was more of an effort. He read an applied science – agriculture – at St Peter's College (which then was only affiliated to the university) at a time when socially you had to be a Duke's son to get away with studying agriculture. After Oxford, Thatcher followed the law and politics. Wright went into engineering and the civil (secret) service. For the next thirty years they were both patronized by the grandees and mandarins of their professions. 'Isn't it fascinating to watch a technical expert do his stuff?' the traitor Antony Blunt once remarked as Wright knelt at his feet unscrambling a tape recorder.[2]

Class infestations ran rampant through Wright's book. He spent a great deal of time on the public-school backgrounds of Kim Philby, Guy Burgess, Donald Maclean, and Antony Blunt and what he termed their 'public-school vowels'. He had a real rage on the social score. He once rounded on Blunt whom he was questioning, saying, 'I remember my father driving himself mad with drink, because he couldn't get a job. I remember losing my education, my world, everything.'[3] He spent a great deal of effort being elected to a second-class London club. He made the mistake of thinking that class in Britain has mainly to do with birth when it was mainly to do with education. As an electronics expert and technician he was not a part of the top civil service stream or of its top social set. He was firmly on the other side of the glass that separates the practically trained from

[1] Interview, Lord Harris, 21 May 1990.
[2] Peter Wright, *Spycatcher* (New York, Viking, 1987), p. 221.
[3] Ibid., p. 264.

the philosopher kings. He felt betrayed by those from privileged backgrounds in high office. He thought he was concerned with traitors when in fact he was concerned with the cliquish, intellectual, self-referential nullity of the civil service mandarinate.

Margaret Thatcher probably shared many of Wright's perceptions, but she correctly identified civil service complacency and inefficiency as the target of her ire and did not waste time wondering if Sir Roger Hollis was a traitor (he was not, as every Soviet defector in a position to know has confirmed). She seized upon the publication of Wright's book as an opportunity to make a principled stand for official secrecy – Wright had taken an oath to be silent about his secret service – and simultaneously to rap the service across the knuckles. On the strict ground that Wright was breaking the terms of his contract by publishing *Spycatcher*, there was a case in law against him. She in fact had little choice but to prosecute. Not only was a matter of law involved, but also the fact that civil servants are paid for by taxpayers to look after the Crown's interests and thus should not be able to exploit the experience for private gain. At the time, she was ridiculed for giving Wright more publicity and guaranteeing the success of his book. The political commentator, Hugo Young, reflected the sort of Establishment view that infuriated Thatcher and her people. He wrote that she should have eliminated Wright's motive in publishing by buying him off,[1] completely missing the points that inaction on her part would have encouraged revelations from others, and that to have bought Wright off would have created a precedent where disgruntled officials could look forward to blackmailing Governments in return for their silence.

She knew how self-protecting and self-promoting the civil service is: 1982–3 had witnessed Intelligence inefficiency with the failure to predict the Argentine occupation of the Falkland Islands. She believed in 'proper' secrets, knowing that secrecy is a tremendous contributor to the mystique of politics and the civil service. So she gave herself to the illumination of secrets that she did not think were proper even if they were possessed by proper secret agencies.

[1] *Guardian*, 8 September 1987.

In the *Spycatcher* affair she said to the secret service in effect, 'The secret of your inefficiency is an improper secret.'

Robert Armstrong was her chosen whipping boy. She sent him to Australia to represent the Government in court against Wright. She did not send a Law Officer or a Minister. By sending the Cabinet Secretary who was also the Prime Minister's principal adviser on security and Intelligence, she was ensuring that the civil service took the blame for Wright's revelations. Armstrong, bashing a photographer at Heathrow with his briefcase on the way (he clearly realized that he was being set up), went to Sydney and returned defeated in court and with his public reputation in tatters. He was particularly damaged by a reply he gave in court under cross-questioning when he had to correct an earlier statement. He did so with the remark that he had been 'economical with truth', which was to dog him ever after. As he pointed out in a letter to *The Times* some years later on his last day in office, he had been quoting Edmund Burke.[1] But such erudition, typical of a top-flight civil servant, was lost on most people at the time. Armstrong had done his duty faithfully and loyally, and in doing so had actually made a very important stand for the probity of the civil service. He had demonstrated the service's commitment to serve its political masters. In the future a Government of a different complexion could expect similar loyalty, even if great discomfort was involved.

A traditional Prime Minister would have acted very differently. He would have made cloying statements of confidence in Hollis and sad, ponderous statements about Blunt. He would not have prosecuted Wright, instead taking the line that the less publicity, the better. He would have declared, 'We have the best secret service, second to none' and that our civil service 'is the envy of the world'.

But Thatcher was no traditional Prime Minister. She was conspicuously not given to *obiter dicta* extolling the secret and civil service: her dinner in 1980 with Bancroft and his colleagues had made that clear. She was also no advertisement for open government. So she was fighting on two fronts. She was simultaneously standing up for secrecy and embarrassing the secret service and the mandarinate. She was winning in a secret way.

[1] Letter, *The Times*, 5 January 1988.

252

The affair revealed that the chief politician in the land, for the first time in British history, was not prepared to protect the civil service. If it was inefficient or made mistakes, Thatcher was prepared to stand aside for the blame to be pinned on the officials responsible. She believed that exposing inefficiency to pitiless publicity was proper. Wright had taken civil service hostages with his book. He had in effect said that if he were prosecuted, reputations would be tarnished and pettiness and inefficiency would be revealed. Thatcher, in reply, said, 'Shoot the hostages.'

Apart from Armstrong, whose first loyalty was always to the traditions of the civil service, there were two civil servants who really did become Thatcher people: Bernard Ingham and Charles Powell. And the Westland affair made this clear to all.

Ingham was, at first sight, an unlikely admirer. A bluff York-shireman, he was a professional journalist, writing for the *Yorkshire Post* and then the *Guardian* in the 1950s and 1960s. In the early 1960s, as a member of the Labour Party, he had stood for election to Leeds City Council, and according to his unofficial biographer, Robert Harris, wrote a polemical column for the Leeds Labour Party's the *Leeds Weekly Citizen*, under the pseudonym 'Albion'.[1] 'Albion' liked coining nicknames. Sir Alec Douglas-Home became 'Sir Alec Strangelove' and was accused of 'arrogance, which is an hereditary, though not exclusive, disease of those reared in the main forelock-touching belts of Great Britain'.[2] The 'Albion'/Ingham of the 1960s was much closer to the Ingham/Thatcher's press officer of the 1980s than might have been realized: the fury with class attitudes was something he shared with most of Thatcher's people. In 1967 he had joined the civil service as the press officer for the Prices and Incomes Board, subsequently becoming director of information at the Ministries for Employment and Energy. At Energy, he attracted the patronage of the Labour Minister, Tony Benn, who in 1978 moved Ingham away from press relations to become under-secretary for energy conservation.

Just over a year later he was summoned to Number Ten by Margaret Thatcher to become her press secretary. It was a job he

[1] Robert Harris, *Good and Faithful Servant: The Unauthorized Biography of Bernard Ingham* (London, Faber & Faber, 1990), pp. 1–5.
[2] Ibid., p. 1.

was not sure he wanted, but he found at his first meeting with the new Prime Minister that her offer and his acceptance were assumed. It was the start of a notable run. Ingham was to stay with her to the end, becoming more and more committed to her with every year, forming the longest full-time relationship between a civil servant and a Prime Minister in British history. 'He was quite professional,' said a colleague in Number Ten. 'He was very strong on what is proper and what is not proper, and he would come in and say, "These are things it is not proper for me to deal with." He was rigorous about the use of Government money and what was policy and what was Party political business. He had set rules about what could be done and what couldn't be done.'[1]

Ingham saw Thatcher through every crisis, taking her side without any apparent hesitation, gaining notoriety for his belligerent off-the-record and Lobby briefings to journalists. He played a crucial part in the Westland crisis as the official in Number Ten who approved – or at least made it appear approved – the leaking of the Solicitor General's letter. He was criticized by the Select Committee investigating the affair, but Margaret Thatcher stood by him. While she probably had little choice but to do so, it was clear to all that she depended upon him and would doubtless have supported him in almost any circumstances. 'Bernard Ingham has presided over her achieving the lowest image rating ever in the history of British Prime Ministers,' said a media adviser, angrily. 'And she says he's lovely. If he worked for me, I'd fire him! Even if you liked him, you'd have to fire him because he's clearly incompetent. But she wouldn't.'[2] 'A lot of people say what he does and has done is wrong,' said a Number Ten aide, 'but he can justify it. He can give chapter and verse for everything.'[3] 'The thing about you and me, Bernard,' Thatcher once said to him, 'is that neither of us are *smooth* people.'[4]

Charles Powell was the other civil servant closest to Thatcher. The son of an Air Vice Marshal who fought in Coastal Command during the Second World War, he was a choirboy (and head boy) at Canter-

[1] Interview, 20 December 1990.
[2] Interview, 5 December 1990.
[3] Interview, 20 February 1990.
[4] Young, *One of Us*, p. 166.

bury Choir School. The Powell family, originally Welsh, had provided a long line of country parsons until the Air Vice Marshal broke ranks. At Oxford, Charles read Modern History, and then entered a career as a high-flyer in the Foreign Office. In 1964, a year after entering the Diplomatic Service, he married an Italian girl, Carla, whom he had met at university. In the mid-1960s he served in Helsinki for just over two years and, with his wife, learnt Finnish (one of the most difficult European languages). He subsequently served in Washington DC and Bonn, and played an important part in the 1979–80 negotiations leading to an independent Zimbabwe. In 1980 he was appointed UK counsellor to the European Community, a job that by all accounts he disliked. In 1984 he became private secretary (overseas affairs) to the Prime Minister (not principal private secretary: that was Andrew Turnbull from the Treasury). Very quickly, he became a Thatcher insider. 'What she desperately needs are people who make her feel really at ease, 'said a member of the Policy Unit, 'and there's no doubt that Powell's wife has this effect, and also Powell has great knowledge of foreign affairs and seems to be quite clever, so that he's not only made himself indispensable on that side, but his wife has made herself indispensable in the relaxation sense. His wife probably has a Tim Bell relationship with her: making her laugh, basically.'[1]

Powell's brother, Christopher, worked on Labour Party advertising during election campaigns, but Charles was devoted to Thatcher. It was a feeling clearly reciprocated by the Prime Minister. On one occasion on a visit to Moscow, Thatcher took Powell rather than her Foreign Secretary at the time, Geoffrey Howe, to a dinner with Gorbachev. In Number Ten he developed a reputation for cutting through bureaucracy and getting things done, often by acting directly and not through Foreign Office channels, much to the distress of his colleagues there. He played a crucial role in forming Thatcher's view in 1985 that Mikhail Gorbachev was a new type of Soviet leader that the West could work with, and that *perestroika* was an initiative that should be supported. In 1990 he personally (and accurately) predicted that the Soviet Union would abandon its objections to a united Germany in NATO. He was never regarded as a

[1] Interview, 25 May 1990.

255

Thatcher yes-man, and demonstrated an ability to put his own stamp on minutes and papers, forwarding to the Prime Minister articles and ideas that he believed to be of value, even if she did not. 'He put in to her Fukiyama's "End of History" article,' an aide recalled. 'She thought it was a load of rubbish.'[1] In July 1990 a memorandum Powell wrote following a meeting at Chequers to discuss German reunification and the nature of German history was leaked to the press. It began with an account of the German character that started with '*angst*' and ended with 'sentimentality', and caused a row. The consensus of opinion was that the memorandum had been leaked so as to inflict damage on Powell who, after more than five years in Number Ten (and no sign of departing), was seen as becoming quietly powerful in his own right.

Charles Powell also played a crucial part in the Westland affair. Together with Ingham, he acted to shield the Prime Minister from direct involvement in the nastier elements of the saga. He was the first person in Number Ten to know that the Solicitor General was writing a critical letter to Heseltine. In evidence to Armstrong, he maintained that he had told no one else about it and that he had 'accepted' that its contents would be leaked.[2] His proper function should have been to inform his superiors, the permanent private secretary or Sir Robert Armstrong, of what he knew, and not to have 'accepted' that the letter would or should be leaked. 'The officials had protected the leader,' wrote Hugo Young about Westland, 'letting her know only what she needed to know, and associating themselves with blind loyalty in increasingly frenzied attempts to unhorse Michael Heseltine. For this, Powell in particular came in for some heavy private criticism among his colleagues in the Whitehall mandarinate. They thought his involvement in such political savagery quite reprehensible. One permanent secretary told me that he considered Powell should have been severely punished for exceeding his proper function.'[3]

'There is no doubt that Powell and Ingham's careers in the civil service are finished when she leaves,' stated a member of the Policy

[1] Interview, 20 February 1990.
[2] Young, *One of Us*, p. 446.
[3] Ibid., p. 456.

Unit in early 1990.[1] 'There is a difference between Bernard Ingham and Charles Powell,' said another Number Ten insider at the same time. 'Bernard is now approaching retirement – he'll be sixty years old in 1992 – so in a way the question of whether or not he can serve someone else or if someone else will have him is irrelevant. The question of whether or not Charles Powell will go back to the Foreign Office is much more pertinent. He's already stayed on far longer than anyone else in his position, and that was at her request. He gave up an ambassadorship and the prospect of promotion to the top of the FO. He's very close to her, and she's very fond of him.'[2]

When Margaret Thatcher resigned as Prime Minister, Bernard Ingham announced his resignation. Charles Powell stayed on in Number Ten with John Major because, as the link between the working levels of the Foreign Office and the Prime Minister, he was considered too central to plans and arrangements to move right away. Powell had liaised closely with Major when he had been Chancellor on the preparations for the December 1990 Rome Summit of European leaders. For six years he had been closely involved with British policy on Europe, and it made sense to keep him on for the Summit only three weeks after Thatcher's departure. Another reason for his staying on was that the pressure of international affairs at the time was particularly acute because of the impending war in the Persian Gulf with Iraq over the invasion of Kuwait, and the Number Ten Press Office let it be known that Powell would be expected to remain in post at least until after the Gulf crisis. He left in March 1991.

Both Powell and Ingham felt that Margaret Thatcher and they could make a difference to the country. They were pursuing objectives that they considered were utterly central to the national interest, and they were prepared to see their careers damaged in consequence. They were affected by the times, responding to crisis rather than to Thatcher. Thatcher, who also responded to crisis, welcomed them in what became for all of them a common struggle. Both men received knighthoods in her resignation honours' list.

[1] Interview, 25 May 1990.
[2] Interview, 20 February 1990.

257

THIRTEEN

A Chancellor goes

On 25 October 1989, the same day that Brian Clough said he would prefer to kiss Mrs Thatcher rather than quit Nottingham Forest, there were other interesting stories in the newspapers. The Prime Minister was in Malaysia, attending the Commonwealth Conference. The Chancellor of the Exchequer, Nigel Lawson, was reported to want the Prime Minister's personal economic adviser, Alan Walters, sacked. In a television interview broadcast the night before, he had described Walters as a 'part-time adviser',[1] suggesting that he could go as easily as he had come.

As the days went by, the story had echoes of the sort of shenanigans expected of a banana republic: the Prime Minister out of the country and the principal Minister, the Chancellor, seemingly making a bid for power. Wednesday, 25 October, was the start of a furious week which ended with the resignations of Nigel Lawson and Alan Walters, and the changing of the three most senior Ministers – Douglas Hurd became Foreign Secretary; the Chief Whip, David Waddington, became Home Secretary in place of Hurd, and John Major, who had been Foreign Secretary for just three months, became Chancellor of the Exchequer. Before becoming Foreign Secretary, Major had been Lawson's number two at the Treasury; his promotion to the Foreign Office was, accurately as it turned out, seen at the time as Thatcher's statement that he was her chosen successor. Lawson's resignation led to Major succeeding Thatcher sooner than anyone realized was likely. Lawson's departure from the Government was the beginning of the breaking up of Thatcher's authority over her Cabinet and over the Parliamentary Party.

The ostensible reason for the fuss was that in an article written for – but not yet published by – an American academic journal of

---

[1] BBC TV, *Nine O'Clock News*, 24 October 1989.

economics, Walters was reported to have said that the Chancellor's wish for the United Kingdom to join the European Monetary System being proposed by the other European Common Market Governments was unsound in economic terms, and that the Prime Minister agreed.[1] If he was saying this with the consent of the Prime Minister, he was passing a vote of no confidence in the Chancellor of the Exchequer, since Nigel Lawson had committed himself to the UK joining the EMS.

Various Conservative Members of Parliament supported the Chancellor and called openly for Walters' resignation. What one may call the British constitution and parliamentary and public opinion do not know quite what to think about external advisers in government. Marcia (now Lady) Falkender was a very significant 'kitchen Cabinet' figure (who, unlike Alan Walters, generated a great deal of personal animosity) in the years of Harold Wilson's second premiership. Lord Cherwell had acted as a lightning-rod for Churchill. The inaccessible prominent adviser is not a figure who easily fits into the constitution, nor a figure who is much liked by parliament and public. Alan Walters was in an awkward position: when a senior Minister draws attention to such a person, irrespective of the issue, the odds tend to be fairly well stacked against the adviser. The usual way of getting around it is to put the adviser in the House of Lords where they can say their piece.

Apart from Walters and the Prime Minister, everyone seemed to have lost sight of the key point. They worked up an anger over a participant in a debate instead of considering what he had to say. In the kerfuffle there was hardly any media coverage to make the Great British Public aware that joining the EMS would be a major policy move, locking the economy into a supranational vice that might be of great benefit but, equally, might not. Joining would mean that the monetary levers at the Government's disposal – notably interest rate fixing – would be committed to maintaining the value of sterling in relation to the Deutschmark (the System's spinal currency), and could no longer be used fully to counteract inflation and unemployment or to fight economic recession. Only fiscal meas-

[1] Sir Alan Walters, 'My Deviationist Economics', written for the *American Economist* and first published in the *Independent*, 26 October 1989.

ures (taxation) would remain fully at the Government's disposal. Membership of the EMS, in other words, would involve a significant surrender of national sovereignty and power.[1]

The pressure from British business and the City of London to enter the EMS had been a crucial factor in the debate over joining. A fundamental change wrought by the Thatcher revolution has been not so much to shift away from manufacturing, but to give new emphasis and support to service industries. Just as the south of England has done better than the north, so activities characteristic of the south have done better than activities historically characteristic of the north. Principal 'south' activities have been the financial services of the City of London. Now, for the first time, Margaret Thatcher appeared to be colliding with the City, and thus with some of the people whom she had 'made' during the previous decade. The Prime Minister who had presided over the 'Big Bang' in the City (when it became fully computerized and the volume of market trading – and thus, in the main, profits – leaped up accordingly) was now acting against joining the EMS which the City, anxious to maintain its centrality as a dispenser of services, wanted to join. The economic realities of the City point to its operating at the highest possible level of activity, and currency assimilation (which is part of what joining the EMS would involve) means just that, through being able to operate in a much bigger uniform currency market. That such assimilation may not be good for manufacturing industry or for aspects of British Government policy is a secondary consideration for the City. What was significant about this collision with Thatcher was that interests which she did a great deal to create and to sustain were finding her not so useful any more.

Once again, however, the journalistic demand to present policy

[1] Definitionally, sovereignty is different from power. But absolute sovereignty would entail the absence of any countervailing power, and since this situation is never the case, the reality is that sovereignty and power overlap.

One consequence of joining the ERM, for example, was apparent when Norman Lamont, Major's Chancellor, as 1991 opened, said that because of increased Government spending necessitated by the conflict with Iraq in the Gulf, taxation might have to be increased and that interest rates (which could be used to help control debt and spending) would have to be kept high in accordance with the EMS agreement (*Independent*, 2 January 1991).

in terms of personalities and conflict meshed with the resentments of disgruntled politicians and prevented a proper analysis of what was going on. That the Prime Minister and Walters – as it now seems – might have been right about the EMS was not addressed. Instead, comment favoured Nigel Lawson's position, with the majority 'City view' in favour of joining the EMS and of high interest rates being frequently cited in support, not least by Opposition spokesmen. Indeed, an assumption that the interests of the City were identical to those of the country at large dominated discussion. No one pointed out that the City's interest is in making money, and to this end City people naturally favour stability and predictability. Substantial financial support, for example, has always come from the City to political parties that favour proportional representation because in a PR system the swings of the pendulum from Right to Left are muted and the more predictable politics of consensus governs.

One of the most interesting aspects of the affair was the backhanded tribute to Thatcherism that Labour's viewpoint represented: the City was no longer being seen as a bunch of purple-faced Old Harrovians smoking cigars in the Livery companies. The 1980s had seen the democratization of the City to an extraordinary degree. The 'Yuppies' with their youth, hard vowels, red braces, striped shirts, designer suits, mobile telephones, computer literacy, and telephone-number incomes dramatically represented this change. And this had an effect on the Labour Party: one could not imagine the Party being magnetized by the 'City view' a decade earlier.

The inside of the Labour Party has not really been anti-City since the war, although the bitterness of 1931 had greatly soured its view before then. In that year, the City establishment at a time of great economic crisis demanded cuts in social benefits when – with many people having been unemployed for years – such cuts were very cruel. No one told the then Labour Government that an alternative would be to cut the pound loose from gold (which had been fixed at too high a sterling price in 1925). The pound was cut loose from gold in September 1931, after the Invergordon mutiny. The City did not collapse, and there is a case to argue that prosperity improved from that moment. Sophisticates in the Labour Party then recognized in the City of that period a set of rather frightened institutionalists who sought, fundamentally, to get on with everyone: Hugh Dalton, Labour's leading financial spokesman in the 1940s, remarked that the Bank of England would be nationalized over a cup of tea. When he was Chancellor after the war, that is exactly what happened. From the early 1930s on, the City has never cared who governs as long as it can have a working relationship with them: Labour as a whole, it seemed, had come to understand that by 1989.

On the morning of Thursday, 26 October 1989, the *Independent* newspaper carried a revealing set of articles. Most appropriate was Alan Walters' article that had apparently been the cause of Lawson's concern. But in the accompanying news story, it emerged that the article had previously not been published anywhere; that the *Financial Times* had obtained a copy from Walters as background material for a profile of him that they were planning; that the newspaper had published some extracts from the article a week before on 18 October, and that the article had been written more than a year earlier at a time when Walters had not been an adviser to the Prime Minister.

The article itself proved to be a retrospective, historical piece about Alan Walters' career rather than the attack on Nigel Lawson's current economic plans which people had been led to believe only days before: the trap of making everything personal had been sprung by Nigel Lawson and the nature of media reporting.

The passage that reportedly caused Lawson anger referred to a debate that had taken place eight years earlier. Walters spoke about two major controversies that had dominated his 1980–82 period as personal economic adviser to the Prime Minister. The first was when in 1981 he had been instrumental in convincing her to cut in half the borrowing requirement of the public sector, thus introducing the biggest budgetary squeeze in peacetime history against the advice of the Treasury and the Bank of England and all conventional wisdom. This was the move that prompted the letter to *The Times* on 31 March 1981, signed by 365 economists including all the living ex-chief economic advisers to the Government, condemning the policy. Subsequently, it should be said, events proved Walters to have been magnificently right.

The second controversy was when 'I found myself in a beleagured but rather select minority. The issue was exchange rate intervention and in particular the advisability of Britain joining the exchange rate mechanism (ERM) of the European Monetary System.' Succinctly expressing his argument against Britain joining the System in a passage which was ignored by most reporters and commentators, Walters continued: 'For more than 35 years I have been convinced that the various forms of pseudo-fixed exchange rates, dignified by various names such as crawling pegs, reference zones, etc., had only deleterious consequences – especially encouraging overvaluation and repression (on the part of dependent currencies such as sterling, the French franc, etc.) and massive capital flight or inflow when the "realignment" was imminent, which would in turn give rise to proposals for more exchange controls and trade barriers.[1] The pressure from Europe and from the British establishment to conform and join the ERM has been enormous.'

Following this passage in Walters' article came his statement of the advice he had given in 1980–82: that to join the EMS before the circumstances were right would be a mistake. This became official Government policy in 1989, uttered frequently by Nigel Lawson and the Prime Minister, and enshrined in the 'Madrid Declaration' of 27 June 1989 (the conditions for British entry to the EMS were substantially drafted by Walters)[2]. He also drew a contemporary parallel: 'But the arguments have never attained even a minimum level of plausibility. My advice has been for Britain to retain its system of flexible exchange rates and to stay out of the

[1] It is very hard to attach such economic moves to an ideological perspective. Samuel Brittan in his *Steering the Economy: The Role of the Treasury* (Harmondsworth, Penguin, 1971 rev. edn), pointed out that when cutting the pound loose from fixed exchange rates was contemplated in 1951, it was regarded as a Radical Right initiative; when the question came up again in the early 1960s, it was regarded as dangerously Left.
[2] Sir Alan Walters, 'Get Thatcher, and They Did', *The Times*, 6 December 1990, and Nigel Lawson, Letter, *The Times*, 7 December 1990. Walters stated that he had devised the Madrid conditions (detailing the 'right' circumstances for entering the EMS) 'at least three days before the meeting'. Lawson stated that he had 'spelled out what were to be the key elements of the Madrid conditions' two weeks before that, and 'Sir Alan's only contribution was to add some further irrelevant conditions which he well knew were unlikely to be met for many years, if ever, and which were rightly disregarded when we did at last join the ERM in October this year.'

present arrangements of the ERM. So far Mrs Thatcher has concurred. (Of course, I would not be opposed, at least on economic grounds, to the development of a proper European currency administered by a European Central Bank preceded by absolutely fixed exchange rates *and* appropriate monetary institutions to support that fixity. But that is another story.) It would not be in Britain's or, I believe, Europe's interest to join the present half-baked system.'[1]

There it was. The EMS system was 'half-baked' in Walters' opinion. Nigel Lawson insisted that this opinion was being aired with Prime Ministerial authority.

The *Financial Times* that same day – 26 October – had a front-page headline story to the effect that the Prime Minister would order Walters to be silent. It seemed as if the Chancellor's anger had forced the Prime Minister to spank her adviser in public.

From these pieces of news, it was clear that either there was far more to the story than had yet appeared or that Nigel Lawson was seizing upon an excuse to embarrass the Prime Minister and Alan Walters. It also seemed fairly certain that most of those who had entered the row had not read the article in question: it had not, after all, been published anywhere until it appeared in the *Independent*. Above all, the squabble of personalities had completely obscured the serious matter of whether or not joining the EMS was a good idea.

Later, Alfred Sherman was to say that without Walters at Number Ten, Mrs Thatcher had been at a loss and unable to control the Chancellor.[2] In 1984, having succeeded Geoffrey Howe as Chancellor immediately after the 1983 general election, Lawson had, in fact, started the reflationary process that led to the high inflation and interest rates that were the backdrop in the autumn of 1989: indeed, some observers had pointed out at the time that the results of Lawson's actions would not be known until 1988/89.[3] In addition, his determination to join the EMS was also criticized by William Keegan, economics editor of the *Observer*, regarded as being more hostile to Government financial policy than commentators in some other Sunday newspapers. Keegan described Law-

[1] *Independent*, 26 October 1989.
[2] *Spectator*, 11 November 1989.
[3] For example, Tim Congdon, *Weekly Economic Monitor*, October 1985.

son's interest in controlling the exchange rate as 'something of an obsession; he subjugated other aspects of policy to the attempt to convince the Prime Minister that it was possible to control the exchange rate, and hence put the pound into the exchange rate mechanism. His over-confidence in 1987–8 led to the dramatic tax-cutting budget of 1988 when the balance of payments and inflation trends were already looking ominous. Reckless expansion, and a complete absence of formal credit controls, led to all the emphasis being put on higher interest rates . . . Mr Lawson has bequeathed a monumental balance of payments crisis to his successor . . . The present exchange rate [£1 – about $1.58; DM2.90] is unsustainable, and Sir Alan Walters was right to question the policy of trying to hold it.'[1]

Lawson used domestic interest rates and intervention in the financial markets to try to keep the pound at about 3 German marks. Thus in June 1988 he had reduced base rates to 7.5 per cent to prevent the pound becoming stronger and exceeding the DM3 parity level. This caused a credit boom (when he resigned, there was about £40 billion of private sector credit outstanding) and an import boom, weakening the pound and encouraging inflation. So, in 1989 he doubled interest rates in a credit squeeze to strengthen the pound.

In the House of Commons some days later, Lawson revealed that he had also faced the Prime Minister's opposition to his attempt to make the Bank of England independent. It might have been pointed out to Lawson that the Bank would almost certainly have stopped him from his 1987–9 pump priming if it had been truly independent. Walters himself had warned the Prime Minister towards the end of 1987 that Lawson's monetary expansion was far too great and ought to be withdrawn quickly, and that the Chancellor was also tagging the Deutschmark. It was to be inferred, from Sherman, that had Walters been an adviser in 1985 and 1986, the rise in inflation would have been forestalled, and that he had been recalled in 1989 to help the Prime Minister in her struggle to control the Chancellor. What was more, Sherman was satisfied, this recall was

[1] William Keegan, 'How Nigel's Boom Led to Doom', *Observer*, 29 October 1989.

the start of a witch-hunt against Walters: exactly by whom he did not say.[1]

Just over a year later, Walters echoed this thought, writing an article, 'Get Thatcher, and They Did,' in *The Times* two weeks after Margaret Thatcher's resignation, in which he said that 'for the get-rid-of-Thatcher gang, I was a splendid intermediate target'. He added that the *Economist* magazine and the political editor of the *Financial Times*, Philip Stephens, were used to spread stories 'at the height of the [November 1990] leadership crisis' by the anti-Thatcher campaign.[2] Nigel Lawson took issue with Walters' article, saying, 'It was the activities of Sir Alan Walters which, by damaging the government, damaged Margaret Thatcher ... Margaret Thatcher was a great prime minister. Sir Alan speaks more truly than he imagines when he writes "perhaps the first step on the slippery slope of Mrs Thatcher's decline was associated with my return to Number Ten in May 1989" – a step I urged her, in vain, not to take, warning her that it was bound to cause the government trouble we could well do without. And so, alas, it did.'[3]

Behind the suspicions of Sherman and Walters lay a shadowland. In the summer of 1989, Thatcher had reshuffled her Cabinet, moving Geoffrey Howe from the Foreign Office to be her deputy and the Leader of the House of Commons, which in turn removed him from certain Cabinet Committees where he had been able to act in concert with Nigel Lawson. The two had formed a strong personal friendship, and supported each other behind the scenes and in comments to the press. Howe had made his anger at being moved widely known, and when he finally resigned from the Government in November 1990, in his resignation speech (during which Nigel Lawson pointedly sat beside him) he acknowledged that he had 'wrestled for perhaps too long' with a conflict of loyalty between the Prime Minister and what he saw as the national interest.[4] But for Thatcher the 1989 summer reshuffle had been a serious act of self-preservation. She left Lawson in place, but with John Major as the new Foreign Secretary she had an economic expert who not

---

[1] *Spectator*, 11 November 1989.
[2] Walters, 'Get Thatcher, and They Did'.
[3] Nigel Lawson, Letter, *The Times*, 7 December 1990.
[4] *Independent*, 14 November 1990.

only took her side against Lawson, but was now also able to debate the Chancellor as an equal. In October, after three months of this, Lawson's frustrations had boiled over.

Nigel Lawson was an extremely intelligent, able, energetic, self-opinionated, noisy journalist and then politician. He had justified self-confidence in his ability to master material. He was not a team-player. He was a brilliant individualist who was very valuable to the Conservative Party and to Thatcher, but who could be replaced easily: there were no 'Lawsonites'. 'I had never, ever had any ambition to be Prime Minister,' he said, 'and so I have never culti-vated people as you have to if you are going to be.'[1] As editor of the *Spectator* in the 1960s, his editorials were arrogant, shrewd, gaullist and belligerent. He represented the vanguard of the post-war revolt against the Atlantic alliance; fixed parities, and the com-mon wisdom on the Welfare State and industrial relations. He was the house smart-alec of the New Conservatives. He was the most independent-minded Minister in a crucial Department that Mar-garet Thatcher had ever had. He was not deferential. He was a dynamic outsider. He had written the February 1974 Manifesto, and then he became an early Thatcherite. He was a man who went his own way, as his fight with Walters and Thatcher showed.

The *Financial Times*, for their planned profile of Alan Walters, had approached an old friend of his, Professor Ezra Bennathan, for biographical material. Bennathan had suggested that Walters unpublished article could be used.[2] It seems probable that someone at the *Financial Times* read the article quickly, thought that Walters' views would be of interest to the Chancellor (if there was a witch-hunt going on, then, perhaps, one of the hunters was at the *Finan-cial Times* and was now reporting back to the Witchfinder General), and sent it to Lawson.

Whispers had begun about Walters' advice being in conflict with Lawson's policy just as the Prime Minister left for Malaya and the Commonwealth Conference. The *Financial Times* carried a story that Walters 'has recently told US bankers and policy-makers that sterling needs to fall to avoid a severe recession in the UK . . . His

[1] Interview, Rt Hon. Nigel Lawson, MP, 21 November 1990.
[2] Ezra Bennathan, Letter, *Independent*, 26 October 1989.

comments concerned some of his American listeners, according to participants, who felt that they had contradicted the message from Mr Lawson about trying to secure a stable pound.'[1] Nigel Lawson later reported that he had obtained 'corroboration of this in a letter from an eminent British economist who happened to be present'.[2] Walters was also said to have criticized the Chancellor's policies at City lunches – although only one lunch (with the Directors of Union Discount) was actually mentioned. Union Discount were horrified: their lunches have been a City fixture for decades, and never before had anything leaked from them. What was more, there was no evidence that Walters had actually said at Union Discount what was attributed to him. Such occasions, with their pledge of discretion, are central to the City's relationship with governments. They depend upon them in order to have an accurate understanding of policy. To many in the City it seemed much more likely that Walters had been set up. There was no secret about his lunching with Union Discount: what could be easier than for witch-hunters to spread rumours therefrom?

That was all before the actual events of late October. The Prime Minister, just back from Kuala Lumpur, found herself in the middle of an autumn storm. She declared her support of her Chancellor's policies, and also her support for her adviser, in the House of Commons on the afternoon of 26 October. 'Advisers advise,' she said, 'and Ministers decide.' Interestingly, what she did not say was that as First Lord of the Treasury she had a direct and superior interest in the Exchequer, and that as Prime Minister, she had every right to take advice from whomsoever she wished.

After Parliamentary Questions on 26 October 1989, at about 5.40 p.m., rumours circulated that Nigel Lawson had resigned on the grounds that he could not continue with Walters second-guessing him behind the door of Number Ten. The rumour was confirmed just before six o'clock. Nigel Lawson had joined the queue of angry middle-aged men who had departed from Margaret Thatcher's Cabinets.

Lawson's resignation, long urged by Sam Brittan, left a legacy

[1] *Financial Times*, 28 October 1989.
[2] Nigel Lawson, Letter, *The Times*, 7 December 1990.

of high interest rates, worrying economic indicators pointing to persisting high inflation, rising unemployment, declining economic growth and the evidence of an historic balance of payments deficit that showed little sign of letting up. For nearly two years, Lawson had acted as if the United Kingdom was already a member of the exchange rate mechanism of the European Monetary System. He had not received Cabinet or Prime Ministerial approval for shadowing the Deutschmark, although Thatcher was, of course, informed about what was going on. 'We had started shadowing the Deutschmark in March 1987,' Lawson pointed out. 'She knew all about that. The Cabinet didn't have much to do with it. There wasn't much discussion in Cabinet about the exchange rate mechanism, but there had been between the Prime Minister and myself. I had seen her privately and talked to her. She had the daily market reports every night. She knew exactly what was happening. And Alan Walters was telling her. It is nonsense to say that she didn't know in advance.'[1] 'I think that history will say that she was wonderful until Nigel Lawson,' said one of her closest advisers pessimistically. 'Until the summer of 1988, until Lawson took control of the situation, and she didn't face up to it. And she was stopped from doing what she wanted to do in 1988, which was to fire him, by whatever: her own instincts, other people, and so on. And unfortunately, most of what she had achieved was undone at that time.'[2]

Unkind souls wondered if Lawson had sought a conflict over Alan Walters so that he could resign before his reputation as Chancellor was further dented by dismal economic performance. He had come in as Chancellor in 1983 with inflation at 4.5 per cent; he left with it at about 8 per cent and rising.[3]

[1] Interview, Rt Hon. Nigel Lawson, MP, 21 November 1990.
[2] Interview, 5 June 1990.
[3] On 6 October 1989, a one-point rise to 15 per cent in base lending rates was signalled by the Bank of England. This, the highest base rate for eight years, was just before the Conservative Party Conference. Lawson admitted that it was 'awkward and embarrassing' so close to the Conference, and he was attacked by Conservative MPs for inevitably losing votes because of raised mortgage rates following on from the increase, and for spending about $2 billion during the previous week in a vain defence of the value of the pound. On 13 October, the *Daily Mail* carried a front page headline, 'This Bankrupt Chancellor', attacking the policies that had required the hike in base rate. At the Party Conference there were constant reports of dissatisfaction with Lawson.

Shortly after Lawson's departure, the resignation of Alan Walters was announced. Although his reasons for going were not made public, he had little choice but to go. It would be very difficult for anyone to accept the position of Chancellor with Walters remaining at Number Ten after Lawson's resignation: a new Chancellor would be seen as a weak yes-man in the circumstances.

Nigel Lawson's letter of resignation showed that he saw himself as the Prime Minister's equal, implicitly denying that she was the captain of the team: 'The successful conduct of economic policy is possible only if there is – and is seen to be – full agreement between the Prime Minister and the Chancellor of the Exchequer.' He was also – and probably correctly – giving no place to the Cabinet's view in his argument. This was between him and her.

The Prime Minister and the Chancellor of the Exchequer dominate most of the Cabinet Committees, which are much more important than the Cabinet as a whole on most matters. So, in a real sense, since the Cabinet became a dignified but not an effective part of the constitution, in any major matter it is likely to be only one or two Ministers and the Prime Minister who determine policy. 'The days are long forgotten when, as with Baldwin, the Prime Minister was titular head but gave his great departmental chiefs a free hand,' John Biffen has observed. 'The two factors which gave the Thatcher Cabinets their cohesion and radical drive were the selected membership of key Cabinet committees and, most important, the indissoluble links between the Downing Street neighbours, the Chancellor and the Prime Minister.'[1] Cabinets very rarely want to play with Prime Ministers: this is a key element in the role of Cabinets, and is an important aspect of the British form of mixed government. Senior Ministers are meant to countervail the Prime Minister a lot of the time.

Lawson's letter continued: 'Recent events have confirmed that this essential requirement cannot be satisfied so long as Alan Walters remains your personal economic adviser.'[2] He was seizing upon

[1] John Biffen, 'The Prime Minister's Rubber-Stamping Ground' *Independent On Sunday*, 22 July 1990. When Jim Prior was moved from Employment to the Northern Ireland Office in September 1981, he made a point of telling the press that he had secured from the Prime Minister an undertaking that he would remain on the key economic Cabinet Committees.

[2] *Independent*, 27 October 1989.

270

something that he could never get for quotation: the whisper he had no doubt heard that 'The Prime Minister does not like Nigel's policy.' At last he had found a habitation and a name for what he had been hearing, one suspects, for some time. Walters became a focus because he was the one person Lawson could put on the record.[1] As is so often the case in politics, fights take place about unlikely things because the likely ones are kept in the shadows.

The Prime Minister's reply provided the first indication that Lawson's attack on Walters was a red-herring, and that the real reason for Lawson's resignation lay elsewhere. She did not mention Walters, instead concentrating on Lawson's political record as Chancellor. 'It is a matter of particular regret,' she wrote, 'that you should decide to leave before your task is complete.'[2] She was indicating that Lawson had resolved to go regardless; she was implying that he was leaving in the midst of economic worries that he had caused and before he had cleared things up. As far as she was concerned, Lawson's departure had far more to do with policy and ambition than with Alan Walters. In politics, policies often become vehicles for ambition, and the drive for an integrated Europe was a juggernaut.

Once Britain's most pressing economic and industrial problems had been redressed in the early 1980s – inflation brought right down; the unions forced back into the bottle – the mice came out to play in no uncertain way. It looked as if senior Ministers, who

[1] On Tuesday 31 October, Nigel Lawson, speaking in the House of Commons, changed his tune about the cause of his departure (although not for long) and confirmed that Sir Alan Walters was not the cause of his resignation, as he had heavily indicated in his letter. Sir Alan's article, Lawson said, 'was of significance only in as much as it represented the tip of a singularly ill-conceived iceberg with all the destructive potential that icebergs possess' (*Independent*, 1 November 1989). He revealed that he had wanted to make the Bank of England independent, but the key policy difference which ultimately led to his resignation, he went on, was with the Prime Minister over the role of exchange rate policy.

Margaret Thatcher might very well have liked an independent Bank of England too. An independent Bank would provide economic discipline. One of the reasons that she seems to like the US system so much is that she knows that no one is to be trusted all the time, and that a certain dispersion of authority is a sensible step to take – as in the US Constitution where there is a balancing of power between the legislative, judicial and executive branches of government. She probably does not really enjoy a situation in which the Treasury and the Bank operate effectively under the same hat.

[2] *Independent*, 27 October 1989.

271

were very unlikely to become Prime Minister but were formidable department heads (the Howe–Lawson axis), were hoping to build their reputations on the next big 'thing': European integration. It could be said that they were looking forward to a point where decisions would be made outside Britain by people like themselves acting in concert with their opposite numbers in the European Commission and in European governments.

The European issue involved a further point. It was a way of channelling certain forces in British politics. The Prime Minister could always appeal to the nation over the heads of her Ministers, but in a Britain more enmeshed in a European framework, that would be less effective. It would not be surprising to find that Howe and Lawson had plans to use European institutions and instrumentalities for a national and economic strategy of their devising, and as a way of cementing their own positions in a European oligarchy of very senior people. And it was also the case that the EMS could be seen – perfectly accurately – as a way of binding Europe together more strongly before new pressures came to bear on it both from within and from the rest of the world. Decisions have to be taken: they may very well be wrong. A large number of people – not just Nigel Lawson and Geoffrey Howe – strongly supported the United Kingdon joining the EMS. It was a major alternative for the British economic future.

With a Prime Minister in power for a decade and seemingly entrenched, frustration was a hallmark of Thatcher's senior colleagues who, as the years passed, had to recognize that their chances of ever becoming Number One were diminishing in favour of a younger generation. Frustration was also inevitable amongst backbenchers. A Government has about one hundred appointments to make, from the Cabinet rank down, thus leaving at least two hundred MPs at any one time without office (in Thatcher's case in 1987–90 it was nearly three hundred). After a decade, and despite shuffles and resignations even on the scale that Thatcher experienced, there were still well over one hundred MPs whom she had never promoted. Naturally enough, frustrated parliamentarians will look for policy bandwagons to clamber aboard in the hope of advancement, and will increasingly be prepared to look for new leadership in the hope of being part of a winning team. Margaret

Thatcher was aware of all this, but there was little she could do about it. Nigel Lawson and Geoffrey Howe were also aware, and their resignations from the Government inevitably played upon the ambitions of colleagues.

Despite his row with Alan Walters and the Prime Minister, however, Lawson was by no means condemned by all Thatcher's people. 'Lawson's greatest sin was to put more money into the economy at the point when he should have been taking it out,' said Nigel Vinson. 'But if he'd gone into the EMS at the point that he wanted to, I think he would have been right. It would have stabilized inflation and we wouldn't have to use interest rates to correct it and it wouldn't have accelerated. I think that Lawson got it more right than wrong. His major tax reforms are elemental in terms of husband and wife tax relief, being taxed independently, the dropping of the top band of income tax to 40 per cent, and other major changes that he's done, all in the right direction.'[1]

However, unlike the mainstream of economic policy where Lawson had been a spokesman for the collective will, the EMS was another matter entirely. While there were many people who supported the idea of joining the EMS, there were also many people in the Government who were not happy about it. Partly because he was seen as being in the mainstream of the Government, by resigning Lawson fuelled a sense that Margaret Thatcher's administration was on the ropes. Lawson's support came principally from political colleagues, the City, and EEC officials. Thatcher was aided not only by Alan Walters, but by Treasury officials who disagreed with the Chancellor. Indeed, Walters was effectively a spokesman for the Treasury view in the argument over EMS membership. The questions that cried to be asked were: 'Why wasn't Lawson overruled?' And 'Is Margaret Thatcher a less formidable Prime Minister than her reputation indicates?'

[1] Interview, Lord Vinson, 30 May 1990.

FOURTEEN

The end in sight

The Lawson affair shed an intense light on Thatcher's style of management, on the divergent views in Europe in the heart of her Government, and on the handful of her people still active around her. It was the preplay to Geoffrey Howe's resignation on 1 November 1990, and the events leading to Margaret Thatcher's departure from Number Ten four weeks later. It also showed that Thatcher's people – the people she could count upon – were behind the scenes, and emerged at their peril into the foreground.

Nigel Lawson called into question the role of advisers generally – not just Alan Walters personally, but the people Thatcher depended upon for advice and sustenance. By doing this, he forced Thatcher to rely upon a smaller circle of permanent officials (principally Bernard Ingham and Charles Powell) by removing from her side one of the outstanding people she liked and trusted most. In the crucial area of management of the economy, Thatcher would be unable to have an official economic adviser in the future (because any Chancellor would have to protest that such an appointment, following the Lawson affair, was effectively a statement of no confidence in the Chancellor by the Prime Minister).

The policies that had produced the worrying economic indicators of 1989 and the high interest rates, rising unemployment and economic recession of 1990–91 had, of course, involved many more people than Lawson. Apart from his personal decisions to shadow the Deutschmark and act as if Britain had joined the EMS, Lawson had been a spokesman for the mainstream of the Government, and at the Treasury had been the official executor of the general will.

Thatcher's extraordinary ability was that she somehow managed to dance above trouble when it came to a crunch. Her ability to distance herself from Lawson, making it appear that the course of the economy was of his making alone, was another example of her doing so. She publicly condemned the rise in inflation, for example, in her final speech to the House of Commons as Prime Minister, declaring, as if she had had nothing to do with it, that: 'There was too much borrowing and inflation rose. That is why we had to take the tough and unpopular measures to bring the growth of money supply within target. Inflation has now peaked and will soon be coming down.'[1] Using the royal 'We', she was consistently able to present herself as a strong-minded saviour. But it was wrong for Lawson alone to be blamed for the worsening economic performance of Britain. Six months after Lawson's resignation the new Chancellor, John Major, acknowledged that 'mistakes had been made' by the Government – rather than just by Lawson – in not dampening inflationary pressures earlier.[2]

If Lawson had been popular in the country as a whole, the outcome might have been different, with not only much more blame being immediately heaped on Thatcher's shoulders, but the effect of his resignation being greater. It was because Michael Heseltine had a degree of popularity nationwide that his resignation in 1986 had been more telling. In 1990, Thatcher's was the most unliked Government in a long time. There are usually people in Front Benches who are substantially loved; with the departure of Willie Whitelaw from her Cabinet, Margaret Thatcher lost that token of popular esteem. But while the country may not have had an affection for her, it did not have any for Lawson either, and this made it easier for her to ride above the storm. Had Lawson been a Whitelaw, it would have been much more difficult for her.

It is easy in retrospect to ascribe to the acts of politicians a coherence that they rarely have. Lawson simply made mistakes in 1985–8 with the Cabinet nodding him on because his record of success up to that point had been sufficiently marked that his colleagues, including the Prime Minister, thought that the Treasury was in good hands. Then in 1988–9, Lawson recognized his mistakes. By October 1989 he had marched himself into a swamp and was probably anxious to find a way out. It does him far too much dishonour as a cynic and honour as a political planner to assume

[1] *The Times*, 23 November 1990.
[2] *Independent*, 18 May 1990.

that matters were coherent. He could not have known that Walters' article was going to float into view, or that it would result in his own resignation (although there was little else that he could have chosen as his ground to resign about). He probably kept on thinking that after the successes he had had, surely a couple of turns of the spigot would put things right again. For him, it was probably like being in a company that had enjoyed great days but no longer did, except that this was not apparent to his colleagues until the money ran out.

For the long term, Lawson was making certain that Thatcher's style of government would be questioned, playing to the sensitivities of frustrated backbenchers and Cabinet Ministers. In the world of politics, having forced a senior adviser out, Lawson could argue that he had forced the Prime Minister to retreat in the interests of greater collective decision-making. The growth in influence and in numbers of advisers around Number Ten over the last three decades is disliked by MPs and Ministers, jealous of their influence. Nigel Lawson probably had almost all his Cabinet colleagues on his side on this point.

Lawson had actually raised a question about the 'primeness' of the Prime Minister, not accepting that it had apparently been settled over the centuries. With him, although everything was seen as personal, the constitutional position was a very real one. And it is a good question that has yet to be fully settled whether there is a House of Commons or a prime ministerial 'Presidency' in Britain. Nineteenth-century doctrine had it that the Prime Minister was 'first' and a magisterial figure in his own right, with powers of formation, dismissal, and elevation, but that Cabinets were strong too and could force a Prime Minister to back down. Lloyd George, who was one of the most formidable (if not, as the historian A. J. P. Taylor maintained, the most formidable) presences in twentieth-century British politics, said in his last years that he had to reckon with his War Cabinet and had never been able to deal with it as easily as Churchill dealt with his. The 'presidential' nature of the premiership was a subtext of Geoffrey Howe's resignation speech, as he remarked that Ministers − not least himself − shared achievements with the Prime Minister. 'Not one of our economic achievements would have been possible without the courage and the leadership of the Prime Minister,' said Howe, going on to refer to his period as her first Chancellor: 'And, if I may say so, they possibly derived some little benefit from the presence of a Chancellor who wasn't exactly a wet himself.'[1]

Throughout the century, there has been a movement in the balance of authority towards Prime Ministers. In the 1960s, there was discussion on whether the Prime Minister had become a 'President', with Ministers united under him by being a category of public servant.[2] The question of Ministers being subservient to the Prime Minister is a presidential one, rather than a parliamentary or collegial one. But people do speak of Harold Wilson and Ted Heath and Margaret Thatcher winning elections, and if that is how people think of it, that is a political reality. The nation may now, in fact, delegate presidential authority to Prime Ministers.

As Prime Minister, Thatcher was always helped by the fact that she was seen as being transparently straight and transparently trying to do the right thing. 'Most politicians are forced into telling lies,' said one of her top media advisers. 'But she doesn't, or, at least, she tells far fewer lies than most. The truth is that to make an omelette you have to break eggs. But nobody ever admits to breaking eggs. They all absolutely deny it. Nobody ever stands up and says, "Yes, you're absolutely right. Certain people will have to lose their jobs; others will become poorer; others will become richer; some of you will have a bad time, and it will be horrible for some people, but in the end it will all come right." And the reason that they don't do that is because it is the conventional wisdom that that is not the way to get elected. They don't have any real belief. They think that doing the right thing is not the way to get elected. They think people are so ghastly, and so pathetic and wimpish, that what you do is lie to them. They actually believe that if you stand up and say, "This is a very unpleasant thing and eggs get broken," people will say "I'm not electing you.".'[3] People never knew where they were

[1] *Independent*, 14 November 1990.
[2] During the 1974 general election campaign, Harold Wilson said that if he returned to Number Ten, there would be 'no presidential nonsense' such as had coloured comment during his first period as Prime Minister. (Peter Hennessy, *Whitehall* [London, Secker & Warburg, 1989], p. 243.)
[3] Interview, 5 June 1990.

with Harold Macmillan and Harold Wilson. No one could ever come alongside Edward Heath. Transparency is usually the mark of the not quite first-rate – of the predictable and manageable politician – and it was very unusual that Thatcher was a first-class politician and yet had this quality. People felt that they knew where they were with her, whether they liked it or not, and that showed in notable contrast to her Cabinet colleagues. Being a first-class politician, and yet in some respects being intensely predictable, is a very rare union.

Thatcher's predictability on the question of British sovereignty in relation to Europe underpinned complaints about her style. The question of sovereignty was to simmer on, despite Thatcher's agreeing to join the exchange rate mechanism (ERM) of the EMS in October 1990. It had boiled up as a major reason for the resignation of Geoffrey Howe. It provided Michael Heseltine with one of his principal arguments against Thatcher in his challenge to her leadership later in the month. 'The truth is that in many aspects of politics, style and substance complement each other,' said Howe, explaining his resignation to the House of Commons on 13 November 1990. 'The real tragedy is we did not join the Exchange Rate Mechanism at least five years ago ... How on earth are the Chancellor and the Governor of the Bank of England, commending the hard ecu [i.e. a single European currency which clearly entailed a European Central Bank] as they strive to do, to be taken as serious participants in the debate? ... It is rather like sending your opening batsman to the crease only for them to find, the moment the first balls are bowled, that their bats have been broken before the game, by the team captain. ... The tragedy is – and it is for me personally, for my party, for our whole people and for the Prime Minister herself, a very real tragedy – that her perceived attitude towards Europe is running increasingly serious risks for the future of our nation.'[1]

Six weeks later *The Times* carried a leader, 'Paying for a Mistake', saying that: 'The key policy decision [Mr Major] made during his period as Chancellor of the Exchequer [joining the ERM] was a mistake, at least in timing and execution', and that rising unemploy-

[1] *Independent*, 14 November 1990.

278

ment (1.7 million in November 1990, the greatest number unemployed for nine years) symptomatic of an economic recession, might force him to acknowledge that this was so.[1] By the beginning of February 1991, opinion generally was changing in favour of the Walters/Thatcher line. The investment company, Goldman Sachs, and the Institute of Fiscal Studies declared that membership of the ERM had a 'systematically perverse' effect on domestic monetary policy: i.e., that the Government had surrendered control over interest rates. Instead of lowering them to encourage reflation in a recession, they were being kept high to preserve the value of sterling in relation to the Deutschmark in the ERM exchange rate band.[2] 'We are deeply concerned about the state of the economy,' declared Alan Walters and five other leading monetarist economists in a letter to *The Times* on 13 February 1991. 'The principles of good monetary policy imply that interest rates should have been cut significantly by now . . . Failure to cut them is increasing the risks of a depression which could get out of control . . . The exchange-rate mechanism obstructs this course. Ideally, we should leave it, in order to adhere to soundly-based monetary targets, the best long-term guarantee of a sound currency.' When the same day the Bank of England announced a reduction of ½ per cent in interest rates, it simultaneously stated that this step was conditional upon sterling's value in the ERM band.

Howe, Lawson, and many others in the Conservative Party, in the City, and in business were prepared to sacrifice large measures of sovereignty in order for the United Kingdom to enjoy a leading role in the creation and eventual operation of a far more united and centrally controlled Europe. Margaret Thatcher was also prepared to surrender sovereignty to a more and more united and centrally controlled Europe: the difference was that she was kicking at every step. 'I fear the Prime Minister increasingly risks leading herself and others astray in matters of substance as well as style,' said Howe.[3] 'Howe indictment could

[1] *The Times*, 14 December 1990.
[2] This squeezed the money supply, thus further deepening the recession. And with sterling pegged to the Deutschmark which was rising in value, and with a UK–German trade deficit, the effects were even more severe.
[3] *The Times*, 14 November 1990.

be mortal blow to Thatcher' was the front-page headline in the *Independent* the following day.

Of course, the question is always which surrender of sovereignty should be engaged in as regards the currency system. To be on the Gold Standard, for example, would also be a surrender of sovereignty.[1] Doing the rounds of the Central Banks asking for loans to maintain the value of sterling can be every bit as much a surrender as that involved in joining any particular currency system. In 1975 and 1976, when the International Monetary Fund was called upon to support the pound, a series of requirements were attached to the loans by the IMF, including notification of policies for conservation and new energy production; consulting the Fund before introducing new, or intensifying existing, restrictions on trade; cutting public expenditure, the reductions in the public sector borrowing requirement. In an international economy, the question is *how* you surrender sovereignty while keeping as much range of choice as possible.

The subtext of joining the EMS was British weakness. What Howe and Lawson did not say was more important than what they did say. First, it was absolutely the last moment to seek the continuation of the American alliance: America is losing interest, and there is little left of the Anglo-Saxon elite in the USA who thought they were honorary citizens of Britain. Secondly, Howe and Lawson both felt, rightly or wrongly, that Britain is so weak in the European combination, that British advance in the 1980s merely maintained relative weakness compared to France and Germany and prevented Britain from being much weaker still. Thirdly, the emphasis on service industries in the 1980s was too great: manufacture is still the core of world greatness. But both Howe (a

[1] The limitations on sovereignty are market limitations. The limitations through the gold standard derive from the millions of individual 'micro' transactions by anyone dealing in gold denominated currency or in gold as a commodity. If a country's gold reserves flow out, certain consequences follow on internal pricing. There is a difference between contracting sovereignty (i.e. to the judgement of the market), and surrendering sovereignty to someone else. 'Free enterprise' does not mean an entrepreneur is free to impose whatever price (or product) he chooses: sovereignty is always qualified. A Government that submits to the gold standard is yielding to millions of micro judgements which is quite different from a Government putting itself under the tutelage of the French or German Government. People talk as if the one is like the other, but it is not.

lawyer) and Lawson (a journalist) are in the service sector. They both sat in a Cabinet that strongly supported service activity and basked in the smiles of the brothers Saatchi.

The jelling of Lawson's and Howe's view of her style was the principal cause of Thatcher's own departure. Ministers and back-benchers were able to rationalize opposition to her continued leadership on the grounds that she was listening to unelected officials more than to Ministers and parliamentarians, and that her style had become too abrasive, too autocratic, and was an election loser. 'The very close relationship between me and Margaret Thatcher continued for a long, long time,' said Nigel Lawson, reflecting on Thatcher's style, 'throughout the Opposition period and my time as Financial Secretary and Energy Secretary and for most of my time as Chancellor. We are very close. It was only after the 1987 election that the drift apart began. Geoffrey Howe had been a rival candidate for the leadership in 1975, and she continued to see him as a potential rival. That's the way she is. After the 1987 election, I was written up in a number of places as being the man who had really won the election, and she suddenly started to see me as a rival and her attitude changed. You know how press gossip is. They talked about me being a potential Prime Minister in several papers. It was all very ill-informed, but nevertheless she began to see me in a different light altogether, and began to distrust me politically for that reason.'[1]

Certainly, Thatcher's manner irked Ministers and MPs. When Lawson told her he intended to resign, she had not consulted her deputy, Howe, preferring the counsel of two of her people – Bernard Ingham and Charles Powell – to her senior political colleagues. This was taken (probably correctly) as yet another sign that Thatcher was isolated in power, unable to confide in her Ministers, and depending for personal support and advice on her people, who were appointees. Additionally, in debate she was a master of detail, and demanded that Cabinet Ministers themselves be expert in the affairs of their departments. As she insisted on television policy was hammered out in Cabinet Committees. Policy had been agreed in this way and had not been altered by advisers. 'I enjoy a good

[1] Interview, Rt Hon. Nigel Lawson, MP, 21 November 1990.

argument,' she declared. 'I enjoy dealing with the facts.'[1] She repeatedly demonstrated that she preferred accuracy to pleasantness. It was in this combination that her colleagues, nearly all from a generation that saw politics as part of a man's world, and nearly all imbued with the cult of the amateur which has coloured British politics and management for generations, found Thatcher's style so difficult to deal with. 'Some people find it difficult to argue with a woman Prime Minister, and shrivel up,' Douglas Hurd explained. But if you persevere, he continued, then if you were master of your case she would take note.[2]

She was also literal minded, and this, too, was irksome. When she said something, she meant it literally; when she was told something, she understood it literally, thus cutting through irony and assumption, the double helix of British upper-middle-class male conduct. The famed 'British understatement' was not for her, and nor were the class attitudes that went with it.

Margaret Thatcher was able to avoid being pinned down, partly because there could not be fraternity between her and her Ministers. The degree to which she, as Prime Minister, had power and her male colleagues did not became vastly more underlined than in the days when Wilson or Heath could be seen laughing with other men in their Cabinets. The biological distinction threw all sorts of other distinctions into high relief: one could not imagine another Minister banging her on the back. It focused her authority, not diminished it. And this did a great deal to diminish the authority of Ministers, not least because there was still a feeling that men dominated by a woman were wimps.

Her technique of constantly questioning people, never letting up, was a very valuable one (especially in a woman in command of men). Churchill, who showered his Ministers and military commanders with endless demands for information, acted similarly. One of the great shocks for Thatcher was her discovery of the fraudulent nature of the male world: that men are not all upright, tough, clear-minded – rather the reverse, in fact. And so questioning was a way of keeping them off balance. It is often easier for a

[1] *The Walden Interview*, ITV, 29 October 1989.
[2] Douglas Hurd, *Panorama*, BBC TV, 30 October 1989.

woman to crack the whip indirectly, by asking a man a question that he cannot properly answer. The person being questioned, even as he answers, becomes increasingly aware of his own ignorance. 'I hope she doesn't ask me about X!' is their inner thought. It keeps people permanently reminded of their inadequacies without saying it to their faces, and permanently under assessment: they are as good as their last answer. Thatcher was a trained barrister, and knew that anyone who answers questions is giving hostages to fortune.

The technique emphasizes the fact that in most relationships there is one who questions and one who is questioned, and after childhood the one who questions has the adult role. It also maintains distance: she was the smallest person in the Cabinet; she was the weakest physically; she was the one who had to think of her appearance when the wind blew. Asking questions is an effective way of combating the 'Don't trouble your head about that' male response to women.

Constant questioning also prevented a matter being regarded as settled until she said it was settled. It meant that things had to come through her hands and were clearly defined. It brought the power to decide right back to her. Howe and Lawson were trying to get out from under this by allying themselves to the external momentum of the EEC.

This was a key to Lawson's and Howe's behaviour. The whole tenor of their resignations was, 'I'm not going to be dominated.' It was an emotional response. In Lawson's case, matters probably went further than he intended. He probably thought he was engaged on a tactical, not a strategic manoeuvre, and then one thing led to another, or perhaps he was weighed down by increasing awareness that his own medium-term financial strategy had gone off the rails. He probably did not recognize that the Walters article was going to be so heavily emphasized (a point suggested by the matter of his speech in the House of Commons following his resignation, when he discussed the nature of Ministers, relationships with the Prime Minister and policy matters, rather than his disagreement with Walters, as reasons for his departure). It was a fairly thin news period, and the newspapers played it up. Lawson probably thought that he would embarrass

Walters and the Prime Minister, and that it would end there. Instead, it became a situation which neither the Prime Minister nor Lawson could escape. That was largely a media consequence, and the affair was an example of how media intervention can make a difference. What began as a purely bureaucratic and Whitehall intrigue on Lawson's part suddenly went out of control when everyone started looking.

Geoffrey Howe's relationship with Thatcher made his resignation particularly intimate. He had been, in effect, a Thatcherite before Thatcher, convinced of the need for monetarist measures in 1974. He had been an effective and successful Chancellor, and had proved to be far stronger than colleagues expected when it came to arguing for the 1981 Budget. But as Nigel Lawson pointed out, she always saw him as a rival. 'Geoffrey once popped his head round the door to ask her something,' an aide recalled. 'He stayed at the door: he didn't come into the room. He kept his hand on the door handle, and he shuffled uncomfortably. He was never at ease with her. I've forgotten what it was he wanted to know or to tell her. But when he closed the door and left, she turned to the rest of us – three of us – and pointed at the door where he'd been. "Nineteen votes!" she cried. "Nineteen votes!" That was the number of votes he'd got in the 1975 leadership election.'[1] 'The only time that she was a bully was when she would beat up Geoffrey,' another Number Ten insider said. 'It was two consenting adults agreeing to torture and to be tortured in privacy, both agreeing and both consenting for years and years and years. She did inflict torture, and he did receive it. I'm sure a judge would have said in court that no civilized human being can possibly imagine that these two things could be done willingly by two consenting adults. She would handbag him, and he would cower to receive it – actually cower. She loved to humiliate him, and he loved to receive it. He would curl up in a ball.'[2]

In her July 1989 Cabinet shuffle when she sacked Howe as Foreign Secretary and instead made him Deputy Prime Minister

[1] Interview, 20 February 1990.
[2] Interview, 2 January 1991.

284

and Leader of the House, she did so without consulting him first. 'She didn't handle Geoffrey at all well,' said Ian Gow a month after this event. 'At their first talk she did not offer the chairmanship of two Cabinet Committees; she did not offer the title, such as it is, of Deputy Prime Minister. And if, of course, she had started off the talk by saying, "Geoffrey, you know how much I owe to you, how much I hate doing reshuffles. Parliamentary proceedings are going to be televised. I must have somebody of real stature in the high-profile parliamentary job as Leader of the House. I want you to become chairman of these Cabinet Committees. I want you to be Deputy Prime Minister, and we'll put that out in the changes. But I'm going to ask you to leave the Foreign Office." But that wasn't how it was done. It was done as a confrontation, and not between people who ought to be trusted and close friends. That's why Geoffrey was wounded. That was very, very bad. And I'm afraid that the omens for Geoffrey and Mrs Thatcher working happily together are not good. As I look ahead I am filled with foreboding.'[1]

According to a Minister, in the last Cabinet meeting Howe attended before he resigned, Thatcher treated him with scorn and derision. As Leader of the House, Howe was responsible for Government business: 'There was some Bill that hadn't been scheduled properly following the Queen's Speech. "How can this Bill not be ready?" she demanded, and she suddenly went for Geoffrey. It was complete humiliation. She treated him so badly that that was finally it.'[2]

Michael Heseltine's resignation as Secretary of Defence over Westland Helicopters had been for different reasons. It also did damage to Thatcher's authority, but it made him the strongest Conservative challenger to her leadership. Whatever the rights and wrongs of the helicopter argument, it was clear that Heseltine had been wronged by a campaign of press leaks, and by leaving her Cabinet in protest (rather than being pushed) he established himself as independent of her and, as time passed, of her policies.

Once an argument ceases to be behind the Cabinet door, it is

[1] Interview, Ian Gow, MP, 8 August 1989.
[2] Interview, 30 January 1991.

very difficult for it to continue without someone quitting or losing face as a consequence. And when this happens, as with the facing-down of Barbara Castle in 1969 over *In Place of Strife*, it is recognized that a good deal of virtue has gone out of the Government.

But there was another side as well. In May 1988 Thatcher had an all but public argument with Lawson over exchange rate policy, providing the occasion of her remark, 'There is no way in which one can buck the market!' In the Members' Lobby of the House of Commons at the time, she was seen wagging a finger at her Chancellor in a public rebuke. But Lawson stuck to his guns, intervening in the international currency markets to support sterling, and she let him. He was expert in his case, and although she did not agree, he had convinced her that he knew what he was doing and was able to argue his corner against all comers. It was hailed as a victory for Lawson over the Prime Minister.

Enoch Powell was to point out that by intervening in the international financial markets to maintain the exchange rate of sterling (i.e. bucking the market), 'Nigel Lawson has followed a course which re-created inflation and thereby destroyed the record of growing industrial peace that had been the Government's most signal achievement.'[1] But the real question was: with other nations intervening in the market on behalf of their currencies, could Britain be the only one that did not? 'Let them bid their currencies up, and we'll take advantage of depreciation!' was effectively Thatcher's answer: a depreciating currency raises exports and diminishes imports. And was industrial peace a Government achievement? What about the drop in inflation world wide (largely a consequence of US action in suppressing its inflation in the late 1970s/early 1980s, 'the Volker recession')? The Government removing itself from industrial relations might have increased problems: industrial relations were vastly worse in the 1920s and 1930s when the Government intervened much less.

Margaret Thatcher tried to have matters both ways: she yielded to Howe, a Minister with a powerful pro-Europe constituency, on the Single European Act which embodied a general commitment

---

[1] *Daily Telegraph*, 28 October 1989.

to seek European monetary union, and then said she had done so because of the pressure he and others had brought to bear. At the time, Nigel Lawson was extremely uneasy about the signing of the Act: he considered that it had not been properly examined or debated in Parliament, and that Howe and Thatcher had conceded qualified majority voting as the way of dealing with European Community matters without sufficient discussion.[1] He also considered that the plan of Jacques Delors, President of the European Commission, for monetary union (of which the EMS was a part) was misconceived.[2] Lawson's later conversion to the EMS was, many suspected, an alibi for his failure to control the money supply. While the Act was an issue, however, Howe, with Lawson following, stood in an excellent position of unifying all bodies of opinion who wanted it. To put it crudely, anti-European opinion was disorganized; pro-European opinion was organized. Thatcher bought time for herself by yielding, and immediately started saying that she had not wanted to sign the Act, becoming a leader against the policy of her own Government. She shifted from being stalled on the penny against it to being stalled on the penny for it. Lawson or Howe, on a matter where Thatcher knew her own mind, should have known that she would never really accept the Act. On her part, signing the Act was politics, not intellect.[3]

Lawson's resignation gave a tremendous push to the drift towards entering the EMS, because Thatcher chose to take it that way. Just as Jim Callaghan would not stand up to the unions, she, having built up the service sector (the City is the predominant service centre) was not prepared to stand up to it as it pushed for opportunities in its own interests. She either had to say, 'Drop dead, City of London,' or she had to say, 'If the City gets any

[1] Private information.
[2] Interview, 24 August 1990.
[3] What was almost completely ignored in the press was that these incidents showed that Margaret Thatcher could be persuaded to go along with a policy that she did not agree with as long as she was convinced that its proponents had thought things through. She might regret it later, and might start opposing her own formal policies, but she was persuadable. Peregrine Worsthorne's editorial in the *Sunday Telegraph*, 29 October 1989, recognized her persuadability, but was an exception.

angrier, we're in trouble, so we'd better join the EMS since they want it so much.' She chose the latter course. In October 1990 when Thatcher finally agreed to enter the exchange rate mechanism of the EMS after a well-publicized row with John Major, her gracelessness in the matter was a political move on her part: entering the EMS but appearing to be in opposition to it, so that if it went wrong she would not be blamed. She was also being a representative of millions of British people who felt exactly the same way. Margaret Thatcher spoke for them even when she gave in to City and European pressure.

The Lawson affair highlighted another pressure on Thatcher: the consequences of her managerial style. She had a history of trying to hold on to senior Ministers rather than of sacking them: indeed, many felt that Lawson should have been moved from the Chancellorship in her July Cabinet shuffle. Keith Joseph, for example, argued that Lawson had misjudged his policy in 1988 and that the argument between him and the Prime Minister 'should have been brought to a head' sooner – not necessarily by Lawson's firing or resignation.[1] Similarly, it was considered by insiders that she had held on to other ex-Ministers, notably John Biffen, Norman Tebbit and Michael Heseltine, far longer than was necessary.

The criticism that should have been levelled at her was one of management. By holding on to people who not only disagreed (there should always be room for disagreement in a team – that is what a liking for good argument is all about) but who also acted in effect unilaterally, she could be seen as indecisive, encouraging people to think that her objections had disappeared, or that she had accepted a deviation from the letter of agreed policy when in fact she had not. Despite appearances, her willingness to act on the advice of colleagues actually brought her into more difficulties than if she had acted in the imperious manner popularly ascribed to her. The question echoed: 'Is she as formidable as is supposed?' If she had sacked Lawson after the first serious disagreements in 1988 (although it must be said that Lawson was then at the height of his popularity in the Conservative Party), the problems she had in

[1] Lord Joseph, *Newsnight*, BBC TV, 30 October 1989.

November 1989 would not have occurred. But during peacetime, Prime Ministers devote themselves to not losing senior Ministers. Macmillan and Attlee were the two who did fire senior Ministers outside of a change of Government, and in both cases their action was seen as panicky. Churchill did not purge his Government until the war was going badly in 1942.

Margaret Thatcher understood that firing Ministers is a reproach on Prime Ministers who are also Party leaders. The instinct of Prime Ministers is to conciliate and compromise with Cabinet Ministers. Prime Ministers know that to lose a strong personality is to lose a personality to play off against other strong personalities who always have the Prime Minister in their sights from the backbenches and from the Opposition benches. To lose senior Ministers is to narrow the sights on the Prime Minister. Thatcher's experiences demonstrated something else: that to hang on to Ministers too long can also be a grave mistake.

Prime Ministers tend to fire incompetents, not rivals. Macmillan purged no one who could be regarded as an alternative Prime Minister. When Kurt Schumacher, the post-war chairman of the West German Social Democrats, was once asked if former members of the Hitler Youth should be allowed into the Socialist Youth Movement, he took the view that of course they should be: that it is characteristic of totalitarian regimes that they try to exact complicity of all their citizens. Prime Ministers want to exact complicity of the strongest of their Party, not of the weakest. In a parliamentary system, you do not want strong people standing behind you, waiting to strike you.

Margaret Thatcher had been in the House during the debate in 1963 following the resignation of John Profumo as Secretary for War who admitted that he had lied to the House of Commons about his involvement with a party girl. The Profumo affair also involved a suspicion that a Soviet diplomat might have secured secrets from him. Five years earlier Thorneycroft, Powell and Birch had resigned. In 1960, Macmillan brought Thorneycroft back as Minister of Aviation and – with almost equal status (a tremendous slap at Thorneycroft, this) – Enoch Powell as Minister for Health. Only Nigel Birch remained outside the Government, on the backbenches. The Profumo debate was a moment of high drama: the

Government could have fallen and the Prime Minister was fighting for his political life.[1]

Birch, a dandy figure, stood up and spoke. 'Nigel Birch was mortally hostile to Macmillan,' remembered Enoch Powell. 'He had been Secretary of State for Air at the time of Suez, and what he saw at that time made him a mortal enemy for ever of Harold Macmillan.'[2] Now he laid into Macmillan's leadership of the country and the Party with a rawhide whip, quoting Robert Browning's biting poem, 'The Lost Leader':

> Let him never come back to us
> There will be doubt, hesitation, and pain.
> False praise on our part, the glimmer of twilight,
> Never glad confident morning again.

Macmillan slumped in his seat. No such devastating remark in the circumstances could have come from the Front Bench. And Margaret Thatcher was there.

Her fear, no doubt, was that when the knife was to be plunged

[1] A gathering of events and circumstances made this so. Macmillan had led the Conservatives to their third consecutive election victory in 1959. It was also the Party's fourth consecutive election in which it had increased its number of seats in Parliament. A euphoric sense had surrounded the Prime Minister in 1959–60. Then a reaction set in. The economy, artificially heated by the politically-inspired 1959 Budget, began to show worrying indicators. The policy of exiting from Empire upset many people and raised new questions: Dean Acheson, who had been Truman's Secretary of State, remarked in 1962 that 'Britain has lost an Empire and not found a role.' It was a remark that infuriated British diplomats, largely because it was unanswerable. The Party lost a series of by-elections. Swinging England had begun in the early 1960s, and so had the television satire boom. Public mocking of Macmillan seemed a national pastime. He reshuffled his Cabinet in July 1962, dismissing seven out of twenty-one Cabinet Ministers, including the Chancellor of the Exchequer. He thought he was losing touch, and the reshuffle was an attempt to bring in new and younger people. The Party thought he had lost his nerve. Then, having steamrollered Conservatives into acceptance of the European Economic Community, Macmillan was slapped in the face in January 1963 by de Gaulle delivering his first 'Non!' Four days later the leader of the Labour Party, Hugh Gaitskell, died. Harold Wilson succeeded Gaitskell, and in the summer of 1963 was enjoying a tremendous honeymoon with the media. Spy scandals percolated, with one (the Vassall case) accompanied by the resignation of a junior Minister. All this coloured the atmosphere of the debate: many MPs thought that Macmillan was on the ropes.

[2] Interview, Rt Hon. J. Enoch Powell, 1 November 1989.

between her shoulder blades, it would come from behind: from the backbenches. And it did. Howe's resignation speech in November 1990 was correctly seen at the time as a powerful attack on her. Alone of her ex-Ministers, he framed a speech that argued for an alternative view of the country's future and thus was able to say, in effect, 'Never glad confident morning again' as long as Thatcher remained Prime Minister. She tried to keep her most powerful critics in Office: she thought she had succeeded with Howe, and was surprised (but not alarmed) when he told her he was determined to go because of her 'nightmare vision' of Europe which he did not share.[1] She was being protective of herself in holding on to people. She was a reverse Walpole. Walpole threw people out rather than share any power. She, in contrast, was prepared to share Office and to some degree power. Lawson and Howe had pressed too much for power, so she shuffled Howe and broke their Cabinet Committee power base, but did not fire them. She tried hard – but not too hard – to keep Lawson in the tent; she did not try very hard to keep Howe in. Doubtless she had a certain contempt for her Ministers: the way they could be held by limousines and status and country houses and London apartments and all the rest, and this dulled her awareness to some extent. Howe's speech was the surprise, right between her shoulder blades.

Within days of the speech, Michael Heseltine declared that he would challenge Margaret Thatcher for the Party's leadership. He came to the contest with clean hands. Heseltine was not compromised to the same degree as Howe and Lawson, who were perceived as having put up with prolonged undercutting by Thatcher (and her press secretary, Bernard Ingham). He had fallen out with Thatcher on a very specific issue that he had used to enunciate a vision of Britain-in-Europe. Following on from Howe, he was consistent and persuasive in presenting himself as a 'European' candidate in 1990. He did not come from any particular part of the Party, but instead reflected an age group (the men in their fifties who were already being retired by Thatcher and who would be too old to challenge for top appointments if she remained the leader through the next general election) and those Conservative

[1] *Independent*, 14 November 1990.

MPs with majorities of less than 8,000 (many of whom understood the opinion poll evidence to mean that they might lose their seats if Thatcher led the Party into another general election).[1]

Heseltine appealed to anger, frustration, age, envy, Europe, a new decade, ambition, the knowledge that the Labour Party would not remain a beatable force forever, and the eighty-odd MPs in a Parliamentary Party of 370-plus who are always unhappy. He also enabled MPs who were dissatisfied on serious grounds with Thatcher's leadership to express their concern in a serious way: unlike Sir Anthony Meyer, the only previous challenger, Heseltine was seen as a potential Prime Minister. This combination, coupled with her loyalty to her Party, was sufficient to oust Thatcher.

[1] Following the murder of Ian Gow by the IRA in August 1990, there was a by-election in his Eastbourne constituency. The Liberal Democrats won, overturning Gow's 16,000 majority, thus lending weight in the weeks before the November 1990 leadership contest to the view that Thatcher was now an electoral liability.

FIFTEEN

Endgame

The collective wisdom of elected politicians is nothing to sneeze at. When the Conservative Parliamentary Party changed the Party's leader, replacing Thatcher with Major, it was an act of ruthless political expediency rather than a mistake or the consequence of a plot. This is not to say that there were no mistakes or plots. There was, for example, a conscious effort on the part of certain Cabinet Ministers to make Thatcher resign: on the night before she announced her resignation, Chris Patten co-ordinated a number of his colleagues to tell her to stand down and then twisted Douglas Hurd's arm to make him stand for the leadership.[1] Parties do not exist for Prime Ministers; Prime Ministers exist for Parties. Thatcher butchered Heath; Thatcher's Cabinet butchered her.

There comes a point when a Government has done all that voters want it to do. For it to do more, even more of the same, is to make the country say 'Enough'. Thatcher had been in power for eleven and a half years, and leader of the Conservative Party for fifteen and three-quarter years. Opinion polls reflect the background noise of politics: what constituents think. Thatcher may well have done as much as the country wanted her to do, which is what the opinion polls were indicating. She was becoming mechanical, and more dominating. Over the last 150 years, there has never been a Party in power for more than fifteen years at a stretch. Thatcher was bidding to be in continuous power for thirteen and a half years, and had declared her intention of going on for a fourth term in Office if she won the next general election, which could have meant her being Prime Minister continuously for over eighteen years. The Conservative Party, like all Parties, wants to stay in power for as long as possible. Its innate wisdom signalled that if Margaret

---

[1] Private information.

Thatcher remained leader, the country might well have said at the next general election, 'We'll try something else.'

Immediately after the results of the first ballot in the 1990 leadership election had been announced, Thatcher declared her intention to fight on. She had received the support of fifty-five per cent of the Parliamentary Party compared to forty-one per cent for Heseltine. Twenty-four hours later, she consulted the men in grey suits (as the Party's elder statesmen were now called) and her Cabinet colleagues about her course of action. Two-thirds of the Cabinet advised her to stand down; four Ministers – Chris Patten, Kenneth Clarke, Norman Lamont and Malcolm Rifkind – went further and suggested that they might not be able to support her continued candidacy.[1] All the arguments about her being a divisive leader and that she might not win against Heseltine on the second ballot were deployed, as was the opinion poll evidence suggesting that the Party would lose the next general election if she remained leader. But this was not enough to make her change her mind and stand down. What tipped the balance was when colleagues she knew to be her friends said to her that after speaking to Cabinet Ministers they, too, thought that although she would probably defeat Heseltine's challenge if she stayed on, the Parliamentary Party would be deeply divided under her leadership, perhaps sufficiently to deny a fourth general election victory. By standing down she made way for a candidate – Major – who she felt was likely to carry on her policies, who was considered to be a unifier, and who had a good chance of defeating Heseltine, who was not a Thatcherite. 'I have concluded the unity of the Party and prospects of victory in a general election,' Thatcher's resignation statement on the morning of Thursday, 22 November 1990 said, 'would be better served if I stood down to enable Cabinet colleagues to enter the ballot for the leadership.'[2] John Major and Douglas Hurd – who had been Thatcher's sponsors for both the first and second ballots – then entered the race. On Sunday, headlines in newspapers announced that Nigel Lawson and Geoffrey Howe were backing Michael Heseltine. On 27 November

[1] Private information; *Daily Express*, 20 December 1990. Patten was Environment Secretary; Clarke was Education Secretary; Lamont was Chief Secretary, and Rifkind was Scottish Secretary.
[2] *Guardian*, 23 November 1990.

1990 in the second ballot, Heseltine had 131 votes, Douglas Hurd had 56, and John Major came within two votes of outright victory with 185. Within minutes of the results being announced, Heseltine and Hurd conceded victory to Major and withdrew from the contest. This prevented a third ballot being held, and the next morning Thatcher gave the Queen her resignation and John Major received the seals of office as Prime Minister and First Lord of the Treasury.

If the Cabinet thought that the Party was going to win the next general election with Thatcher as leader, they would not have cracked her nerve in a matter of hours. They would have closed ranks against Heseltine. What they did showed that they were reasonably certain that the country had had enough of Thatcher, and they persuaded her of this.

Thatcher went because she was potentially beaten. It was a preemptive blow. No Prime Minister had ever been pulled down by his own Party in mid-career before. The Conservatives had won (with massive majorities in 1983 and 1987) every general election that Thatcher led them into. She lost only in the opinion polls. Her resignation revealed a new political fact: that in the age of polls, at least for a Conservative Prime Minister, losing a series of them had become tantamount to losing a general election, especially when there are nuclei of opposition within the Parliamentary Party. Since 1937 only two Party leaders – Churchill for the Conservatives and Harold Wilson for Labour – had returned to Number Ten having been defeated in a previous general election. Thatcher's departure showed that an American pattern of presidential politics was being established: being beaten in an election or in the opinion polls equates to being finished.

Thatcherism was possible because of the bankruptcy of the post-1945 consensus, and because the sense of emergency that had infested the twentieth century had exhausted voters and politicians. The wars, tensions and fears of the sixty years from 1914 had sustained acceptance of the primacy of the State in the British democracy. This primacy was seen as necessary to deal with the emergencies of the period. From it came the worst and best aspects of socialism. Margaret Thatcher and her people were in the vanguard of such awarenesses, and – through her – they seized their moment.

But there was an unresolved paradox extending across the range of Thatcher's policies. The drive to extend market principles ran into the wall of traditional attitudes, as debates on the Green Belt, education, the National Health Service, and Sunday trading demonstrated.

Thatcher herself, and a substantial number of her supporters, did not want the social consequences that flow from greater freedom and opportunity. They did not want to permit more abortions or pornography or to let people exist in squalid poverty if they could not succeed in the market place. She wanted to replace old regulations with new ones: she did not want to be rid of regulation altogether. 'That's the other side of her,' observed an adviser, 'which is where people are most critical of her, and perhaps with justification: she had to be pragmatic.'[1] She and her people were not Tories. She was a mixture of a lower-middle-class success story; of unconventionality – because she was the first woman Party leader and Prime Minister, not because she was unconventional by nature – and of turn-of-the-century business impatience with shibboleths. Here her father shone through her. She was not a crisp, worldly Grey or Chatham: she had conventional social views. She had been much the same all her life, and proved remarkably indifferent to the aristocratic or to the royal embrace.

Unlike many of her people, Thatcher believed in first principles rather than ideologies: Hayek was conspicuously absent from her lips in office. She was an old-fashioned patriot; most of her people were far more international in cast. She was not trying to make a new world: she believed that hard work, keeping your word, being enterprising, and living by impersonal rules – the principles of her father's shop in Grantham – were still good. She was concerned to exercise power in the service of authority. She wanted a world in which the copybook maxims flourished, and despite all the complaints about her, she was much less a giver of orders than determined that people ought to be sensible and get on. She had the defects of her qualities. 'She needed lots of people to think, to work with her,' said Alfred Sherman, 'and the minute she didn't have them, her strength of will which was her great asset became her

[1] Interview, 5 December 1990.

great liability. The Thatcher era was over while she was still there. One reason why they got rid of her was that they thought if they're not going to have Thatcherism, why have Thatcher? Entering the ERM was the end of Thatcherism. She fell because of her mistakes and because of being right, and of the two, being right was more damaging.'[1]

There was no fund of affectionate stories told about Thatcher. The country held her in respect as Prime Minister, but with no personal warmth. And that was rather her attitude towards her country too. The British people made a rational assessment: Margaret Thatcher did not like them that much. She remembered the enthusiasm they had for people, policies and remedies she considered to have been completely wrong. Her election to national leadership was a confession of failure by the country which, accordingly, was prepared to take punishments from her. She possessed a few certainties and drove them home. A great deal that she is credited with she did not bring about: the world turned, and she with it.

A third Industrial Revolution has effectively taken place since 1960. There has been a move away from manufacturing in the whole of the developed world. There has been an enormous development of international connections of all sorts. There has been a tremendous move to service industries, and to small, specific institutions. In the 1960s, the developed world was ready for the move to the small – the comprehensible company; greater devolution of political power; community awareness and pride; greater respect for the artisan. The 1970s were a time of reaction to the big – trade unions; the State; the media. Margaret Thatcher and her people embodied radical impatience. They denounced the gold-leaf encrustations on the British political, social and cultural system, and inferentially they denounced the system as a whole. They felt they had come in to save the country, and that the governing elites that dominated political, social and cultural life, and that ridiculed Thatcher and her people, needed to be taught some sharp lessons. They amplified a mood. They were spot-on for the moment and for the long term on the decentralization of initiative. But the

---

[1] Interview, Sir Alfred Sherman, 10 December 1990.

emphasis of the Thatcher years on service industries had already begun to look misplaced by the late 1980s.

One of Margaret Thatcher's great claims to authority was the way she apparently responded to crises, from the Falklands War to the 1984–5 miners' strike. In the 1990s, trade unions are a diminished force in British society. The transformation of the coal and steel industries in the 1980s was symbolic. She suffered from her own success. No one was waiting for Britain to implode in 1990. She commanded a great deal of authority when she came into Number Ten because she owed no favours and because she had won the leadership of the Conservative Party against all expectations except, perhaps, her own. Up to the mid-1980s, people were holding their breath about Thatcherism, and she was in a tremendous position because only a post-Thatcherite Minister would have been acceptable as her successor, and it was too early for that person to exist.

Much was made of the poll tax as a cause of Thatcher's departure. It was bad judgement on her part to try to settle local government finance: every other government had shied away from trying. Her attempt was a political and an administrative mistake. She had demonstrated excellent political acumen in the breaking of union power in the early 1980s. That was her great achievement. She showed her touch by waiting for the right time to spring the trap. At that time she had her vital people with her in Number Ten as advisers and in the Policy Unit, devising tactics and strategy. Refusing to amend the poll tax showed that she was losing her political touch. By then, most of her vital people had gone. When a Prime Minister becomes inflexible, the end is always near.

In December 1990, as John Major began his premiership, the central question he faced was to what extent he was able to find points of difference with Thatcher's policies. He chose to represent himself as an emollient Thatcherite. He was reported to regard Iain Macleod as his political hero, a One Nation Tory, economically 'dry' but socially liberal,[1] and he began talking about 'society' – something Margaret Thatcher had declared was meaningless. 'I am my own man,' Major said, 'and on that basis I see no need to beat

---

[1] *Guardian*, 28 November 1990.

my own chest.'[1] He then proceeded to be conciliatory and talk his way apart from Thatcher. He went to the December 1990 European summit meeting in Rome and told the House of Commons on his return that the proposal he had made in 1989 for a hard-ecu parallel currency (which Thatcher had supported) was a path to European economic and monetary union, but refused to rule out the alternative adoption of a single Euro-currency (something Thatcher was considered to have opposed).[2] Within three weeks of entering Number Ten, his Government announced spending increases of more than £200 million, all on politically sensitive issues. An extra £81 million more would be spent on hospitals; £42 million more would be paid in compensation to haemophiliacs who had contracted AIDS through National Health Service blood transfusions; £96 million would be spent on finding beds for London's homeless. In addition, reductions were made in the poll tax.[3] Seven weeks later, a planned £300 million clean-up of council estates was announced, and rises of 11–18 per cent in public sector pay was approved – well in excess of inflation – and exactly opposite to Thatcher's stand against the civil service strike a decade earlier which had signalled her determination to control public spending and inflationary settlements. The Ribble Valley by-election on 7 March 1991 saw the tenth safest Conservative seat in the country returning a Liberal Democrat with a five-thousand-vote majority. The upset was blamed on anger at the poll tax, and Major immediately made plain his intention of scrapping the tax. It was good politics to buy off trouble – Thatcher had acted similarly in 1983 and 1987 – but Thatcher's people worried that electoral tactics were actually the substance of Major's politics, and that there was a steady

[1] Ibid.
[2] *The Times*, 19 December 1990.
[3] People who had to leave their homes because of old age, illness or disablement, or to look after another person, were removed from liability. So were people who had an empty property awaiting sale after repossession by a mortgage lender, or who had self-contained premises difficult to let separately. The clergy, agricultural workers, and members of the armed forces who lived in homes provided by their employers would be charged only half the tax. No tax would be liable on the first six months a property was empty and unfurnished, and no tax would be paid for the first six months after a grant of probate or letters of administration where the person liable for the charge was acting as a personal representative. Previously, tax was payable after three months in both cases.

search underway for a new Conservative–Labour consensus. They formed the Conservative Way Forward organization in March 1991 'to mobilize support in the Conservative Party for the ideas and values of Margaret Thatcher'.[1] 'This is a vehicle for people who believe in what Margaret stood for,' said a member of the CWF's council. 'All the time Mrs Thatcher was leader it was not thought necessary. Now there is a gap in the party.'[2]

Thatcher and her people identified the issues that were key in the minds of the electorate. She did not indulge the electorate: she knew that people respond to a lead. There was a 'trust the people' attitude about her, which was underestimated by her critics. On the day that Thatcher announced her resignation, three Ministers broke down and cried in Cabinet and two people chained them-selves to the railings outside Michael Heseltine's London house in protest: no other British Prime Minister ever had quite such a demonstration of support. Opinion polls taken in the days after-wards showed a massive leap in Thatcher's popularity, suggesting that while people may have been angry with her (especially about the poll tax), they did not want her to go. 'What was clear from the poll evidence even before she went, when she was hitting real lows in popularity,' said one of her election advisers, endorsing the view that by losing her the Conservative Party might have lost a vote winner, 'was that people might have been angry with her, but they trusted her to sort it out. They were saying, in effect, "Maggie, you cocked it up, now go and fix it." They weren't saying, "Maggie, get out."'[3] Lord Randolph Churchill said that 'trust the people' should be a principle of Tory Democracy: by that he meant that the people should be trusted to follow the aristocracy. But in Margaret Thatcher's case it was much more systemic. She believed that most people want to work, want to create for their own, but not in complete selfishness, and that they are benefited by their larger sense of being British. Her views struck a deep chord with the key socio-economic C2 group of voters. 'We did some proper group research just before the local election results, with C2s,' said a media

[1] Conservative Way Forward, founding statement. The CWF's council included Keith Joseph, Cecil Parkinson (chairman) and Norman Tebbit.
[2] *Mail on Sunday*, 10 March 1991.
[3] Interview, 5 December 1990.

adviser in June 1990. 'And in it we did games with them: you've gone to the doctor and you're in the waiting room and there are two doors, one marked "Dr Kinnock" and one marked "Dr Thatcher". What happens? They all say, whatever their persuasion, "If we go through that door marked Dr Thatcher, we're going to get a cold, clinical examination and at the end of it she's going to say, 'You're drinking too much, smoking too much, eating too much, not taking enough exercise. Now get out of here and take care of yourself and stop bothering the State with this petty indulgence.' If you go through that door, marked Dr Kinnock, you're going to get a big grin and be cuddled and be sympathized with, and he's going to give you a painkiller and send you away." And you ask them, "Which door are you going to go through?" And they say, "Thatcher, of course."'[1]

The question is, where do the public and the private interest meet? The average Thatcher voter was terribly proud to be British. He was prepared to pay for a scientific coup by a State-owned British laboratory: individual effort was by no means supreme in his thinking. He felt that most (but not all: some are scroungers and wastrels) Britons who fell on misfortune ought to be assisted (it could happen to him). He did not like trade unions transcending this sense of community into a predatory attitude. He was by no means as individualistic as an American conservative. He had a higher sense of the fitness of Government to provide certain services such as health and education than Americans do. Sections of Thatcher voters were more prepared to enforce certain beliefs, and to vote for the sort of people who would give problems to American evangelical Christians.

In the mid-1950s the people who were most staunchly white-hot Conservatives woke up and found they were living in a world in which the Fabian consensus had triumphed: improved social services; colonial independence; alliance with the USA; nationalization, were all in train. In 1975 Thatcher's people were seen as angry theorists, as a reaction to failure and not as having a positive programme. The voice of experience was that Selsdon Man could not come out of his cave. The common wisdom was, 'Well,

[1] Interview, 5 June 1990.

they tried to do that in 1970, and look what happened.' When Thatcher's people asserted themselves, they looked as though they were an opposition within the Opposition; that the Party that could not stay in office was tearing itself apart. Yet, at the very moment that the consensus of collectivists and accommodationists seemed supreme, it came under radical challenge and fell apart in five or six years. Now it can be said that it does not matter who is in power; that Thatcherism, on a majority of the positions that it exercised itself over, has set the agenda for the next decade: the idea of a National Plan is dead – no one is proposing one; challenge to entrenched attitudes is underway; no one is arguing that the trade unions should be as powerful as they were in the 1970s. A tradition of onslaught on British institutions has been established, instead of one of industrial strife.

In the 1990s the people who insisted they were class warriors have woken up to discover that they are in a Thatcher consensus. They are not going to renationalize; they are not going to set up as a socialist republic off the coast of Europe; they recognized that they have to win the vote of the new service middle classes – that they cannot rely on working-class loyalties. It is not a question of winning over the Conservative working man: they have to deal with the grandchildren of the Labour working men who want to own country homes. 'They won't turn the clock back more than a third of the distance,' judged Alan Walters about a future Labour Government. 'They can't. She's changed the Labour Party far more than the Conservative Party.'[1] That change was only partly Thatcher. It was perhaps more that she was quicker than most to see the way the world was turning: an increasingly large middle class; increasing internationalism; increasing disenchantment with any kind of socialist model; increasing dispersion of initiative; diminishing number, and thus power, of labour-intensive industries; the authority of technology.

After the mid-1980s when most of Thatcher's people had resigned as advisers or had grown apart from her (usually because their advice was no longer congenial), she secured greater individual authority and power. In July 1990 during a lunch with the directors

[1] Interview, Sir Alan Walters, 25 May 1989.

of an independent broadcasting and production company, she spoke about Boris Yeltsin's recent visit to London. 'I said to Mr Yeltsin when he came by,' she said, '"Mr Yeltsin, we are very fond of Mr Gorbachev, and we wouldn't want anything bad to happen to him. My view has always been, even with quite a small country like our own, that you need half a dozen good people to make things work. If I'd ever had half a dozen good people it would have been all right."'[1] She had no faith in most of her Cabinet colleagues as successors, or in them as being right: if left to themselves, she did not think they would do the right things – the things she would do. So she made sure that they did not have much power and, ultimately, this was what so many of them complained about. By the end, she had surrounded herself with civil servants, just as Edward Heath had. Heath's civil servants were men who were already there, and who stayed on in their positions under Harold Wilson and Jim Callaghan. In Thatcher's case they were junior men whom she brought forward faster and further than their careers would normally have allowed. Not since the premiership of Lloyd George had that been done. Ultimately, many of her people felt that in consequence she was increasingly removed from them and the ideas she needed to sustain her political vitality, and was instead dependent upon officials whose first thought was to please her rather than to tell her ugly truths.

Democracy likes to change Governments. There are always ideologues who will argue that their Party has been or will be out of office because it has not been true to itself; that the country will respond to certainty; that the country is really full of people who want nationalization or the re-establishment of the British Empire. But Parties win elections and then ideologues meet the political realities: that one-third of their Party are hardliners and that the rest want to hold office.

Thatcherism may be happier out of Office and in opposition within the Conservative Party. But when Margaret Thatcher left Number Ten, the bridge between radical ideas and politics went. One of the most startling features of her regime as Prime Minister was the access that new ideas and initiatives had to the most senior

---

[1] Private information.

levels of power. In 1979 if a leading politician had publicly spoken of privatizing the Trustee Savings Bank or Rolls-Royce or the steel or water or the telephone or electricity industry, he would have been ridiculed by most commentators: to a significant degree, this was the experience of Keith Joseph. By 1991, the privatization of all these had become facts.

After the Second World War, the Japanese went for economic dynamism and a great deal of social restraint; Britain went for the opposite: very little social restraint and little dynamism which, in a real sense, produces repressive tolerance. Britain remained Britain – a right little, tight little island – in a fairly leaden way, which was a furiously frustrating business for Margaret Thatcher. This was what she was at war with.

But she did not think that was at all what she was struggling with. She did not recognize how far the Left had its tap-root in piety. The British Left is fundamentally Christian in outlook – there are more important things than money – with a medieval critique in a very real sense: the Schoolmen detested usury. The Left talk about production for use, not gain, and have powerful support for this view in all sections of British society. However, there is no system or doctrine that is fully adequate, so that striking the balance between human solidarity and individual freedom and effort is the continuing task of civilization. Margaret Thatcher sought a balance in espousing both intense individual effort and intense patriotism. But there were many people who would regard patriotism as something of a luxury. And there were very large numbers of patriotic people who did not greatly like competitiveness.

Margaret Thatcher accomplished one of the greatest of all political acts: she established new habits of enterprise, of work, and of political debate. This went deeper than tactics and strategy: it involved a massive change in the attitudes and assumptions of the British voter. She had communicable enthusiasm that brought together unlikely people. She showed that it was not class treason for millions of people who had traditionally voted Labour to vote Conservative. In 1983 for the first time, a majority of trade union members who voted did not vote Labour. She was, in fact, one of the great coalition-builders of British politics, and politics is about coalitions. Despite the attacks of political opponents, she was not

Mrs Gradgrind and the country did not think she was. The distance between her and her people was because she was quintessentially a politician, and because, unlike her, they did not have to think in several worlds simultaneously.

There was an unarticulated feeling that Margaret Thatcher had exhausted her repertoire by the time she resigned as Prime Minister. Her colleagues in the House of Commons clearly felt it. Diaghilev used to call Cocteau in and say, *'Jean, étonnez-moi!'* Voters did not feel that Mrs Thatcher could astonish them much more. Some of her people were even more pessimistic. 'She was going to lose the next election,' said Norman Strauss. 'That was an absolute certainty. She was a busted flush intellectually in terms of what was required for the job. It was really all over in 1983. It took so much longer to be over because of Labour.'[1] Robert Blake, writing a fortnight before Thatcher resigned, suggested that sycophancy had dulled her touch and that a divided Party that would lose the next election was a consequence. He drew a comparison with Lloyd George: 'Bonar Law told the editor of the *Manchester Guardian* after the fall of Lloyd George in 1922: "My experience is that all Prime Ministers suffer by suppression. Their friends do not tell them the truth; they tell them what they want to hear . . ." Bonar Law was right. The Prime Minister ought to pay more attention to her critics and less to her yes-men. And history, for what it is worth – not much perhaps to the Prime Minister – suggests that she will lose the next election unless she can produce a united party to fight it.'[2]

Even with a decade of inadequate Labour Opposition, it was remarkable that Thatcher lasted so long. Her authority had been that of someone who has done something fairly astonishing quite a few times: she confronted organized labour, won a war in the South Atlantic, took triumphant part in the facing down of the Soviet Union. 'In 1979, 1983, 1987, they needed Mrs T to slay dragons, fight the unions, undo Labour economic failure, create the environment for prosperity, wipe out socialism, strengthen our defences, expand choice, opportunity and freedom,' said one of her closest media advisers. 'Now in 1990 many of the dragons are

[1] Interview, Norman Strauss, 11 December 1990.
[2] Robert Blake, 'Suffering by Suppression', *Spectator*, 10 November 1990.

perceived to be slain, i.e., trade unions, communism, socialism, unemployment. The economic dragon was slain. It re-emerged, only because of the Government's perceived errors. The new dragons are perceived to be of the Government's own making, i.e., the Community Charge, the trade gap, interest rates, the mortgage rate, Tory splits, Europe. The result of this is that people no longer knew what they needed Mrs T for, other than to correct the Government's own errors. Telling them they need the Prime Minister to sort out the economy may be believed, but there are no votes in it, because people believe it's the Government's fault it has gone wrong.'[1]

There was, however, still unfinished business in Thatcherism that her people still believe in and that her successors may explore. 'I feel we should have gone faster,' Sir John Hoskyns said, looking back. 'She herself said as much in an interview a couple of years ago. That was always my worry.'[2] The idea of Britain becoming a pacemaker in the international economy is seen to be way down the road in the future. Britain has to some extent been an exemplar to developing countries about increasing initiative. But when you see how well Germany does with many more restrictions than in Britain, we have to recognize that the propensity to work and discipline is central. And in Britain, work is still a bore. Not many people, even working for themselves in Britain, work eighty-hour weeks. The British still enjoy their leisure more – and are very inventive with it and invest heavily in it (British television, DIY, video-renting, for example). The British get on with each other amazingly well. They are an accommodating people, and this works against greater commitment to effort.

A major area of unfinished business arose because privatization did not result in the spread of share ownership that was hoped: in 1991, over eighty per cent of shares in British firms were owned by institutional investors, a proportion which had grown during the Thatcher years. It was (and is) encouraged by the tax system, and by the growth of pension funds chasing shares. Nor did Thatcher make any attempt to change the tax system which, most

[1] Interview, 5 December 1990.
[2] Interview, Sir John Hoskyns, 7 December 1990.

unThatcheritely, rewards people for amassing debts through mortgaging their homes. Despite decrying State power, the proportion of national income taken up in taxation also grew during the Thatcher years.

'One element of policy that developed in a way quite unforeseen was the privatization policy,' said Ian Gow in 1989, providing a Thatcherite recipe for the future. 'And we still have further giant steps to take: notably the railways and the mines. I think we still have enormous strides to make about wider share ownership, and still further strides to make on trade unions, law reform, and maybe – if you can get inflation down, which we did, below three per cent – it is no more difficult to bring inflation down by three points from eight to five than from three to nothing. I think that we will see a further extension of share ownership on quite a big scale, and I think still further initiatives about getting rid of the remaining council houses. There are five million council houses still.'[1]

A decade was spent in making sure that Britain did not fall apart. National decline, both relatively and absolutely, was slowed. 'I saved your life,' Thatcher could say. 'But I didn't get you out of bed.' Thatcher never accepted that Britain's future was as an appendage to Germany or Europe. Her successors can throw Britain wholeheartedly into Europe, or take the country out. Europe is emblematic of the issues Thatcher made her own: freedom and responsibility versus central regulation.

Britain no longer needs someone to beat the unions off: the 1970s will not be re-enacted. Thatcher was a victim of her success here. She was probably the last great spokesman for the American connection. In the years since 1987, Britain has started treating Europe as truly real: not as the place over the water, but as something that Britain is part of. Ambitious people no longer think of a non-European alternative: the functionaries, the higher civil servants, politicians generally, businessmen, the City, are thinking in European terms. The unreality of the American connection; the reality of the European connection which is organic; the collapse

<hr>

[1] Interview, Ian Gow, MP, 8 August 1989.

of the Left and of unionism, all meant that an exorcist was no longer needed.

One of her people was at a dinner party in the spring of 1990. He was arguing the case for free market principles, and someone said, 'Yes, the free market is all very well, but you don't mean absolutely free?'

'Yes, I do,' said Thatcher's person.

'What? No regulation at all?'

'None!'

'What do you mean? We all could die?'

'Yes.'

'What? You must be mad!'

'Everything should be freed, so that people can do exactly what they want to do.'

'Good God, old boy, it would be chaos!'

'The difference between you and me,' said Thatcher's person, providing a summary of the genuine idealism so many of her people passionately feel, 'is that I think people are basically good, and that they will find the right way. Whereas you think people are basically evil.'[1]

---

[1] Interview, 5 June 1990.

APPENDIX ONE

Thatcher's Ministers: those she sacked and those who resigned

January 1981:   Norman St John-Stevas (Chancellor of the Duchy of Lancaster and Minister for the Arts), sacked.

Angus Maude (Paymaster General), resigned.

September 1981:   Mark Carlisle (Education), sacked.

Lord Soames (Lord President of the Council and Leader of the House of Lords), sacked.

Sir Ian Gilmour (Lord Privy Seal), sacked.

April 1982:   Lord Carrington (Foreign), resigned.
Humphrey Atkins (Lord Privy Seal), resigned.

January 1983:   John Nott (Defence), resigned.

October 1983:   Cecil Parkinson (Chancellor of the Duchy of Lancaster and Chairman of the Conservative Party), resigned.

June 1983:   Lady Young (Lord Privy Seal and Leader of the House of Lords), sacked.

Francis Pym (Foreign), sacked.

David Howell (Transport), sacked.

September 1984:   Lord Cockfield (Chancellor of the Duchy of Lancaster), sacked.

Jim Prior (Northern Ireland), resigned.

September 1985:   Patrick Jenkin (Environment), sacked.

Peter Rees (Chief Secretary to the Treasury), sacked.

Lord Gowrie (Chancellor of the Duchy of Lancaster and Minister for the Arts), resigned.

January 1986:   Michael Heseltine (Defence), resigned.

Leon Brittan (Trade and Industry), resigned.

May 1986:   Sir Keith Joseph (Education), resigned.

June 1987:	John Biffen (Lord Privy Seal and Leader of the House of Commons), sacked.
	Michael Jopling (Agriculture), sacked.
	Lord Hailsham (Lord Chancellor), sacked.
	Nicholas Edwards (Wales), resigned.
	Norman Tebbit (Chancellor of the Duchy of Lancaster and Chairman of the Conservative Party), resigned.
October 1987:	Lord Havers (Lord Chancellor), resigned.
December 1988:	Lord Whitelaw (Lord President of the Council and Leader of the House of Lords), resigned.
July 1989:	George Younger (Defence), resigned.
	Lord Young (Trade and Industry), resigned.
	John Moore (Social Security), sacked.
	Paul Channon (Transport), sacked.
October 1989:	Nigel Lawson (Chancellor), resigned.
January 1990:	Norman Fowler (Employment), resigned.
March 1990:	Peter Walker (Wales), resigned.
July 1990:	Nicholas Ridley (Trade and Industry), resigned.
November 1990:	Sir Geoffrey Howe (Deputy Prime Minister and Leader of the House of Commons), resigned.

Fifteen Cabinet Ministers were sacked by Margaret Thatcher in the period 1979-90; twenty-one resigned.

Thatcher's resignation
honours list

Ever since Harold Wilson's resignation honours in 1976 which were sub-
mitted on lavender paper and in the handwriting of Marcia Falkender,
Prime Minister's resignation honours lists have been called the 'lavender
list'. Wilson's honours were controversial: he was seen as rewarding
cronies and contributors to Party funds (one of whom – Lord Kagan –
subsequently spent a term in prison), and as having devalued the system.
Margaret Thatcher was accused of devaluing the system because she also
rewarded prominent contributors to Party funds.

The baronetcy awarded to Denis Thatcher was at his wife's request, but
was separate from her resignation list. Margaret Thatcher's becoming a
member of the Order of Merit upon her resignation was the Queen's own
decision.

Nearly all Thatcher's people who had not been honoured over the
previous eleven years received honours in the resignation list. Some who
had already been honoured received an additional honour. It was reported
that Thatcher had included the novelist Jeffrey Archer in her list, but that
his name had been removed by the Scrutiny Committee (established in
the wake of Wilson's resignation list) as unsuitable; it was also reported
that John Major had asked Thatcher to include Archer but that she had
refused on the grounds that the novelist had done sufficient work for the
Party to deserve an honour in the normal course of events, and that she
was putting on her list people who would not otherwise be honoured.

LIFE PEERS Dame Joan Seccombe, vice-chairman of the Conservative
Party; Mr Brian Griffiths, head of the Prime Minister's Policy Unit; Sir
Hector Laing, president of United Biscuits; Mr Peter Palumbo, chairman
of the Arts Council; Sir Jeffrey Sterling, chairman of P & O and special
adviser at the Department of Trade and Industry; Sir Gordon White,
chairman of Hanson Industries; Sir David Wolfson, chairman of Haigside
Ltd., and of Next.

DAMES AND KNIGHTS Mr Timothy Bell, chairman of Lowe Bell Communications; Mr George Gardiner, MP for Reigate; Mrs Jane Gow, widow of Ian Gow;[1] Mr Bernard Ingham, Prime Minister's press secretary; Mr Geoffrey Leigh, chairman of Allied London Properties; Mr Nicholas Lloyd, editor of the *Daily Express*; Mr Peter Morrison, MP for Chester and the Prime Minister's Parliamentary Private Secretary; Mr Gerrard Neale, MP for North Cornwall; Mr Michael Neubert, MP for Romford; Mr Charles Powell, Prime Minister's private secretary (foreign);[2] Miss Sue Tinson, associate editor of Independent Television News.[3]

COMMANDER OF THE ORDER OF THE BATH (CB) Mr Andrew Turnbull, Prime Minister's principal private secretary.[4]

COMMANDER OF THE ORDER OF THE BRITISH EMPIRE(CBE) Mr John Catford, Prime Minister's appointments secretary; Miss Joan Hall, former MP for Keighley and member of the Council of Buckingham University; Dr John Henderson, Margaret Thatcher's personal physician; Mr Brian Hitchen, editor of the *Daily Star*; Mrs Olga Polizzi, member of Westminster City Council; Mr Harvey Thomas, Conservative Party director of presentation and promotion.

OFFICER OF THE ORDER OF THE BRITISH EMPIRE (OBE) Mrs Marjorie Sherman, for charitable services; Miss Christine Wall, head of the news department of the Conservative Party; Mr John Whittingdale, Prime Minister's political secretary.

MEMBER OF THE ORDER OF THE BRITISH EMPIRE (MBE) Mrs Jean Dibblin, Prime Minister's senior personal secretary; Mrs Susan Goodchild, Prime Minister's invitations secretary; Mrs Dorothy Haynes, curator/housekeeper at Chequers; Mrs Margaret King, Aquascutum fashion director; Mr Robert Kingston, Margaret Thatcher's personal

[1] Created a Dame Commander of the Order of the British Empire (DBE). As a member of an Order of Chivalry, Gow's 'knighthood' was superior to all the others – except Charles Powell's and Sue Tinson's – which were Knights Bachelor (i.e., knights unassociated with an Order).
[2] Powell was created a Knight Commander of the Order of Saint Michael and Saint George – KCMG – the Order associated with Foreign Office honours. The Order ranks below the Order of the Bath and above the Order of the British Empire.
[3] Like Jane Gow, Sue Tinson was created a Dame Commander of the Order of the British Empire.
[4] CB ranks immediately below a Knight Bachelor and is the most senior of the non-title chivalric honours.

detective; Mrs Amanda Ponsonby, Prime Minister's personal assistant; Mrs Janice Richards, head of the garden rooms at Number Ten; Mrs Sherry Warner, senior cook at Number Ten.

BRITISH EMPIRE MEDAL Mrs Edwina Booker, cleaner at Number Ten; Mrs Alma Dew, telephonist at Number Ten; Sergeant Theresa Duda, WRAF, assistant house manager at Chequers; Mr Peter D'Emanuele, messenger at Number Ten; Mr Alfred Heath, custody guard supervisor at Number Ten; Mrs Doris King, messenger at Number Ten; Mr Anthony Yandle, deputy house manager at Number Ten.

INDEX

318